AF771264

Macintosh Human Interface Guidelines

Addison-Wesley Publishing Company

Reading, Massachusetts Menlo Park, California New York
Don Mills, Ontario Wokingham, England Amsterdam Bonn
Sydney Singapore Tokyo Madrid San Juan
Paris Seoul Milan Mexico City Taipei

Apple Computer, Inc.

Apple Computer, Inc.
20525 Mariani Avenue
Cupertino, CA 95014
408-996-1010

Simultaneously published in the United States and Canada.

ISBN 0-201-62216-5
1 2 3 4 5 6 7 8 9-BA-9695949392
First Printing, November 1992

The paper used in this book meets the EPA standards for recycled fiber.

Contents

Chapter 6 Dialog Boxes 175

Chapter 7 Controls 203

Figures and Tables

About This Book

Macintosh Human Interface Guidelines describes the way to create products that optimize the interaction between people and Macintosh computers. It explains the whys and hows of the Macintosh interface in general terms and specific details.

Macintosh Human Interface Guidelines helps you link the philosophy behind the Macintosh interface to the actual implementation of interface elements. Examples from a wide range of Macintosh products show good human interface design, including individual and iterative examples. These examples are accompanied by descriptions and discussions of why to follow the guidelines. This book also contains examples of how *not* to do human interface design; they are marked as such and appear with a discussion that points out what's inappropriate and how to correct it.

Who Should Read This Book

This book is written for people who design and develop products for use with Macintosh computers. If you are a designer, a human interface professional, or an engineer, this book contains information you can use to design and create products that fit the Macintosh model. It provides background information that can help you plan and make decisions about your product design.

Even if you don't design and develop products for the Macintosh, reading this book will help you to understand the Macintosh interface. This book is appropriate for managers and planners who are thinking about developing Macintosh products, as well as people who are interested in human interface design in general.

This book is written with the assumption that you are familiar with the concepts and terminology used with Macintosh computers and that you have used a Macintosh computer and some Macintosh applications.

What's New in Macintosh Human Interface From Apple

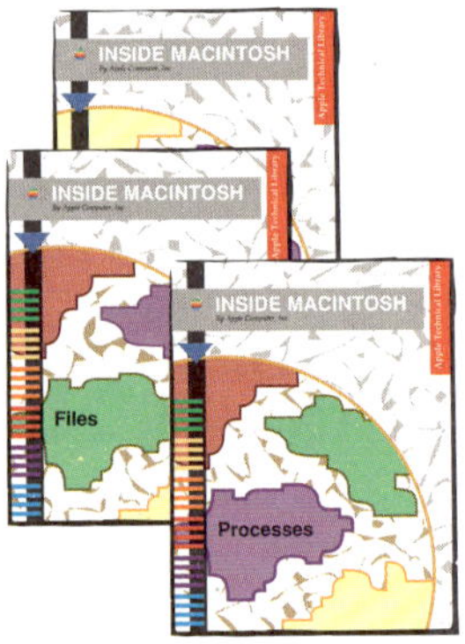

In previous years, the human interface guidelines were published in *Inside Macintosh*, in *Human Interface Guidelines: The Apple Desktop Interface*, and in *Human Interface Notes*. This book contains all the current human interface guidelines pertaining to all types of products that work with Macintosh computers.

In the current *Inside Macintosh*, you'll find human interface information and guidelines included in the individual chapters about each topic, such as the Edition Manager or the Dialog Manager. These chapters also have technical implementation information about the Macintosh Operating System. *Inside Macintosh* doesn't contain the philosophy of the Macintosh interface or the rationale about how to use the interface elements properly, so to create your product, you'll need *Inside Macintosh* and this book.

About *Making It Macintosh*

Making It Macintosh: Macintosh Human Interface Guidelines Companion is a CD-ROM–based accompaniment to *Macintosh Human Interface Guidelines*. *Making It Macintosh* contains animated examples of common problems developers encounter when they implement the Macintosh interface, presents solutions to these problems, and discusses how you can approach similar problems. You can use *Making It Macintosh* and *Macintosh Human Interface Guidelines* together, or you can consult each separately. For information about ordering *Making It Macintosh*, see the back of this book.

What's in This Book

This book contains three major sections. You can read it from start to finish or use it as a reference in which to look up specific pieces of information that you need to know. The paragraphs that follow describe the type of information you'll find in each part of the book.

The Basic Philosophy

The first part of this book presents the key design principles and considerations for developers to keep in mind when creating a product that works with Macintosh computers. It suggests ways to incorporate human interface into your product design and decision-making processes.

It also describes how to involve users in your product design process to ensure that you've built a product that serves your users well and conforms to the guidelines.

The Interface Elements

The second part of this book defines various parts of the Macintosh interface. It presents examples of the right and wrong ways to use interface elements and behaviors and contains specific implementation information you can use while you're creating a product. This part of the book also shows how to combine interface elements with behaviors, aesthetics, and language to create a superior product.

Appendixes

The appendixes provide additional information about the topics discussed in this book. Appendix A describes resources such as professional societies and conferences from which you can get additional information. Appendix B is a bibliography that presents major works on topics discussed in the book. Refer to this appendix when you want to find where to get more extensive information or training on a topic such as color or menus. Appendix C provides a checklist for you to use when evaluating your product to make sure it meets the intent and purpose of the Macintosh human interface guidelines. The glossary, which follows the appendixes, provides definitions for terms used in the book. At the end of the book is an index, which will help you locate information about specific topics.

Visual Cues Used in This Book

In this book you'll find visual cues to certain types of information.

- This symbol indicates an example of the correct way to use an interface element.

- This symbol indicates an example that is OK or is an improvement to a poor example. It would still be useful to consider making improvements to this type of example.

- This symbol indicates an example of the wrong way to use an interface element. It specifically calls out common mistakes.
- **Boldfaced text** indicates that a new term is being defined and that a definition of the word appears in the glossary.

Fundamentals

This part of *Macintosh Human Interface Guidelines* presents the philosophy and psychology behind the Macintosh interface. Read this part to learn about the design principles and considerations that developers can use to create an excellent human interface. You can find out how to incorporate good human interface into your design and decision-making processes and how to involve users throughout the design process. You can also read about how to work with and go beyond the guidelines while maintaining their spirit and intent.

This part contains the following chapters:

- Human Interface Principles
- General Design Considerations
- Human Interface Design and the Development Process

Human Interface Principles

Human Interface Principles

At Apple Computer, products are designed with a number of basic principles of human-computer interaction in mind. This chapter discusses the human interface design principles that describe key considerations for the design decisions you make for your product.

Having technical knowledge of the Macintosh user interface is a key factor in product design, but understanding the theories behind the user interface can help you create an excellent product. This chapter provides a theoretical base for the wealth of practical information on implementing the Macintosh interface elements presented in Part Two.

The Human Interface Design Principles

This section presents a set of principles useful for designing products for Macintosh computers. The reason for defining a set of design principles is to help you build a product that meets the standards of the Macintosh computer. Also, these principles can help clarify what you can do in order to design a product based on what is known about people and how they operate in the world.

You'll undoubtedly find out that you can't design in accordance with all of the principles all of the time. In that type of situation, you'll have to make a decision based on which principle or set of principles is most important in the context of the task you're solving.

Metaphors

You can take advantage of people's knowledge of the world around them by using metaphors to convey concepts and features of your application. Use metaphors involving concrete, familiar ideas and make the metaphors plain, so that users have a set of expectations to apply to computer environments. For example, people often use file folders to store paper documents in their offices. Therefore, it makes sense to people to store computer documents in computer-generated folders that look like file folders. People can organize their hard disks in a way that's analogous to the way they organize their file cabinets.

The desktop is the primary metaphor for the Macintosh interface. It appears to be a surface on which people can keep tools and documents. Several other metaphors are integrated into the desktop metaphor. It makes sense in the context of a desktop environment to include folders and a trash can (even though most trash cans don't sit on the desktop). Menus are an extension of the desktop metaphor. People can connect the idea of making choices from a computer menu with making choices from a restaurant menu. Although people don't keep restaurant menus on the edge of their desks, using the term *menu* in the computer environment reinforces the idea that people can use computer menus to make choices.

Metaphors in the computer interface suggest a use for something, but that use doesn't define or limit the implementation of the metaphor. For example, a paper file folder has a limited storage capacity, but a folder on the Macintosh doesn't have to be constrained by the same limitations. Computer folders can hold a limitless number of files (up to the storage capacity of the hardware), and this is an advantage that the computer can offer. Try to strike a balance between the metaphor's suggested use and the ability of the computer to support and extend the metaphor.

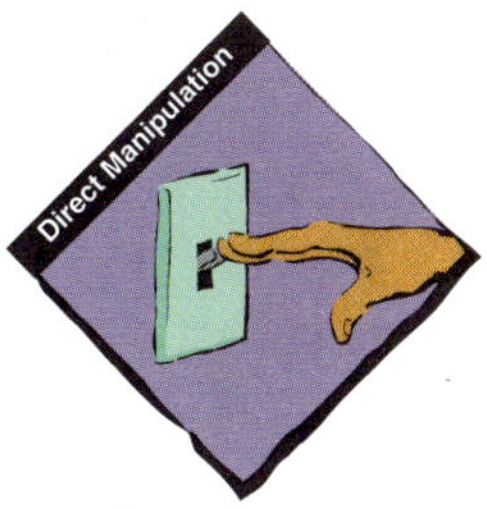

Direct Manipulation

Direct manipulation allows people to feel that they are directly controlling the objects represented by the computer. According to the principle of direct manipulation, an object on the screen remains visible while a user performs physical actions on the object. When the user performs operations on the object, the impact of those operations on the object is immediately visible. For example, a user can move a file by dragging an icon that represents it from one location to another or can position a cursor in a text field by directly clicking the location where the cursor should be placed.

Figure 1-1 shows a folder icon being dragged across the desktop as an example of direct manipulation on the computer.

Figure 1-1 Direct manipulation

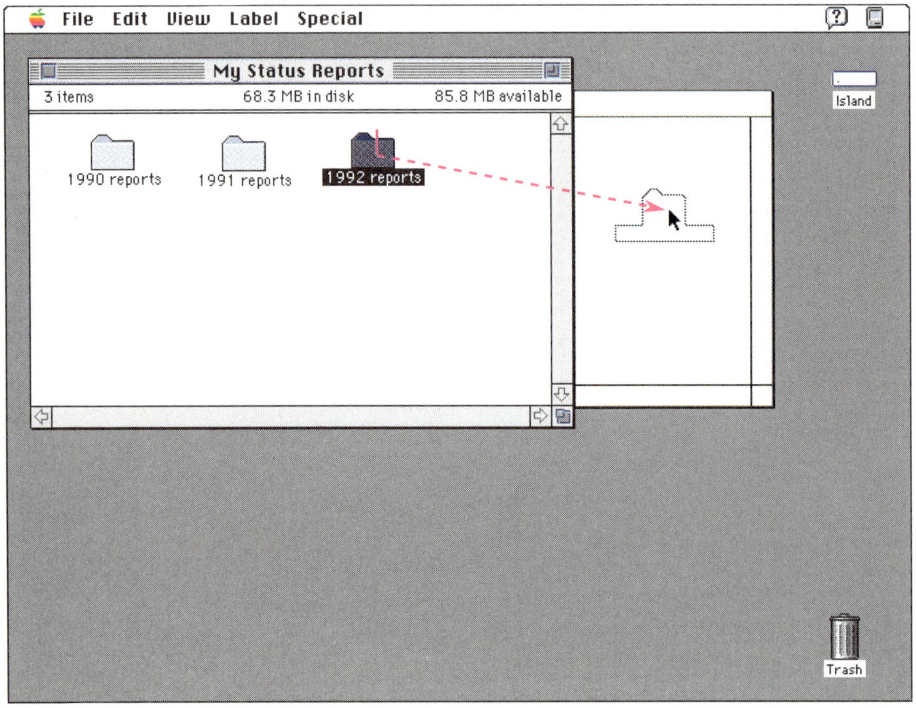

In addition to expecting physical results from their actions, users want their tools to provide feedback. For example, when a drawing tool is moved, a line appears in the document on which the user is working. Users want to see what actions are available at any given moment. If grave consequences might follow from any of those actions, they want to know about those consequences—before any damage is done and while they can still change their minds. They want clues that tell them that a particular command is being carried out, or, if it cannot be carried out, they want to know why not and what they can do instead. Users also want topics of interest to be highlighted.

Animation, when used sparingly, is one of the best ways to show a user that a requested action is being carried out. For example, animated pointers reassure the user, during a lengthy process such as saving a large document to disk, that the computer is completing the task without any problems.

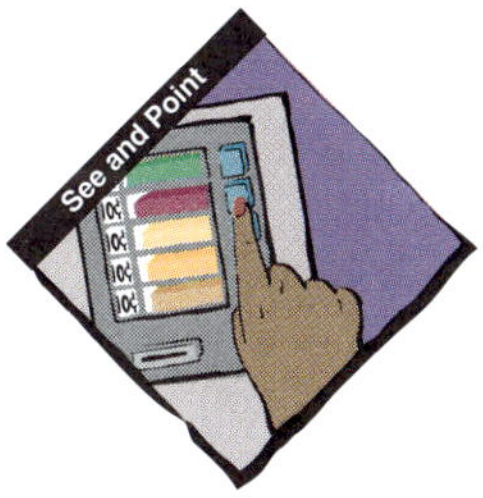

See-and-Point

On the desktop, users perform actions by choosing from alternatives presented on the screen. Users interact directly with the screen, selecting objects and performing activities by using a pointing device, typically a mouse, to point at elements on the desktop.

The Macintosh desktop works according to two fundamental paradigms. Both paradigms share two basic assumptions: that users can see on the screen what they're doing and that users can point at what they see. The paradigms are based on a general form of user action: noun-then-verb.

In one paradigm, the user selects an object of interest (the noun) and then chooses the actions to be performed on the object (the verb). All actions available for the selected object are listed in the menus, so users who are unsure of what to do next can refresh their memory by scanning through the menus. At any time, users can choose any available action without having to remember any particular command or name. For example, a user clicks a document icon (the noun) and then prints (the verb) the document by choosing Print from the File menu.

In the second paradigm, the user drags an object (the noun) onto some other object that has an action (the verb) associated with it. On the desktop, for example, the user can drag icons to the Trash, to folders, or to disks. The user doesn't choose an action from the menus, but it's clear what happens to one object when it's placed on another object. For example, dragging a document icon to the Trash means that the user wants to discard that document. For this metaphor to work, the user must recognize what an object such as the Trash is for, so it is especially important that objects look like what they do in the real world. If the document icon didn't look like a piece of paper with text and the Trash didn't look like the place to discard something, the interface would be more difficult to use.

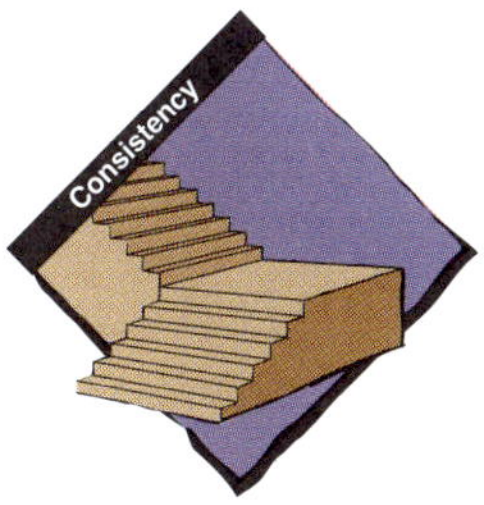

Consistency

Consistency in the interface allows people to transfer their knowledge and skills from one application to any other. Use the standard elements of the Macintosh interface to ensure consistency within your application and to benefit from consistency across applications.

Effective applications are consistent in a number of different ways. Consistency in the visual interface helps people learn and then easily recognize the graphic language of the interface—for example, once users know what a checkbox looks like, they don't have to learn another symbol for making choices. Consistency in the behavior of the interface means that people have to learn how to do things such as clicking and pointing only once; then they can explore new applications or new types of features using skills that they already have. In general, consistency benefits the typical user, who usually divides working time among several applications, and it benefits software developers because their users can build on prior experiences with elements in other applications when learning how to use a new application.

The following are some questions you can ask yourself when thinking about consistency in your product.

Is your product consistent

- within itself?
- with earlier versions of your product?
- with Macintosh interface standards?
- in its use of metaphors?
- with people's expectations?

Note that the most difficult kind of consistency to achieve is matching people's expectations. Because you often face a wide audience and a range of expertise, it's difficult to meet the expectations of everyone. You can address this problem by carefully weighing the consistency issues in the context of your target audience and their needs.

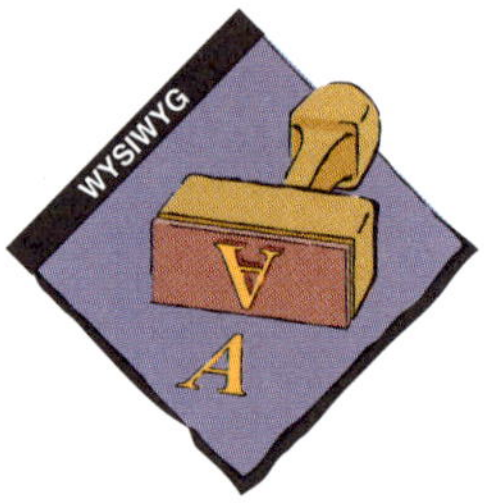

WYSIWYG (What You See Is What You Get)

Don't hide features in your application by using abstract commands. People should be able to see what they need when they need it. For example, menus present lists of commands so that people can see their choices instead of having to remember and type command names.

People should be able to find all the available features in your application. If you find a need to initially "hide" features, do it in a way that gives people information about where they can find more choices. A stepped interface, by revealing relevant information to users in steps, shows the choice most users want most of the time while providing a way for the user to get more choices. For information on stepped interfaces, see the guidelines in the section "Using Progressive Disclosure" on page 35 in Chapter 3, "Human Interface Design and the Development Process."

Make sure that there is no significant difference between what the user sees on the screen and what the user receives after printing. Let the user be in charge of both the content and the format (spatial layout as well as font choices) of the document. When the user makes changes to the document, quickly and directly display the results; the user shouldn't have to wait for a printout or make mental calculations of how the document shown on the screen will look when it appears on the printed page.

User Control

Allow the user, not the computer, to initiate and control actions. People learn best when they're actively engaged. Too often, however, the computer acts and the user merely reacts within a limited set of options. In other instances, the computer "takes care" of the user, offering only those alternatives that are judged "good" for the user or that "protect" the user from having to make detailed decisions. This approach mistakenly puts the computer, not the user, in control.

The key is to create a balance between providing users with the capabilities they need to get their work done and preventing them from destroying data. For situations in which a user may destroy data accidentally, you can help the user by providing warnings, usually in the form of an alert box, to notify users of a potentially undesirable situation and still allow them to proceed, if they confirm that this is what they want. This approach "protects" users but allows them to remain in control.

Feedback and Dialog

Keep users informed about what's happening with your product. Provide feedback as they do tasks and make that feedback as immediate as possible. When a user initiates an action, provide some indicator, visual or auditory (or both), that your application has received the user's input and is operating on it. Provide as much information as possible about how long operations take. When your application can't respond to user input because it's processing a different task, inform the user of what to expect and describe any delays, why they occur, and how long they'll take. Also, tell the user how to get out of the current situation whenever possible.

Provide direct, simple feedback that people can understand. Most people would not know what to do if they saw this message "The computer unexpectedly crashed. ID = 13." It would be very helpful if the message spelled out exactly which situation caused the error—for example, not enough memory was available for the computer to complete the task—so that the user could understand how to avoid the situation in the future.

Figure 1-2 shows an example of a message that doesn't do anything to help the user and an example of a message that provides useful and helpful information to the user.

Figure 1-2 An example of a bad message and an example of a helpful message

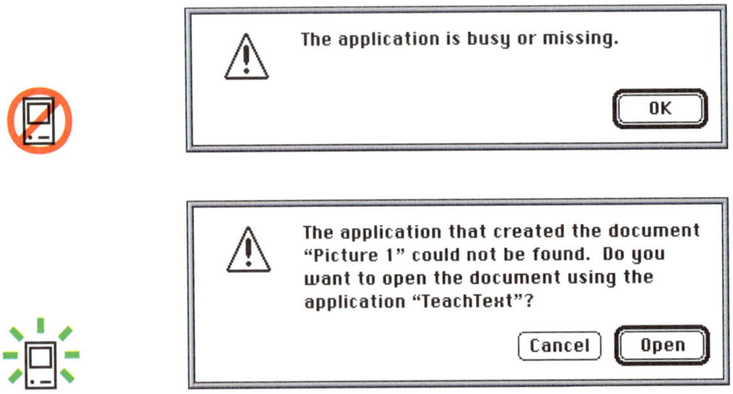

Forgiveness

You can encourage people to explore your application by building in forgiveness. Forgiveness means that actions on the computer are generally reversible. People need to feel that they can try things without damaging the system; create safety nets for people so that they feel comfortable learning and using your product.

Always warn people before they initiate a task that will cause irretrievable data loss. Alert boxes are a good way to warn users of this kind of situation. Note, however, that when options are presented clearly and feedback is appropriate and timely, learning how to use a program should be relatively error-free. This means that frequent alert boxes are a good indication that something is wrong with the program design.

Perceived Stability

Computers often introduce a new level of complexity for people. If people are to cope with this complexity, they need some stable reference points. The Macintosh interface is designed to provide a computer environment that is understandable, familiar, and predictable.

To give users a visual sense of stability, the Macintosh interface provides the desktop, a two-dimensional space on which objects are placed. It also defines a number of consistent graphics elements (menu bar, window border, and so on) to maintain the illusion of stability. Note that it is the *perception* of stability that you want to preserve, not stability in any strict physical sense.

To give users a conceptual sense of stability, the interface provides a clear, finite set of objects and a clear, finite set of actions to perform on those objects. Even when particular actions are unavailable, they are not eliminated from a display but are merely dimmed.

Aesthetic Integrity

Aesthetic integrity means that information is well organized and consistent with principles of visual design. This means that things look good on the screen and the display technology is of high quality. Since people spend a lot of their time working while looking at the computer screen, design your products to be pleasant to look at on the screen for a long time. You may want to consider investing some of your resources in a graphic designer; the skills a graphic designer can bring to your product design are well worth the expense.

Keep the graphics of the display simple. The number of elements and their behaviors should be limited to enhance the usability of the interface. Graphics—icons, windows, dialog boxes, and so on—are the basis of effective human-computer interaction and must be designed with that in mind. Don't clutter the screen with too many windows, overload the user with complex icons, or put dozens of buttons in dialog boxes.

Make sure to follow the graphic language of the interface and don't change the meaning of standard items. For example, if you sometimes use checkboxes for multiple choices and other times for exclusive choices, you dilute the meaning of the element.

Don't use arbitrary graphic images to represent concepts. When you add nonstandard symbols to menus, dialog boxes, or other elements, the meaning may be clear to you, but to other people the symbols may appear as something different and distracting. If you need symbols other than standard ones, use graphic images that convey meaning through representation, analogy, or metaphor. For more information on designing additional appropriate symbols, see the section "Extending the Interface" in Chapter 3, "Human Interface Design and the Development Process," beginning on page 38.

Figure 1-3 shows an example of how confusing arbitrary symbols can be and how much clearer a simple menu with standard symbols can be.

Figure 1-3 Don't use arbitrary graphic elements

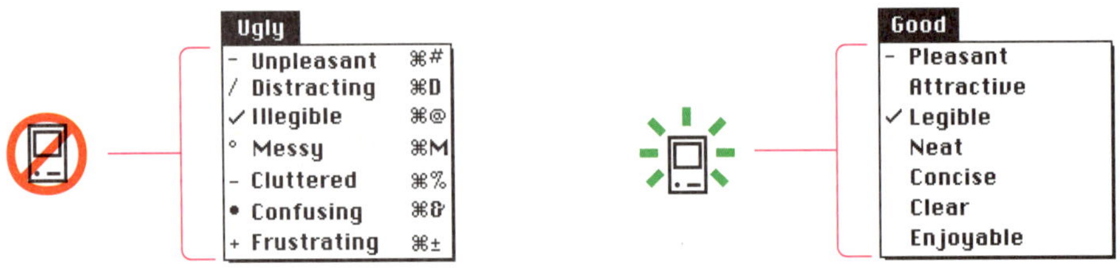

In general, match the graphic element with users' expectations of its behavior. Push buttons appear as though they push in rather than slide sideways. Indicators in sliders slide along to change values. These behaviors map to people's expectations of how these elements behave.

Give users some control over the look of their computer environments. This allows them to display their own style and individuality. It also reduces the burden on the designer of trying to create an interface that appeals to every user. When a user sets up his or her computer environment in a certain layout, it should stay that way until the user changes it.

Modelessness

For the most part, try to create modeless features that allow people to do whatever they want when they want to in your application. Avoid using modes in your application because a mode typically restricts the operations that the user can perform while it is in effect. It locks the user into one operation and doesn't allow the user to work on anything else until that operation is completed. In contrast, modelessness allows the user to perform more than one operation at a time and thus gives the user more control over what he or she can do on the computer and in an application. As much as possible, you want to preserve the user's ability to be in control of the task and the order of operations.

This is not to say that you should never use modes in applications. Sometimes using a mode is the best way out of a particular problem. Most acceptable modes fall into one of the following categories:

- Long-term modes, such as doing word processing as opposed to graphics editing. In this sense, each application is a mode.

- Short-term "spring-loaded" modes, in which the user must constantly do something to maintain the mode. Examples are holding down the mouse button to scroll text or holding down the Shift key to extend a text selection.
- Alert modes, in which the user must rectify an unusual situation before proceeding. Keep these modes to a minimum.

Other modes are acceptable if they do one of the following:

- They emulate a familiar real-life situation that is itself modal. For example, choosing different tools in a graphics application resembles the real-life choice of physical drawing tools.
- They change only the attributes of something, not its behavior. The boldface and underline modes of text entry are examples.
- They block most other normal operation of the system to emphasize the modality, as in error conditions incurable through the software (for example, a dialog box that disables all menu items except Close).

If an application uses modes, there must be a clear visual indicator of the current mode, and the indicator should be near the object most affected by the mode. A good example is the changing pointer in many Macintosh graphics applications; depending on the function ("mode") the user has selected, the pointer looks like a pencil, a paintbrush, a spray can, or an eraser. It should also be very easy for users to get into or out of the mode (such as by clicking a different palette symbol).

Additional Issues to Consider

This section discusses several other issues that are helpful to think about when you design your product.

Knowledge of Your Audience

Identifying and understanding your target audience are among the most important first steps when you start designing your product. To create a product that people can and will use, study the people who make up your target audience.

It's useful to create scenarios that describe a typical day in the life of a person you think uses the type of product you're designing. Think about the different work spaces, tools, and constraints and limitations that people deal with. You can also visit actual work places and study how people do their jobs.

Analyze the steps necessary to complete each task you anticipate people wanting to accomplish. Then design your product to facilitate those tasks, using a step-by-step approach by thinking of how a person might get from one place to the next in a logical fashion.

Involve users throughout the design process and observe them working in their environment. Use people who fit your audience description to test your prototypes and development products. Listen to their feedback and try to address their needs in your product. Develop your product with people and their capabilities, not computers and their capabilities, in mind. For more information, see the section "Involving Users in the Design Process" in Chapter 3, "Human Interface Design and the Development Process," beginning on page 41.

Accessibility

The computer should be accessible to everyone who chooses to use it. There are likely to be members of your target audience who are different from the "average" user that you envision. Users will undoubtedly vary in their ages, styles, and abilities. They may also have physical or cognitive limitations, linguistic differences, or other differences you need to consider. Identify how the individuals in your target audience differ and what special needs they may have.

Make it easy for users to interact with your product using different input devices and output devices. If you develop specialized hardware and software for people with physical limitations, work with application developers so that your products are supported by their software.

Make your application accessible to people around the world by including support for worldwide capabilities in your designs from the beginning of your development process. Take stock of the cultural and linguistic needs and expectations of your target audiences. For more information, see the section "Worldwide Compatibility" beginning on page 16 in Chapter 2, "General Design Considerations."

More information about universal access appears throughout the book where appropriate. For specific information, see the section "Universal Access" beginning on page 24 in Chapter 2, "General Design Considerations."

General Design Considerations

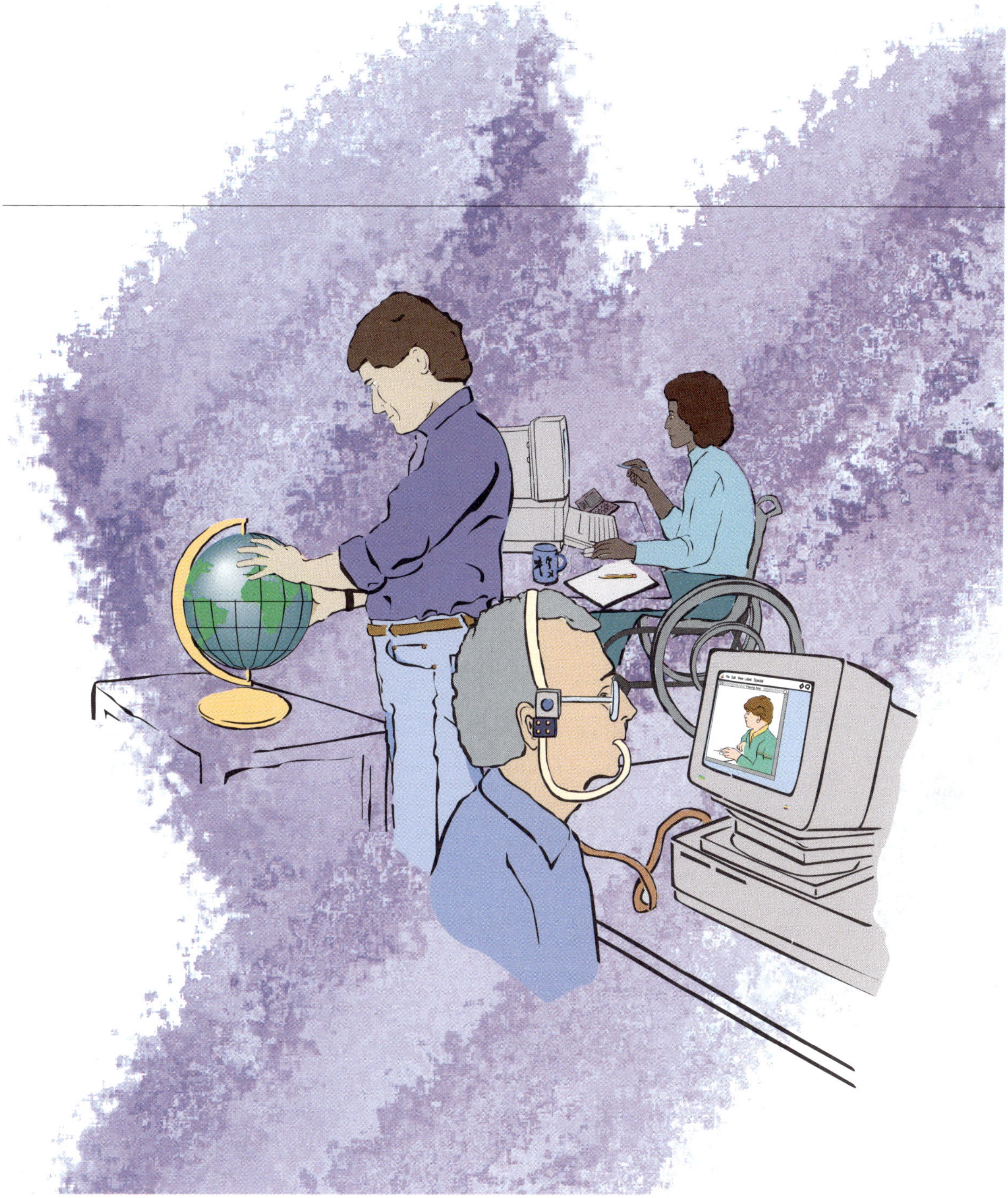

General Design Considerations

This chapter discusses several areas to consider as you begin your development process. These considerations cover three broad areas:

- worldwide compatibility—support for multiple script systems and multicultural sensitivity to your target audience
- universal access—provisions for people with disabilities to use your software by means of alternative input devices or output devices
- collaborative computing—support for people working in groups on local networks or people using computers over remote networks

If you are aware of the factors that influence worldwide compatibility, universal access, and collaborative computing, you can plan ahead. By incorporating support for these capabilities from the beginning of your development process, you can save time, money, and development problems and end up with a product that is immediately useful to a wide range of people.

Worldwide Compatibility

Macintosh system software is designed to address the complex problems you'll encounter when you design your applications to be compatible with regional, linguistic, and writing system differences around the globe. The Macintosh script management system (which is one or more script systems, the Script Manager, and other text-handling managers) allows your application to handle text in many different languages.

It's much easier to include worldwide compatibility from the beginning of your development process than to try to incorporate support for script systems after your product is complete. This may mean that you create your application so that it is easy to localize, or adapt for use in a specific area. Localizing software involves translating an application's menus, dialog boxes, alert boxes, and content areas into a language or regional dialect.

The following sections outline a number of issues to consider before you develop software for worldwide use. For a complete description of the issues and a discussion of technical implementation, see *Inside Macintosh: Text* and *Inside Macintosh: Overview*. These books discuss the routines that assist you in developing your application for worldwide use. See *Guide to Macintosh Software Localization* (available from APDA) for details on script systems and the localization process. See the section "APDA" on page 332 in Appendix A, "Resources," for information about how to contact APDA.

Cultural Values

Make sure that visible interface elements can be localized for other regions around the world. Whenever you design a user interface, consider that differences exist in the use of color, graphics, calendars, text, and the representation of time in various regions around the world. For example, different cultures use different objects to store documents. In the United States, file folders are flat and have tabs that can indicate the contents of the folder. In Europe, file folders are more like narrow cardboard boxes. You may want to localize elements of the user interface, such as graphics or the colors of text in versions of your application designed for different regions.

Graphics have the potential to enhance your application, but they can also be offensive. In addition to colors, cultures assign varying values and characteristics to living creatures, plants, and inanimate objects. For example, in the United States the owl is a symbol of wisdom and knowledge, whereas in Central America the owl represents witchcraft and black magic. It's a good idea to avoid the use of seasons, holidays, or calendar events in software that you expect to distribute worldwide. Also avoid using graphics that represent holidays or seasons, such as Christmas trees, pumpkins, or snow—or be sure that the symbols can be localized.

Different calendars are used to mark time around the world. The United States and most of Europe observe time according to the Gregorian calendar. The traditional Arabic calendar, the Jewish calendar, and the Chinese calendar are lunar rather than solar. Often time is marked according to one calendar for business and government purposes and according to a different calendar for religious events. Make your application flexible in handling dates; you also may want to provide the user with a way to change the representation of time. Use the text utilities to handle numbers, dates, and sorting.

Resources

It's essential to store region-dependent information in resources so that text the user sees can be translated during localization without modification of your application's code. When you create resources, consider text size, location, and direction. Text size varies in different languages. Also, depending on the script system, the direction of text may change. Most Middle Eastern languages read from right to left. Text location within a window should be easy to change.

Use the Macintosh script management system to handle these situations. See *Inside Macintosh: Overview* and *Inside Macintosh: More Macintosh Toolbox* for more information on using resources to store data the user sees.

Language Differences

Translating text is a delicate task and can often cause confusion, so be wary of using colloquial phrases or nonstandard usage and syntax. Carefully choose your words for command names in menus and for messages in dialog boxes, alert boxes, and help balloons. When translated, text can become up to 50 percent larger than U.S. English text. Text needs room to grow up, down, and sideways. Figure 2-1 shows Finder menu bars in several languages. Compare the different lengths of the menu titles that have the same meaning.

Figure 2-1 Menu bars in different languages

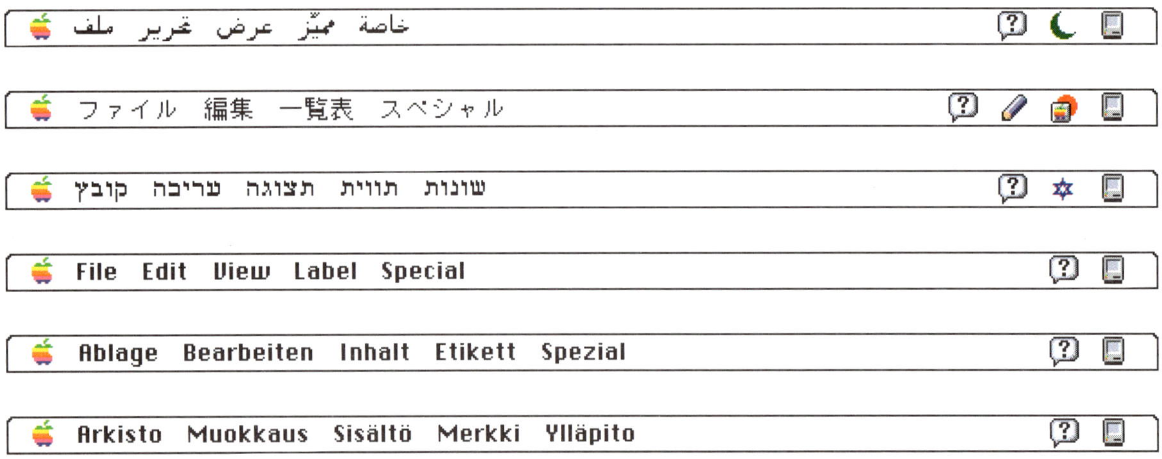

Potential grammar problems may arise with error messages and the user programming structure of languages such as HyperTalk. Use complete sentences whenever possible. Don't use phrases that you then concatenate to create sentences. The word order of messages may become completely different in translation, rendering such a message nonsensical when translated. For example, word order in German usually places the verb at the end of a sentence. See *Inside Macintosh: Text* for information on technical implementation.

Text Display and Text Editing

Macintosh system software allows users to display different scripts at the same time. A script system consists of resources that support a writing system for a human language. Writing systems may differ in the direction in which their characters and lines flow, the size of the character set used, and whether certain characters are context dependent. Whenever a user installs a non-Roman script system, at least two scripts are available, the Roman script that is present on all Macintosh computers and the non-Roman script.

No matter what level of worldwide text support you provide, it's important to avoid four common assumptions:

- Characters aren't necessarily 1 byte; they can be 2 bytes.
- Text isn't always left-aligned and read from left to right.
- Text isn't always read by a person; it may be spoken through a text-to-speech converter.
- System and application fonts aren't always Chicago and Geneva.

For specific instructions on how to handle 2-byte character codes, cursor controls, multiple sets of numerals, tokens, and highlighting mixed-directional text, see *Inside Macintosh: Text*. In addition, see that book and the chapter on worldwide software in *Inside Macintosh: Overview* for thorough discussions of text display and editing.

Default Alignment of Interface Elements

When dialog boxes are localized, the text in the dialog box may become longer or shorter. Also, the alignment of controls in the dialog box may vary with localization. For example, Arabic and Hebrew are written from right to left, so the alignment of items in an Arabic or a Hebrew dialog box is generally right to left, just as dialog box items in English or Russian are generally left to right. Figure 2-2 shows examples of English and Arabic dialog boxes.

Figure 2-2 English and Arabic dialog boxes

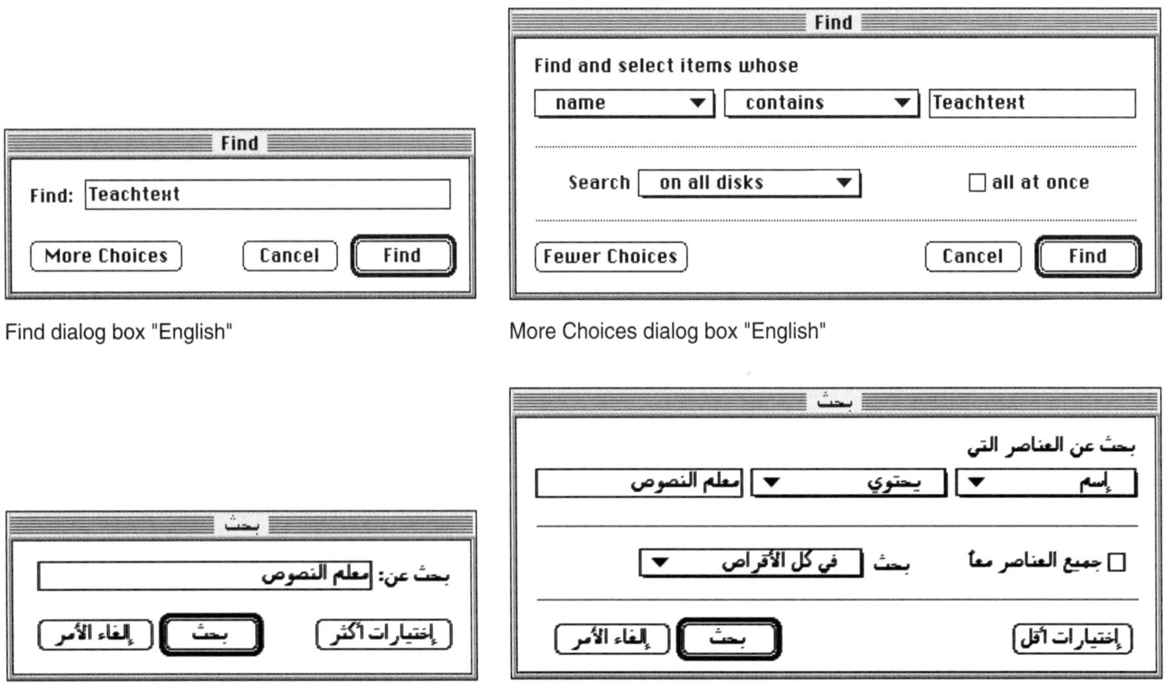

Find dialog box "English"

More Choices dialog box "English"

Find dialog box "Arabic"

More Choices dialog box "Arabic"

When the alignment of items is reversed, it's important that the elements appear vertically aligned. Therefore, when you create dialog box items, make sure that their display rectangles are the same size. Figure 2-3 shows examples of the incorrect and correct ways to size display rectangles in a dialog box.

Figure 2-3 Dialog boxes with display rectangles that are different sizes and the same size

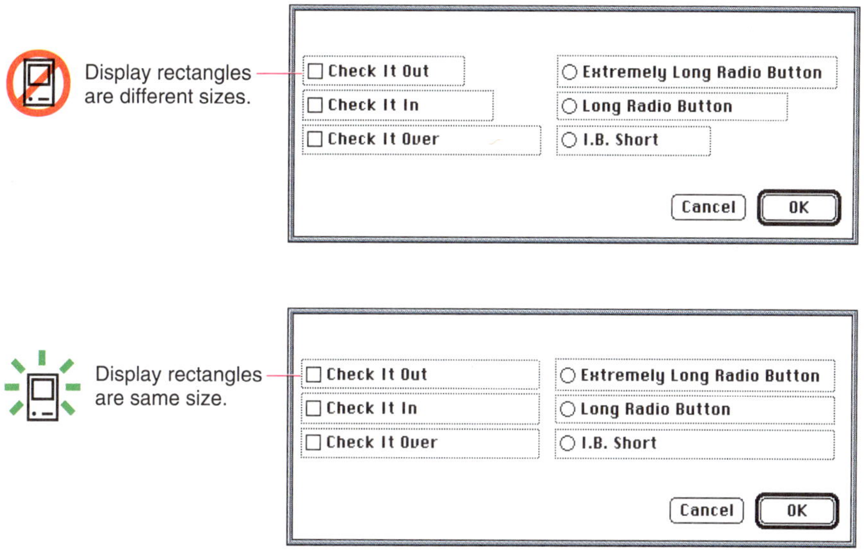

Figure 2-4 shows the same dialog boxes with the alignment of their elements reversed, as they would appear in a right-to-left script system. This figure shows that when the controls are reversed, they don't align properly, which is why it's important to create display rectangles of the same size.

Figure 2-4 Right-to-left alignment of dialog box items

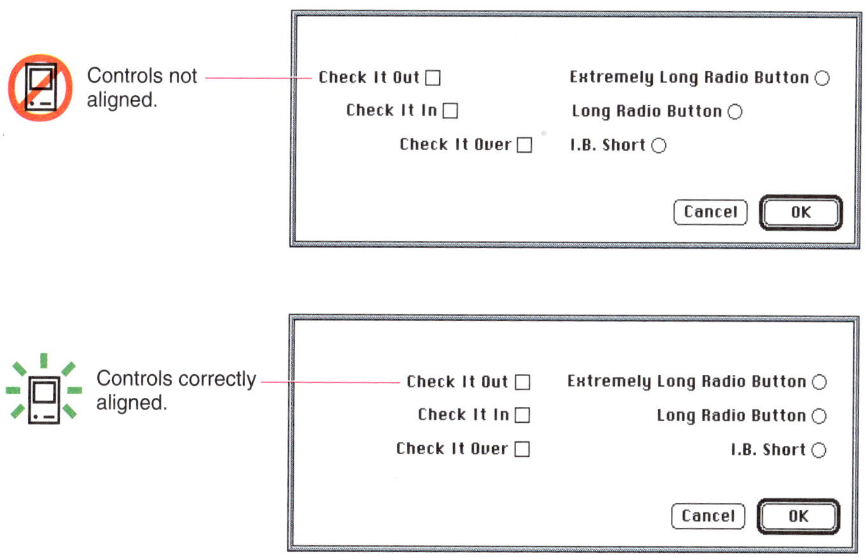

Another common problem occurs when dialog box items are longer than the boundaries of the dialog box. In this case, when the text direction is reversed, the text appears outside of the dialog box and isn't visible on the screen. Be sure to make your dialog box items shorter than the width of the dialog box.

Keyboards

As stated previously, users can install multiple script systems. If the Operating System determines that all conditions are met, it enables the script system, making it available to users. A script system can contain more than one keyboard layout that maps character codes to keys on a physical keyboard, and it can support more than one attached physical keyboard. Double-byte scripts contain input methods (which allow users to enter double-byte characters) and keyboard layouts. See *Inside Macintosh: Text* for information on installing and enabling script systems and keyboard resources.

The Operating System adds a Keyboard menu when more than one script system is present or a localizable resource flag is set. This menu simplifies the user's access to input methods, keyboards, and scripts. The icon for the Keyboard menu appears between the icons for the Help menu and the Application menu. A small keyboard icon appears next to each keyboard layout name, and the icon of the active keyboard layout appears in the menu bar. As Figure 2-5 shows, the Keyboard menu displays a list of installed keyboard layouts for each enabled script system. For double-byte scripts, the Keyboard menu displays a list of input methods instead of keyboard layouts.

A keyboard icon represents a localized keyboard layout or an input method. If you develop keyboards, keyboard resources, or input methods, you must provide customized icons like these. For detailed guidelines about how to design a keyboard icon, see "Keyboard Icons" on page 252 in Chapter 8, "Icons."

The Keyboard menu groups the keyboard layouts and input methods by script system. These groups are separated by dotted lines on black-and-white screens or gray lines on color screens. Figure 2-5 shows an example of the Keyboard menu with the keyboard icon and layout for the active script system, and the script boundary area of the menu. Only one keyboard layout or input method, and one physical keyboard are active at a time; the active condition is indicated by a checkmark in the menu.

Figure 2-5 The Keyboard menu

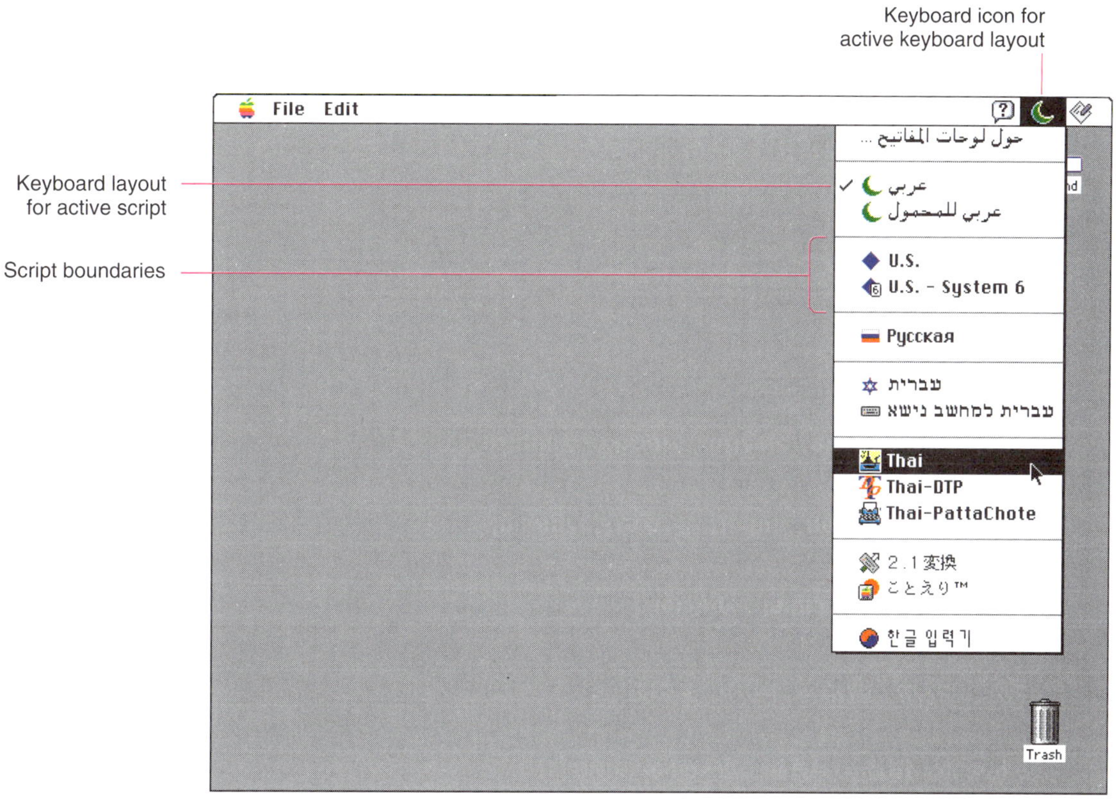

Fonts

When you write software that supports non-Roman scripts, don't make assumptions about font sizes; let the user choose them. For example, system or application fonts may be preset to 12 or 18 points. A font with a resource ID of 0 is not always set to Chicago, nor are system fonts always Chicago and Geneva. Use system and application fonts when the user cannot choose the font, but *don't* hard code Roman values. If you must assign font sizes, use the Script Manager to get a script system's appropriate fonts and sizes. Use the proper font names as defined by worldwide system software. Whenever possible, display font names in the proper script and font in your Font menu.

In some scripts and fonts, diacritical marks may extend beyond the ascent line. Other fonts, such as Japanese fonts, contain glyphs that extend to the boundaries of the enclosing rectangle of the font, or to *both* minimum-y and maximum-y lines. Leave room for space between lines of text and between the top and bottom lines of any enclosing rectangle. See *Inside Macintosh: Text* for more information. Figure 2-6 shows some glyphs that demonstrate the boundaries you need to allow for in lines of text.

Figure 2-6 The boundaries of a font

Universal Access

Providing universal access means creating products that all people can use, including people who have a disability. Approximately forty-three million people in the United States alone have some type of disability. Computers hold tremendous promise for people with many kinds of disabilities. In terms of increasing productivity and mobility, computers can have a far greater impact on people with a disability than on other users.

It's a good idea to build in support for universal access for several reasons. First, United States law mandates that computer manufacturers that provide office equipment to their organizations and agencies provide access for users with a disability. Second, it makes sense to plan ahead and incorporate support for universal access from the beginning of your design process rather than having to add it after your product is done.

When you think about designing for the wide range of abilities in your target audience, think about increasing the amount of productivity for the entire audience and be careful not to overcompensate for the special needs of certain members of the group. Don't add features for disability access that get in the way of able users. The features you include should be additional ways to access the hardware or software, not primary ways of input and output that make it more difficult for other, nondisabled users.

In general, if you follow the design principles described in Chapter 1, "Human Interface Principles," beginning on page 3, you will meet the needs of most of your users. This section describes the main categories of disabilities and gives suggestions for specific design solutions and adaptations you can make. For more information, contact Apple's Worldwide Disability Solutions Group.

People With a Physical Disability

People who have a physical disability that requires additional access methods include individuals with congenital anomalies, spinal cord injuries, or progressive diseases and individuals who are without the use of a hand or an arm. People in this group mainly have difficulty with computer input devices, such as the mouse or keyboard, and with handling storage media.

If you create hardware, make sure that you don't impose any physical barriers to storage media that would impede someone with limited or no use of the hands or arms. For example, a disk drive with a latch would be difficult to open for a user who interacts with the computer by holding a pencil in the mouth.

If you can provide a mouse method and an alternative keyboard method for accomplishing tasks in software or hardware, you can accommodate most people's physical needs. (Note that this doesn't mean you should assign a keyboard equivalent to every menu item.)

People With a Visual Disability

People with a visual disability have the most trouble with the output display, the screen. Fortunately, the software capability to handle different text sizes can make it easier to support people with a vision disability. You can design your software with a "zoom" feature that increases the size of characters or graphics on the screen.

Color-vision deficiencies create problems for many people. Don't create software that uses only color coding to convey important information. Color coding should always be redundant to other types of cues, such as text, position, or highlighting. If you allow users to select the colors your software uses to convey information, they will choose colors that are visually appropriate for their needs.

People With a Hearing Disability

People with a hearing disability cannot hear auditory output at normal volume levels or at all. If important cues are given with sound, they should be visually available as well. Software should never rely solely on sound to provide important information. If you don't automatically supplement all audible messages with visual cues, allow the user to choose visible messages instead of audible ones. For example, in the Speaker Volume control in the Sound control panel, the system beep can be set to 0, which has the effect of flashing the menu bar instead of playing a sound to notify the user of a warning condition. Figure 2-7 shows the Sound control panel with its Speaker Volume control set to flash the menu bar as a visual clue.

Figure 2-7 The Sound control panel

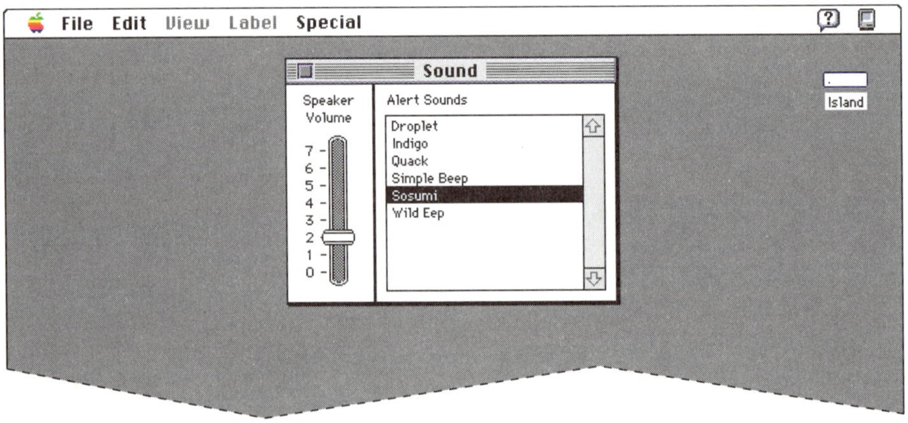

To indicate activity, hardware should have visible lights in addition to the sound generated by the mechanisms. Hardware that specifically produces sound should facilitate external amplification. For example, including a jack for external speakers or headphones allows people to amplify sound to an appropriate level.

People With a Speech or Language Disability

People who have a speech or language disability may have normal to above-average cognitive ability but no capacity for oral communication. The speech or language disability may be caused by an injury or a stroke, for example. These people use computers for augmentative and assistive communication. For example, they can use a computer to generate speech. Many people with speech or language disabilities are not able to use the standard keyboard and mouse because of some associated physical disability. To address the needs of these people, augmentative and assistive communications software is designed to be used with a variety of alternative input devices. Such software communicates with applications, windows, dialog boxes, and the desktop by *emulating* keyboard and mouse input. Don't create any barriers in your application to this type of communication, such as designing your application to communicate *directly* with the hardware (especially the keyboard and mouse), or the augmentative and assistive software won't work with your product.

People With a Seizure Disorder

Some people with a seizure disorder are sensitive to certain flicker frequencies, which may cause them to go into seizure. To avoid this problem, avoid refresh rates in the range from 10 to 50 Hz. The most problematic part of this frequency range is from 15 to 30 Hz.

Collaborative Computing

Collaborative computing is a shared computing environment or application that facilitates communication and teamwork among groups of people. These people have specific needs that may have ramifications for your software.

When you design products for use by groups of people, the products should follow all the standard guidelines and principles of the desktop interface. There are several additional concerns to consider when you design collaborative or multiuser interfaces. Your main concern is to ensure a good user experience for groups of people.

Concern for Other Users

When people work in groups, sharing information among computers over networks, usually one person controls some resource that other people are using simultaneously. A **shared resource** may be a document with data in it, an application, a storage medium, or some other resource. The user in control of the shared resource needs to be aware of the consequences to other current users, particularly in situations in which the user in control wants to cease sharing or disconnect other users from the shared resource. Create a structure that allows clear communication about the shared resource between the users in a group. Figure 2-8 shows an example of a message that users receive when they are connected to a file server that is closing down. Receiving such a message allows them to finish up their work and disconnect without losing any data.

Figure 2-8 A shutdown message

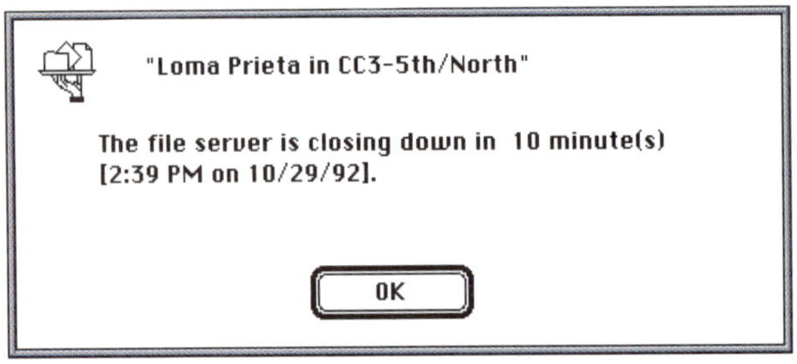

User Identification

When people share information, it is important to be able to identify all the people who are participating in the collaboration. You should allow the owner of shared resources to be able to obtain as much information as possible, such as the name, location, and access privileges, about the people who are using the shared resource. Finding out that another person is using a machine as a "guest" provides no useful information and prevents the owner from further communication in case of a problem or situation that requires it.

Access Privileges

Collaborative products typically allow users to share data with other people, providing different access rights to different people. For example, one user may want to allow some people to change a document and allow other people simply to read it. The owner may want to restrict some people from seeing the document at all.

Provide a simple, clear way to assign access privileges to shared information and then clearly display to users what those assigned privileges are. One typical problem with multi-user programs is that they have an interface that makes it easy to provide unintentional access to other users without making this mistake apparent. Try to avoid this compromised security state by making it clear to users what information is shared and available to others.

Passwords

In addition to access privileges, password schemes often protect shared resources such as collective data. When you provide a password system, make the interface to it as clear as possible. Follow these guidelines concerning passwords:

- Allow passwords to contain both alphabetic and numeric characters.
- Allow passwords to be as long as is practical.
- Never display the password on the screen in clear text, not even while the user is typing it. A common method of providing feedback to the user is to display a bullet character for each character that the user types. When the user edits a password, the Delete key erases one character in a system that displays a character for each character typed.
- Provide a way for the user to verify the password when it is entered or changed. Requiring the user to enter the password two times minimizes the possibility of a typing error. If a person makes a mistake in entering the password but doesn't have to verify it, he or she will then be denied access to the data.

Figure 2-9 shows the initial dialog box a user sees when connecting to an AppleShare file server. It shows the password field with bullets in it to represent typed characters.

Figure 2-9 The AppleShare connect dialog box

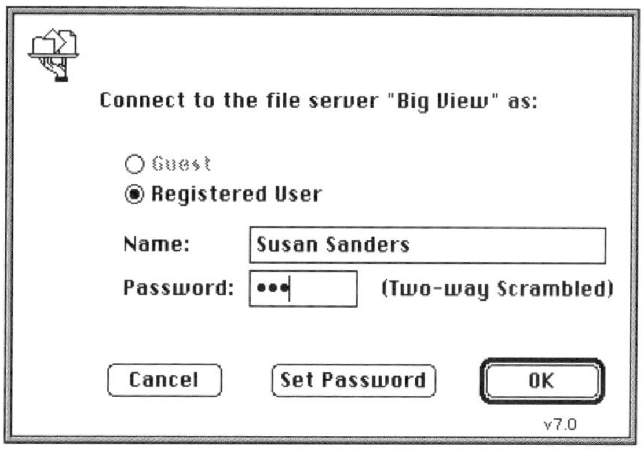

Data Encryption for Security

When people share information with collaborative or networking products, users need to be able to trust that the information is secure from unwanted intruders. If data is stored on a communal file server or if it is sent across network connections, it may easily be inspected by unauthorized users. Therefore, you should encrypt sensitive data, such as passwords, in some way to prevent this intrusion from happening. Make sure you let the user know whether their data has been encrypted or not; they need to know if their data is protected from other users.

Clear Communications

Collaborative computing extends the interface from the realm of human-to-computer communication to human-to-human communication. When people communicate over a network, certain aspects of everyday social interaction, such as voice inflection, gesture, facial expressions, and body language, are lost. You can enhance people's ability to communicate clearly on the computer by supporting the ability to include contextual clues, including font styles and sizes, punctuation, colors, graphics, sounds, and animation.

Displaying the Current State of Data

When many people work on the same data, it must be clear to everyone what is happening at all times. Because some data may be visible to more than one person at a time but editable by only one person, you need to provide a visual clue about the current state of the data. (Make sure that the visual clue is accessible to users with a visual disability, particularly if they require the aid of some kind of special device or software.) The current state of the data may vary from moment to moment or from session to session. If one person is editing the data, other people should not be able to edit it at the same time. It is very important to make clear to all users which information they may change and which they may not. If you can provide more information to users about why some information is presently unavailable for change, it will save them from wasting time trying to change unavailable information, for example.

When there is a change to data that is visible to more than one user at a time, display the change immediately. For example, on an AppleShare volume several people may have windows open that display the contents of the volume. If one user creates a document on the volume, its icon appears immediately in all the open windows on the volume. Such feedback is very important to people who are working cooperatively.

Communicating With Other Environments

In collaborative communications, users may be interacting with other kinds of computers and computing environments. In most cases, these environments have human-computer interfaces very different from that of the Macintosh computer, and they may operate in vastly different ways. To whatever extent possible, Macintosh software should operate according to the user interface guidelines and should be consistent with other Macintosh applications.

When people working on different kinds of computers or in different computing environments communicate with one another, be aware that messages may lose a lot of their contextual clues. For example, if the person on the receiving end does not have the fonts that the sender has, the message sent may appear quite different than anticipated. As much as possible, try to preserve the integrity of communication in order that messages seen by collaborators are as similar as possible. If you know that some data will be lost when it migrates from one system to another, notify the user on the receiving end.

Network Transparency

Most collaborative products are based on a number of sophisticated networking and communications technologies. The details of networking and data transport can be very complicated, technical, and often arcane. Ideally, make your product as self-configuring as possible so your users won't need to confront the technological details of the network. Also, try to make interacting with remote resources as simple as using local resources.

CHAPTER 3

Human Interface Design and the Development Process

This chapter discusses aspects of the product development process, including ways you can incorporate human interface design into that process. First, this chapter presents several issues to consider when deciding on the features you want to include in your product. Second, this chapter provides suggestions for how to make your product simple and easy to use; too often, users are confused by unnecessary complexity in an application. Next, this chapter describes how to extend the interface when your application requires functionality that isn't covered by existing user interface elements. Finally, this chapter discusses the benefits of involving users throughout the entire phase of your product development process.

Design Decisions

For design decisions regarding features in your application, you need to weigh the costs, which are not all financial, against the potential benefits. Every time you add a feature to your application, think about the following factors:

- Your application gets larger.
- Your application gets slower.
- Your application's human interface gets more complex.
- You spend time in development rather than refinement of existing features.
- Your application becomes more difficult to document.
- You increase the number of possible user errors.
- Every new feature can have an impact on an existing feature.

This section presents several additional factors you'll want to take into consideration when adding features to your product.

Features Inspired by Market Pressures

Remember to think about your users and keep their interests foremost when making your design decisions. Market pressures can sometimes cause developers to try to implement features that they feel are necessary, even when they don't have the resources to develop those features fully. Because a good review in the press can make an application successful, developers are sensitive to meeting the expectations of reviewers as well as their target audiences. Many times reviews include information on whether or not applications have certain features and the right number of new features. The pressure of competition is intense, and developers may often feel that they must make decisions based on market pressures.

Feature Cascade

When deciding whether or not to add features to your product, think about whether the benefits to users of additional capabilities outweigh the additional development efforts, growth in size, and reduction in running speed that the features would cost. If you are developing a simple application, it's very tempting to include additional features that users claim they want. It takes a lot of restraint to stick to the original intent of the application. Watch out for feature cascade, because it can often reduce the overall effectiveness of and add unwanted complexity to your application.

The 80 Percent Solution

During the design process, you may discover problems with your product design. You can use the 80 percent solution to help determine how to solve those problems. The 80 percent solution means that your design meets the needs of at least 80 percent of your users. If you try to design for the 20 percent of your target audience who are power users, your design will not be usable by the majority of your users. Even though those 20 percent are likely to have good ideas and probably think a lot like you, the majority of people may not be like the 20 percent who are elite users of your product. Involving a broad range of users in your design process will help you find the 80 percent solution.

Managing Complexity

The best approach to developing software that is easy to use is to keep the design as simple as possible. (The general design guideline that simple design is good design applies directly to the discipline of human-computer interactions.) The challenge that users desire is to solve their problems using the tools that you design to facilitate their work. The more you can do to simplify the interface and your product for your users, the more likely it is that you will build a product that meets their needs and expectations.

Using Progressive Disclosure

Progressive disclosure is one way to reduce the complexity of your designs. It allows you to present the most common choices to users while initially hiding more complex choices or additional information. Progressive disclosure helps you develop your interface so that it is easy for novice users to learn and includes the features and power that advanced users desire.

For dialog boxes, you can implement progressive disclosure and thus reduce the complexity of your design by presenting only the most common options in the dialog box that appears initially on the screen. There are a couple of techniques you can implement to allow users to see more options. The most standard method of letting users see more choices is including a button named More Choices in the lower-left corner of the dialog box. When the user clicks the button, the dialog box expands to display more information and the button name changes to Fewer Choices. This method is very clear and predictable. People know how to use buttons, and the labels let people know right away that they have access to more information if they don't see what they're looking for. Figure 3-1 shows an example of a dialog box that implements this method of progressive disclosure.

Figure 3-1 An expanding dialog box

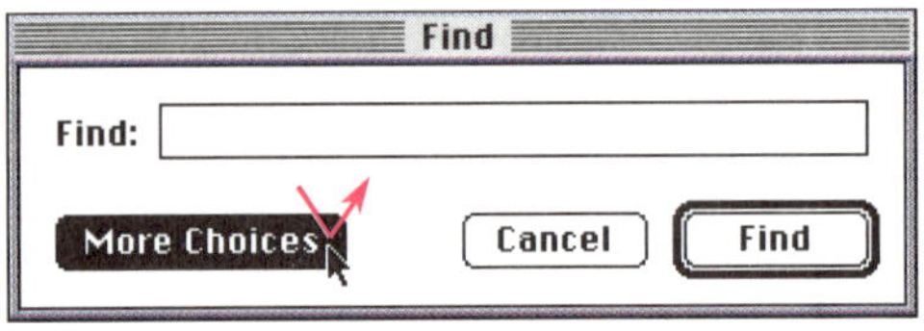

1.

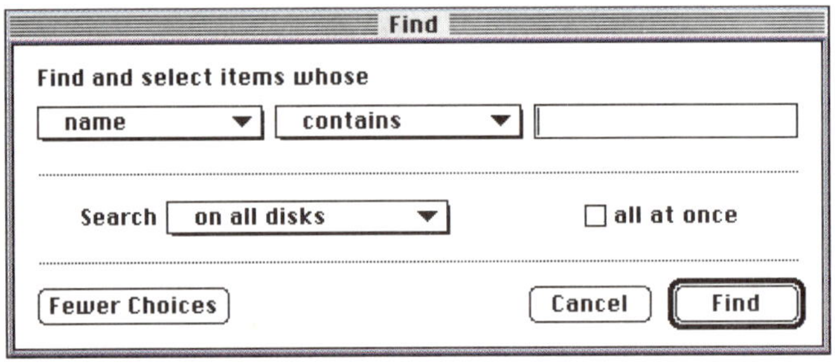

2.

If you include a More Choices button in a dialog box, it's best to extend the bottom of the window to accommodate the additional information. You could move a side of the window without causing too much change in the perceived stability of the window. However, avoid expanding the window symmetrically in all directions, because this behavior destroys the user's initial sense of the window being one object with some of it not visible. In general, it's best to keep all controls visible at all times. Also, if the larger state of the dialog box won't fit on the screen when the More Choices button is selected, move the dialog box the minimal amount necessary to make it fit on the screen. When the user clicks the Fewer Choices button, keep the dialog box in its new position; *don't* move it back to its original position on the screen.

Figure 3-2 shows the directions in which a window or dialog box can grow to disclose more information.

Figure 3-2 Directions a window can expand

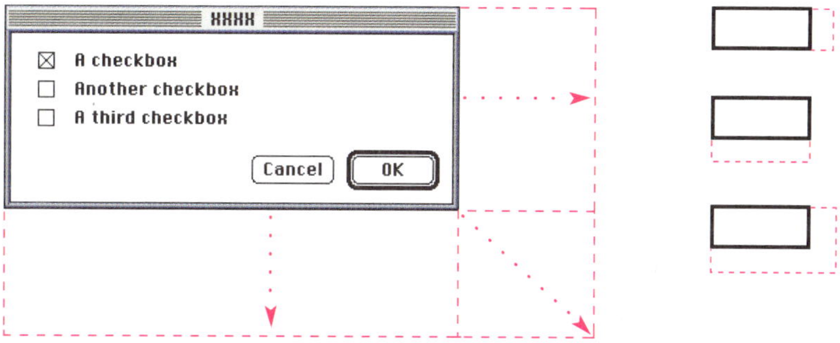

OK to expand in these directions.

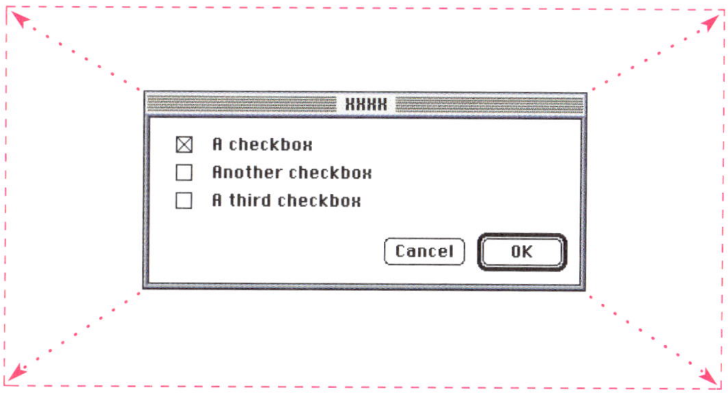

Don't do this.

Implementing Preferences

Preference settings are user-defined parameters that your software remembers from session to session. Preferences can be a way for your application to offer choices to users about how the application runs. Preferences often affect the behavior of the application or attributes of the content created with the application.

In order to reduce the complexity of your application, make decisions about which features to implement as preferences based on what your users really need. The key is to implement as preferences only those features that your users find useful. In other words, avoid creating one large dialog box with all the preferences you can think of. Instead, eliminate the settings that are special cases of a behavior or an attribute and build in flexible features as a part of your application.

A preference should be a setting that the user changes *infrequently.* If you provide choices to users that they will change many times in a work session, you should implement those choices in a menu or other interface element to which the user has easy, modeless access. By choosing the right way to implement a feature, you can give users the flexibility to choose, in their own language, their preferred method of working.

Extending the Interface

This section describes how to extend the Macintosh user interface when your application needs an element that doesn't already exist. When a need arises that can't be met by the standard elements, you can extend the user interface by creating combinations of standard elements or new elements. This section contains information on how to determine when it's appropriate to go beyond the guidelines, how to use the existing interface elements to build new elements, and pitfalls to avoid when you design additional interface elements.

When to Go Beyond the Guidelines

People rely on the standard Macintosh user interface for consistency. Don't copy other platforms' user interface elements or behaviors in the Macintosh because they may confuse users who aren't familiar with them.

There are times when the standard user interface doesn't cover the needs of your application. This is true in the following situations:

- You are creating a new feature for which no element or behavior exists. In this case, you can extend the Macintosh user interface in a prescribed way.
- An existing element does almost everything you need it to, but a little modification that improves its function makes the difference to your application.

The sections that follow present the guidelines that describe how to extend the Macintosh user interface guidelines.

Build on the Existing Interface

When you need to extend the user interface, the best place to begin is with the already defined visual and behavioral language. Look carefully at the elements that are defined in this book. Think about what the appearance means to people (the look) and how they expect the element to behave (the feel). Visual cues, like the drop shadow and the arrow on a pop-up menu, are triggers for people. These cues help people recognize elements that they can use. People also learn to associate certain behaviors with specific elements. For example, people recognize push buttons by their rounded rectangle shape. They look for a label that identifies the action the button causes. This particular appearance distinguishes a push button from other types of elements. When people click a button, they expect the button to be highlighted to indicate that the action takes effect. People may also expect that clicking a button has additional behaviors related to it, including dismissing a dialog box or changing the content area of the active document. Mixing visual cues is confusing to users. For example, adding a drop shadow to a push button makes the push button look like a pop-up menu.

Don't Assign New Behaviors to Existing Objects

The previous section describes how to use elements from the existing user interface. When you do use existing interface building blocks, use them in the standard way. Make sure you do *not* change the behavior for standard elements. When you need a new behavior, design a new element for it. If elements behave differently in different situations, the interface becomes unpredictable and harder to figure out.

Consider an example of a palette that includes a subpalette. You might think of using the ellipsis character to indicate that the palette will display additional choices. However, using this symbol to indicate a subpalette gives it a meaning other than the standard meaning. In menus, the ellipsis character means that the user must provide more information before a command will operate. It doesn't mean that more information appears when the user chooses the item. This incorrect use of the ellipsis character is shown in Figure 3-3.

Figure 3-3 An incorrect subpalette indicator

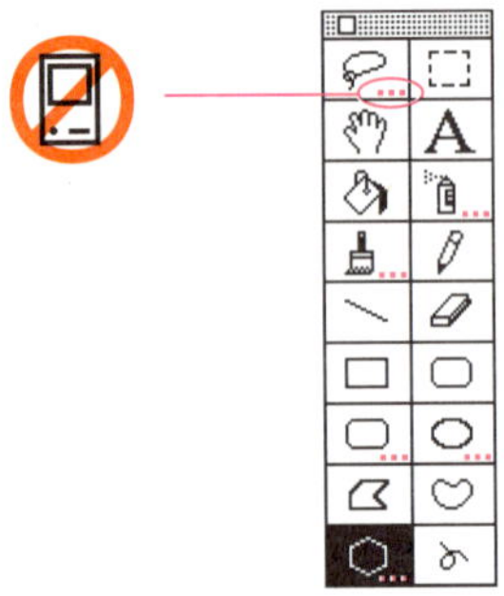

A better idea would be to use a right-pointing triangle; using it to indicate a subpalette would be analogous to using it to indicate a submenu. Figure 3-4 shows a triangle being used to indicate a subpalette.

Figure 3-4 A better subpalette indicator

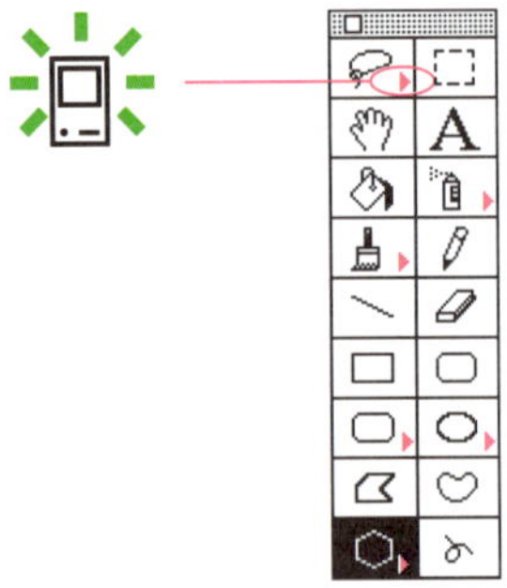

Create a New Interface Element Cautiously

As a general rule, be cautious about creating a new interface element because you may end up introducing unnecessary complexity to your product. Before you create a new interface element, make sure that you can't use existing elements to achieve the desired result. Involve users during the design process of the new element, because they can help you tell whether it's intuitive or not.

Involving Users in the Design Process

The best way to make sure your product meets the needs of your target audience is by exposing your designs to the scrutiny of users. You can do this during every phase of the design process to help reveal what works about your product as well as what needs improvement.

When you give people an opportunity to use your product or a mock-up of it, they will inevitably find some undiscovered flaws. You can implement significant changes to your product during its evolution and thereby save yourself lots of time and money and save your users from frustration. By identifying and focusing on users' needs and experiences, you can create products that are easier to assemble, learn, and use. These improvements can translate into competitive advantages, increased sales, and enhanced customer satisfaction.

Define Your Audience

There are several steps to involving users in your design process. The first step, done at the beginning of a project, is to define the users and then do an analysis of the target audience. You want to determine what these people are like, how they might use a product like yours, if they have any similar products, and what features they would desire in your product. By doing some research on your target audience, you can find out if what you're including in or adding to a product is desirable and useful.

Analyze Tasks

The second step is to analyze the tasks people will be doing with your product. You need to do a task analysis for each task you anticipate that your users will do. Look at how they perform similar tasks without a computer to help. Then look at how the computer can facilitate the tasks. To help plan a task analysis, imagine a scenario in which a user uses your product. List each task a person might perform in that scenario, then break each task apart into its component steps. This allows you to identify each step that a person goes through in order to complete the task. Order the steps according to how people do them. When you feel you have all the steps listed and ordered, read the list back to someone and see if that person can use the steps you've listed to accomplish the task.

Build Prototypes

For the third step, apply the information you've collected about your users, their skills, and the tasks you envision them performing to create a prototype of your design. Prototyping is the process by which you develop preliminary versions of your design to verify its workability. You can use a variety of techniques to construct prototypes of your design. Creating storyboards is one technique—you draw out the steps your users will go through to accomplish a task using your product. Another technique is to build a simulation of the product in prototyping software that animates some features or demonstrates how the product will work.

Observe Users

Once you have a prototype drawn or mocked up, you can begin to show it to people to get reactions to it. The fourth step, called user observation, lets you test the workability of your product design by watching and listening carefully to users as they work with your prototype. Although it is possible to collect far more elaborate data, observing users is a quick way to obtain an objective view of your product. Before you do any testing, take time to figure out what you're testing and what you're not. By limiting the scope of the test, you're more likely to get information that will help you solve a specific problem. You can use the information you gather about your target audience to help you pick participants for your user observation; find people who have the same demographic background and experience level as the typical user in your target audience. Your participants will work through one or more specific tasks. These tasks can be based on the task analyses that you performed earlier in the design process. After you determine which tasks to use, write them out as short, simple instructions. Your instructions to the participants should be clear and complete but should not explain how to do things you're trying to test. See the following section, "Ten Steps for Conducting a User Observation," for more information about how to conduct a user observation; it includes a series of sample steps on which you can base your own user observation.

During the user observation, record what you learn about your design; you'll be using this information to revise your prototype. Once you've revised your prototype, conduct a second user observation to test the workability of the changes you've made to your design. Continue this iterative process of creating prototypes and conducting user observations until you feel confident that you've fully addressed the needs of your target audience.

Ten Steps for Conducting a User Observation

The following steps provide guidelines that you can use when conducting a simple user observation. Remember, this test is not designed as an experiment, so you will not get quantitative data that can be statistically analyzed. You can, however, see where people have difficulty using your product, and you can then use that information to improve your product.

Most of these steps include some explanatory text that contains sample statements that you can read to the participant. Feel free to modify the statements to suit your product and the situation.

1. **Introduce yourself and describe the purpose of the observation (in very general terms). Most of the time, you shouldn't mention what you'll be observing.**

   Set the participant at ease by stressing that you're trying to find problems in the product. For example, you could say something like this:

   - "You're helping us by trying out this product in its early stages."
   - "We're looking for places where the product may be difficult to use."
   - "If you have trouble with some of the tasks, *it's the product's fault*, not yours. Don't feel bad; that's exactly what we're looking for."
   - "If we can locate the trouble spots, then we can go back and improve the product."
   - "Remember, we're testing the product, not you."

2. **Tell the participant that it's OK to quit at any time.**

   Never leave this step out. Make sure you inform participants that they can quit at any time if they find themselves becoming uncomfortable. Participants shouldn't feel like they're locked into completing tasks. Say something like this:

   - "Although I don't know of any reason for this to happen, if you should become uncomfortable or find this test objectionable in any way, you are free to quit at any time."

3. **Talk about the equipment in the room.**

   Explain the purpose of each piece of equipment (hardware, software, video camera, tape recorder, microphones, and so forth) and how it will be used in the test.

4. **Explain how to think aloud.**

   Ask participants to think aloud during the observation, saying what comes to mind as they work. By listening to participants think and plan, you'll be able to examine their expectations for your product as well as their intentions and their problem-solving strategies. You'll find that listening to users as they work provides you with an enormous amount of useful information that you can get in no other way.

Some people feel awkward or self-conscious about thinking aloud. Explain why you want participants to think aloud and demonstrate how to do it. For example, you could say something like this:

- "We have found that we get a great deal of information from these informal tests if we ask people to think aloud as they work through the exercises."
- "It may be a bit awkward at first, but it's really very easy once you get used to it. All you have to do is speak your thoughts as you work. If you forget to think aloud, I'll remind you to keep talking. Would you like me to demonstrate?"

5. Explain that you will not provide help.

It is very important that you allow participants to work with your product without any interference or extra help. This is the best way to see how people really interact with the product. For example, if you see a participant begin to have difficulty and you immediately provide an answer, you will lose the most valuable information you can gain from user observation—where users have trouble and how they figure out what to do.

Of course, there may be situations in which you will have to step in and provide assistance, but you should decide what those situations will be before you begin testing. For example, you may decide that you will allow someone to struggle for at least three minutes before you provide assistance. Or you may decide that there is a distinct set of problems on which you will provide help. However, if a participant becomes very frustrated, it's better to intervene than have the participant give up completely.

As a rule of thumb, try not to give your test participants any more information than the true users of your product will have. Here are some things you can say to the participant:

- "As you're working through the exercises, I won't be able to provide help or answer questions. This is because we want to create the most realistic situation possible."
- "Even though I won't be able to answer your questions, please ask them anyway. It's very important that I capture all your questions and comments. When you've finished all the exercises, I'll answer any questions you still have."

6. Describe in general terms what the participant will be doing.

Explain what all the materials are (such as the set of tasks, disks, and a questionnaire) and the sequence in which the participant will use them. Give the participant written instructions for the tasks.

If you need to demonstrate your product before the user observation begins, be sure you don't demonstrate something you're trying to test. For example, if you want to know whether users can figure out how to use certain tools, don't show them how to use the tools before the session. Don't demonstrate what you want to find out. For example, rather than showing the participant what the final design outcome looks like and asking an opinion, you can show before and after screen shots and ask what the participant observes about each one.

7. **Ask if there are any questions before you start; then begin the observation.**

8. **During the observation, remember several pointers:**
   - Stay alert. It's very easy to let your mind wander when you're in the seventh hour of running subjects. A great deal of the information you can obtain is subtle.
   - Ask questions or prompt the participant. Make sure you have a tester protocol that spells out how frequently you prompt and what you say. Your interruptions shouldn't be frequent, but when a participant is hesitating or saying, "Hmmm," ask what the participant is thinking about.
   - Be patient; it is very easy to become impatient when someone is taking a long time. The participant is doing you a favor and is probably somewhat nervous. Anything you can do to alleviate the participant's insecurities and put the participant at ease will provide you with much richer data.

9. **Conclude the observation.**

   Do the following when the test is over:
   - Explain what you were trying to find out during the test.
   - Answer any remaining questions the participant may have.
   - Discuss any interesting behaviors you would like the participant to explain.
   - Ask the participants for suggestions on how to improve the product.

10. **Use the results.**

    As you observe, you will see users doing things you may never have expected them to do. When you see participants making mistakes, your first instinct may be to blame the mistakes on the participant's inexperience or lack of intelligence. This is the wrong focus to take. The purpose of observing users is to see what parts of your product might be difficult to use or ineffective. Therefore, if you see a participant struggling or making mistakes, you should attribute the difficulties to faulty product design, not to the participant.

Be sure to schedule time between your sessions to make notes and review the session. Jot down any significant points. If you used videotape or audio cassette tape, mark in your notes the specific parts of the tape that you may want to review.

To get the most out of your test results, review all your data carefully and thoroughly (your notes, the videotape or cassette tape, the tasks, and so on). Look for places where participants had trouble and see if you can determine how your product could be changed to alleviate the problems. Look for *patterns* in the participants' behavior that might tell you whether the product was understood correctly.

It's a good idea to keep a record of what you found out during the test. You don't need elaborate video equipment; a hand-held video camera will work. In fact, you don't even have to use video equipment. You can use a tape recorder to record what is spoken during the session. The important point is that you create some kind of objective, factual record of the session that you refer to later. That way, you'll have documentation to support your design decisions and you'll be able to see trends in users' behavior. You might want to write a report that documents the process you used and the results you found. After you've examined the results and summarized the important findings, fix the problems you found and test the product again. By testing your product more than once, you'll see how your changes affect users' performance.

The Interface Elements

The second part of *Macintosh Human Interface Guidelines* defines the elements and behaviors of the Macintosh interface. It presents examples of each concept and examples of the right and wrong ways to use interface elements and behaviors. Use this section to find specific implementation information while you're creating a product. This part of this book also shows how to combine the pieces of the interface with behaviors, aesthetics, and language to create a superior product.

This part contains the following chapters:

- Menus
- Windows
- Dialog Boxes
- Controls
- Icons
- Color
- Behaviors
- Language

Menus

This chapter describes the kinds of menus you can implement in your application—pull-down menus, scrolling menus, hierarchical menus, pop-up menus, palettes, and tear-off menus. It also describes in detail the appearance and behavior of these menu types including how menu items should be worded and what symbols you can use in menus. This chapter defines the items in the standard menus most applications use and the standard keyboard equivalents for those menu items.

Menus present lists of menu items—commands, attributes, or states. The user can browse through menus or choose an item. Menus appear in several forms in the interface. Pull-down menus are available in the menu bar. Hierarchical menus include submenus that descend from pull-down menu items. Some menus can be torn off from the menu bar to become palettes. Pop-up menus generally appear in dialog boxes. See *Inside Macintosh: Macintosh Toolbox Essentials* for information about implementing menus in your application.

In the Macintosh interface, people use a specific syntax for completing actions. First they select an object, then they choose a command to act on that object. This order of operation occurs in the Finder and in applications. Figure 4-1 shows this standard syntax.

Figure 4-1 The standard order of actions

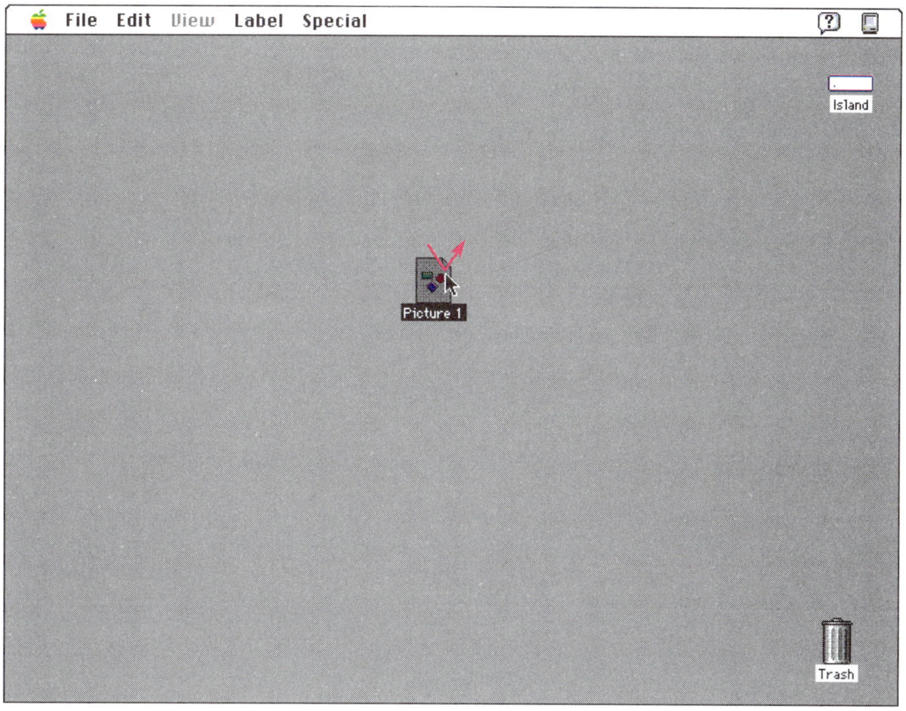

1.

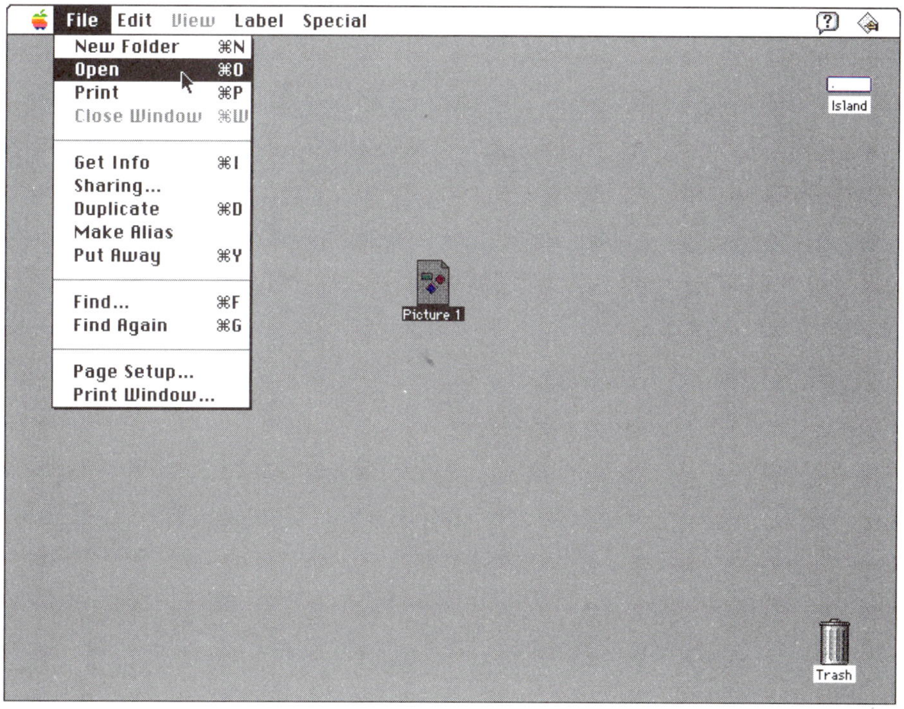

2.

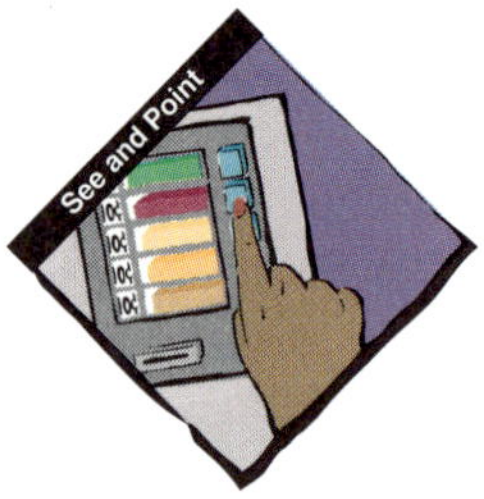

Menus are based on the principle of see-and-point. People don't have to remember command names because they can see all the options at any time and choose any available option. The menu bar also reflects the principles of perceived stability and aesthetic integrity. The menu bar provides a stable location for people to look for commands. It remains at the top of the screen no matter what the user is doing. To maintain the visual clarity of the interface, only the menu bar is visible until the user pulls down a menu to look at its contents. This feature allows people to concentrate on the main attraction, the content of the screen, while giving them easy access to the menus. Each application, each desk accessory, and the Finder have their own menu bars, containing standard menus and their own application-specific menus.

The Menu Bar

The **menu bar** extends across the top of the screen and contains words and icons that serve as the title of each menu. It should be visible and always available to use. Nothing should ever appear on top of the menu bar or obscure it from view. The menu bar should always contain the standard menus—the Apple menu, the File menu, the Edit menu, the Help menu, and the Application menu. The Keyboard menu is an optional standard menu that appears when the user installs a script system other than the Roman Script System. The titles of the standard menus never change. (The titles of the Apple, Help, Keyboard, and Application menus are icons rather than words.) The standard menus are described in the section "Standard Macintosh Menus," beginning on page 98.

You can include as many menus in between these standard menus as are essential to your application and as fit on the smallest screen on which your application runs. It's a good idea to leave some room in the menu bar, both for localization and for menus added by third-party products such as utilities. Figure 4-2 shows the menu bar as it looks when the Finder is the current application, and points out the space you have for application-specific menus.

Figure 4-2 A menu bar

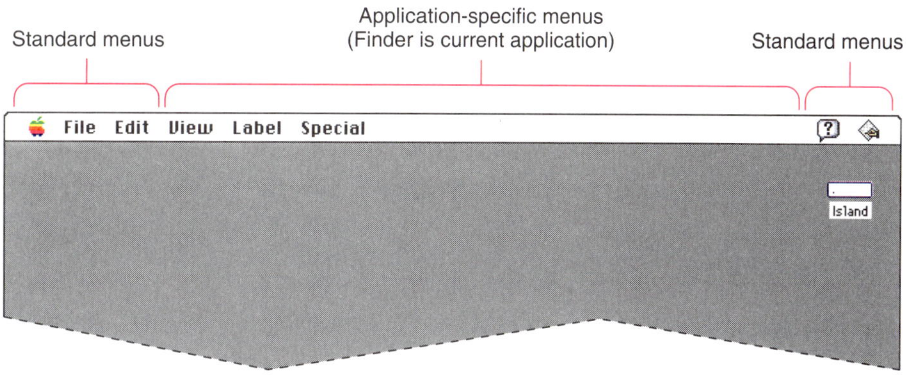

The width of the menu bar depends on the screen size of the user's monitor. Figure 4-3 shows menu bars of three different widths and how much space is used by the Finder's menu titles on each screen.

Figure 4-3 Three menu bars

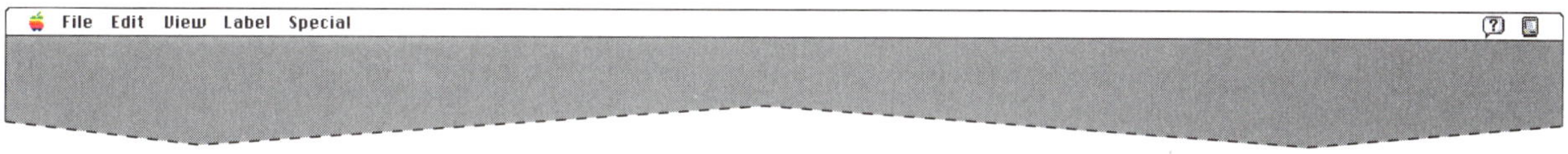

19-inch screen

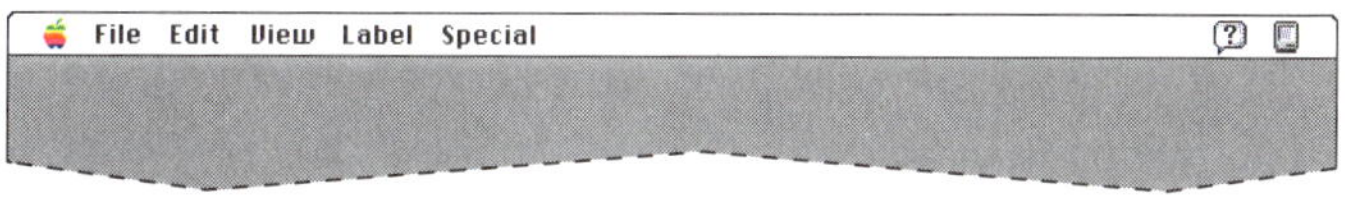

13-inch screen

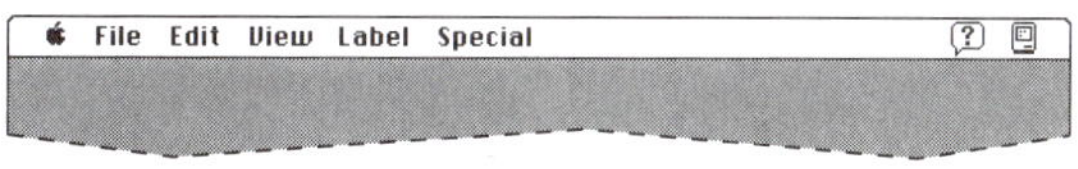

9-inch screen

Your application's menu titles should remain constant. This constancy adds to the user's sense of perceived stability of the interface and helps users identify applications when they switch from one to another. For a menu title, use a word that reflects the category of the commands in each menu. For example, the Edit menu contains commands that change, or "edit," a document's contents. When you choose menu titles, think about the word lengths in different languages so that your menu titles will fit in the menu bar even in the longest case when you localize them. Figure 4-4 shows the Finder menu bar in six different languages. You can see the variation in the length of simple menu titles. See *Guide to Macintosh Software Localization* for lists of standard menu titles in different locales around the world.

Figure 4-4 The Finder menu bar in six languages

Menu titles always remain visible. If *all* the operations in a given menu are currently unavailable (that is, the user can't choose them), dim the title by drawing it in gray. The user can still open the menu and see the names of the operations when a menu is dimmed. Figure 4-5 shows a menu bar with an unavailable menu.

Figure 4-5 An unavailable menu

The menu bar should be visible at all times to provide a visual anchor for people and to provide access to menus. If your application can display screen-sized presentations, you may implement a feature where the user displays the presentation without the menu bar being shown. If you do decide to implement this feature, you must provide a way, such as a keyboard equivalent, for the user to make the menu bar reappear and this method must be clearly visible on the screen and accessible to users when the menu bar isn't. For instance, you could include a button labeled "Menu Bar" somewhere on the screen so that the user only has to click it to get to the menu bar.

Menu Behavior

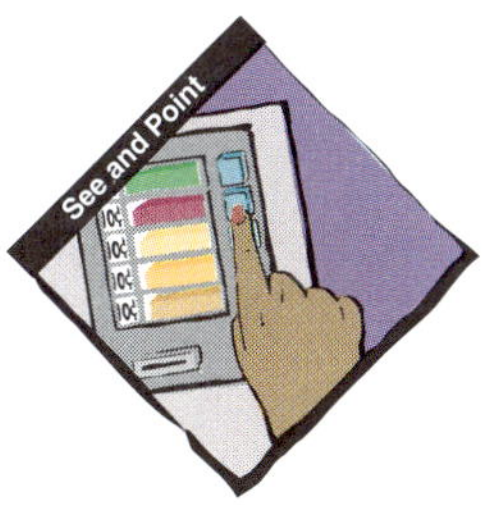

When people want to use menus on the Macintosh, they usually select an object and then choose a menu item. This behavior follows the paradigm of identifying what the user wants to act on and then specifying the action by choosing a menu item. To use a menu, the user first positions the pointer on a menu title and then presses the mouse button. While the mouse button is down, the application highlights the menu title and displays the menu. Nothing actually happens until the user chooses a menu item.

Figure 4-6 shows an example of an open menu.

Figure 4-6 Opening a menu

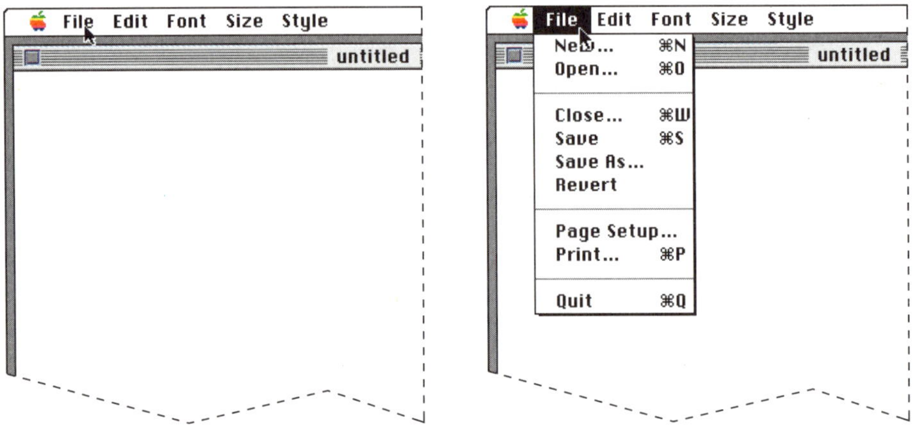

1. Pointer in menu title

2. Mouse button down

People can look at menus without having to complete any action. Sometimes people scan menus to find out what features are available. Other times, people look for a certain command by some context, such as looking for the third item with an ellipsis character in a menu. The user can move the pointer anywhere on the screen (except back into the menu bar) without losing sight of the menu, as long as the mouse button is down. To close a pull-down menu, the user returns the pointer to the menu bar, or moves the pointer away from the menu and releases the mouse button. Pull-down menus allow people to browse through the features in an application.

To choose a command, the user drags the pointer down the list of menu items, and as the pointer appears over each item, it is highlighted. When the user releases the mouse button while an item is highlighted, the item blinks briefly, the menu disappears, and the operation associated with the menu item runs. You must continue to highlight the menu title until the operation is complete.

While an operation generated by a menu item takes place, you need to provide feedback to the user about what is going on. You can display the animated watch cursor for immediate feedback if an operation will last only a short length of time. If the operation takes a bit longer, display a status dialog box to give the user more feedback about the operation under way. If an operation takes a long time, be sure to implement it asynchronously so that it can run in the background. After the operation is completed, return the menu title to the unhighlighted state. Figure 4-7 shows the use of a cursor change to provide feedback.

Figure 4-7 A feedback technique

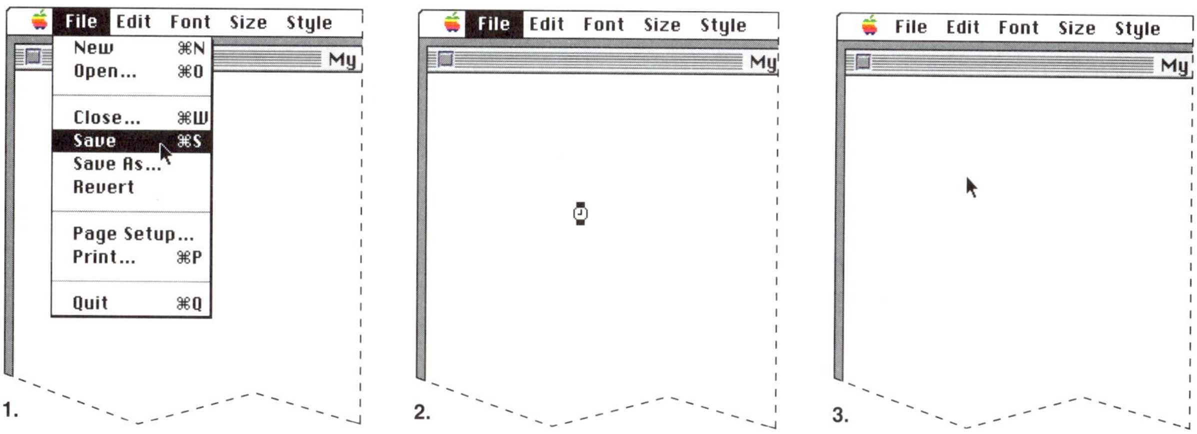

Keep in mind when you decide your timing issues that people have built-in expectations about how long they want to wait for an operation to be completed. Try to provide your users with feedback that lets them know that the computer is still working.

Sometimes people may switch to a different application to do something else while waiting for the current operation in your application to finish. In this case, the user wouldn't see a cursor change, and it may be best to use a more visible form of feedback such as a status dialog box. The paragraphs that follow describe two situations in which different kinds of feedback were chosen based on the context and the users' expectations in each situation.

When a Find operation lasts longer than approximately four seconds, the Finder displays a "Searching" message in a dialog box. For a Find operation, people typically want to do something with the target of the command, so they wait for its completion rather than go on to another task. If the search operation takes more than a few seconds, it's good to provide additional feedback that the search is taking place.

When the user chooses Empty Trash, however, the Finder waits approximately eight seconds, about twice the amount of time for the Find operation, before displaying the "Emptying Trash" dialog box. The end result provides the user with a skinny receptacle and more disk space. Users may be willing to wait for a longer amount of time for the Trash to empty because they usually aren't waiting to do something with the result of the command.

The previous paragraphs described typical behavior that occurs when a user chooses a menu item from a pull-down menu. In the case that a menu item displays a window that contains editable text, such as a modal dialog box, make the menu bar active and enable the Edit menu and other appropriate menus. Don't continue to highlight the menu title of the item that displayed the dialog box—as long as the user can use at least one of the menus, you shouldn't keep a title highlighted.

Menu Elements

Menu elements include words or icons that name menu items, keyboard equivalents, dividers, and marks. Menu items usually apply to the current selection, although some may apply to the whole document or window. Figure 4-8 shows an enlarged menu and points out its features.

Figure 4-8 A typical menu

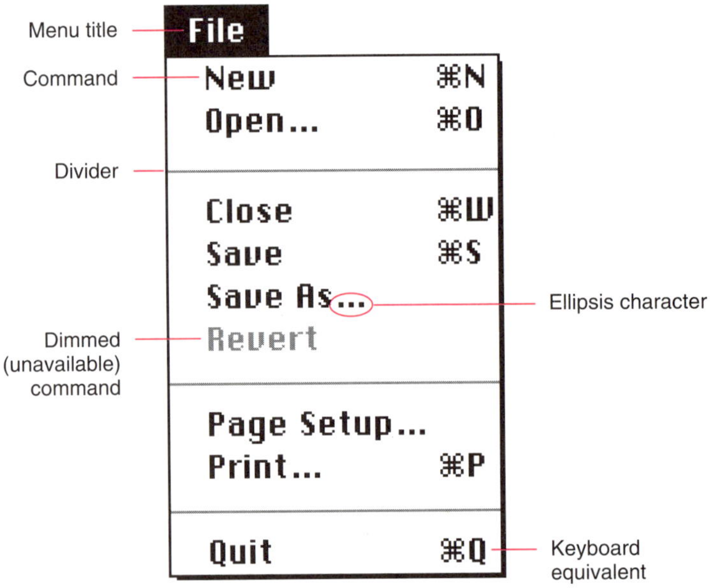

Menu Item Names

This section describes the two major categories of menu items—commands and attributes—and gives examples for you to follow in deciding how to name menu items for your application.

You can use different parts of speech to name your menu items depending on what effect they have when the user chooses a specific item. For menu items that act as commands, use verbs (or verb phrases) that declare the action that occurs when the user chooses the item. Some examples are Save, which means *save my file*, and Copy, which means *copy the selected data*. Your menu command names should fit into a similar sentence.

If the item changes an attribute of a selected object, use an adjective (or adjective phrase) that describes the change. Adjectives in menus *imply* an action. They should fit into the sentence "Change the selected object or objects to . . . " For example, when people think of choosing a font style such as bold, they might think, "Change the selected text to bold," as they choose the adjective from the menu. Figure 4-9 shows a menu that contains adjectives as items.

Figure 4-9 A menu with adjectives

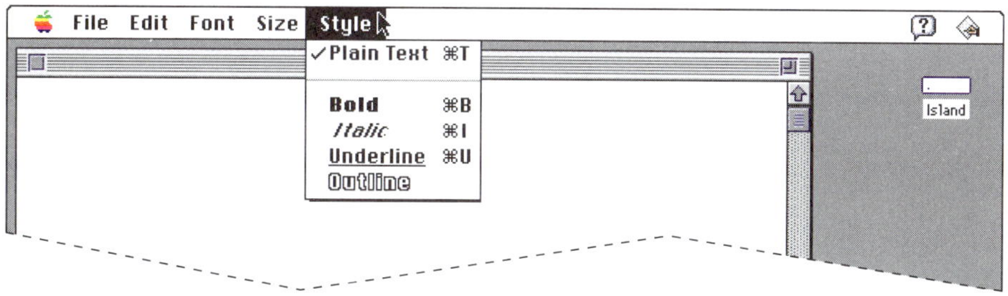

Use one word for menu item names when possible. Capitalize the first letter of the first word of each command and capitalize the important words in phrases. For more information on the style of language in the interface, see the section "Style" beginning on page 306 in Chapter 11, "Language." It presents the rules for capitalization and usage of language. Figure 4-10 shows a menu with the items properly capitalized.

Figure 4-10 Command names properly capitalized

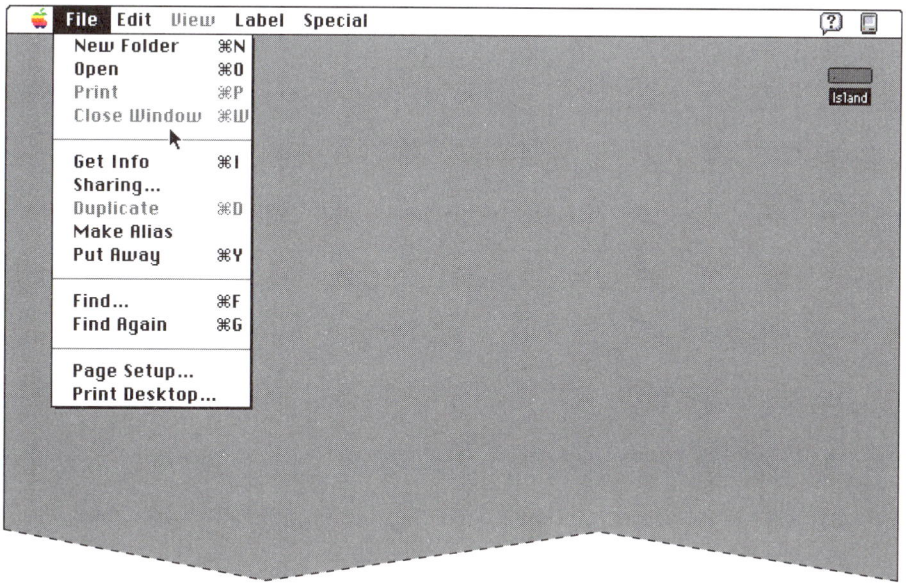

Menus created using the standard menu definition in the Macintosh Toolbox display menu items in the system font, which is 12-point Chicago in the Roman version of system software. The system font for the primary script system varies depending on the version of localized system software installed in the user's computer when multiple script systems are installed. When a menu item is unavailable, it is displayed in gray letters. When a user moves the pointer over the dimmed item, it isn't highlighted. Figure 4-11 shows this behavior.

Figure 4-11 Unavailable items aren't highlighted

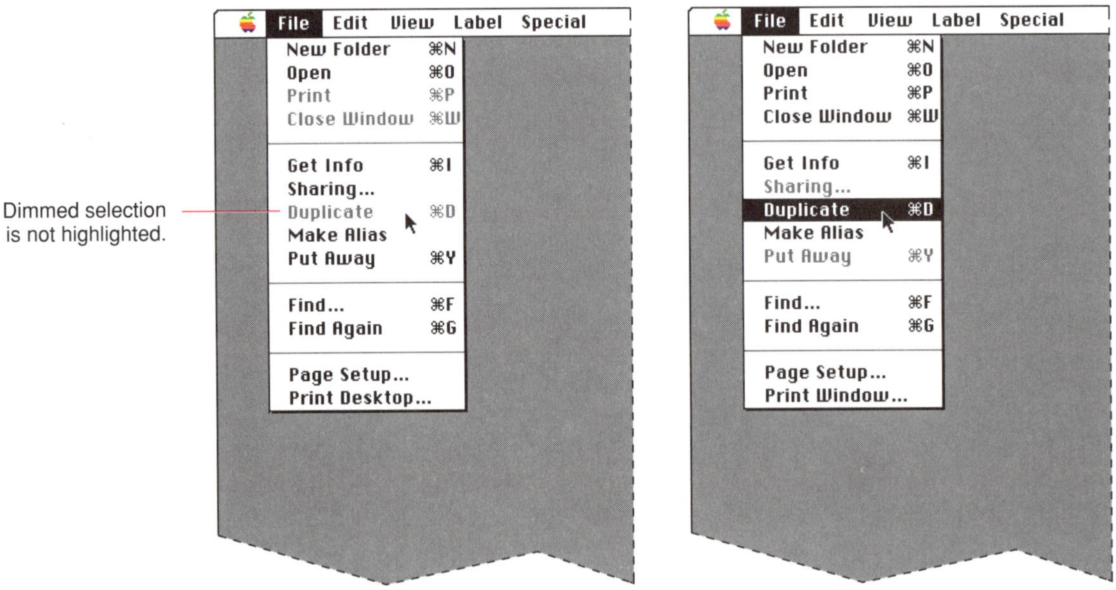

Grouping Items in Menus

The items in a menu should be logically related to each other and to the menu title. Grouping items in a menu breaks up the menu visually so that it's easier to quickly locate items. This technique lends visual clarity to the interface.

Logical grouping of menu items is the most important aspect of arranging your menus. In general, place the most frequently used menu items at the top of the menu. Put the least frequently used items at the bottom of the menu. However, create groups that make sense to the user rather than simply grouping all the most-used items at the top of the menu.

Group actions together and attributes together in a menu that contains both types. In a menu that contains a single type of item, group actions or attributes that are related. For example, in the Edit menu, the commands that allow a user to do simple text editing are grouped as a set. Group attributes that are interdependent either as a **mutually exclusive attribute group** or an **accumulating attribute group.** The Style menu groups the attribute items that affect text appearance as an accumulating group that is separated from the Plain Text item. The Plain Text item turns off all of the other attributes in effect when it is chosen. Figure 4-12 shows these Edit and Style menus with appropriate groupings of items.

Figure 4-12 Menus with appropriate groups

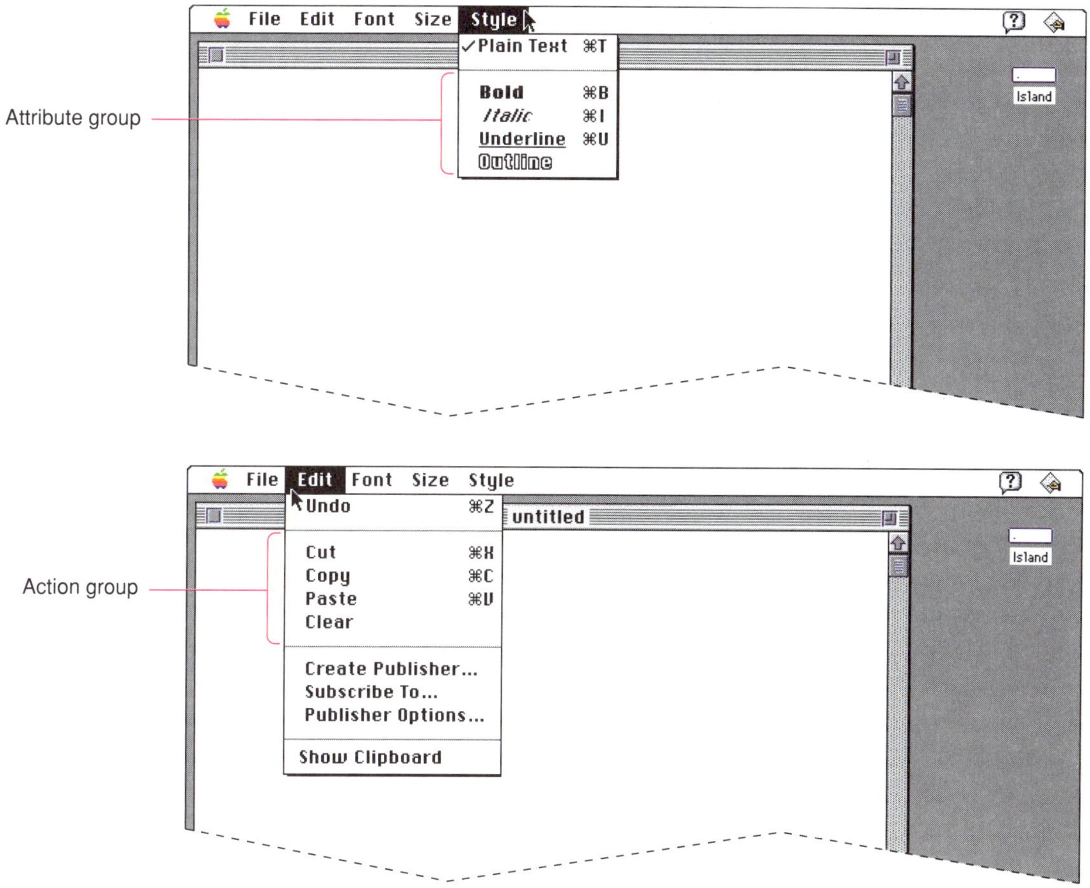

How many dividers to use is partially an aesthetic decision. Remember that the Macintosh interface relies on aesthetic integrity as a means of good communication. Figure 4-13 shows a menu that depicts the right balance of grouping contrasted with two menus that show insufficient grouping and too much grouping. Use this picture as a visual guide when trying to decide how many dividers to use to group items in your menus.

Figure 4-13 Grouping items in menus

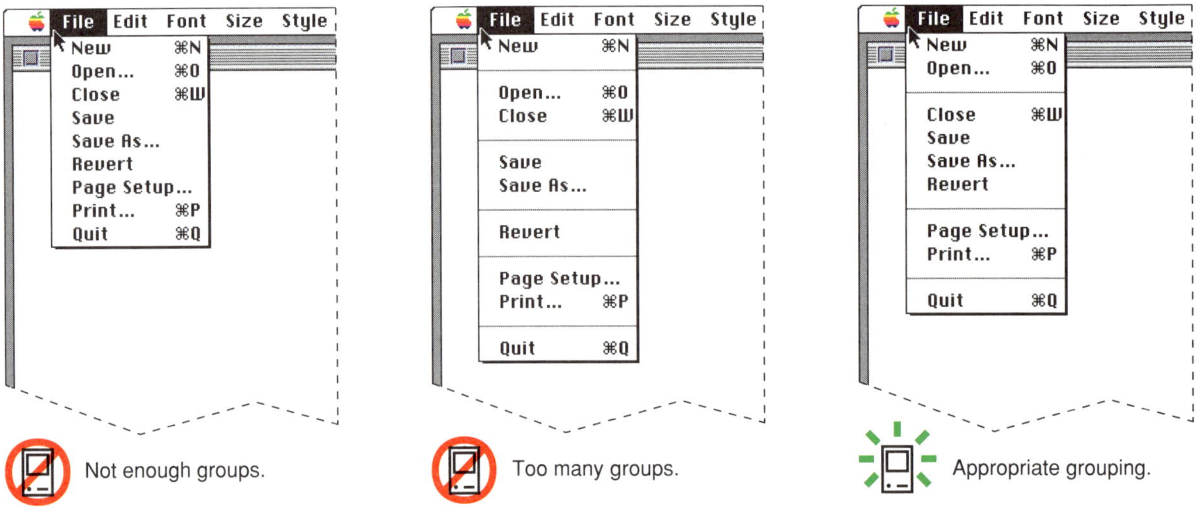

Menu Dividers

Use standard menu dividers to separate groups of commands in your menus. On color and gray-scale screens, a gray line serves as the divider. For display on black-and-white screens, a dotted line appears separating groups of menu items. Figure 4-14 shows these two types of dividers.

Figure 4-14 Standard menu dividers

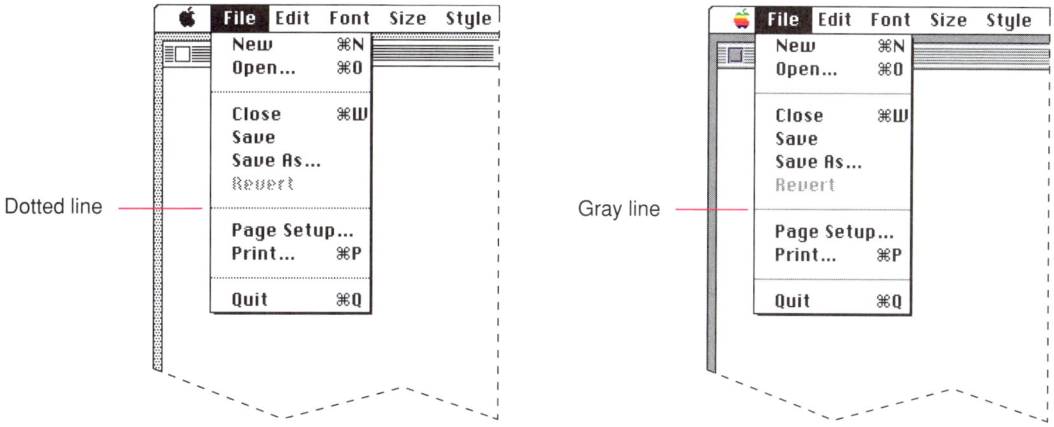

Black-and-white screens

Color and gray-scale screens

Even though the Menu Manager allows you to use other techniques to divide menus, use the standard dividers. For example, don't use a dimmed menu item as a divider. Dimmed items always represent a menu item that is usually available, but, in a certain context is not. Figure 4-15 shows an example of a menu divider you shouldn't use.

Figure 4-15 An inappropriate menu divider

Don't use a dimmed menu item as a divider.

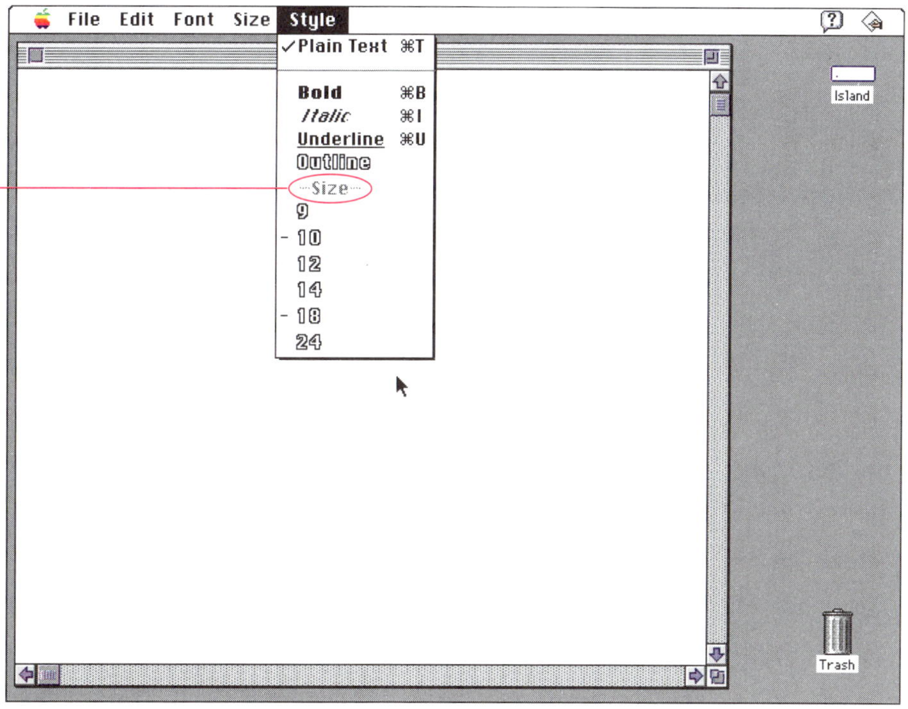

Standard Characters and Text Style in Menus

You can use several standard characters to indicate additional information in menus. Don't use arbitrary symbols in menus because they may confuse people. The standard characters include checkmarks, dashes, and ellipsis characters. In a Style menu, you can display menu item names in different text styles. Figure 4-16 shows a menu with text styles and a checkmark as an indicator.

Figure 4-16 A menu with text styles and an indicator

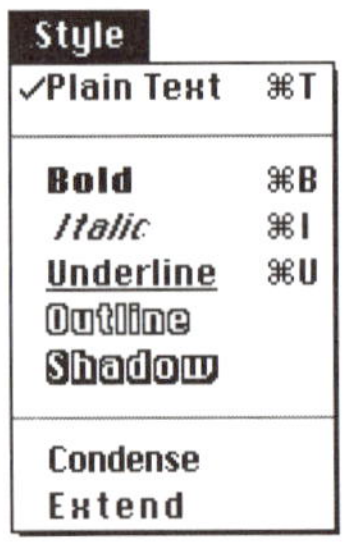

Checkmarks and Dashes in Menus

Checkmarks indicate a setting that applies to an entire selection. Dashes indicate settings that apply to only part of a selection.

In a mutually exclusive attribute or action group of commands, only one item is in effect at any one time. (In dialog boxes, mutually exclusive options are represented by radio buttons.) In a menu, use a checkmark to indicate the item that's in effect. For example, the Left, Center, and Right commands in a graphics menu are a set of three commands, only one of which can be in effect at any time. A checkmark indicates which item is in effect for the current selection. When the user chooses a new menu item, move the checkmark to that item. Figure 4-17 shows how to correctly use a checkmark to mark a choice in a mutually exclusive group of items.

Figure 4-17 A checkmark to indicate a choice in a mutually exclusive group

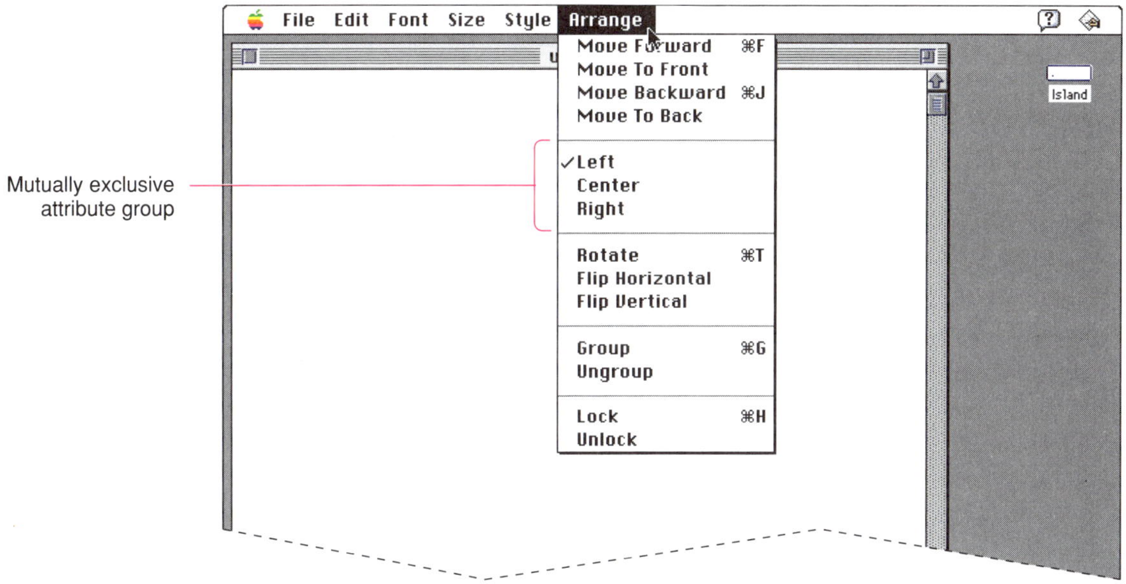

In an accumulating (nonexclusive) attribute group, any number of attributes can be in effect at the same time. (In dialog boxes, these options are represented by checkboxes.) Figure 4-18 shows a Style menu when all the selected text is bold.

Figure 4-18 A checkmark to indicate a choice in an accumulating attribute group

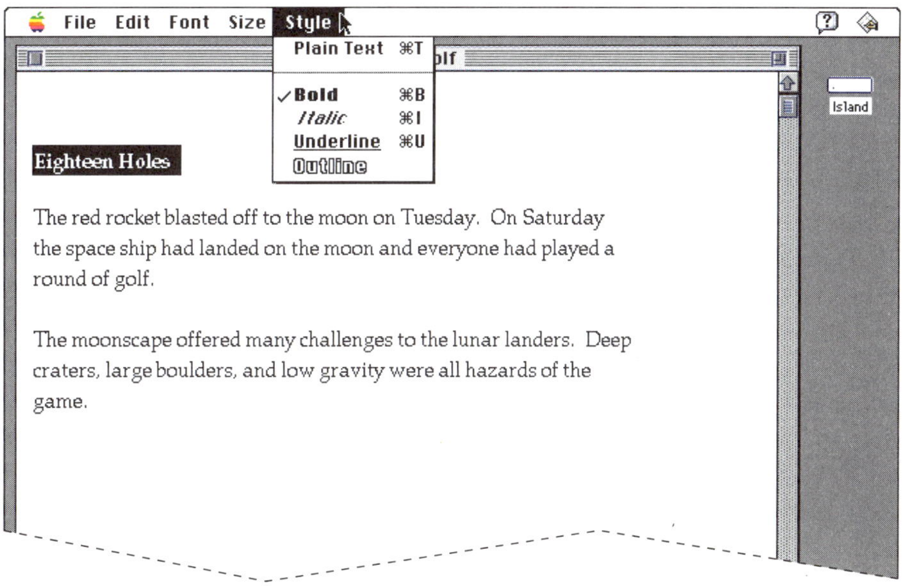

Use dashes to indicate that an attribute applies to only part of the selection. For example, if a selection of text appears in two different styles, display a dash next to each style name. Figure 4-19 shows this state.

Figure 4-19 Dashes to indicate partial attributes in an accumulating attribute group

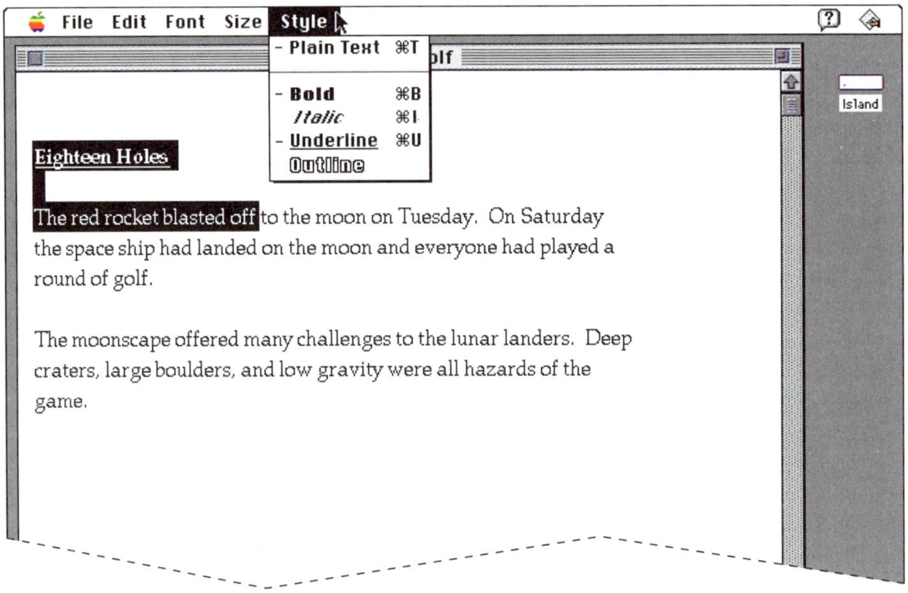

You can use a combination of these marks when appropriate. Figure 4-20 shows an example where the entire selection is bold, part of the selection is also italicized, and part of the selection is underlined. (This technique of using many styles in text is not recommended for best readability.)

Figure 4-20 Several attributes in effect

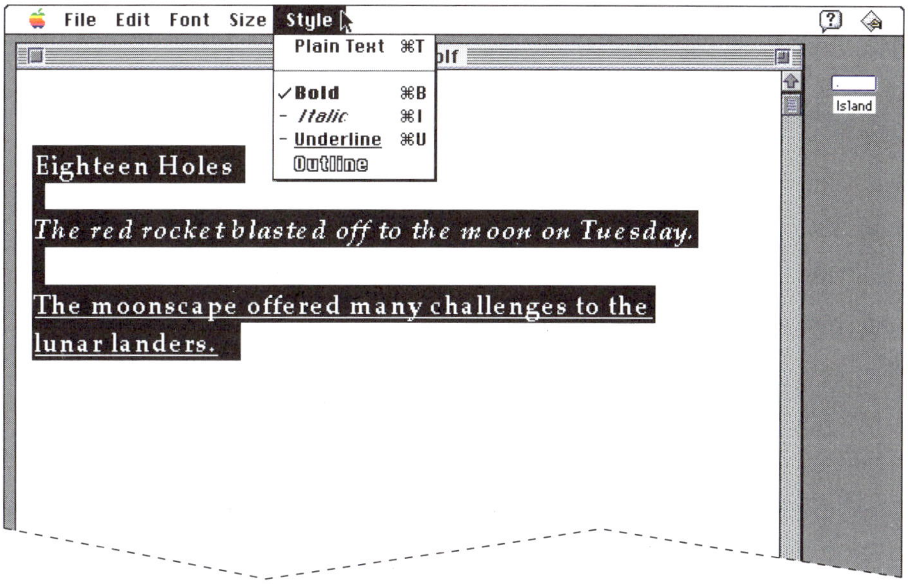

The Ellipsis Character in Menus

The ellipsis character (…) after a menu item means that the command needs more information from the user before the operation executes. To generate this character in your application's menus, type Option-; rather than three unspaced periods; the spacing is slightly different. The ellipsis character is often misused to indicate a wide variety of behaviors. The only time they should be used is to let the user know that a command will need more information to execute, as opposed to a command that executes immediately with no further information.

This section contains several examples that demonstrate the correct and incorrect ways to use the ellipsis character in menus. The Find command in the Finder's File menu is an example of the correct presence of the ellipsis character. The command needs more information from the user about what to look for. The ellipsis character lets users know that they will have an opportunity to provide more information before the command executes.

Figure 4-21 shows a menu item with the ellipsis character correctly used.

Figure 4-21 The ellipsis character means more information is required

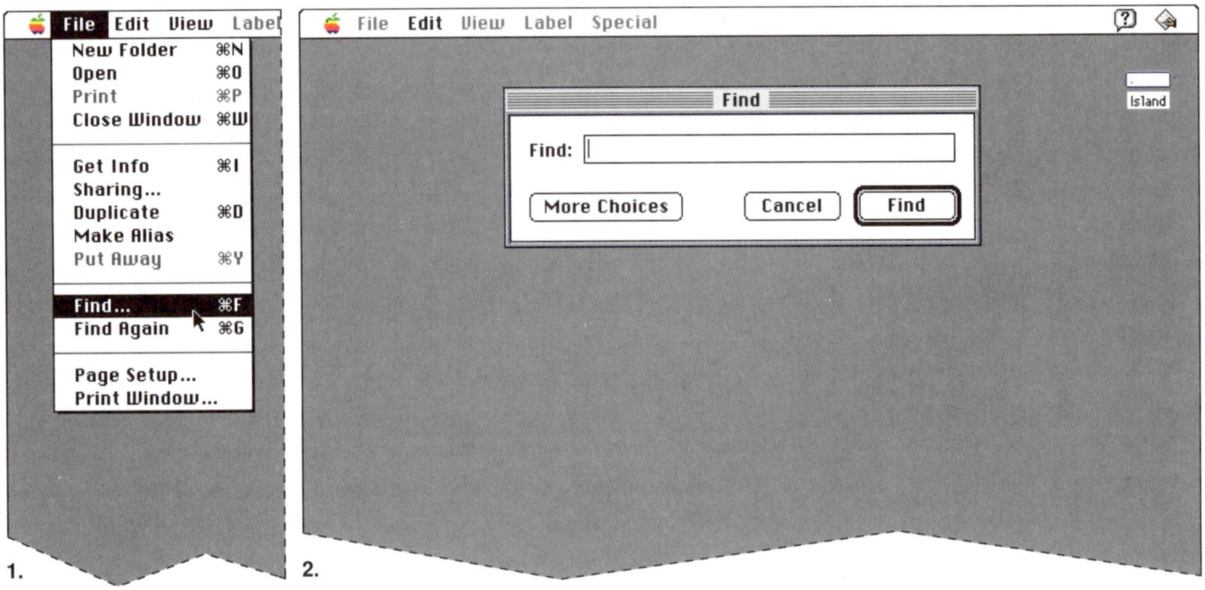

Don't use an ellipsis character with a command that never displays a dialog box asking for more information, but executes immediately. This use definitely confuses the meaning of the ellipsis character and makes the interface unpredictable. When a user chooses a command and expects to see a dialog box that never appears, it may seem like something is wrong. Try to be consistent in your implementation of interface elements like the ellipsis character.

Figure 4-22 shows the incorrect use of the ellipsis character after a command that never displays a dialog box, and the menu as it should appear.

Figure 4-22 Don't use the ellipsis character with a command that doesn't require more information

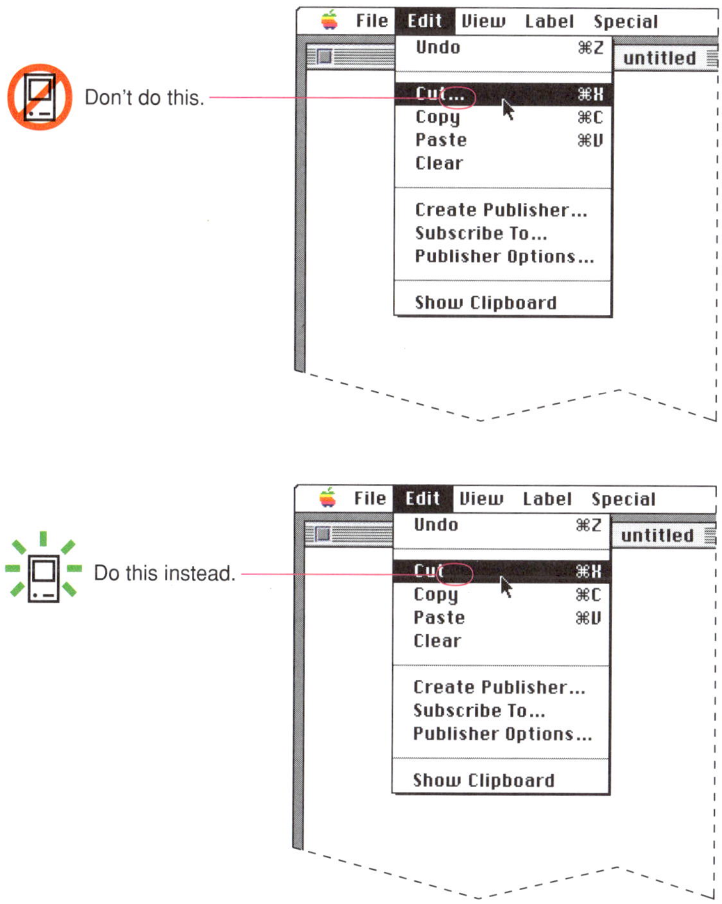

The ellipsis character *doesn't* simply mean that a dialog box or window will appear. For example in the Finder File menu, the Get Info command doesn't have an ellipsis character and *shouldn't*. When you select a Finder object and choose Get Info, a window appears displaying information about the object. The window appearing simply completes the command. The command doesn't require additional input from the user before it executes.

Figure 4-23 shows the correct absence of the ellipsis character, even in the case where a window appears as the result of a command.

Figure 4-23 The absence of the ellipsis character means no more information is required

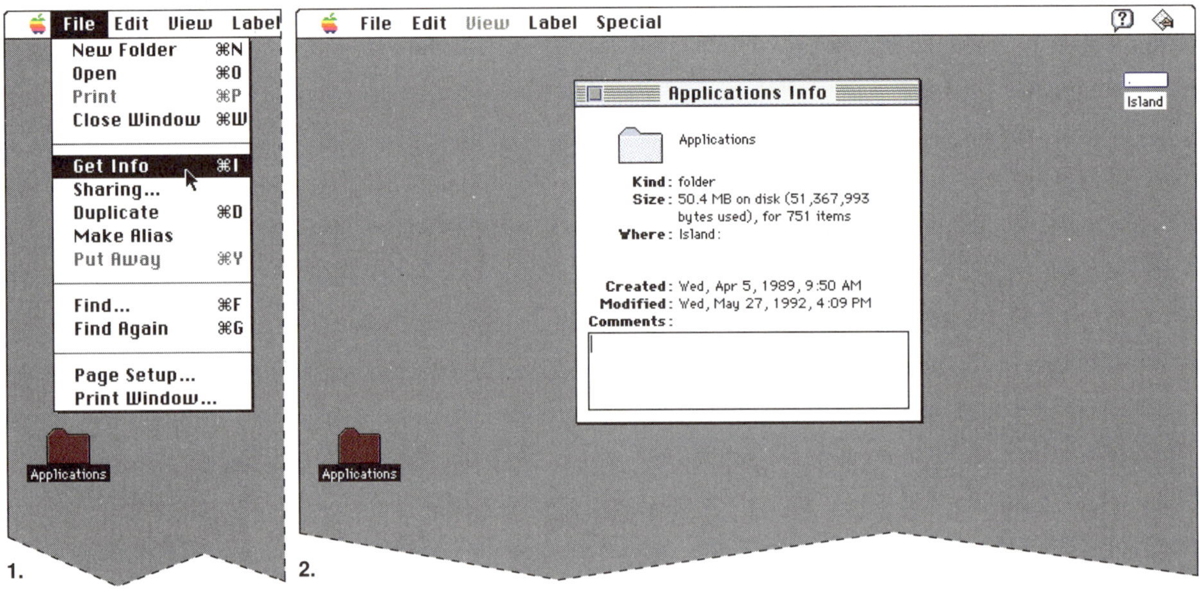

Don't use an ellipsis character if the command displays an alert box to warn the user of a potentially dangerous action, especially if the command displays an alert box *only* sometimes. In this case you are simply giving the user an opportunity to cancel a potentially dangerous action (such as causing a loss of data), not asking for more information. Figure 4-24 shows the correct absence of the ellipsis character with a command that displays an alert box.

Figure 4-24 The ellipsis character doesn't mean an alert box appears

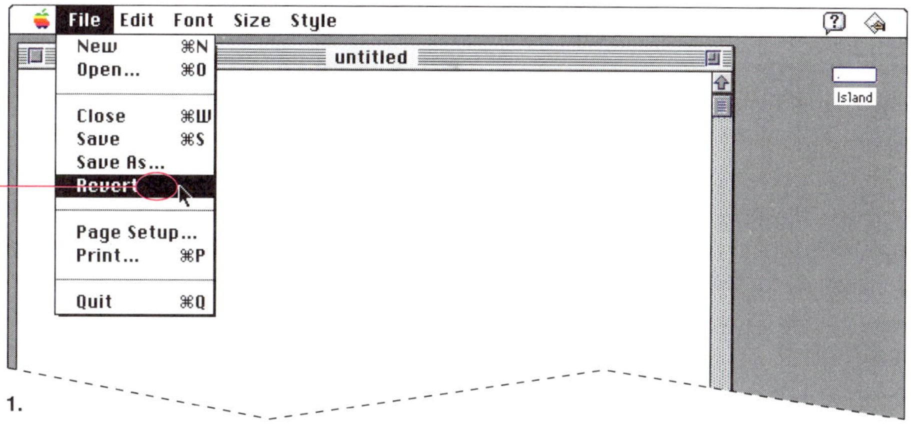

1.

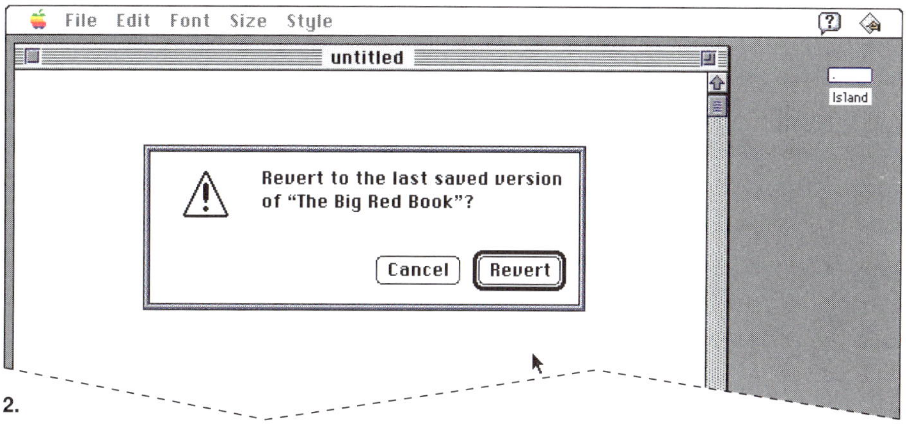

2.

A Diamond Mark in the Application Menu

When your application is running a background task and you need to notify the user of something that needs attention, you can use various techniques provided by the Notification Manager to get the user's attention. At the minimum, display a diamond-shaped mark next to your application's name in the Application menu to indicate that it is the application that is asking for the user's attention and alternate a small icon in the menu bar with the icon for the Application menu. In general, you should use the small icon that corresponds to your application or system extension, so that the user gets an additional visual clue about which application is requesting attention.

Figure 4-25 shows an example of a notification symbol in a menu.

Figure 4-25 The Application menu with a notification symbol

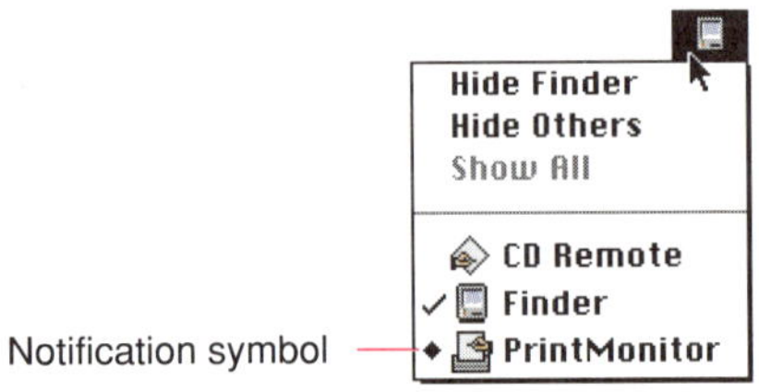

There are other notification techniques as well. You can also play a sound and put up an alert box to notify the user. See *Inside Macintosh: Processes* for more information on notification techniques and implementing the Notification Manager.

Avoid Nonstandard Marks in Menus

Don't use any nonstandard marks or arbitrary graphic symbols in menus. They only add visual clutter to the menu and people won't necessarily understand the significance of the nonstandard marks—for example, they won't know what a circle, addition sign, or tilde in a menu means. Figure 4-26 shows some marking techniques to avoid.

Figure 4-26 Don't use arbitrary symbols in menus

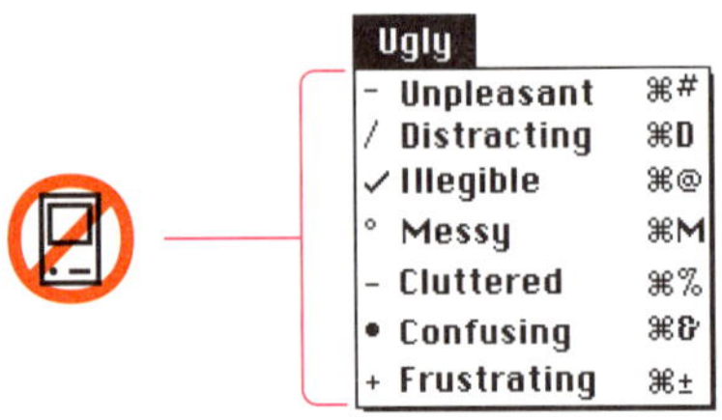

Text Styles in Menus

You can use text styles in a Style menu to indicate the effect of choosing a certain text attribute. This use is only appropriate in Style menus. Figure 4-27 shows an appropriate Style menu. Outline style is also used in the Size menu to indicate installed sizes of bitmapped fonts and all sizes of TrueType fonts that are available.

Figure 4-27 A Style menu with text styles

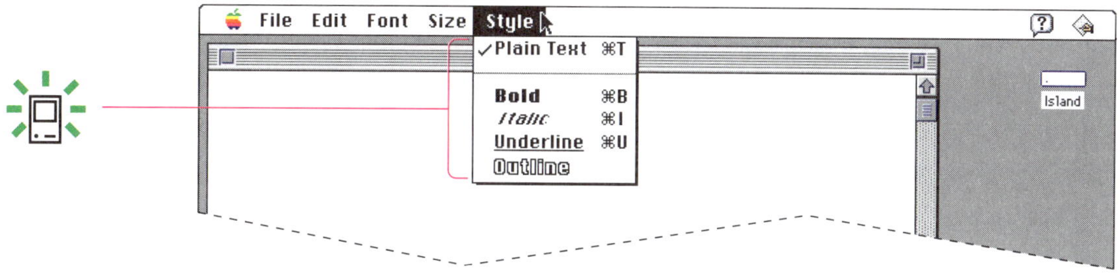

Use the standard wording for style items. These items are one type of toggled menu item. With this type of toggled menu item, the first time the user chooses the item, it sets the selected object to that attribute. The second time the user chooses the item with the same object selected, the effect is reversed. See the discussion of toggled menu items in the next section, "Toggled Menu Items," for more information. Figure 4-28 shows the effect of choosing a style menu item.

Figure 4-28 The effects of the two states of a Style menu item

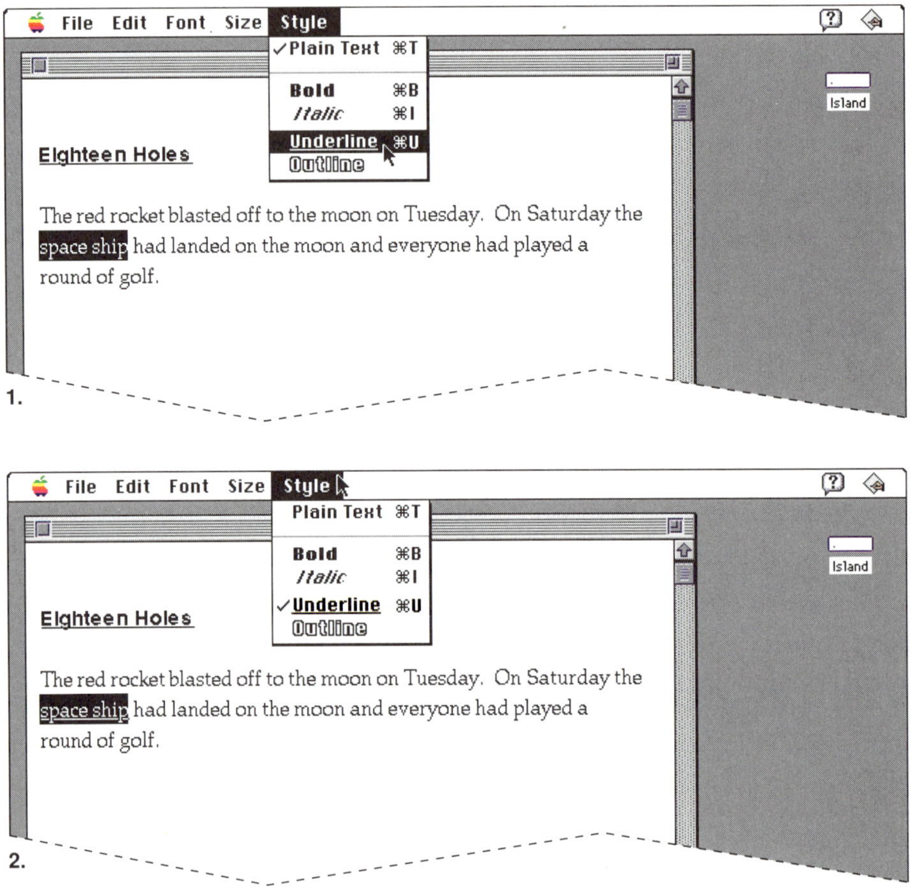

Don't use text styles to indicate additional information, not style related, about menu items. This technique may distract and confuse your users. It may also disrupt the visual clarity of the interface.

Don't use both arbitrary marks and text styles to try to pack your menus with meaningful information. Use plain 12-point Chicago for menu commands on an unlocalized Roman system and add standard marks only where they belong. (Use keyboard equivalents on only the most often used items and follow the guidelines in the section "Keyboard Equivalents" on page 128 for assigning them.) Figure 4-29 shows an extreme example of an overburdened menu and an appropriate standard menu. For more information about providing text style choices, see the section "The Style Menu," which begins on page 124.

Figure 4-29 A menu with nonstandard marks and extraneous text styles and a menu all in plain text style

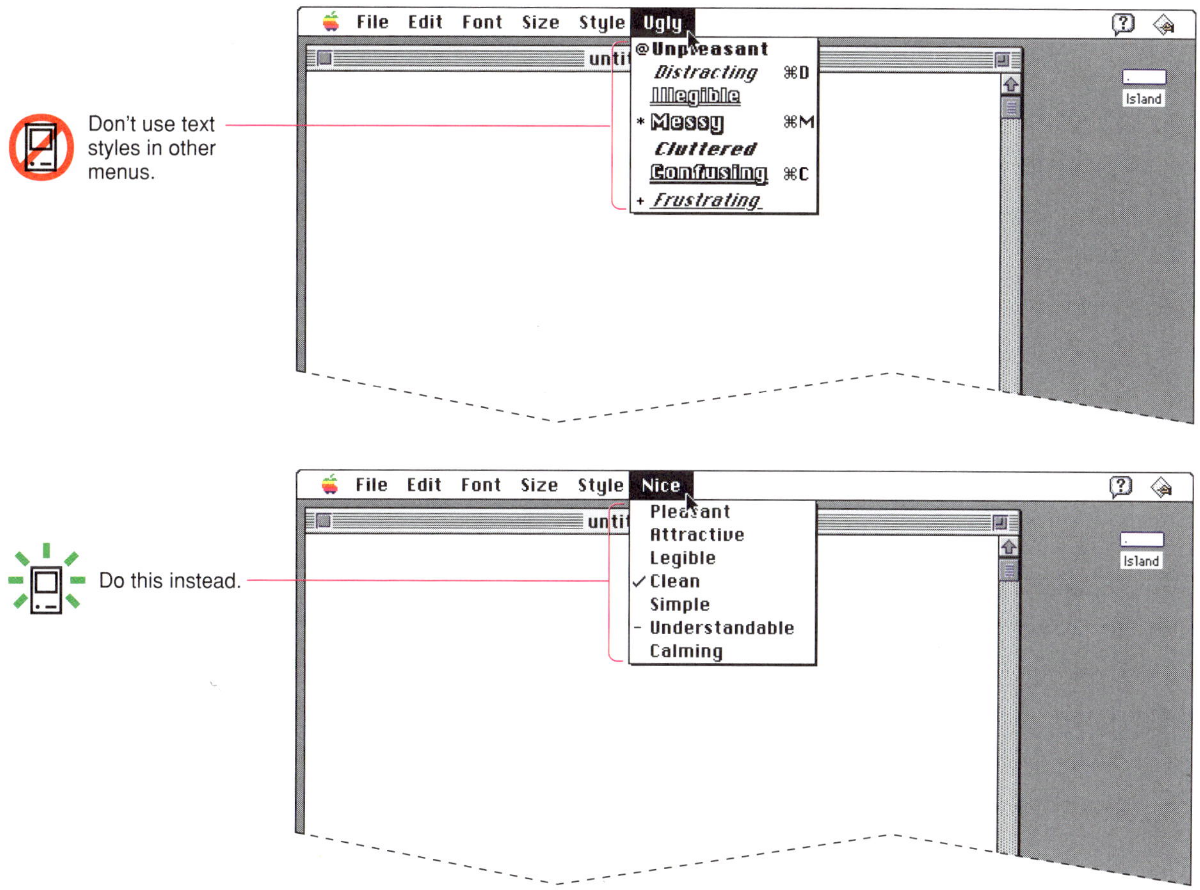

Toggled Menu Items

A **toggled menu item** changes between two states each time a user chooses it. It's like a toggle light switch, when you flip it one way, the light turns on. When you flip the switch the other direction, the light turns off.

There are three types of toggled menu items. In one type, there is one menu item and its name changes to reflect the current state of the item. An example of this type is the command Show Ruler, which changes to Hide Ruler when the ruler is visible in the document. Another type of toggled menu item has one menu item that has a checkmark next to its name when it is in effect. An example of this type of item is a style attribute like Bold. The third type of toggled menu item has a group of two menu items that are opposite states. The state currently in effect has a checkmark next to its name.

If you have room in your menu, it's a good idea to use two menu items that describe opposite states. The user can see both items at once, and there's less chance of confusion about the effects of the menu items. Set the items off using dividers to indicate that this is a related set of menu items. Use a checkmark to indicate the active item, as described in the section "Checkmarks and Dashes in Menus" on page 64. Figure 4-30 shows a set of properly constructed toggled menu items.

Figure 4-30 A set of toggled menu items

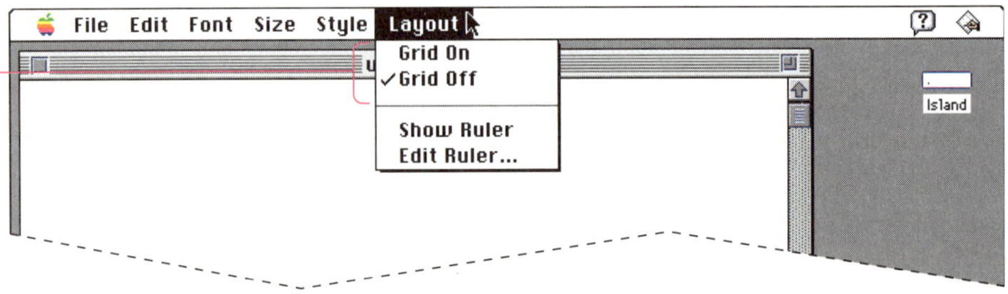

If you don't have room in your menu for two items, you can use one item (which describes a specific action) and change its name to the opposite action when it's chosen. When you use a toggled menu item that is only one item, you must be sure that the name of the command is completely unambiguous. The command names should be verbs that express opposite actions. In the previous example, you could change the phrase Grid On to Turn Grid On. The command becomes Turn Grid Off in the opposite state. Figure 4-31 shows this solution.

Figure 4-31 A single toggled menu item whose name changes

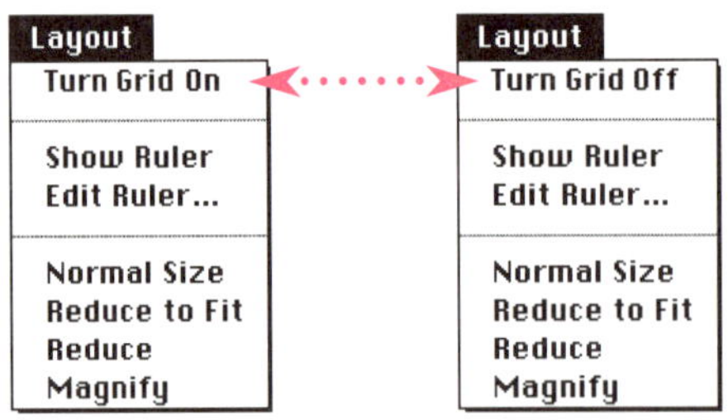

In this menu, Turn Grid On clearly means that the grid appears when the user chooses the command. Then the command name changes to a clear statement of what happens as a result of choosing the Turn Grid Off command.

Try not to use phrases that could have ambiguous meanings. For example, does Use Grid mean that

- the grid is on?
- this command turns on the grid?

Figure 4-32 shows two different expectations of what the user might see when the Layout menu is opened after choosing the command Use Grid. In this example people have to choose the command, see what happens, and look at the menu to see what the meaning of Use Grid is.

Figure 4-32 An ambiguous toggled menu item

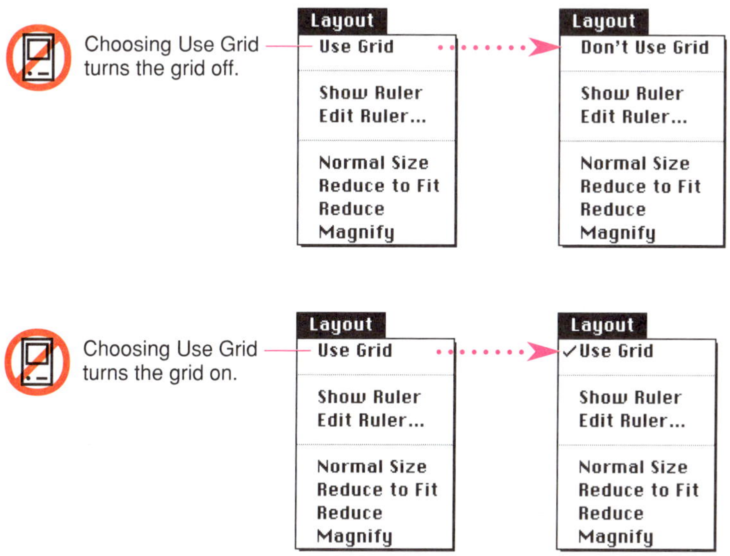

Don't use one menu item with a toggled checkmark to indicate the presence or absence of a feature like a grid or a ruler. It's unclear whether the checkmark means that the feature is in effect or whether choosing the command turns the feature on. In the example shown in Figure 4-33, a checkmark next to Grid On could mean the grid is on, but the absence of a checkmark wouldn't be a clear indication that the grid is off. Because any change to the user's content or working environment should be visible on the screen (in the application or in the Finder), not hidden, don't use the menu as an indicator of the current state by placing a checkmark next to a single, ambiguous menu item.

Figure 4-33 An incorrect use of a checkmark to indicate a state

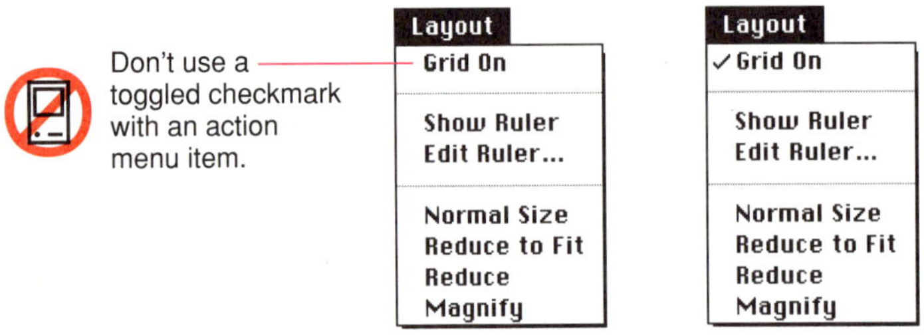

Scrolling Menus

Scrolling menus contain more menu items than are visible on the screen. (For a nonscrolling menu, you can usually use between eight and twelve menu items and still have a menu that is easy to use and to navigate.) Scrolling menus should exist only when a user adds many items to a customizable menu like the Font menu.

If a menu becomes too long to fit on the screen, an indicator appears at the bottom of the menu to show that there are more items. When the user starts to scroll, an indicator appears at the top of the menu to show that some items are no longer visible in that direction. When the user drags past the last visible item, the menu scrolls to show the additional items. When the last item is shown, the downward-pointing indicator disappears. Figure 4-34 shows this behavior.

Figure 4-34 A scrolling menu

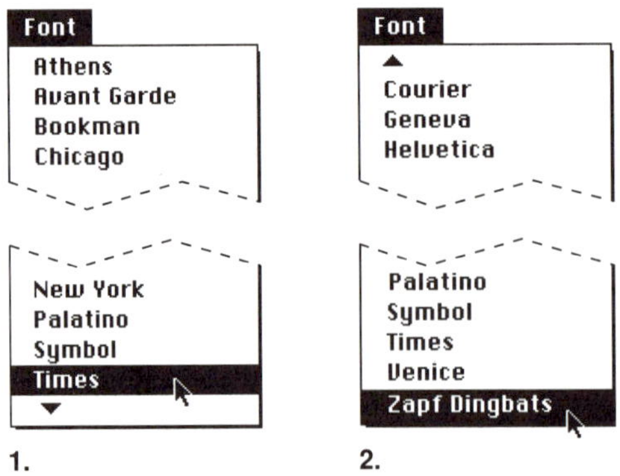

Figure 4-35 shows the menu scrolling in the opposite direction.

Figure 4-35 The menu scrolling in the other direction

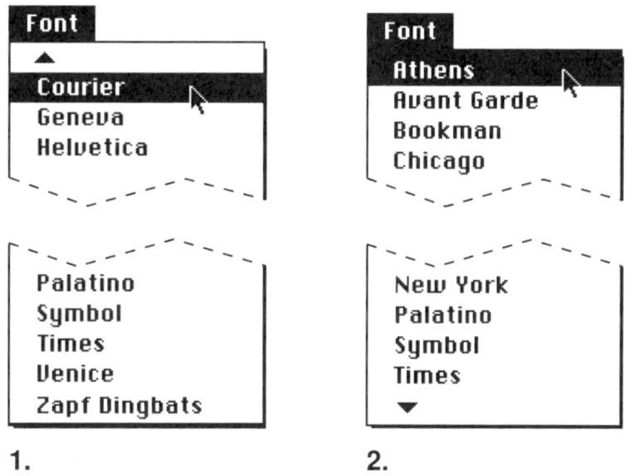

If the user drags back up to the top, the menu scrolls back down in the same manner. If the user leaves the menu and comes back to it later, it appears in its original position, with the hidden items and the indicator at the bottom.

Hierarchical Menus

Hierarchical menus are menus that include a menu item from which a submenu descends. You can offer additional menu item choices without taking up more space in the menu bar by including a submenu in a main menu. When the user drags the pointer through a menu and rests it on a hierarchical menu item, a submenu appears after a brief delay. To indicate that a submenu exists, use a triangle facing right, as shown in Figure 4-36.

Figure 4-36 A hierarchical menu

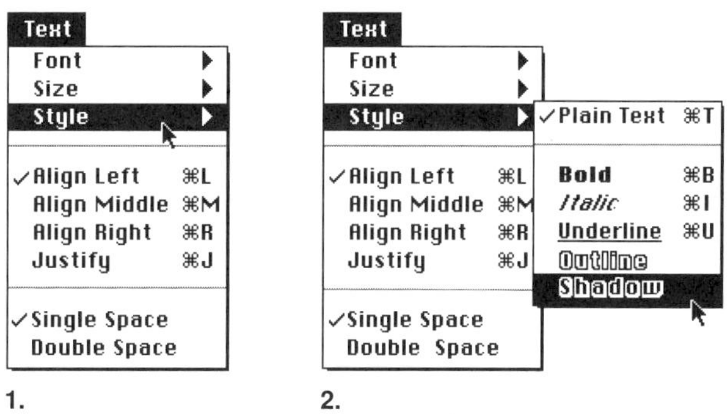

Submenus add complexity to the interface. They hide choices from people by adding a layer to menus. They are physically more difficult to use than menus that pull down from the menu bar. You should use a submenu only when you have more menus than fit in the menu bar. Figure 4-37 shows an example of unnecessary submenus.

Figure 4-37 Don't use submenus unnecessarily

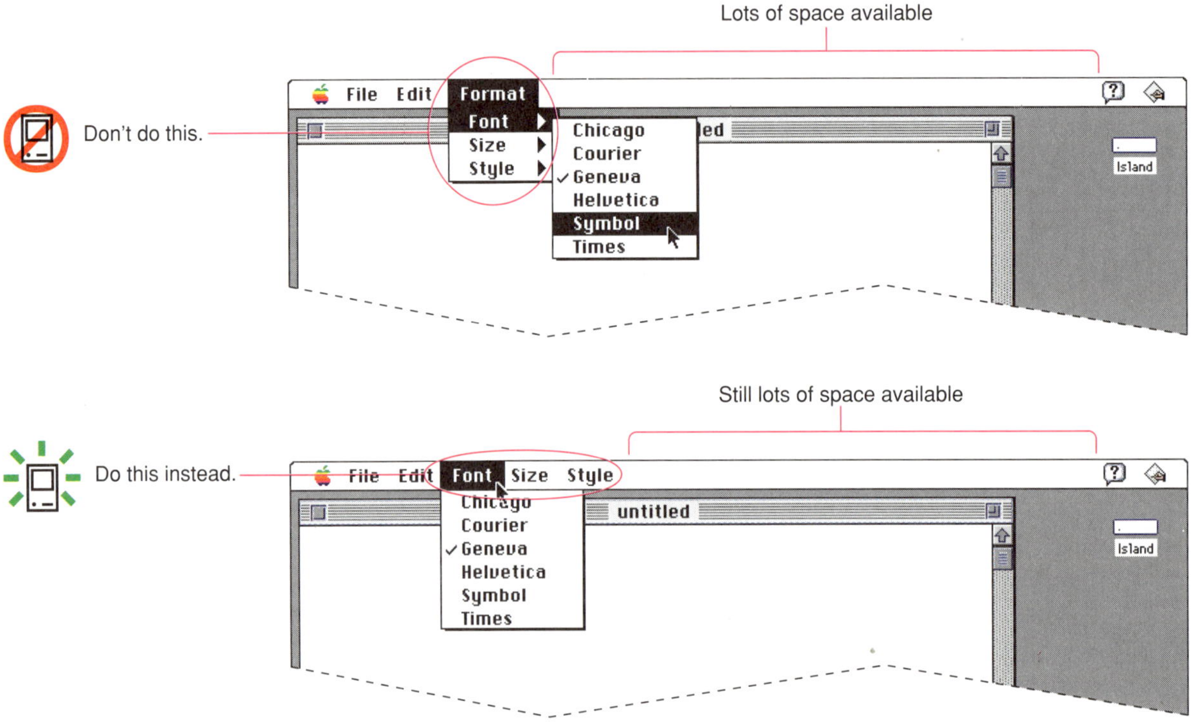

When you use submenus, include them in a menu with a logical relationship to the choices they contain. In the example shown in Figure 4-38, the submenus are in the logical menu. However, since there is still space available in the menu bar, it's questionable whether the submenus should exist. They would be more visible as main (pull-down) menus in the menu bar. Fonts should always be in their own separate menu because users often have very long lists of fonts.

If you find that there is still a lot of space between your last menu title and the standard menus (Help menu, Keyboard menu, and Application menu), it's best to continue to use standard pull-down menus instead of hierarchical menus.

Figure 4-38 shows an example of a 9-inch screen that still allows room for more menus. The Size and Style submenus would fit in the menu bar.

Figure 4-38 A menu bar on a 9-inch screen with space for more menu titles

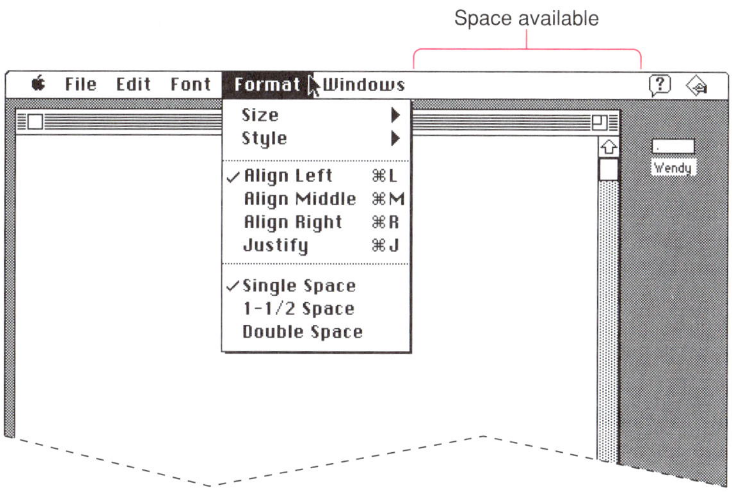

Hierarchical menus work best for providing a submenu of attributes. A menu item that's the title of a submenu should clearly represent the choices it contains. It's much easier to identify a set of attributes than a set of verbs (actions). Figure 4-39 shows the difficulty of naming a menu item so that it serves as a descriptive title for a submenu of commands. The figure also shows an appropriate title for a submenu of attributes.

Figure 4-39 Examples of submenu titles

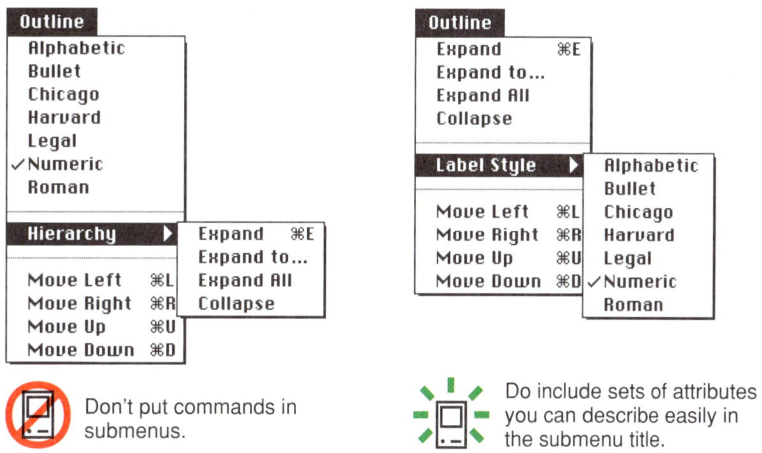

A main menu can contain both standard menu items and submenu titles. You may assign keyboard equivalents to menu items in either a main menu or a submenu. Follow the guidelines presented in the section "Keyboard Equivalents," which begins on page 128.

Never use more than *one level* of submenus. A submenu at the second level would be buried too deep in the interface and would unnecessarily create another level of complexity. Also, it takes more time for the user to use and peruse a hierarchical menu than a pull-down menu. It is physically difficult to use a second level of submenus without slipping off the first submenu. Figure 4-40 shows an example of a technique to avoid using with submenus.

Figure 4-40 Avoid more than one level of submenus

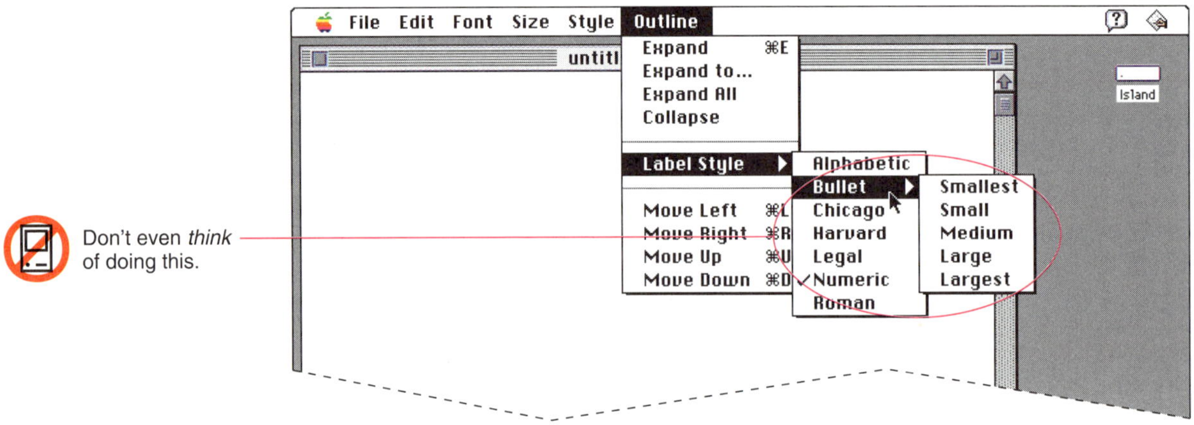

Pop-Up Menus

Pop-up menus present a list of mutually exclusive choices in a dialog box or window. Pop-up menus are used as a means of selecting one choice from a list of many. Figure 4-41 shows a standard pop-up menu. A pop-up menu typically has a title that appears to the left of the menu in script systems that read from left to right. The menu itself looks like a rectangle with a drop shadow. The menu contains the text of the current choice and a triangle indicator that identifies this element as a pop-up menu.

Figure 4-41 A pop-up menu and its parts

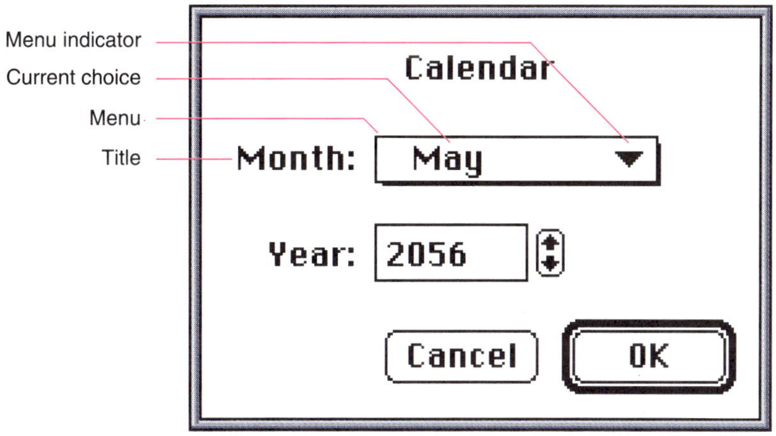

Pop-up menus act like other menus: the user can drag through them and choose an item, which then flashes briefly and appears as the current choice in the menu. The user can also move outside the menu to leave the current value active. (If a pop-up menu reaches the top or bottom of the screen, it scrolls like other menus.)

Pop-up menus work well for presenting a number of mutually exclusive choices. However, they hide these choices from view. You should use a pop-up menu when the user doesn't need to see all the choices all the time in a dialog box or window. You can use a pop-up menu when you have from 5 to 12 items. If your item list fits in this range, it's a good idea to use a pop-up menu because the user will be able to see all the choices when the menu is open and won't have to scroll through the menu to see additional choices. If you have more than 12 items, use a scrolling list instead. Users would have a hard time scrolling a pop-up menu to see all the choices and then reversing the scrolling direction to choose the item they wanted.

Figure 4-42 shows a pop-up menu in a dialog box and the same menu when it's open.

Figure 4-42 Opening a pop-up menu

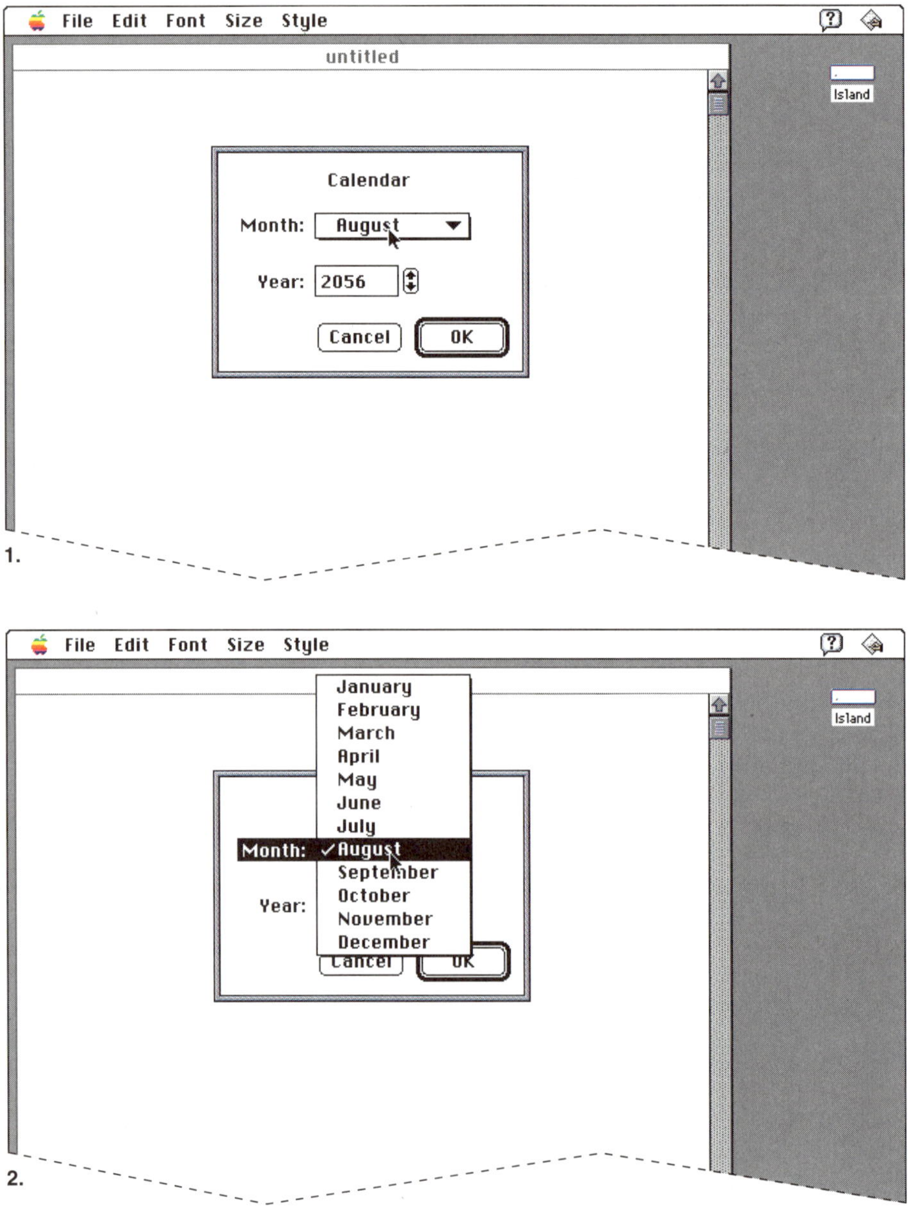

If you need to show only a few choices, consider using another interface element instead of a pop-up menu. Figure 4-43 shows such a situation. Since there are only three types of columns to choose from, and the user can make an exclusive choice, it makes more sense to use radio buttons for the choices. The radio buttons don't take up much more space than the pop-up menu would and they're always visible when the dialog box is open.

Figure 4-43 Pop-up menus versus radio buttons

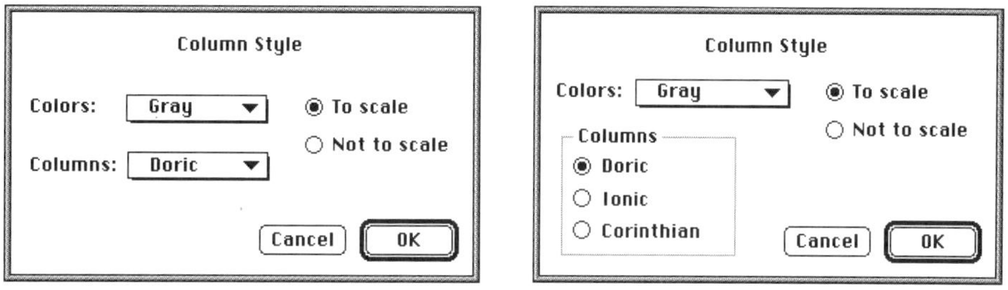

Choices are hidden. Choices are visible.

Pop-up menus provide a list from which only a single selection can be made. These choices could be expressed as nouns (things) or adjectives (states or attributes). Don't use pop-up menus when more than a single selection is needed. Allowing multiple selections from a pop-up menu gives the user ambiguous feedback. The user knows only the current selection, not all of the settings currently in effect. This forces the user to open the menu to know what all the settings are.

Don't use pop-up menus for accumulating attribute lists like text style choices. Style menus provide multiple choice lists, which should be presented either as checkboxes in a dialog box or pull-down menus. If you put a multiple choice menu in a dialog box, you would destroy the ability of the menu to provide feedback in the menu text. You would be hiding essential information from the user, who would only be able to see it when the menu was open. You can use checkboxes to provide a set of "many-from-many" choices.

Figure 4-44 shows an example of a pop-up menu with more than one choice in effect. The figure also shows one correct way to provide the same choices by using checkboxes. You could also provide this same set of choices with a pull-down menu.

Figure 4-44 Pop-up menus versus checkboxes

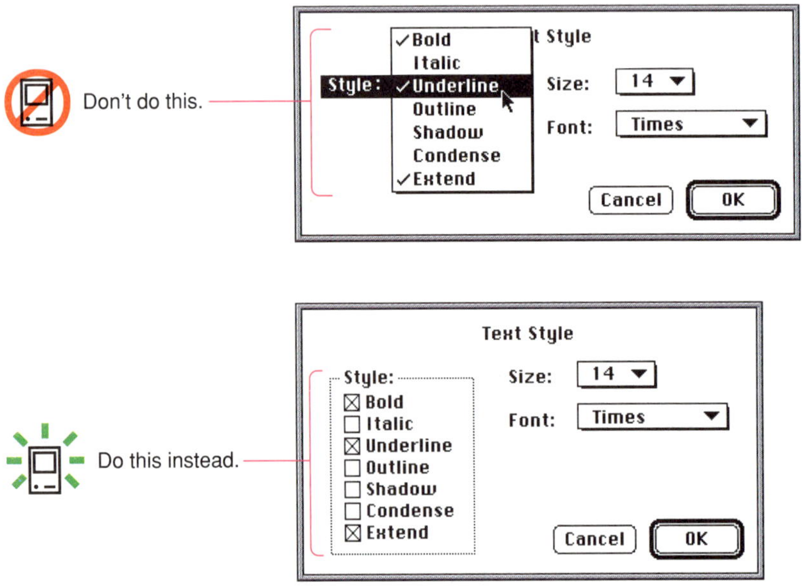

Never create a hierarchical pop-up menu. Doing so would hide choices too deeply in the interface. It would also create an element that would be far too physically difficult to use.

Pop-up menus are *not* a means of providing more commands. Therefore they shouldn't contain actions (verbs). If there were a pop-up menu that contained commands, there wouldn't be a logical choice to display as the current choice. Figure 4-45 shows this dilemma. Commands aren't persistent choices, they are always available and aren't current as soon as they finish operating. In other words, don't use a pop-up menu to present choices that should appear in pull-down menus. Since the choices in a pop-up menu aren't visible at all times, the menu items shouldn't contain keyboard equivalents.

Figure 4-45 Don't use pop-up menus for commands

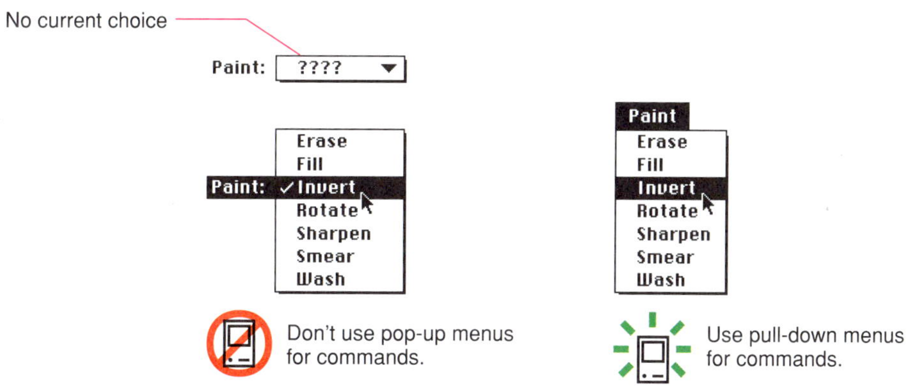

Standard Pop-Up Menus

The standard pop-up menu looks like a rectangle with a one-pixel border. It has a one-pixel drop shadow and contains a downward-pointing triangle similar to the triangle used to indicate a scrolling menu. Figure 4-46 shows a simple pop-up menu.

Figure 4-46 A standard pop-up menu

When the user presses the mouse button while the pointer is over the pop-up menu or its label text, the triangle disappears and the other choices appear. When the mouse button is released, the triangle reappears. An exploratory press in the menu to see what's available doesn't select a new value.

While the menu is open, its title is inverted. If several pop-up menus are near each other, the inverted title makes it clear which menu is being chosen from. The open menu shows a checkmark next to the current selection. When a user makes a new choice in the pop-up menu, it becomes visible as the current choice in the menu after it closes.

Figure 4-47 shows four simple steps that show how a user makes a choice from a pop-up menu.

Figure 4-47 Using a pop-up menu

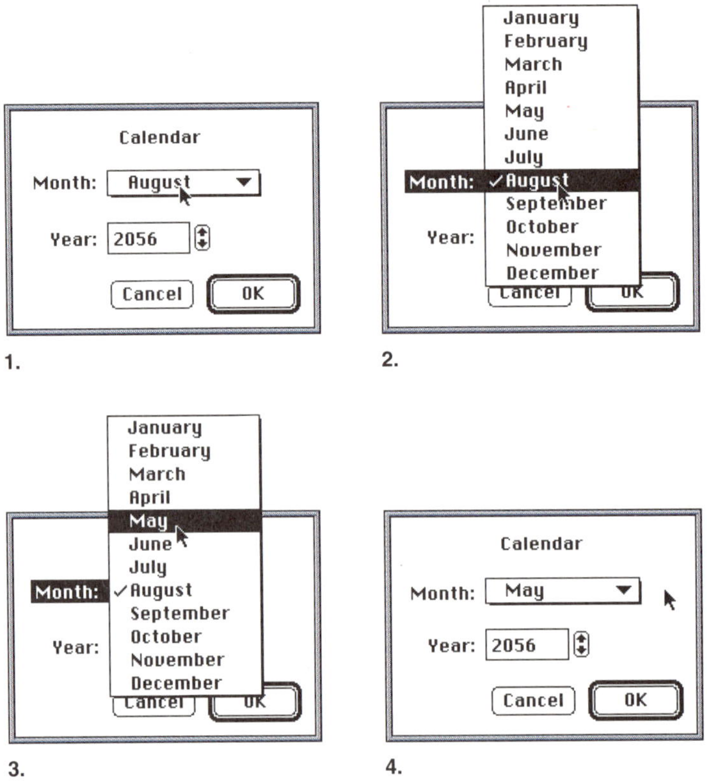

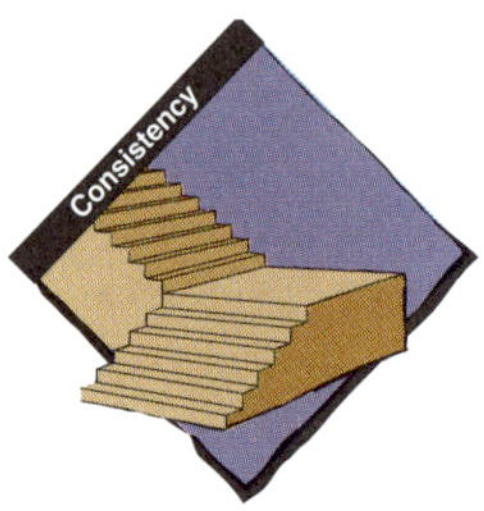

Be sure to use the same font for the closed state and the open state of a pop-up menu. If the menu looks different when it's open, you destroy the illusion that it is one object that expands and contracts. It's best to use 12-point Chicago, plain in pop-up menus. However, if it's necessary to use another font, use it in both states of the menu to maintain a consistent and stable appearance. In most cases you should use a 12-point font in pop-up menus. In rare cases you may find it necessary to use a 9-point font. However, keep in mind that it may not be possible to localize a 9-point font.

Figure 4-48 shows the incorrect and the correct way to use fonts in pop-up menus.

Figure 4-48 Correct and incorrect use of fonts in pop-up menus

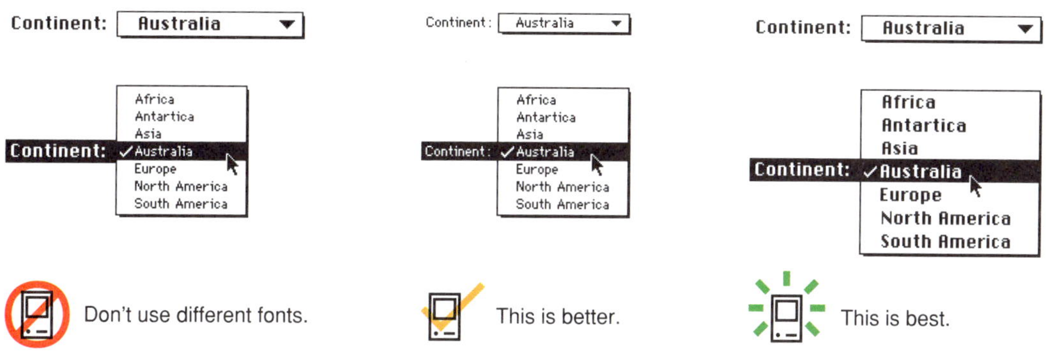

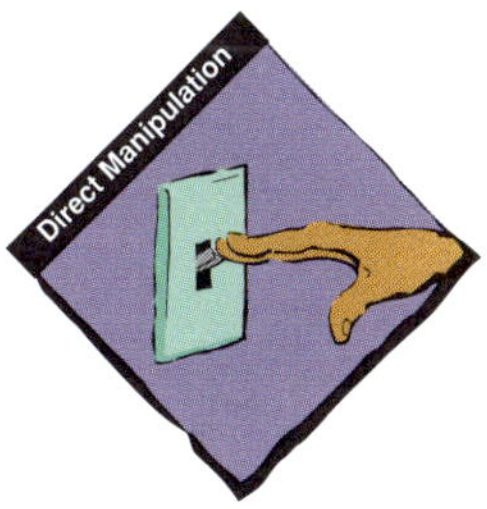

It's very important to create and maintain the illusion that a pop-up menu is one object. Ideally, it should be the same width when it's open as when it's closed. It's OK to have a pop-up menu be wider when it's open. In no case should you create a pop-up menu that appears narrower than the normal state. If the menu does appear narrower in the open state, the menu looks and feels like two separate objects. This appearance would destroy the sense of direct manipulation that users get as they use single objects. Figure 4-49 shows two pop-up menus that violate the guideline that a pop-up menu maintains the illusion of being one object. In the third example in Figure 4-49, the pop-up menu still appears to be one object, even though it is larger in the open state than it appears in the closed state. The final example in Figure 4-49 shows the best case of a pop-up menu that appears as though it is always one object when the user is opening, using, or closing it.

Figure 4-49 Pop-up menu behavior

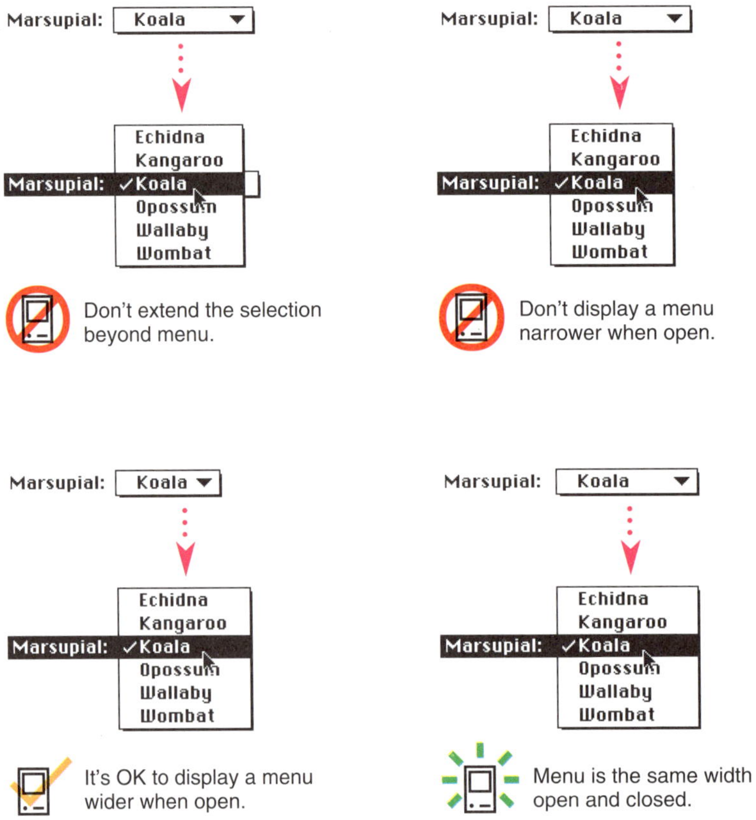

When you use the pop-up menu control definition function, you always get the correct appearance and behavior for pop-up menus. However, sometimes developers find new ways and places to implement pop-up menus. If you must do this, at least maintain as much of the standard appearance of the pop-up menu as possible. For instance, always draw the triangle as a visual indicator of the menu. Otherwise there is no clue that some text in your interface is a pop-up menu.

Figure 4-50 shows an example of a hidden pop-up menu and how to make it more visible.

Figure 4-50 A hidden pop-up menu

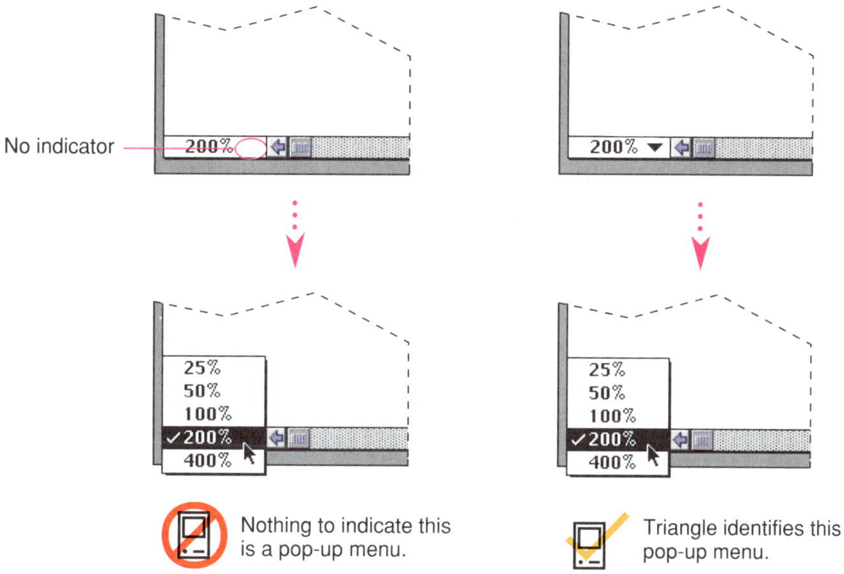

Type-In Pop-Up Menus

Sometimes it is useful to display a list of likely choices but still allow the user to type in a choice that you can't anticipate. Keep in mind that all preset choices should be visible so that people can make choices with mouse actions. The type-in option should be an additional choice when appropriate, not a requirement. You'll need to handle error checking and feedback for the typed data, as you would for a text entry field.

If the user types in an item that is already in the menu, place a checkmark next to the menu item. When the menu is open, highlight the item in the text box and the corresponding item in the menu. This behavior prevents a quick look in the menu from accidentally wiping out the previous value. It also reinforces the idea that choosing a different value in the menu changes the value in the text box. You don't need to highlight the title of the menu in this situation. The standard pop-up menu lends itself readily to this extension, as shown in Figure 4-51.

Figure 4-51 A type-in pop-up menu

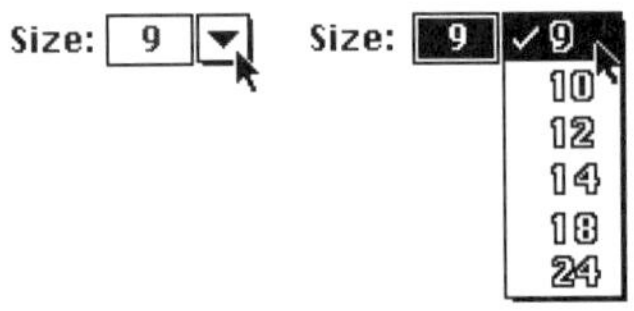

If the value typed into the text box does not match any of the items in the pop-up menu, add the type-in value as the first item and separate it from the standard values by a gray or dotted line, as shown in Figure 4-52. This item disappears from the menu when the user selects a standard value from the pop-up menu. Separating the custom item from the standard items makes a clear distinction between the items that are always available and the typed-in value, which is only temporary.

Figure 4-52 A type-in pop-up menu with user's choice added

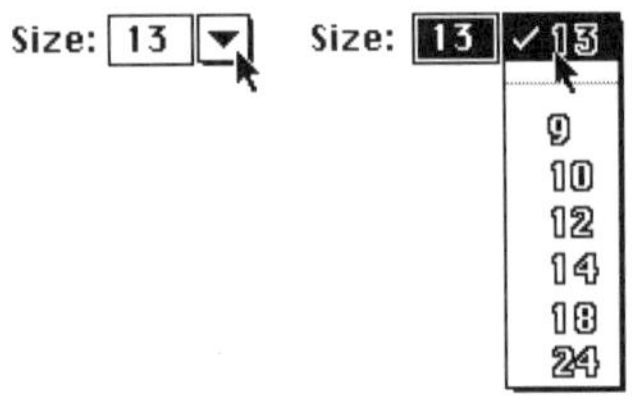

Tear-Off Menus and Palettes

A **tear-off menu** is a menu that a user can detach from the menu bar by pressing the mouse button while the cursor is over the menu title and dragging beyond the menu's edge. These menus are usually called **palettes.** Palettes can also be part of a standard document window. Sometimes palettes pop up from an item in a tear-off menu. You can create tear-off menus and palettes to provide sets of colors, patterns, or tools to users. Use symbols such as icons, patterns, characters, or drawings to provide easy access to features of your application.

Figure 4-53 shows a tear-off menu that becomes a palette and a palette that popped up from a torn-off menu.

Figure 4-53 A tools palette and a color palette

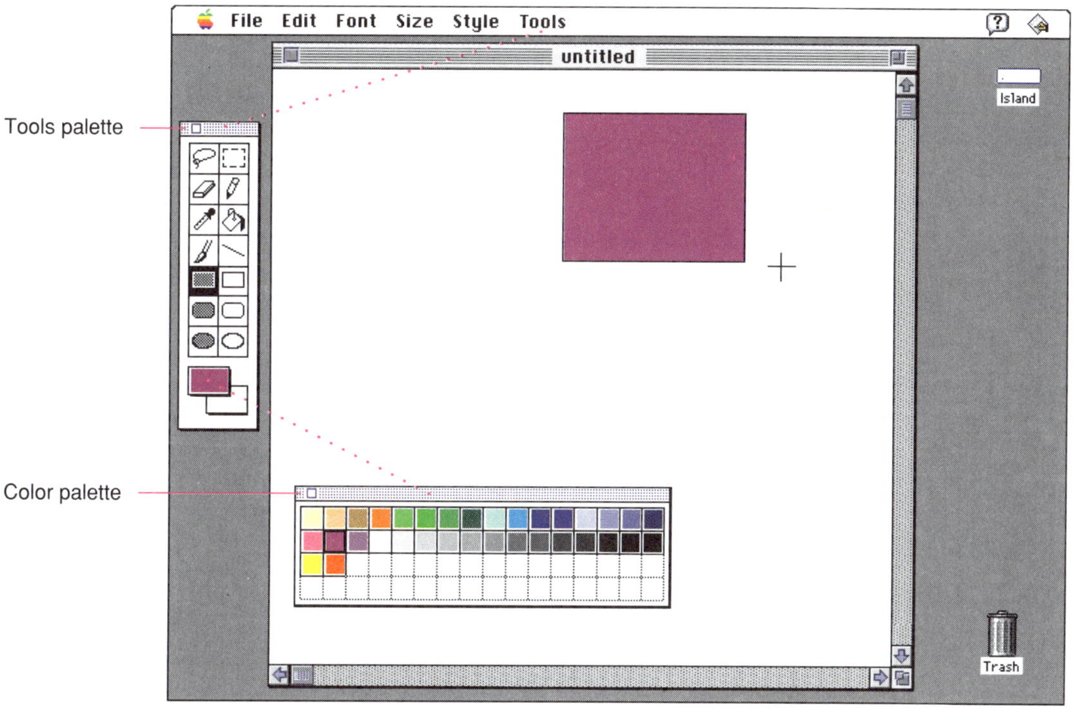

Tear-Off Menus

A tear-off menu allows users to move a menu around the screen like a window. Tear-off menus save desktop space because the user can place them on top of a document or move them to a convenient position. If you implement a tear-off menu rather than a fixed palette in a window, you allow the user to have a larger workspace in document windows. Users can also choose to leave the menu in the menu bar, or tear it off and close it when necessary. Tear-off menus give the user more flexibility than fixed palettes do.

When the user drags a tear-off menu three pixels away from the menu bar, the menu separates from the menu bar and floats on the desktop. Even after a user tears off a menu, it is still available from the menu bar, however. Figure 4-54 shows the process of tearing off a menu and positioning it on the desktop. Note that if the user tears off a menu while the same menu floats on the desktop in its torn-off state, the torn-off menu on the desktop disappears; only one copy of a tear-off menu can appear on the desktop at a time.

Figure 4-54 Using a tear-off menu

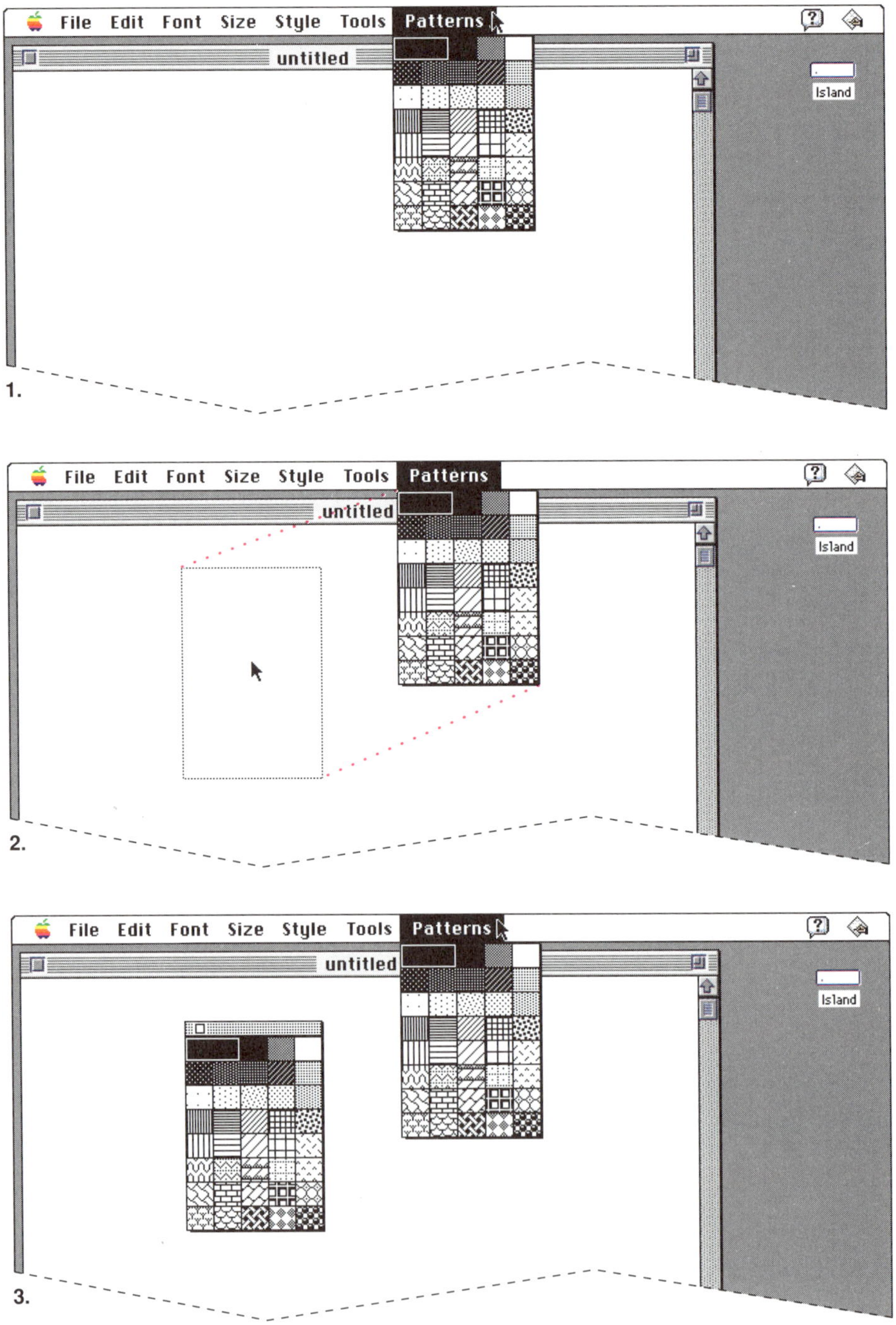

The user can choose an item from a tear-off menu simply by pulling down the menu like any other menu, then dragging the pointer to the desired item and releasing the mouse button. You need to provide visual feedback about the current selection regardless of the content of the tear-off menu. In a tear-off menu that contains tools, highlight the currently selected tool. In a tear-off menu that contains patterns or colors, you can outline the currently selected item and include a preview area that shows that item. When the user clicks a new item, change the selection to that item. For tear-off menus that contain text items such as buttons, a single click selects the item. You also need to provide tracking feedback in tear-off menus. That is, as the user drags over the items in a tear-off menu, each item should be highlighted or outlined when the pointer is over it. Only one item can be active at a time. A tear-off menu behaves the same way when it is attached to the menu bar and when it is torn off and on the desktop.

Tear-off menus behave like utility windows and document windows. Users can drag them around the screen and close them with a close box. Tear-off menus have a drag region with a 25 percent black-and-white pattern and a close box. Tear-off menus are always on top of document windows. If your application can have more than one menu torn off at a time, then you must determine their order of appearance based on user actions. Figure 4-55 shows an example of a tear-off menu on top of a window.

Figure 4-55 A tear-off menu on top of a document window

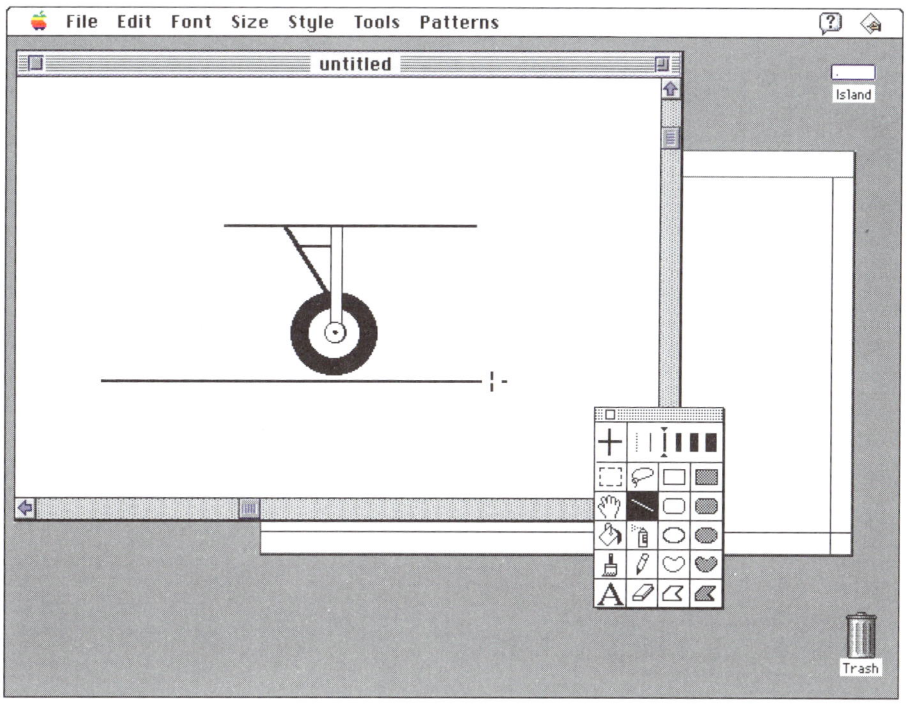

Palettes

You can use icons, patterns, colors, characters, or drawings that represent an operation in a palette. You need to provide visual feedback about the current selection in a palette. In a palette that contains tools, highlight the currently selected tool. In a palette that contains patterns or colors, you can outline the currently selected item and include a preview area that shows the current selection. When the user clicks a new item, change the selection to that item. You also need to provide tracking feedback in palettes. That is, as a user drags over the items in a palette, each item should be highlighted or outlined when the pointer is over it. Only one item can be active at a time. (If your application uses only one palette for multiple open windows, then the palette reflects the settings for the active window.) Figure 4-56 shows some palettes and the feedback they provide to show the currently selected tool or pattern.

Figure 4-56 Palettes and feedback

In a palette of tools or patterns, you can change the pointer shape to give additional feedback about the current selection. People can change a selection immediately by clicking another item. Figure 4-57 shows a tool palette and the corresponding pointers that provide additional feedback to the user about which tool is active.

Figure 4-57 A tool palette with the corresponding pointers

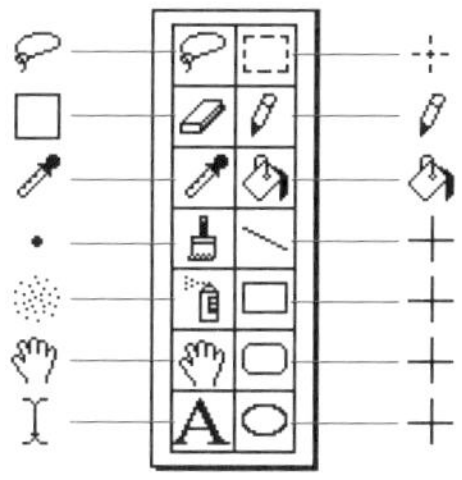

If you include tool palettes as part of your windows, put them on the left side of the window or along the top of the window underneath the title bar. Using these positions keeps the palettes from conflicting with standard window controls. Don't put palettes in areas where users expect standard controls like scroll bars or the close box. Figure 4-58 shows a window with a tool palette in an appropriate location.

Figure 4-58 A tool palette in a window

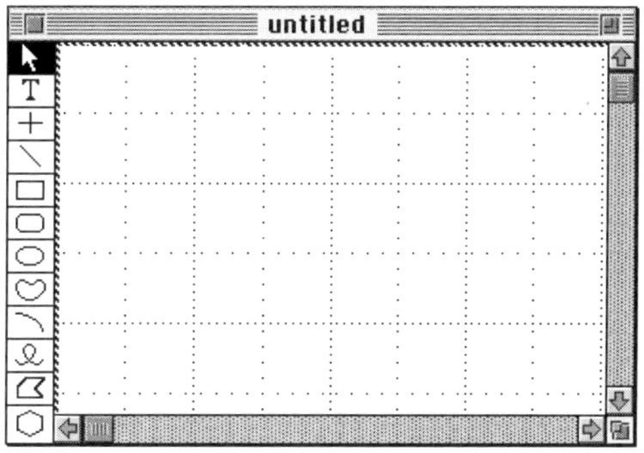

If the palette is part of a window, then the user has less area for content, especially on a small screen. Also parts of the palette may be concealed if the user makes the window smaller. If a palette is not part of a window, then it takes up extra space on the desktop.

Standard Macintosh Menus

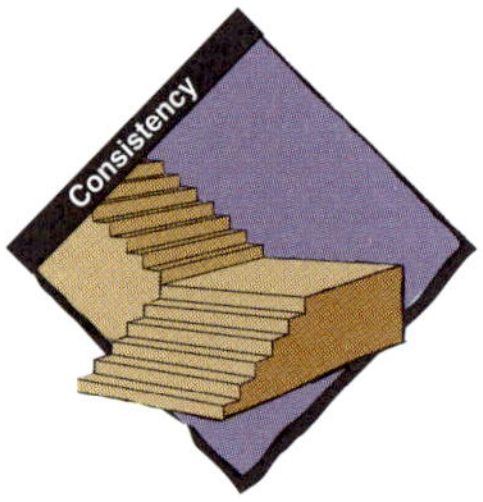

This section describes the style and contents of standard menus for Macintosh applications.

The Apple Menu

The **Apple menu** contains all items that the user puts in the Apple Menu Items folder. They appear in alphabetical order in the menu, separated from the About menu item by a gray line. This menu also displays small icons for each item. Figure 4-59 shows a sample Apple menu.

Figure 4-59 An Apple menu

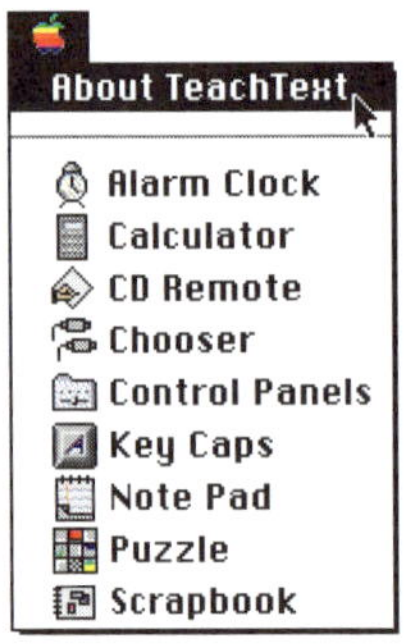

About

You can include an About item in the Apple menu. When the user chooses this item, display a dialog box that contains your application's name, version number, and copyright information. You can include additional information in the dialog box if you find it necessary. Include an OK button in the dialog box so that the user can dismiss the dialog box after reading it. If you don't include an OK button, remove the dialog box automatically after a few seconds. Figure 4-60 shows a sample dialog box.

Figure 4-60 An About dialog box for an application

File Menu

The **File menu** provides commands that pertain to housekeeping tasks for documents. It also contains the Quit command. All of the standard operations are described here. If you add additional commands to the File menu, be sure that they fit the category of taking care of documents. Figure 4-61 shows a sample File menu.

Figure 4-61 A File menu

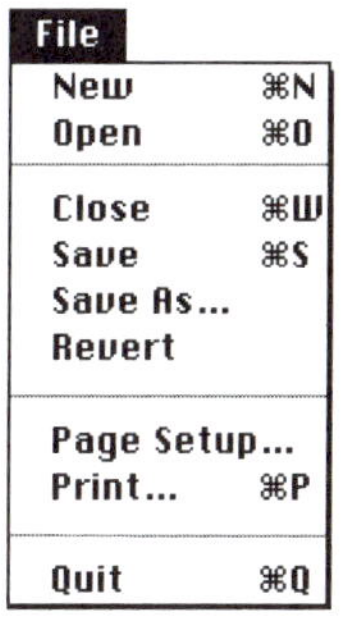

New

The New command opens a new, untitled document for the current application. The user names the document the first time it's saved. If you detect that there isn't enough memory available to open another untitled window when the user chooses this command, display a dialog box that explains why the user can't open another window and suggest a solution. As described in Chapter 5, "Windows," which begins on page 131, always title the first new window "untitled." Some specialized applications require documents to be named when the user creates them. For example, if you are developing a database application, you can display the standard file dialog box for saving documents so that the user can name and save the database document upon creation. For more information on displaying default window titles, see Chapter 5. Figure 4-62 shows the New command and its result.

Figure 4-62 The New command

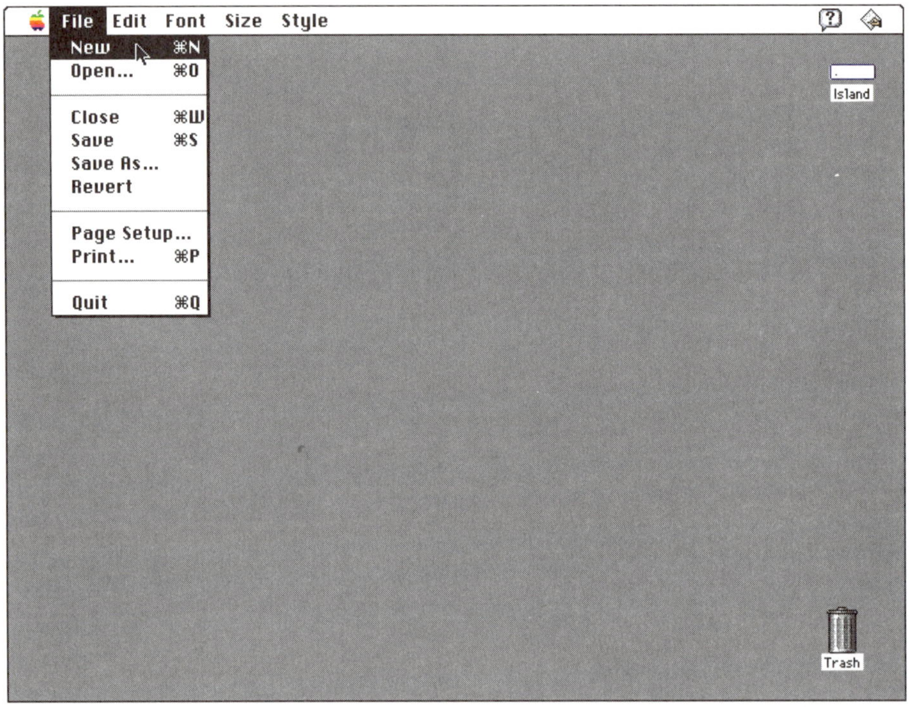

1.

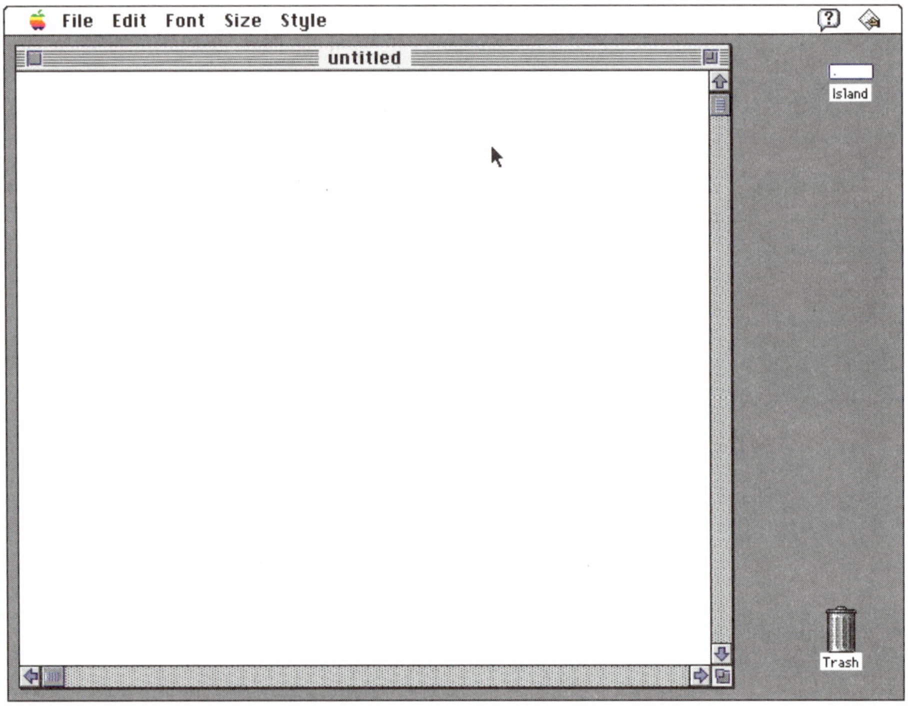

2.

Open

The Open command opens an existing document. When the user chooses Open from within your application, display the standard file dialog box. The user selects a document from the list in the dialog box. You can create a custom filter procedure to display all the documents of the types that your application can handle. When the user selects a document, the application opens it. Figure 4-63 shows the standard file dialog box that appears when the user chooses the Open command.

Figure 4-63 The standard file dialog box for opening files

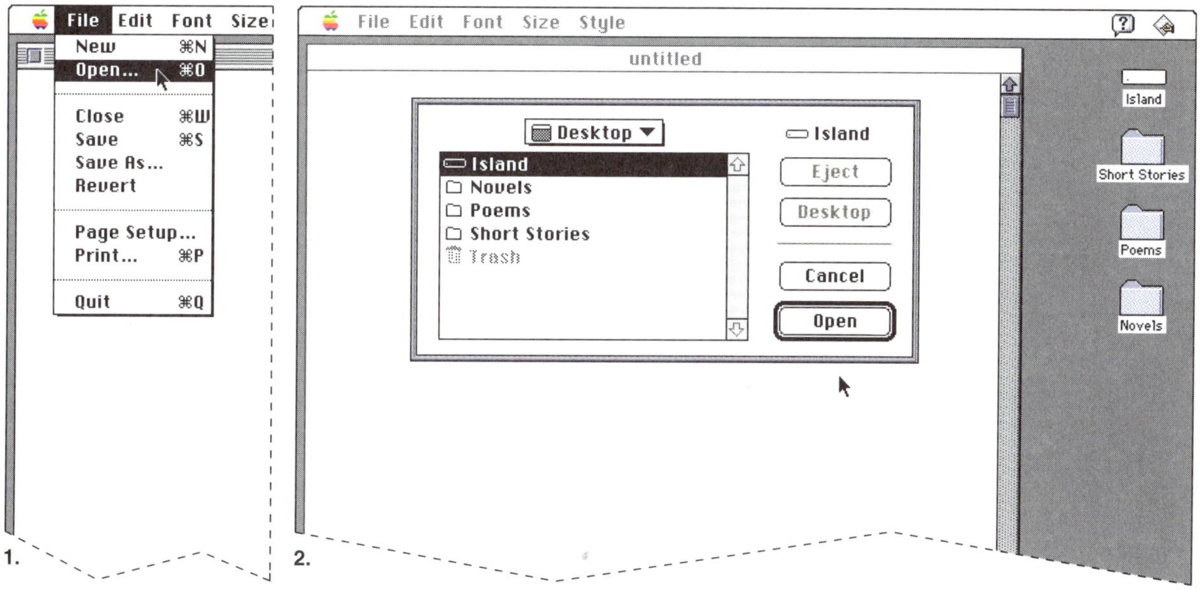

The user can browse through all levels of the file system from the desktop down through nested folders, and back to the desktop. The Eject button allows the user to eject any removable media such as a 3.5-inch disk or a CD-ROM disc. The Eject button is disabled when there are no removable media selected. The Desktop button allows the user to go immediately to the top level of the hierarchy. The Desktop button is disabled when the user is looking at that level, as shown in Figure 4-63.

When the user chooses Open while running an application, the standard file dialog box displays all documents that the application can open. The standard file dialog box displays all documents, folders, and storage devices that are available. When the user selects a document and clicks the Open button or double-clicks a document name, the application opens the document.

When an application starts up by putting an empty, untitled document on the screen, the Open command remains enabled even if the application allows only one open document at a time. In this case, choosing Open from the File menu displays an alert box that informs the user that only one window can be open at a time and asks if it's OK to close the current window. If the user clicks OK, close an empty document or display the save changes alert box for a document with contents; then open the document the user selected. If the user clicks Cancel, the current document remains on the screen in the state it was in before the user chose the Open command.

Note that you shouldn't set a maximum number of documents that your application can open. You should base the limit on the amount of available memory at any given time.

Close

The Close command closes the active window, which may be a document window, a modeless dialog box, a folder, or any other type of window. Clicking in a window's close box provides a mouse-based method of closing windows. The user can also press Command-W to close windows.

When the user chooses the Close command, and the active document has been changed since the last save, display the standard save changes alert box. This alert box is designed to prevent users from accidentally losing data. The standard appearance and layout of the alert box help users quickly identify a potentially dangerous situation. For information about the layout of items in alert boxes, see "Basic Dialog Box Layout," which begins on page 196 in Chapter 6, "Dialog Boxes."

Use the caution alert box, which includes the caution icon in the upper-left corner. This icon indicates to users that they need to carefully consider the alert box message before clicking the default button or pressing the Return key. The caution icon should always be in the same, predictable location so that users easily recognize it as a warning and understand its meaning.

The button names in the save changes alert box correlate to the action users perform by pressing the button. The buttons read Save, Don't Save, and Cancel. Using these verbs reinforces the identity of each possible action to the user. In other words, Don't Save provides much more context for the user than No does.

In order to prevent accidental clicks of the wrong button, you should always keep safe buttons apart from buttons that could cause data loss. Standardizing the location of buttons in a safe configuration provides an additional safeguard for the user. Place the Save button in the lower-right corner with the Cancel button to its left. Place the Don't Save button left-aligned with the message text. Make the Save button the one that is linked to the Return or Enter key. This way, the user is less likely to accidentally click the Don't Save button and cause irretrievable loss of data. Figure 4-64 shows an example of a standard save changes alert box.

Figure 4-64 The save changes alert box

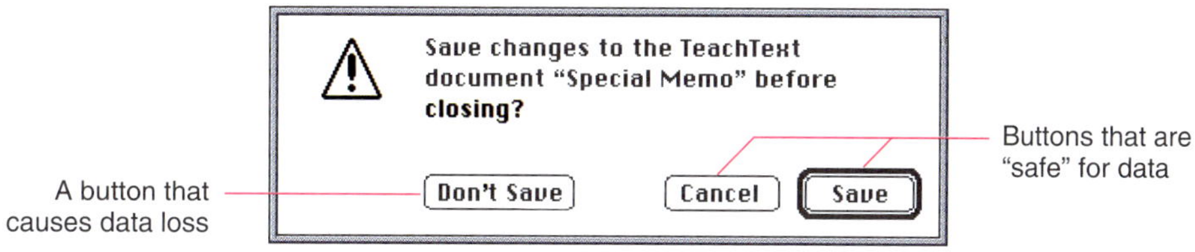

Include the name of your application and the name of the document in the alert box message, as shown in Figure 4-64. When a user chooses the Close command, the message should read, "Save changes to the . . . document . . . before closing?" This wording should change to "Save changes to the . . . document . . . before quitting?" if the alert box appears as a result of the Shut Down command or the Quit command. When a user shuts down the computer, several save changes alert boxes may appear if there are several open, unsaved documents on the desktop. The addition of contextual information to the message helps the user by identifying to which application and document the message refers.

When you display the save changes alert box, center it horizontally either on the screen or over the active window if the window is on a large screen. Figure 4-65 shows the correct placement of the alert box on three common sizes of screens.

Figure 4-65 The correct location of the save changes alert box

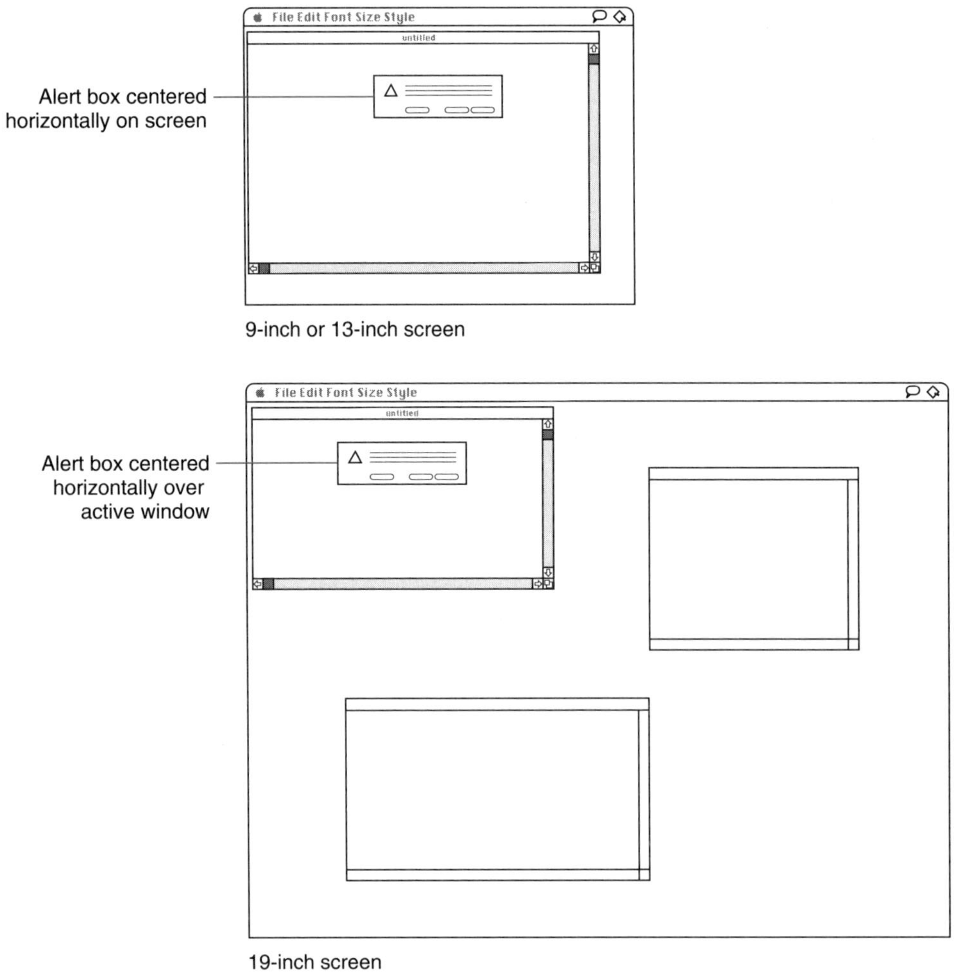

Save

The Save command lets the user save the active document to a disk, including any changes made to that document since the last time it was saved.
Figure 4-66 shows the Save command.

Figure 4-66 The Save command

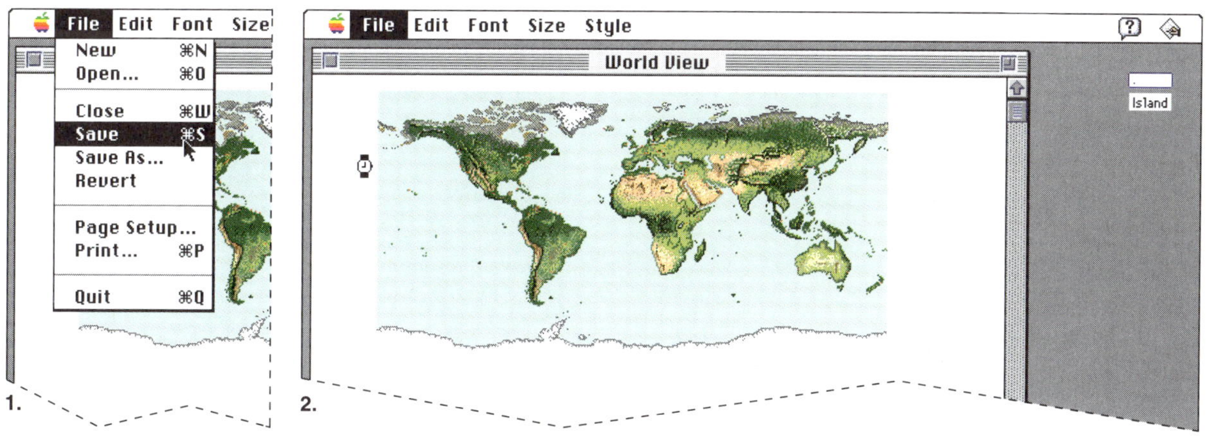

The document remains open. Provide feedback to the user that the document is being saved. Use the animated watch cursor if the save takes approximately one or two seconds. If the operation takes much longer, display a status bar or other message box.

If the user chooses Save for a new untitled document (one that the user hasn't saved yet), display the Save As dialog box described in the next section.

If there's not enough room on the selected disk to save the document, display a caution alert box that says so and suggest that the user can use Save As instead to save the document on another disk. *Don't* destroy the document just because the current disk is full. Figure 4-67 shows a sample alert box for this case.

Figure 4-67 A sample alert box to use when a disk is full

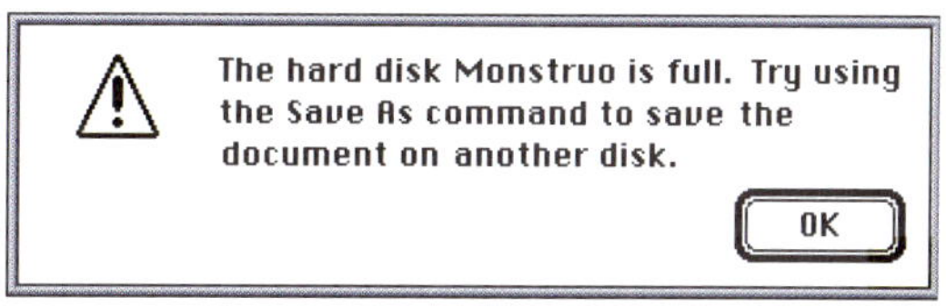

Save As

The Save As command saves a copy of the active document under a new name provided by the user. Figure 4-68 shows the Save As command and its dialog box.

Figure 4-68 The Save As command and dialog box

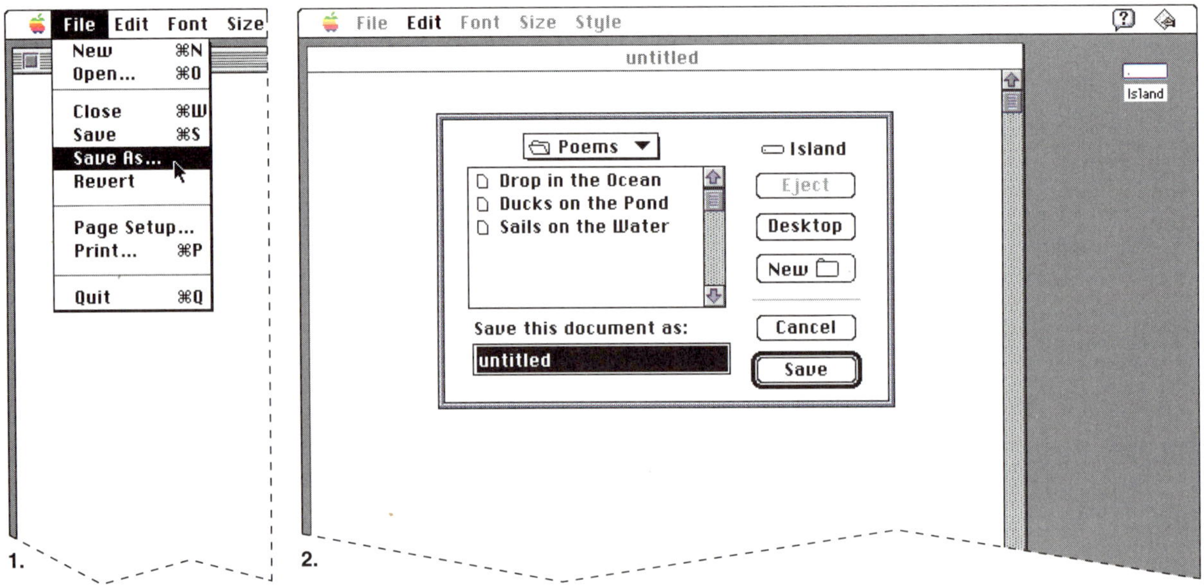

The Save As dialog box allows the user to provide a name for the document and to choose where it will be saved. Leave the document open and active.

When the user opens a document, makes changes to it, and then chooses Save As, don't change the original document. Save the changed version of the document under the new name. The active document is no longer the one the user opened, but rather the new one with the new name.

If the user uses the Save As command to make a new copy of a document, and made no changes to the original document, create a second document exactly like the first one. The user now has two identical documents with different names.

If your application supports stationery, include a Stationery option in the Save As dialog box. A stationery pad is a template of the original document with whatever information it contains. When a user opens a stationery document, open a copy of the template with the name untitled. When the user saves that document, display the Save As dialog box so that the user can name it.

Don't use the Save a Copy command in your application. People may not understand the distinction between the Save As command and the Save a Copy command.

Revert

The Revert command discards all changes made to the active document since the last time it was saved or opened. The document that was last saved to the disk is reopened. When the user chooses Revert, display an alert box that warns the user about the potential data loss this operation will cause. Provide a cancel button so that the user has a way to back out of the situation. Figure 4-69 shows a File menu with the Revert command highlighted and an appropriate alert box.

Figure 4-69 The Revert command

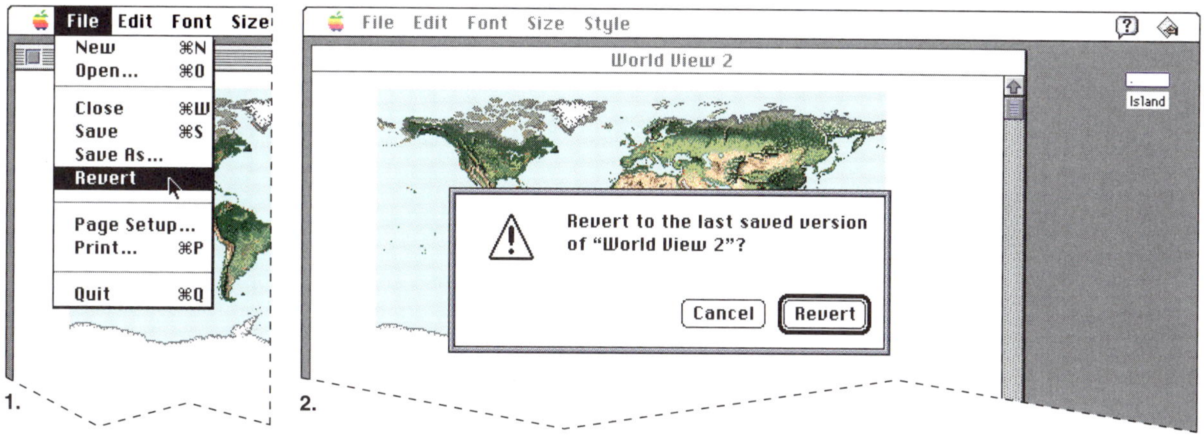

Page Setup...

The Page Setup command lets the user specify printing parameters such as the paper size and printing orientation. Your application can provide other printing options as appropriate. These parameters are saved with the document when the document is saved. Figure 4-70 shows a typical Page Setup dialog box.

Figure 4-70 A Page Setup dialog box

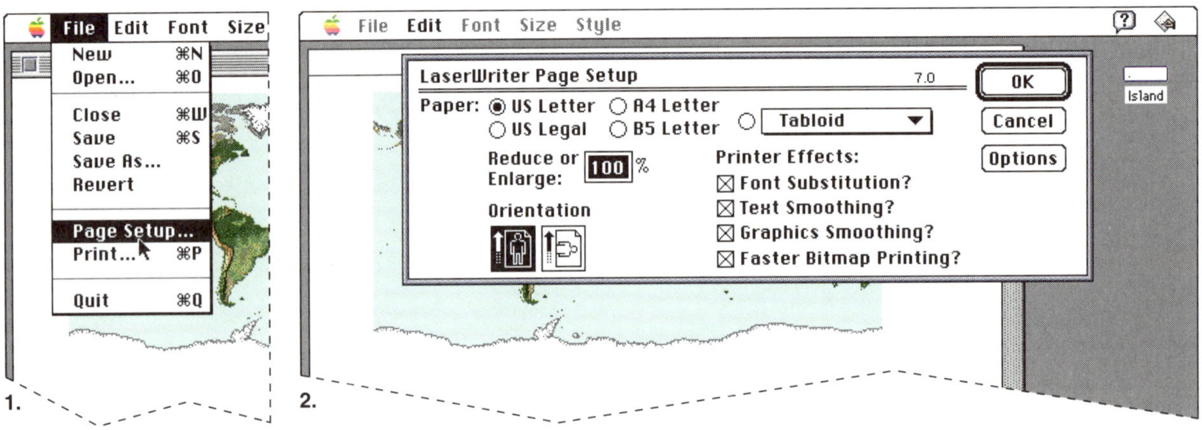

Print...

The Print command lets the user specify various parameters, such as print quality and number of copies, and then prints the document. The parameters apply to only the current printing operation and are not saved with the document. Figure 4-71 shows a typical Print dialog box.

If the user has not selected a printer in the Chooser, display a dialog box when the user chooses the Print command. This dialog box should alert the user of the situation and direct the user to the Chooser to select a printer.

If a document is printed from the Finder, the document is opened and the Print dialog box is displayed. If the application is launched for the purpose of printing the document, the application quits after the printing is complete or canceled. If the application is already running, the application remains active after the printing is complete. This behavior occurs so that the application remains in the same state after printing a document as before the printing was initiated.

Figure 4-71 A Print dialog box

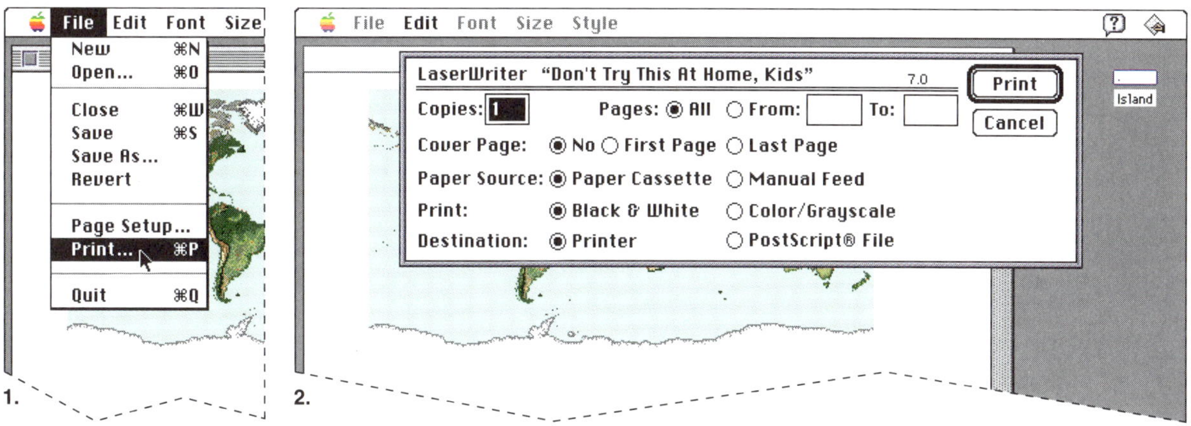

If you find it necessary to add items to the Print dialog box, do so at the bottom of the dialog box. For more information on printing, see the appropriate book in *Inside Macintosh*.

Quit

The Quit command lets the user leave the application and return to the Finder, or another open application. If any open documents have been changed since the last time they were saved, present the standard save changes alert box, once for each open document. This alert box is described in the section "Close" on page 102.

The Edit Menu

The **Edit menu** provides commands that allow people to change, or edit, the contents of their documents. It also provides the commands that allow people to share data, within and between applications, via the Clipboard or the Edition Manager. All applications should support the Undo, Cut, Copy, Paste, and Clear commands. These commands provide standard text-editing abilities, which need to be available in modal dialog boxes such as the Save As dialog box, even though your application itself may not handle these features. You can include a Select All command and its keyboard equivalent if it makes sense for your application.

Figure 4-72 shows an example of a standard, simple Edit menu.

Figure 4-72 A standard Edit menu for an application

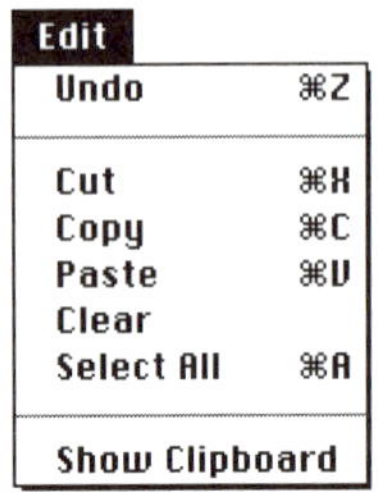

You can add other commands to this menu if they're essential to your application and involve changing user content. You must add the commands after the standard menu commands without changing their order. Figure 4-73 shows how to incorporate commands into the Edit menu without disrupting the standard order.

Figure 4-73 Adding commands to the Edit menu

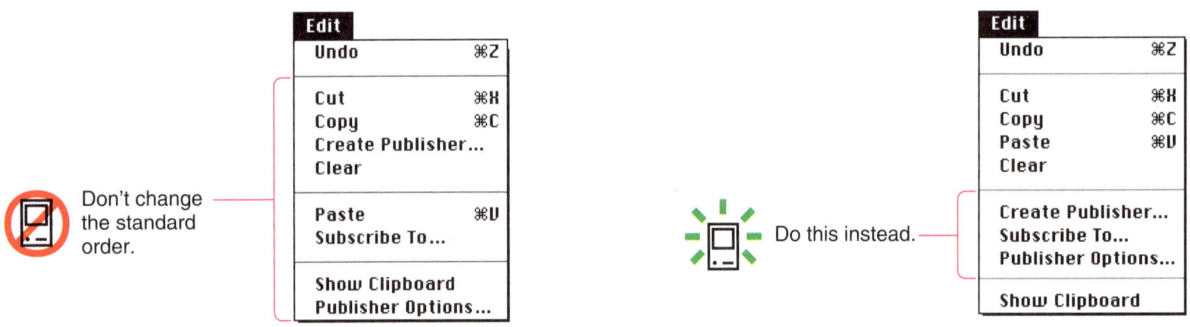

In addition to the standard commands, if your application implements the capabilities of the Edition Manager, include its commands in the Edit menu, separated from the standard commands by a gray line. Figure 4-74 shows a sample Edit menu that includes the required Edition Manager commands.

Figure 4-74 A sample Edit menu with Edition Manager commands

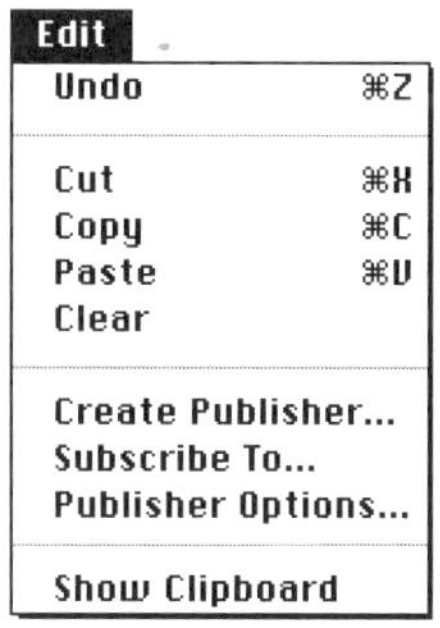

If you find that you need all of the available space in the Edit menu for your application's commands, another way to accommodate the Edition Manager commands is by implementing a submenu. Include a Publishing command in the Edit menu as the title of the submenu. Use the standard indicator for a hierarchical menu, as shown in Figure 4-75, which also shows the submenu with the Edition Manager commands. Because hierarchical menus increase the complexity of your application, it's best to use this approach only when you have no other alternative.

Figure 4-75 A sample hierarchical Edit menu with Edition Manager commands

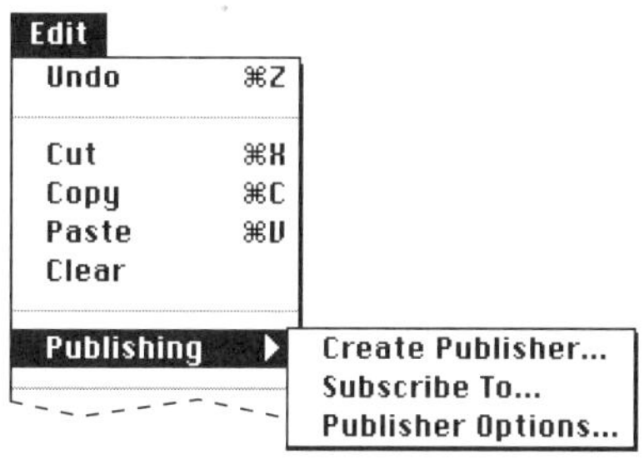

The Clipboard

The Clipboard holds whatever data is cut or copied from a document. It stores the contents until the user replaces them with a new cut or copy operation. The user can change documents, applications, or open a utility without losing the Clipboard contents. Because the contents of the Clipboard don't change when the user moves from one application to another, the Clipboard is used to transfer data among compatible applications and desk accessories. If the user moves the Clipboard file from one disk to another, the contents move with it, replacing any existing Clipboard file on the target disk.

Figure 4-76 shows an example of the Clipboard window with some text in it.

Figure 4-76 The Clipboard

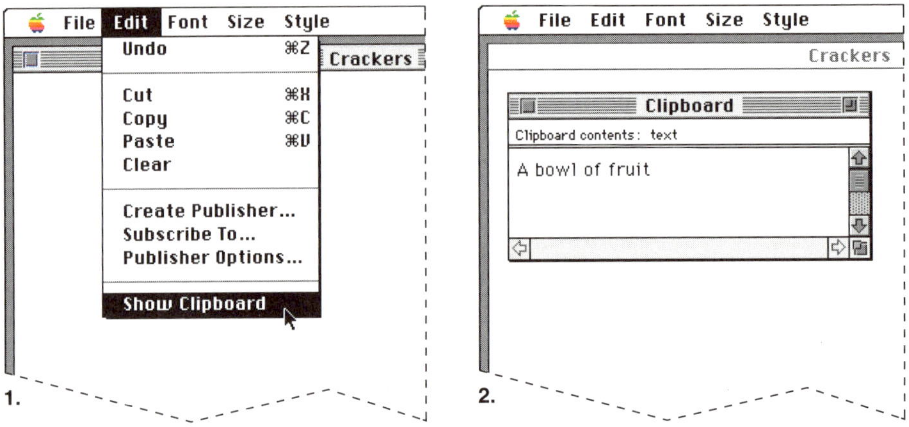

The Clipboard is available to all applications. Your application can show the contents of the Clipboard in a window. The Clipboard window looks and acts like a document window. The contents are visible, but not editable.

Every time the user selects data in the active document and chooses Cut or Copy, store a copy of the selection in the Clipboard, replacing any previous Clipboard contents. Keep the previous contents available in case the user chooses Undo.

Implement the Show Clipboard/Hide Clipboard command in the Edit menu so that the user can display and close the Clipboard window. If the Clipboard is already showing, the user can also use the close box or the Close command to close the window. Show Clipboard and Hide Clipboard are a single toggled item. The Show Clipboard/Hide Clipboard command is described in "Show Clipboard/Hide Clipboard" on page 117.

You should let the user determine when the Clipboard window is open. For example, if the user leaves the window open when quitting your application, the Clipboard should be open when the user restarts it.

In the cooperative, multitasking environment of the current system software, it's important that you hide your application's Clipboard window when your application is not active. In this model, each application has a local Clipboard. Whenever the user switches applications, the contents of the Clipboard are converted to a standard format.

Undo/Redo

The Undo command reverses the effect of the user's previous operation. The Redo command reverses the effect of the last Undo command. Undo and Redo are a single toggled item. In most applications, there is one level of undo operations. The application determines which operations can be undone. Simple operations require your application to store a minimal amount of information about the previous state of the data in order to implement the Undo command. For example, if a user cuts one word from a document, you only need to store the size, the location, the content, and the style of the data. For operations that require you to store the entire state of the document in order to implement the Undo command, it may be more difficult to implement. You should consider the needs of your audience when making difficult decisions about which operations support the Undo command. Remember that your application must be able to redo every undo operation.

In general, support the Undo command for operations that *change the user's contents* of a document. It's nice, but not necessary, to support the Undo command for operations that *don't change the user's contents* of a document. Actions that take a lot of effort to recreate are probably those that a user would most expect to be able to undo. For example, a user might spend several minutes arranging windows on a screen in a specific layout. If that user then accidentally chose the Tile command, the user would expect to be able to recover the original layout by using the Undo command.

Most menu items, regardless of how the user invokes them, should be undoable. Most keyboard input, any sequence of characters typed from the keyboard or numeric keypad, including Delete (Backspace), Return, and Tab should also be undoable.

Operations that may not be undoable include selecting, scrolling, splitting the window, or changing a window's size or location. None of these operations interrupts a typing sequence. For example, if the user types a few characters and then scrolls the document, the Undo operation doesn't undo the scrolling but does undo the typing. Whenever the location affected by the Undo command isn't currently showing on the screen, your application should scroll the document so the user can see the effect of the Undo command.

You should add the name of the last operation to the Undo command. For example, it could read Undo Typing if the user just finished entering some text in a document. If the last operation can't be undone, you should use the phrase Can't Undo and display it dimmed, because it provides more feedback to the user about the current state. The Undo command changes to Redo after the user chooses Undo. You should also include the operation name in the Redo string when possible. If the user chooses Redo, reverse the undo operation.

Figure 4-77 shows an example of the Edit menu with correctly updated Undo and Redo commands.

Figure 4-77 The Undo and Redo commands

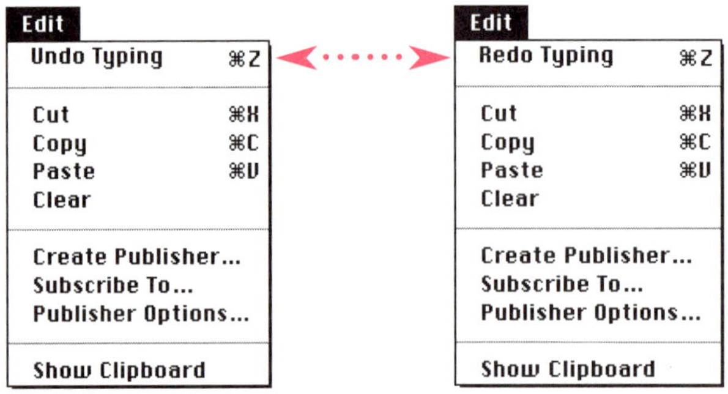

If a user is about to complete an operation that could have a deleterious effect on data and that can't be undone, you should warn the user. For example, if a user is about to destroy a lot of data by replacing every fifth word with a space, display an alert box that says something to the effect of, "You are about to change a lot of your document. You can't undo this operation." The buttons should be labeled Replace and Cancel. If the user is about to make a change that affects only the environment, such as changing a window location, then it's not necessary to display a warning.

The Command-Z combination is reserved as a keyboard equivalent for the Undo/Redo command in the Edit menu. It shouldn't be used for any other purpose.

Cut

The Cut command removes data that the user selects prior to choosing the command. People use the Cut command to delete the current selection or to move it. Store the cut selection on the Clipboard, replacing its previous contents.

Make the area active where the cut selection was. The visual indicators vary by application type. For example, a word processor would display a blinking insertion point at the spot where the text was cut. In an array, the user would see an empty but highlighted cell. If the user chooses Paste immediately after choosing Cut, restore the document to the state it was in just before the cut operation.

The Command-X combination is reserved as a keyboard equivalent for the Cut command in the Edit menu. It shouldn't be used for any other purpose.

Copy

The Copy command makes a duplicate of data the user has selected. Your application puts a duplicate of the selected information on the Clipboard, but leaves the selection in the document. People use the Copy command in conjunction with the Paste command to insert duplicate data in another location.

The Command-C combination is reserved as a keyboard equivalent for the Copy command in the Edit menu. It shouldn't be used for any other purpose.

Paste

The Paste command inserts the contents of the Clipboard in a document at the insertion point. It replaces any current selection. The user can choose the Paste command several times in a row to insert multiple copies of the Clipboard contents. After a paste operation, make the object that was pasted the new selection, unless the user pasted text. In this case, place an insertion point after the inserted text. In either case, leave the contents of the Clipboard unchanged.

People use the Paste command as the last stage of a move or copy operation. Figure 4-78 shows how the Paste command works.

The Command-V combination is reserved as a keyboard equivalent for the Paste command in the Edit menu. It shouldn't be used for any other purpose.

Figure 4-78 The results of using the Paste command

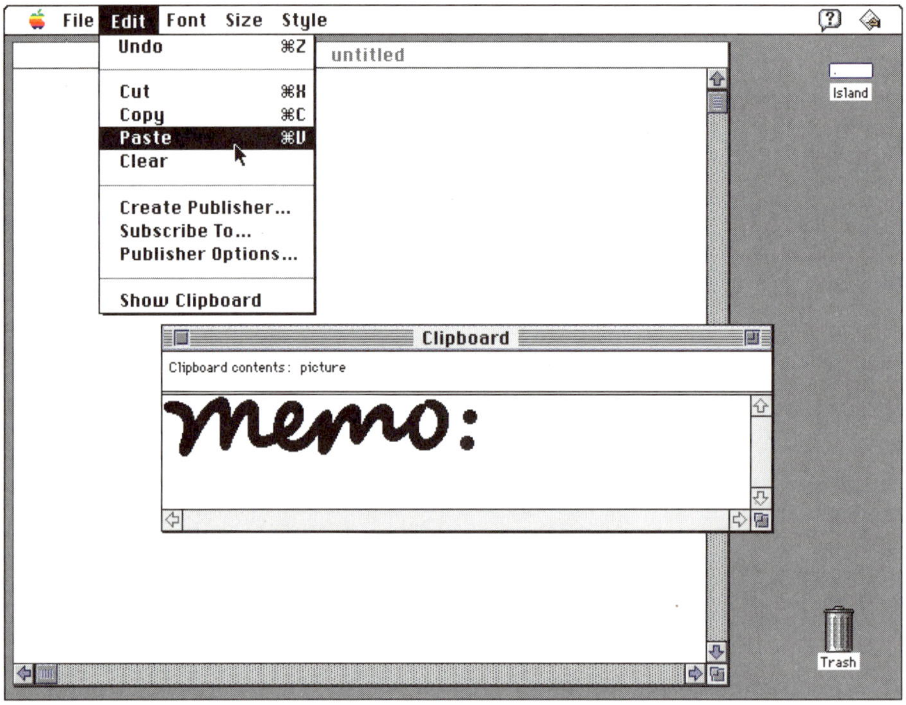

1.

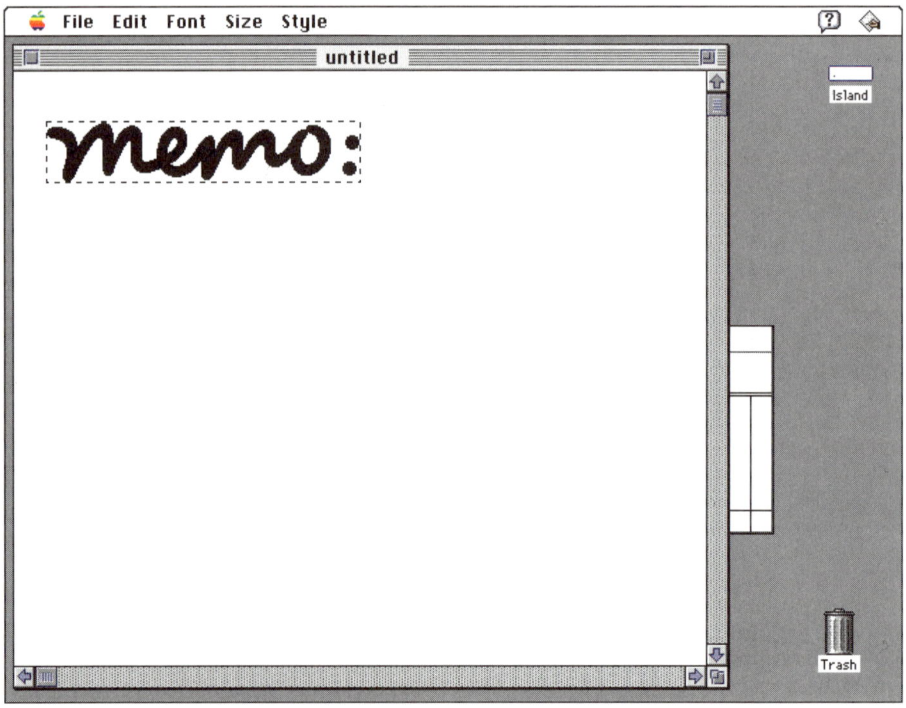

2.

Clear

The Clear command removes data that the user selects just prior to choosing the command. Unlike Cut and Copy, the Clear command does not put the selection in the Clipboard. The Clipboard is unchanged and your application displays the new selection in the same way as it would after a cut operation.

Pressing the Delete (Backspace) key or the Clear key has the same effect as choosing the Clear command from the File menu. (Note that the Backspace key and the Clear key do not appear on all keyboards.)

Select All

The Select All command highlights every object in the document. In a word processor, Select All selects every character as well as all graphics in the document. This command is useful if a user wants to copy or reformat an entire document.

The Command-A combination is reserved as a keyboard equivalent for the Select All command in the Edit menu. It shouldn't be used for any other purpose.

Show Clipboard/Hide Clipboard

Implement the Show Clipboard command in the Edit menu so that the user can display and close the Clipboard window, as described earlier in this chapter in the section "The Clipboard." (If the Clipboard is already showing, the user can also use the close box or the Close command to close the window.) Show Clipboard and Hide Clipboard are a single toggled item.

Show Clipboard changes to Hide Clipboard when the Clipboard window is displayed. The user can also use the close box in the Clipboard window (or the Close command) to hide the Clipboard. Remember to hide your Clipboard window when your application isn't active. Display it again when the user makes your application active by clicking a window or using the Application menu.

Create Publisher...

The Create Publisher command creates an edition based on the selected data. Your application stores this data in an edition file. This information updates automatically when a user saves the document that contains the publisher. The entire Edition Manager interface is described in the chapter "Edition Manager" in *Inside Macintosh: Interapplication Communication.*

Figure 4-79 shows the first two steps of the process.

Figure 4-79 The Create Publisher command and dialog box

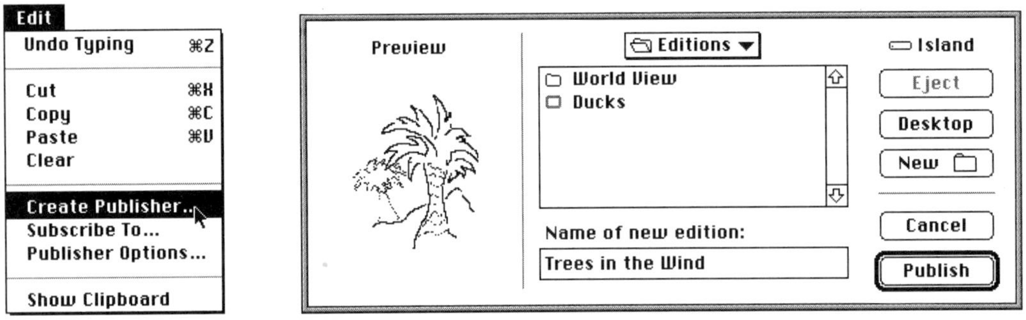

1. 2.

Subscribe To...

The Subscribe To command allows the user to specify which edition to insert in the document. Display the Subscribe To dialog box, as shown in Figure 4-80.

Figure 4-80 The Subscribe To command and dialog box

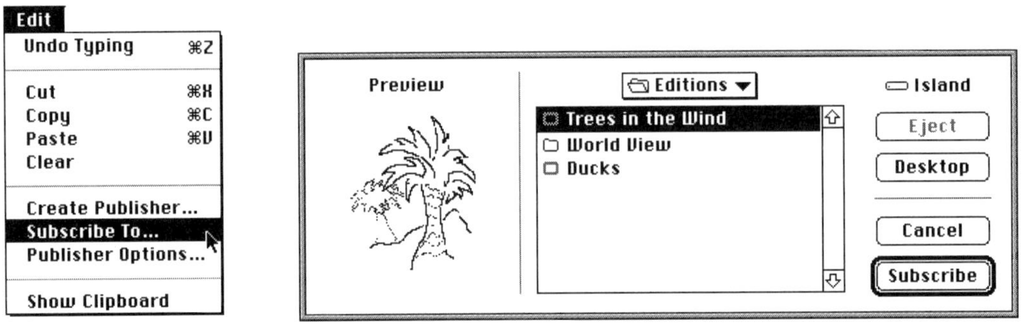

1. 2.

Publisher/Subscriber Options...

The Publisher Options and Subscriber Options commands allow you to provide some choices about publishers and subscribers to the user. Publisher/Subscriber Options is a context-sensitive toggled command; the command name changes to reflect whether a publisher or subscriber is selected. If a user selects a publisher, the command should be Publisher Options. If a user selects a subscriber, the command name should change to Subscriber Options. If no area is selected, the command should appear unavailable in the last state it was in.

Figure 4-81 shows the Publisher Options dialog box. The options apply to the currently selected publisher.

Figure 4-81 The Publisher Options dialog box

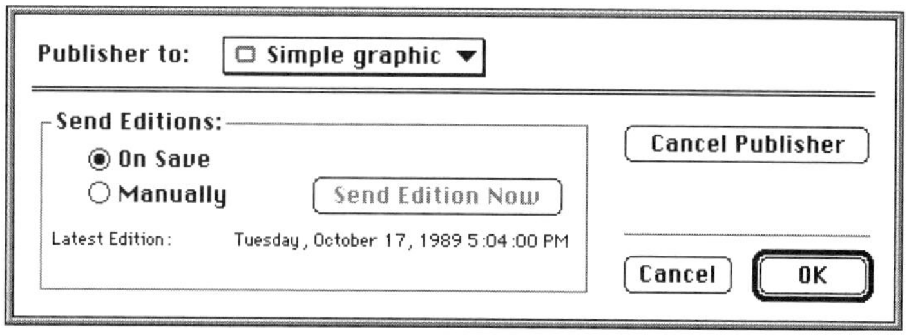

The Cancel Publisher button allows the user to stop sending the information to an edition. The data remains unchanged in the document. The border that denotes a publisher no longer appears when the data is selected.

The Send Editions radio buttons allow the user to specify whether to automatically send a new edition when the document is saved or to send the data to the edition when the user decides to do so. The Send Edition Now button becomes available when the user clicks the Manually button. Then the user must click the Send Edition Now button to specifically send a new edition of a publisher. Information that identifies the latest edition sent appears in the area below the radio buttons.

If you provide additional options to the user, include the controls in the bottom area of the Publisher Options dialog box.

Figure 4-82 shows the Subscriber Options dialog box. The options apply to the currently selected subscriber.

Figure 4-82 The Subscriber Options dialog box

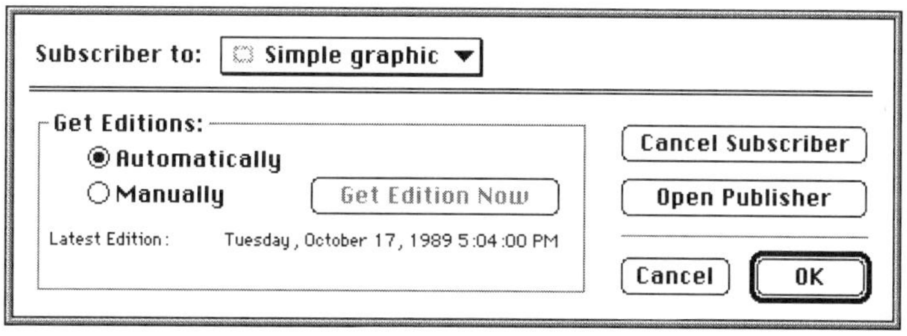

The Edition Manager has no provisions to let users edit subscribers directly because new editions can arrive at any time. This situation could be especially destructive if several users were working over a network with interconnected publishers and subscribers, and new editions arrived that replaced subscribers that had been edited. To make changes to a subscriber, the user must go to the publisher and make changes to it. The user can use the Open Publisher button in the Subscriber Options dialog box. This option locates the document that contains the publisher and opens it, launching the application if necessary. The document automatically scrolls to display the publisher. When the user saves changes to the document, the new contents are written to the edition file and all subscribers are updated. Because the changes are made to the original document, the user can make changes to the data without danger of losing the change in a subscriber. It's important to note that the user must have correct access privileges to the document that contains the publisher for this option to work. If a user doesn't have permission to open a file on a file server or a personal Macintosh, display an alert box to notify the user that the publisher couldn't be opened and why.

The Cancel Subscriber button allows the user to break the connection to the edition. The data remains in the document, but new editions won't be received and the borders that denote a subscriber no longer appear.

The Get Editions radio buttons allow the user to specify when new editions should be received. If the user clicks Automatically, editions arrive as they become available when the document is open or each time the document is opened if new editions are available. If the user clicks Manually, new editions are received when the user selects the subscriber, chooses Subscriber Options, and then clicks the Get Edition Now button. Information that identifies the latest edition available appears in the area below the radio buttons.

If you provide additional options to the user, include the controls in the bottom area of the Subscriber Options dialog box.

The Font Menu

The **Font menu** provides choices of text fonts for users. A font is a set of typographical characters created with a consistent design. All the characters in a font share features such as the thickness of horizontal and vertical lines, the degree and position of curves, and the presence or absence of serifs. Serifs are fine lines added to the main strokes of a letter. The characters in a font can appear in many different point sizes, but all have the same general appearance, regardless of size.

Your application can include a Font menu if you support text in your application. Not all applications need a Font menu, but all word processors should include a Font menu.

Display the names of all available fonts (those residing in the user's System Folder) in your application's Font menu. Fonts appear in the Font menu in alphabetical order, grouped by script system when more than one script is installed. When the script system is installed, the font name of an international font appears in its corresponding script when it is localized. Users install fonts by dragging the font icon to the System Folder icon. Figure 4-83 shows an example of a Font menu.

Figure 4-83 A Font menu

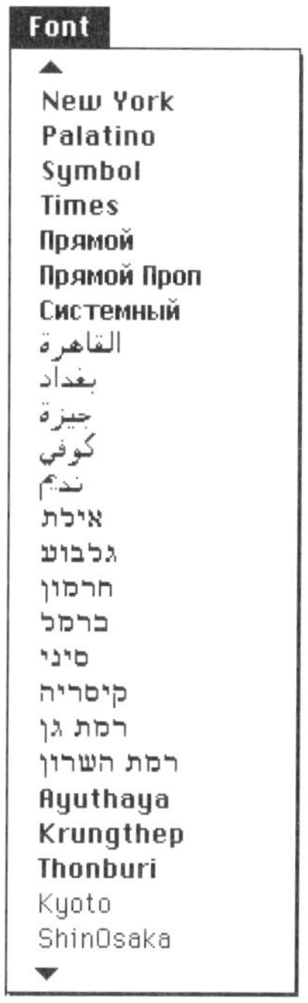

Indicate which font is currently in effect using a checkmark. As described in the section "Checkmarks and Dashes in Menus," which begins on page 64, use dashes to indicate when more than one font applies to the current selection.

Many people have a very large set of fonts, so the font list should never be included with other items in one menu. Your application needs to have a Font menu and separate menus to accommodate lists of attributes such as style and size choices.

Figure 4-84 shows why it's not a good idea to try to group the Font menu with other text-related menus.

Figure 4-84 Don't combine the Font menu with other menus

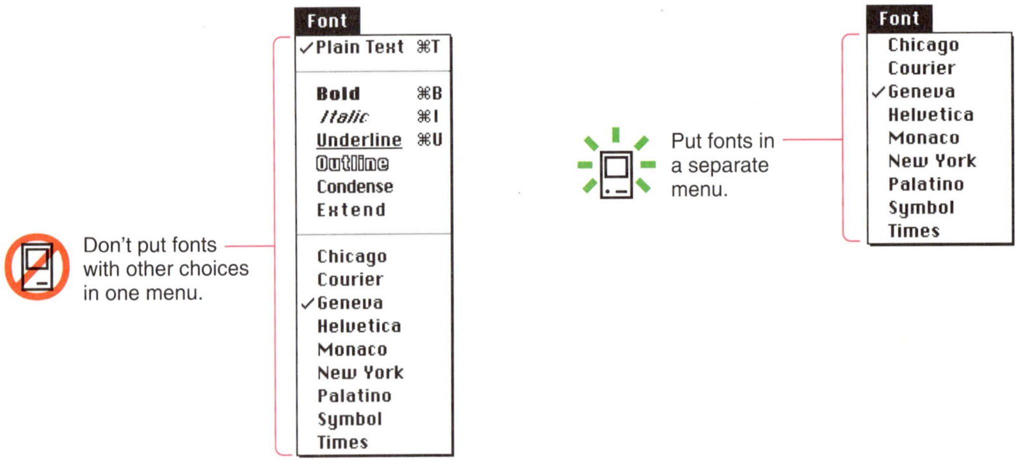

For more information on font considerations, see the section "Worldwide Compatibility" on page 16 in Chapter 2, "General Design Considerations."

The Size Menu

The **Size menu** provides size choices for fonts. Font sizes are measured in points. A **point** is a typographical unit of measure equivalent to 1/72 inch. Indicate the current font size with a checkmark. As described in the section "Checkmarks and Dashes in Menus," which begins on page 64, use dashes to indicate when more than one font size applies to the current selection. Figure 4-85 shows a typical Size menu.

Figure 4-85 A Size menu

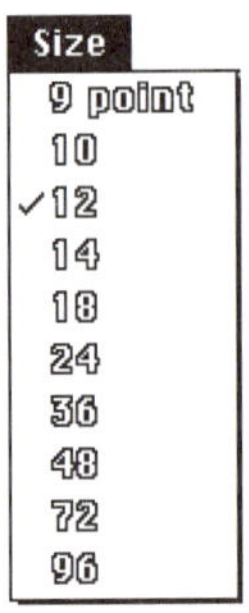

System 7 supports both bitmapped and TrueType fonts. To incorporate basic support for TrueType fonts into your application, provide support for all font sizes in your application. Don't set an upper limit for font sizes. Outline the font sizes in the menu for those sizes that appear in the user's System file. Use plain type for font sizes that aren't in the System file. If a TrueType font is present, outline all sizes of that font that you display in the menu. Provide a way for users to choose whatever font size they desire.

One way that you can support TrueType fonts is to add an Other command to the end of the Size menu. When the user chooses Other, display a dialog box that allows the user to choose any available font size by typing in a text box. If the user enters a font size not currently on the menu, add a checkmark to the Other command and include the font size as part of the Other command name. Show the font size in parentheses after the word Other. If a selection contains more than one nonstandard size, include the word Mixed in parentheses following the word Other. In this case, leave the text box of the font size dialog box blank when the user chooses the Other (Mixed) command. Figure 4-86 displays a sample pull-down Size menu and font size dialog box. See *Inside Macintosh: Text* for more information on supporting fonts in your application.

Figure 4-86 A sample pull-down Size menu and font size dialog box

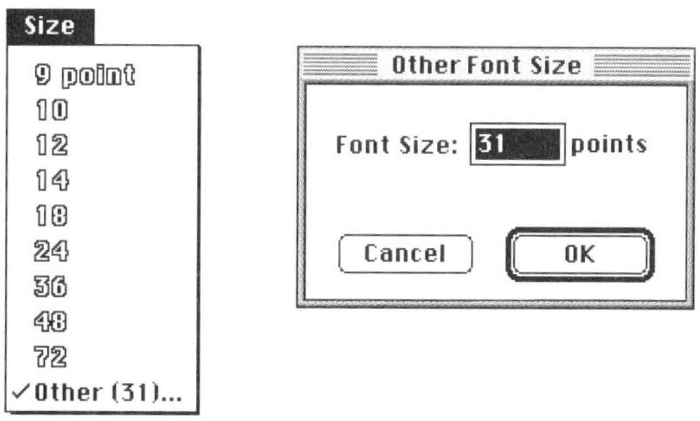

It's possible to implement the Size and Style menus as submenus in a hierarchical menu. For information on doing so and the tradeoffs that you need to consider before implementing the menus this way, see the section "Hierarchical Menus," which begins on page 79.

The Style Menu

The **Style menu** provides style choices for fonts. The menu items in a standard Style menu are Plain Text, Bold, Italic, Underline, Outline, Shadow, Condense, and Extend. You can display these styles in the menus to indicate the effect of choosing the items. Figure 4-87 shows a typical Style menu.

Figure 4-87 A Style menu

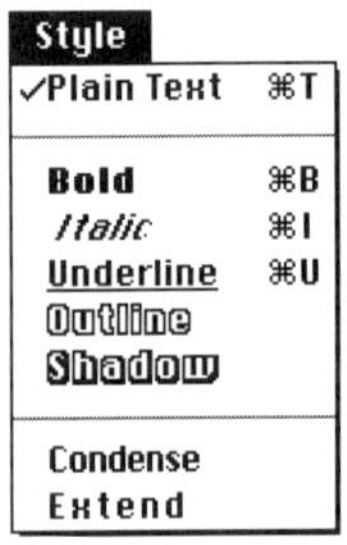

You can also include other style attributes in this menu, such as Superscript, Subscript, Small Caps, and Uppercase and Lowercase. Most style attributes except Plain Text, Uppercase and Lowercase, and Condense and Extend, are accumulating attributes. This means that the user can choose all of them, none of them, or any combination of them. Choosing Plain Text cancels all other style attributes.

Display a checkmark next to each item when it's in effect. The absence of a checkmark indicates that the attribute is not currently in effect. It is important that you toggle on and off each attribute individually. In this way you provide the user with the ability to have multiple attributes in effect and then cancel one of them, without having to cancel them all and start over. For example, if the user made a selection bold, italic, and underline (which is not recommended), he or she could decide to eliminate the underline style but keep the bold and italic styles.

You can assign keyboard equivalents for the Style menu, as described in the section "Keyboard Equivalents," which begins on page 128.

The Help Menu

The Macintosh Operating System includes Balloon Help, an online help system for system software; you can use the Help Manager to implement Balloon Help for your application. The user can turn on Balloon Help from the Help menu. Figure 4-88 shows the Help menu.

Figure 4-88 The Help menu

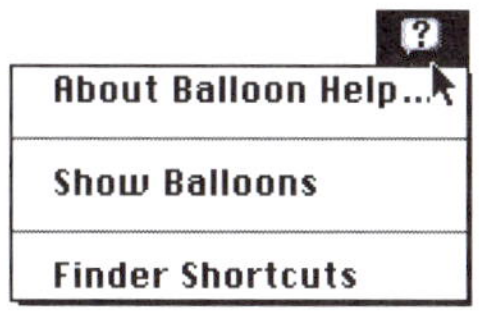

If you provide additional help information for your application, put the help commands that you provide in the Help menu. It's a good idea to include the name of your application next to your help command. For example, you might include a command called WaveWriter Help in the Help menu.

The Keyboard Menu

Users can install multiple script systems. A script system can contain multiple **keyboard layouts** that each map character codes to keys on a physical keyboard, can use input methods that act as a front end processor for text input in 2-byte scripts, and can support more than one attached physical keyboard. See *Inside Macintosh: Overview* for information on installing and enabling script systems and keyboard resources.

The Keyboard menu appears when more than one script system is present or a localizable resource flag is set. This menu simplifies the user's access to script systems, keyboard layouts, and input methods. The icon for the Keyboard menu appears between the icons for the Help menu and the Application menu. A keyboard icon appears next to each keyboard layout or input method name in the menu, and the icon of the active keyboard layout or input method appears in the menu bar. As Figure 4-89 shows, the Keyboard menu displays a list of installed keyboard layouts and input methods for each enabled script system.

Menus

The Keyboard menu groups the keyboard layouts by script system, which are separated by dotted or gray lines. In Figure 4-89, there are several script systems that include keyboard layouts and input methods. Only one keyboard layout or input method and one physical keyboard are active at a time. Indicate the active condition by using a checkmark in the menu.

Figure 4-89 The Keyboard menu

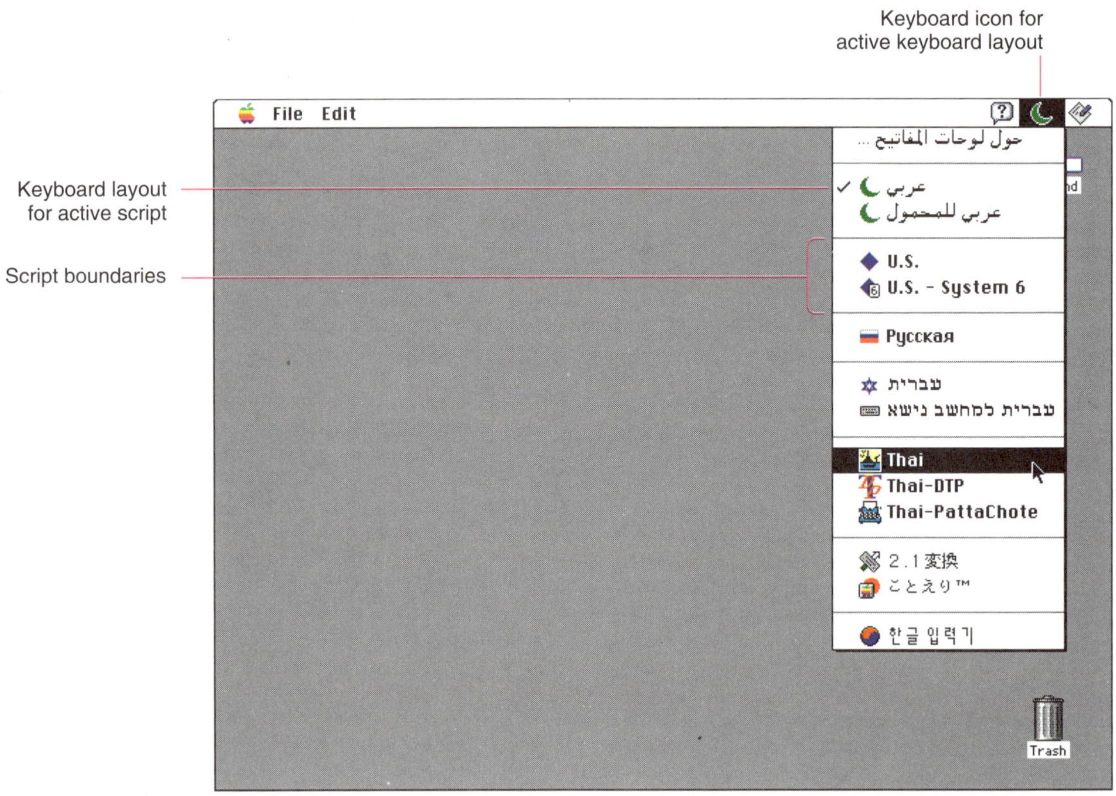

Users can change scripts by using this menu or by using a keyboard equivalent, Command–Space bar, to cycle through the scripts. The user can rotate through keyboard layouts or input methods within a script by using Command–Option–Space bar. Don't use the keyboard equivalents Command–Space bar and Command–Option–Space bar in your application because they are reserved for use by the Script Manager. See the section "Keyboard Equivalents," which begins on page 128, for a complete listing of reserved keyboard equivalents.

A keyboard icon represents a localized keyboard layout or input method. If you develop keyboards or keyboard resources, you should provide customized icons. You need to create a 16-by-16 pixel icon in 1-bit, 4-bit, and 8-bit color.

If you are designing a new keyboard icon, use a symbol to represent a keyboard layout for a region that is larger or smaller than a country or province. For example, a diamond represents the Roman Script System, which is used in the United States, Central America, South America, Australia, and most of Europe. Use the flag of a country or province if the keyboard layout is used only in that area. For example, the Union Jack represents the keyboard layout localized for use in Great Britain. Be sure to use the colors that appear on the nation's flag. You can also add a visual indicator to the flag to show some modification. Use a superscript diamond to indicate a QWERTY transliteration, which is a mapping of sounds from a language to the Roman keyboard layout. See Figure 8-44 in Chapter 8, "Icons," which begins on page 223, for examples of icons with these symbols. Also, see that chapter for more information on designing or creating keyboard and input method icons.

The Application Menu

The **Application menu** displays a list of the applications that are currently running. When the user opens your application, its name and its small icon appear in the Application menu. Users can switch to another application by choosing an item in this menu. They can also hide the open windows of the active application or any other open applications. See Chapter 5, "Windows," which begins on page 131, for more information about how your application should behave when the user makes it the active application or when the user chooses another application while yours is active.

Keyboard Equivalents

Apple reserves several standard keyboard equivalents for standard commands. Table 4-1 and Table 4-2 show the standard Macintosh keyboard equivalents.

Table 4-1 Apple-reserved keyboard equivalents for all systems

Menu	Keys	Command
File	⌘-N	New
File	⌘-O	Open…
File	⌘-W	Close
File	⌘-S	Save
File	⌘-P	Print…
File	⌘-Q	Quit
Edit	⌘-Z	Undo
Edit	⌘-X	Cut
Edit	⌘-C	Copy
Edit	⌘-V	Paste
Edit	⌘-A	Select All
Edit	⌘-period	Terminate an operation

Table 4-2 shows several keyboard equivalents that are reserved for use with localized versions of system software, localized keyboards, keyboard layouts, and input methods. These keyboard equivalents don't correspond directly to menu commands, so there is no menu column with command names in Table 4-2.

Table 4-2 Additional reserved keyboard equivalents for worldwide systems

Keys	Action
⌘–Space bar	Rotate through enabled script systems
⌘–Option–Space bar	Rotate through keyboard layouts and input methods within a script
⌘–*modifier key*–Space bar	Apple reserved
⌘–Right Arrow	Changes keyboard layout to current layout of Roman script
⌘–Left Arrow	Changes keyboard layout to current layout of system script

See the section on keyboard equivalents in the book *Inside Macintosh: Overview* for a discussion of handling keyboard equivalents in other script systems.

The key combinations in Table 4-1 and Table 4-2 are reserved across all applications. Even if your application doesn't support one of the menu commands in Table 4-1, it shouldn't use these keyboard equivalents for another function.

Some applications use other common keyboard equivalents, as shown in Table 4-3. These keyboard equivalents are secondary to the standard keyboard equivalents listed in Table 4-1 and Table 4-2. If your product doesn't support one of these functions, then use these equivalents as you wish.

Table 4-3 Common keyboard equivalents that are not reserved

Menu	Keys	Command
File	⌘-F	Find
File	⌘-G	Find Again
Style	⌘-T	Plain Text
Style	⌘-B	Bold
Style	⌘-I	Italic
Style	⌘-U	Underline

Don't assign keyboard equivalents for infrequently used menu commands. Add keyboard equivalents only for the commands your users employ most frequently.

CHAPTER 5

Windows

This chapter describes document windows, which contain user data, and utility windows, which "float" above other windows and can provide tools or other controls that users can work with while document windows are open. The chapter presents specifications and recommendations about the appearance and behavior of these windows, including how the window frame should look, how the user interacts with windows, how you should display them on the screen, and how they interact with each other. This chapter includes some information about dialog boxes, but you can find more extensive information about dialog and alert boxes, both of which are also windows, in Chapter 6, "Dialog Boxes," which begins on page 175.

Windows provide a way for people to view and interact with their data. Windows have standard appearances that create a sense of perceived stability for people because they have a standard way to view and interact with all the different kinds of data they can create and store on Macintosh computers.

A window is a view into the document—if the document is larger than the window, the window is a view of a portion of the document. The application puts one or more windows on the screen, each window showing a view of a document or of auxiliary information used in processing the document.

Generally there is only one window per document. Multiple windows for the same document can confuse the relationship of windows to icons. The user may wonder, "which window do I close to close the document?" You can provide multiple views to a document by implementing the capability to split windows or by adding utility windows. (See the section "Splitting a Window" on page 170 and the section "Utility Windows" on page 137 for more information.)

Figure 5-1 shows examples of the standard window types, including dialog boxes.

Figure 5-1 Examples of standard windows

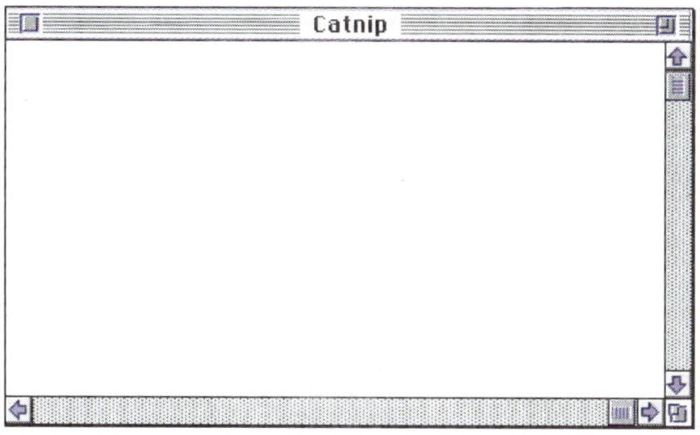

Document window

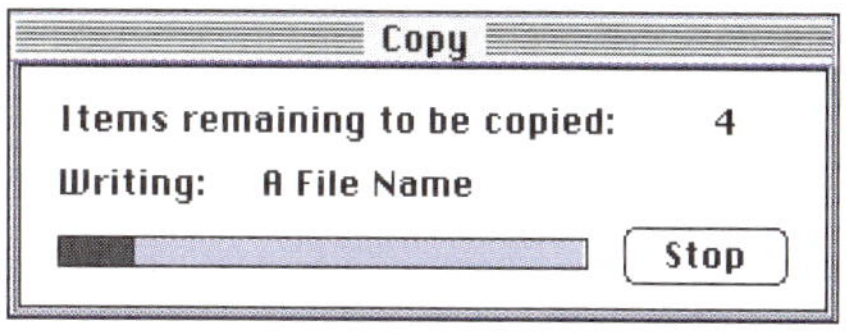

Movable modal dialog box

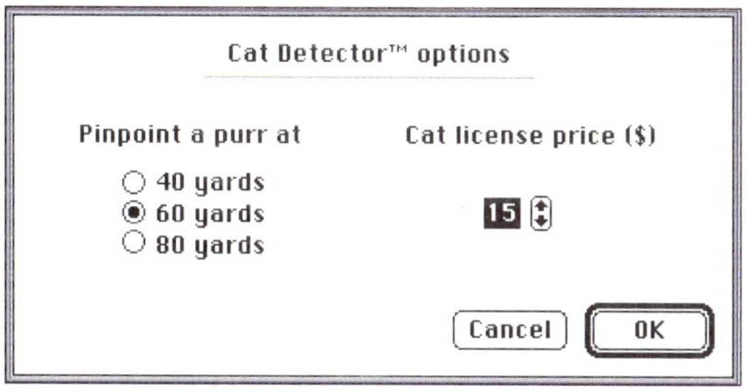

Modal dialog box

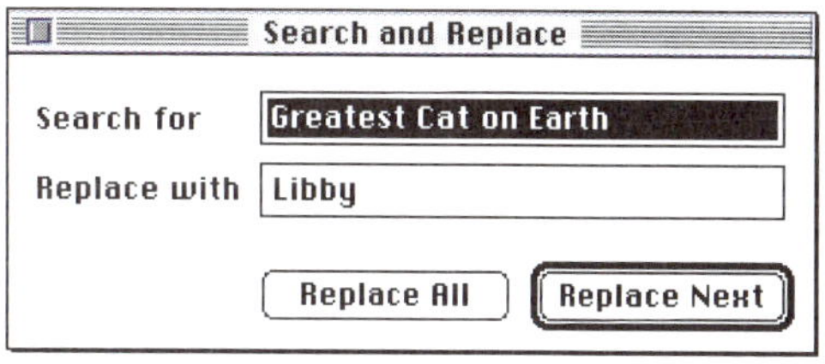

Modeless dialog box

There are conventions for opening, closing, moving, sizing, scrolling, and zooming windows. This means that no matter which application people use, they know how to control windows on the screen and how to adjust windows in the desktop workspace for particular tasks or for their work styles.

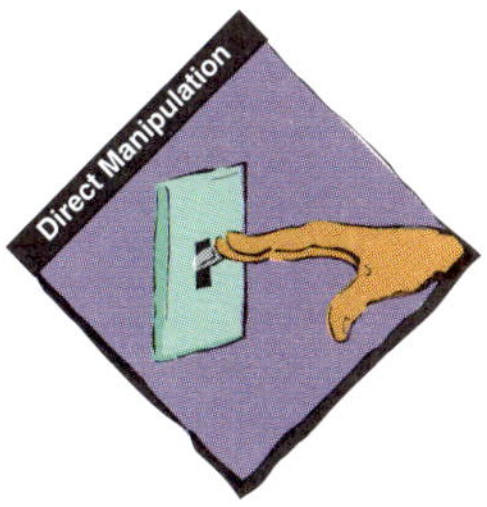

When people manipulate windows on the screen, they see immediate visual feedback. When people move windows, the graphic display keeps up with their movements using a dotted outline to represent the window as it moves on the screen, reinforcing their sense of direct manipulation. When people open and close windows, they see an illusion of such actions. All of these mechanisms emphasize that the user is in control and can directly manipulate "real" interface objects such as windows. See *Inside Macintosh: Macintosh Toolbox Essentials* for information on implementing windows.

Window Appearance

Document windows present a view into the content that people create and store. If the document is larger than the window, the window shows a portion of the document. The Window Manager provides support for the window frame. Your application determines window content and what happens in the content area. Document windows also provide a graphic representation of opening, closing, and other operations performed on documents. Windows are usually, but not necessarily, rectangles.

This section discusses the appearance of document windows and utility windows. The section "Window Behaviors," beginning on page 139, includes information about the behavior of window components as well as information about general window behaviors.

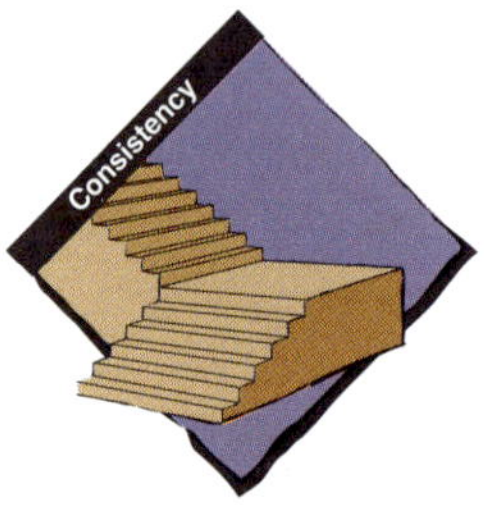

Document Window Controls

Standard document windows have standard structural components. These components include the title bar, size box, close box, zoom box, and scroll bars. Figure 5-2 shows the structural components of standard document windows.

Figure 5-2 Standard document window parts

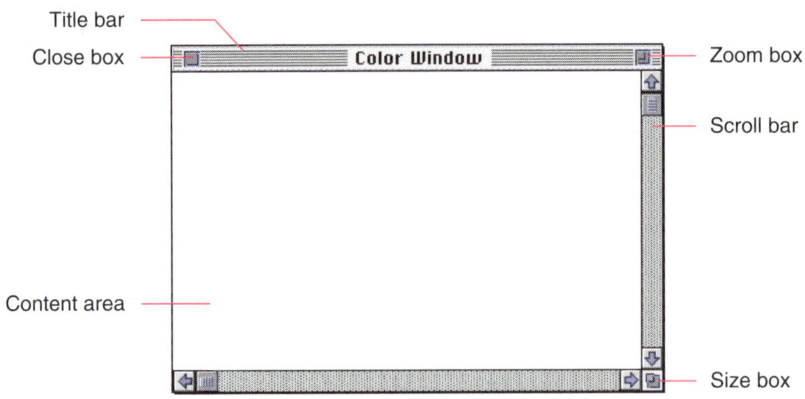

Windows are designed for visual consistency across all monitors from black-and-white displays to 24-bit color displays. For display on color monitors, colors and shades of gray have been added to the frames of windows and to user controls to emphasize those areas that users interact with, such as scroll boxes and arrows, zoom boxes, close boxes, and size boxes. The window content area remains white on all systems and the window contents remain black and white, unless the user assigns color to the content. This updated design takes advantage of the color capabilities of the Macintosh but maintains the consistency of the Macintosh interface.

Use of Color in Windows

Color distinguishes the active window from other windows and enhances the appearance of user controls on the window frame. On color screens, the scroll bars and the racing stripes in the title bar are gray. The user controls—close box, size box, zoom box, and scroll box—are colored to make them more apparent. The borders of inactive windows are gray and appear to recede into the background so that the active window's black frame emphasizes its position in front of the other windows. Figure 5-3 shows the appearance of windows on a color screen.

Figure 5-3 Windows on a color screen

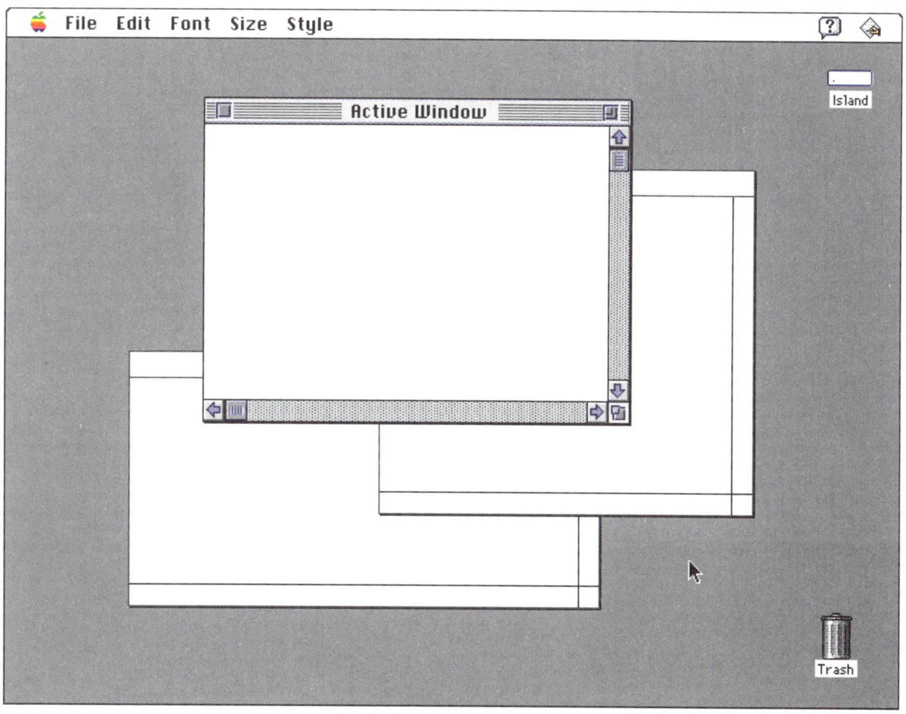

The standard window definition functions display color windows and dialog boxes. The control definition functions for scroll bars, scroll arrows, scroll box, close box, size box, and zoom box have been updated to display these controls in color. If you use the standard window definition functions and standard control definition functions, your application's windows will match the appearance of Macintosh system windows. If you create your own windows, be compatible with the system software appearance by using the standard window color table. Figure 5-4 shows the components of a standard window in color.

Figure 5-4 Standard window components in color

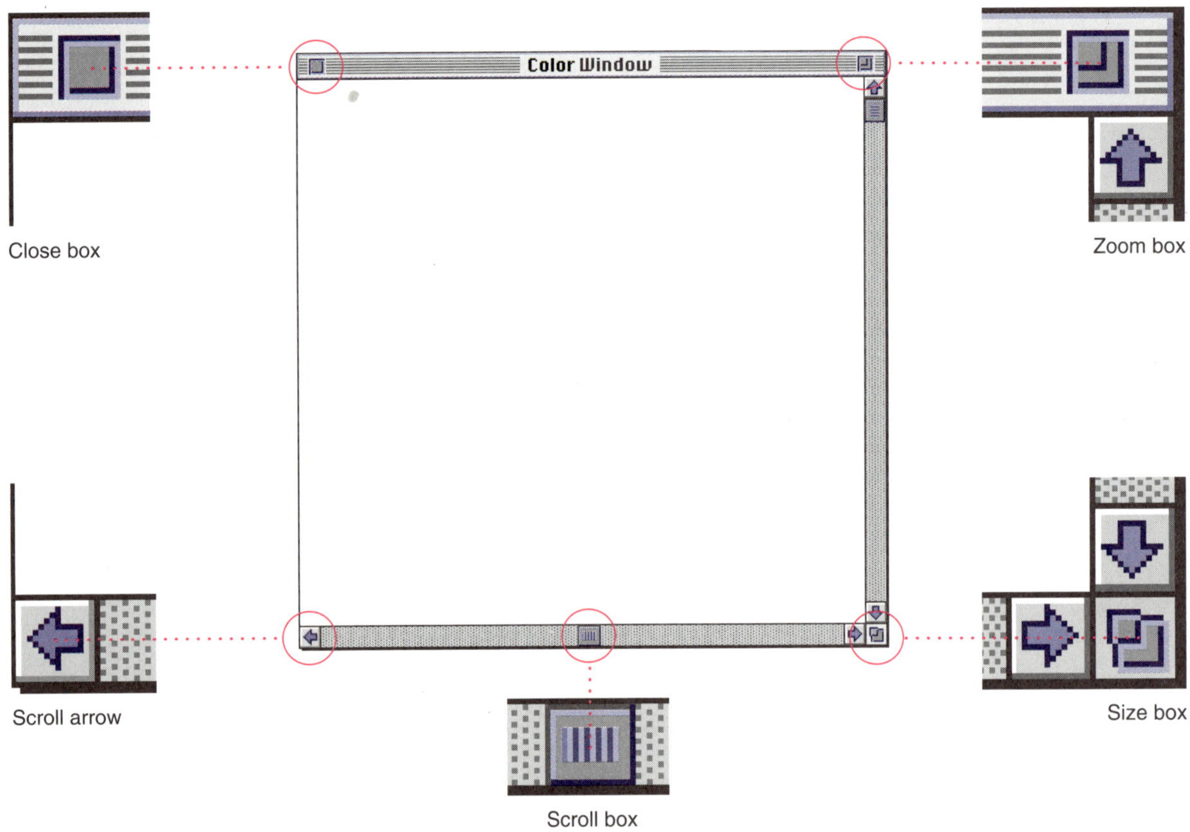

Be aware that users can change the color used in window frames and dialog box frames by using the Color control panel. If you use the standard window color table, you can be sure that any colors you use are consistent with any color that the user can choose from the Color control panel. You can use the

Palette Manager to associate a color palette with a window definition. For more information, see the discussion of the Palette Manager in *Inside Macintosh*. Figure 5-5 shows the Color control panel and the colors that the user can choose to be used in windows and dialog boxes.

Figure 5-5 Colors that the user can choose for windows

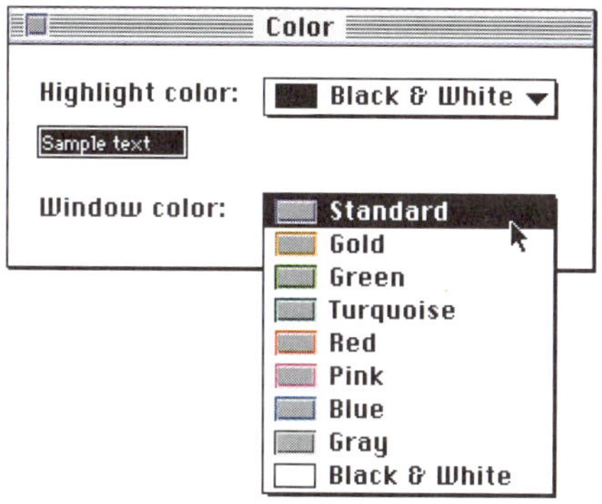

Utility Windows

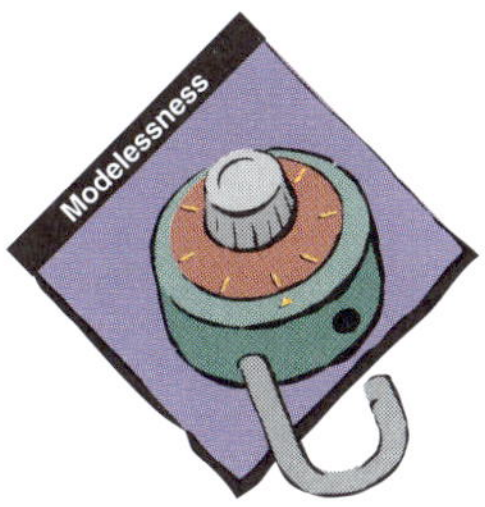

A **utility window** is a small accessory window that provides additional tools or controls to users. A tool palette or a set of text attributes could be implemented in a utility window. Utility windows float on top of document windows. The user can open several utility windows at a time. The user can easily use any utility windows from the active document window. That is, the user doesn't have to click a utility window once to make it active and then click again to make a choice or activate a setting in the window. Figure 5-6 shows an example of a utility window.

Figure 5-6 A utility window

You can create utility windows as a way to present controls or settings that affect the active window. Utility windows are useful for keeping extremely important controls or information accessible at all times in the context of a user task. Don't use utility windows when you can solve this need with a modeless dialog box (the user can make the appropriate settings and then close the dialog box) or by adding controls to the window frame (where appropriate) because utility windows take up screen space, which is a factor especially on smaller screens.

You need to create and maintain any utility windows for your application. Whenever your application is in the background, hide all utility windows. Sometimes applications implement palettes in utility windows. Palettes are discussed in Chapter 4, "Menus," in the section "Tear-Off Menus and Palettes" on page 92.

Most utility windows don't have titles. The standard drag region at the top of utility windows is 11 pixels high. If you create utility windows that have title bars and a title (text), make sure the title bar is at least 19 pixels high, the height of a document window title bar. (If you create a smaller title bar with a title, it can't be localized for areas where the system font is never smaller than 12 points.) Fill the title bar with a 25 percent pattern. Don't use racing stripes in a utility window title bar. You can include a close box and a zoom box on utility windows. If you do include these mechanisms, implement them with standard behaviors, as described in "Closing a Window" on page 152 and "The Zoom Box and Window Behavior" on page 168.

When a user has a document window open and a utility window that accepts text as well, it's difficult to make it obvious where keyboard input will appear. You need to implement a way to clarify to users what they can expect in such a situation. You may use a secondary selection technique, such as outlining the text in the inactive window (or making it gray on a color monitor), to distinguish between the active input area and the inactive one. It's also very difficult to manage the input and editing of text in a utility window. If users are confused about where the text will appear, it's probably a better idea to implement a modeless dialog box with the same capability. Figure 5-7 shows an example of a utility window and a document window that both accept text; this type of situation can be confusing to users.

Figure 5-7 Make it clear where text will appear

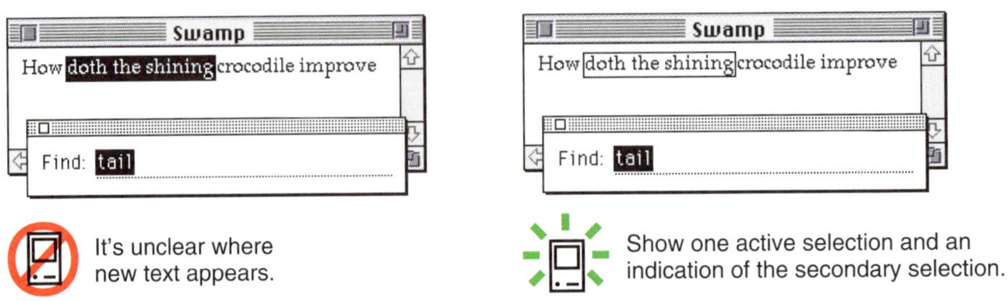

Window Behaviors

Document windows provide immediate feedback about all actions the user takes such as opening, closing, and changing the view of a document. The sections that follow describe these behaviors and appearances.

The Active Window

People can open as many applications and desk accessories as their computer's memory can support, but they interact with only one at a time. The one the user is interacting with is the **active application.** Its small icon represents the Application menu in the menu bar.

As with applications, there can be only one active window at a time. Like the active application, the **active window** is the one the user is currently working in. It is frontmost and visually distinct from the other windows on the screen. The title bar displays racing stripes and the controls in the window frame are visible. On color screens, the controls in the scroll bars are colored. Your application should update the controls, such as the scroll bars, in its frontmost window whenever the user switches to your application. Figure 5-8 shows what the active window looks like compared to other windows on the screen.

Figure 5-8 The active window

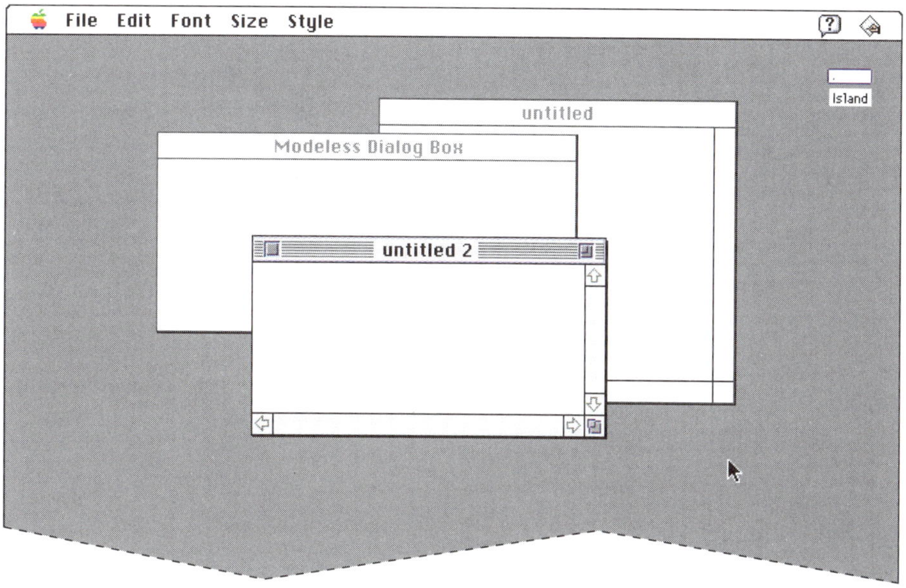

All other windows, whether they belong to your application or another, are inactive. Things can happen to documents in inactive windows, but only the active window interacts with the user. For example, if the user chooses Save, the command affects only the active window.

To make a window active, the user clicks anywhere in its content area or window frame. It appears to the user that the window "moves" to the frontmost plane and any parts that were previously covered by other windows become visible.

When a user clicks in an application window, the click activates the window, but makes no other changes. To make a selection in an application window, the user must click again. This behavior protects the user from losing an existing selection when the window becomes active. When the user activates a window that had been deactivated, reinstate the window just the way it was before the window was deactivated. The scroll box should be in the same position and the same selection, if any, should still be highlighted. Try not to create a great deal of flashing or other visual disturbance when you update windows for your application. This action should take place with as little distraction to the user as possible.

When a window that belongs to your application becomes inactive, the visual characteristics of the active state reverse. The close box, zoom box, size box, scroll box, and stripes in the title bar disappear. Don't display the scroll bars and their associated controls (scroll box and arrows) when a window from your application is inactive; however, the lines that outline the area of the scroll bar itself should remain visible. For example, notice the appearance of the scroll bar in the "untitled" window shown in Figure 5-8; only the outline is displayed. Don't display a selection in an inactive window. Users may have difficulty determining where the next keyboard or mouse action will take effect. (You can use a secondary selection technique, such as an outline on a black-and-white monitor or gray on a color monitor, to indicate where a selection is in an inactive window.) Figure 5-9 shows what can occur when two windows simultaneously display selection information.

Figure 5-9 Don't show a selection in an inactive window

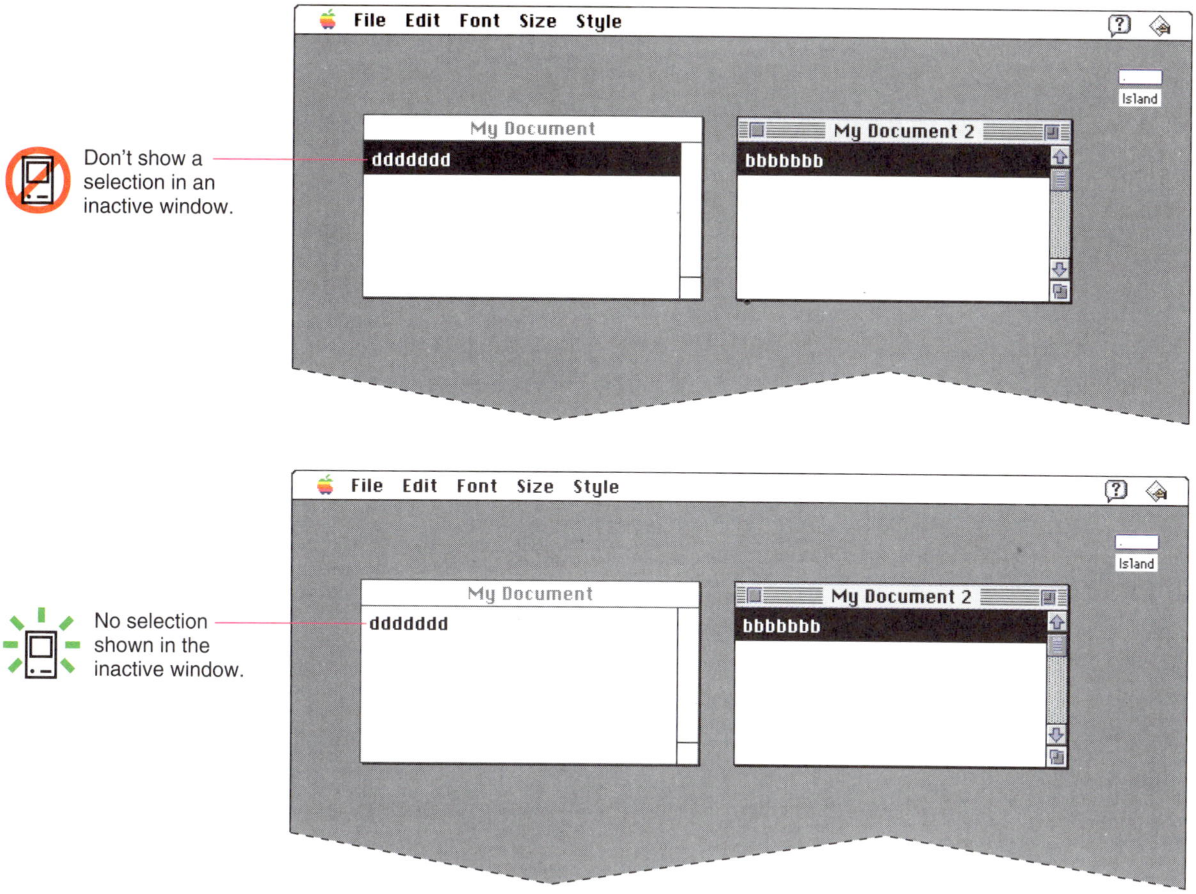

Opening Windows

Users can open windows in a variety of ways including double-clicking a document icon in the Finder, choosing a file from a standard file dialog box, choosing the New command, choosing the Open command, or choosing a command that displays a dialog box. For more information on where to open windows on the screen, see the section "Window Positions" on page 146.

When your application displays a new window, title it "untitled," spelled in lowercase letters. If the user chooses the New command again, without saving the first untitled window, title the second window "untitled 2," leaving a space between the word and the number. Continue to add one to the number in the title as long as the user continues to open new windows without saving previously numbered untitled windows.

Figure 5-10 shows some examples of appropriate window titles for a series of windows that haven't been saved or named.

Figure 5-10 Appropriate window titles for a series of unnamed windows

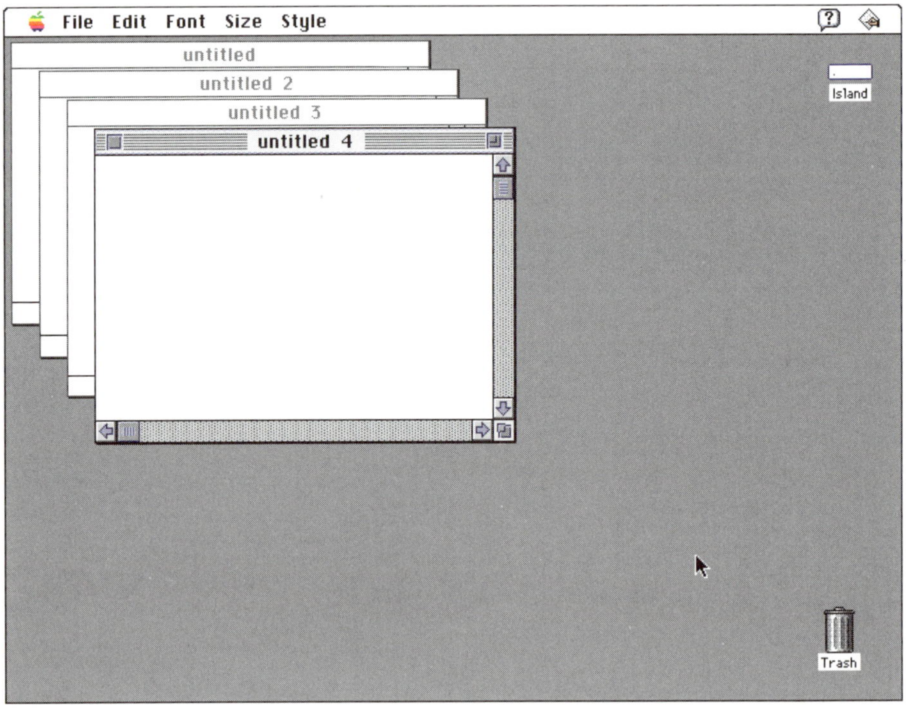

Add numbers to window titles only when there is more than one open, untitled window on the screen. If the user saves the first window, open the next new one as "untitled."

Never capitalize the word *untitled* in a new window title. It makes the window look like it has a name and discourages people from saving the document with a meaningful name. Don't number the first new window with the numeral one. Usually people open only one window, use it, save and name it, and then go on with other work. In this case, numbering one instance of a window doesn't make sense and is distracting. Also, don't add punctuation of any kind to untitled window titles. Figure 5-11 shows several examples of window titles that use naming techniques you should avoid; it includes an example of the right way to title a window.

Figure 5-11 Examples of correct and incorrect window titles

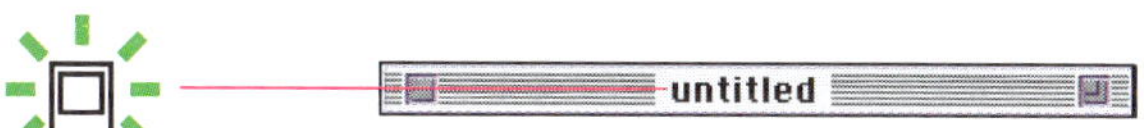

Do use "untitled" for the first new window.

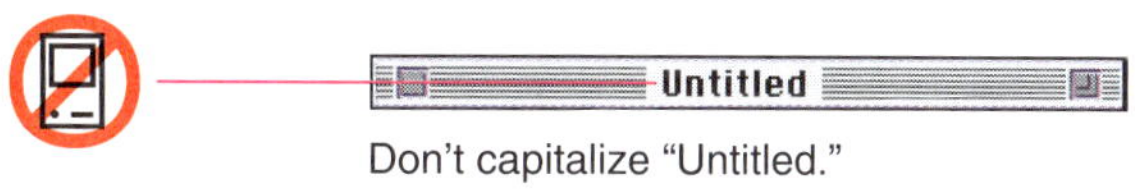

Don't capitalize "Untitled."

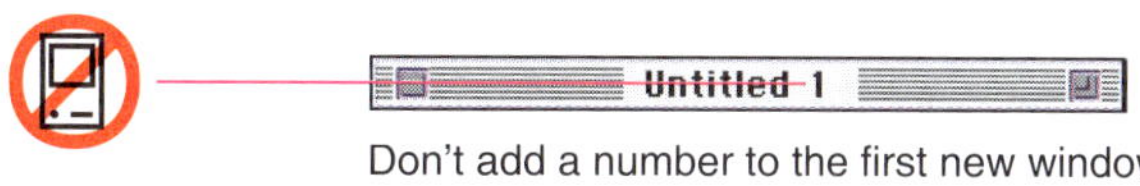

Don't add a number to the first new window.

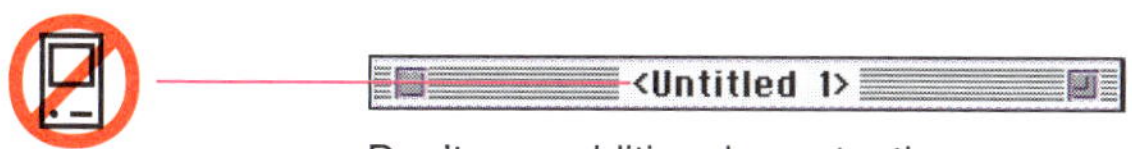

Don't use additional punctuation.

Don't leave a title blank.

When the user opens an existing document, display the name of the document as it appears in the Finder icon. The document and its corresponding window name must match at all times.

Window Display Order

Windows always appear on the desktop in a certain hierarchy of layers. Each application has its own stack of windows within which different types of windows appear in a specified order.

Standard document windows and modeless dialog boxes appear on the lowest level, closest to the desktop and farthest away from the user. Modeless dialog boxes follow the same ordering guidelines as document windows; they typically appear on top of an open document window just as if they were new document windows. Figure 5-12 shows the initial order of document windows and modeless dialog boxes on the desktop; this order remains the same until the user activates the modeless dialog box or one or more of the windows.

Figure 5-12 Display order of document windows and modeless dialog boxes

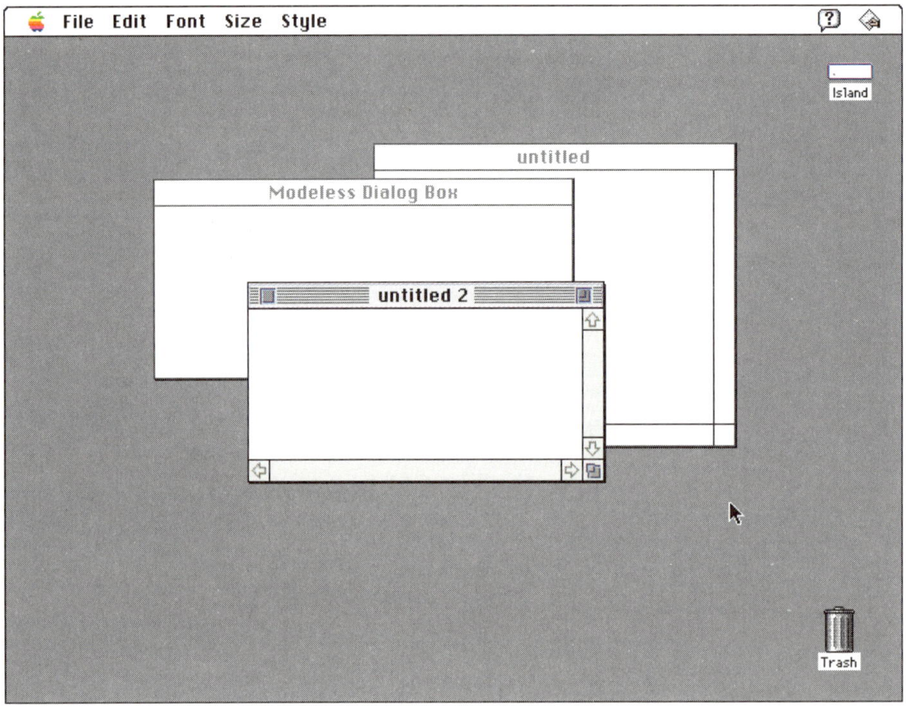

Floating windows, such as utility windows and palettes, appear on top of other document windows and modeless dialog boxes, as shown in Figure 5-13.

Figure 5-13 Adding floating windows to the desktop

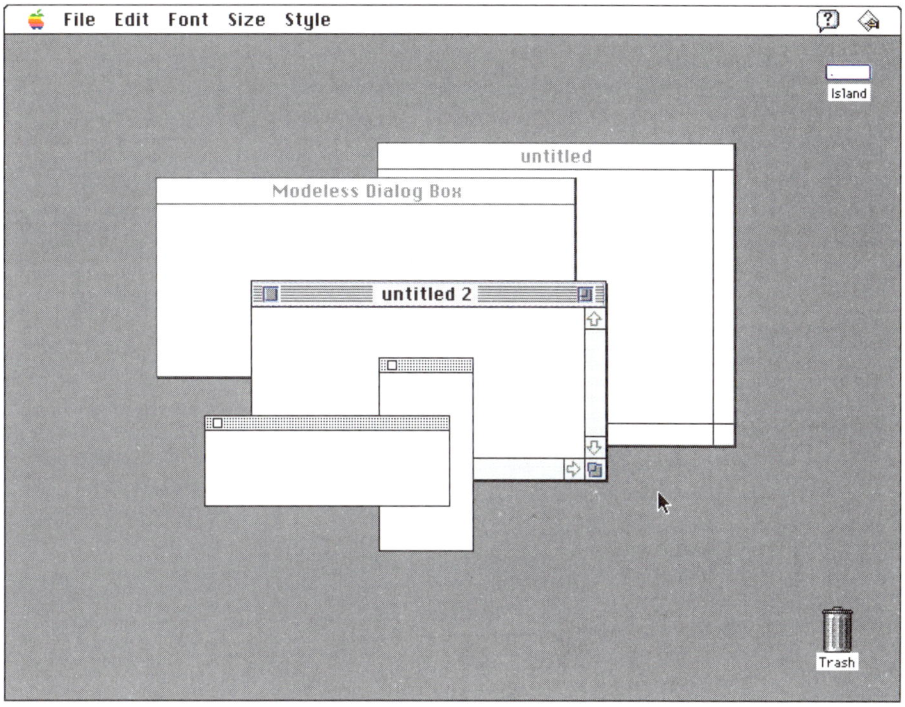

When a user chooses a command that displays either a modal dialog box or a movable modal dialog box, that dialog box appears on top of all modeless windows and utility windows. All the open windows from an application that appear beneath a modal dialog box are frozen in place and inactive, but the user can move the open windows by pressing the Command key and dragging them (one by one) to other positions on the screen (the open windows remain inactive, but the user can now view their contents). To view windows appearing beneath a movable modal dialog box, the user can move the movable modal dialog box (rather than moving the other windows) to another position on the screen.

Figure 5-14 shows a movable modal dialog box on top of all other windows.

Figure 5-14 Adding a movable modal dialog box to the desktop

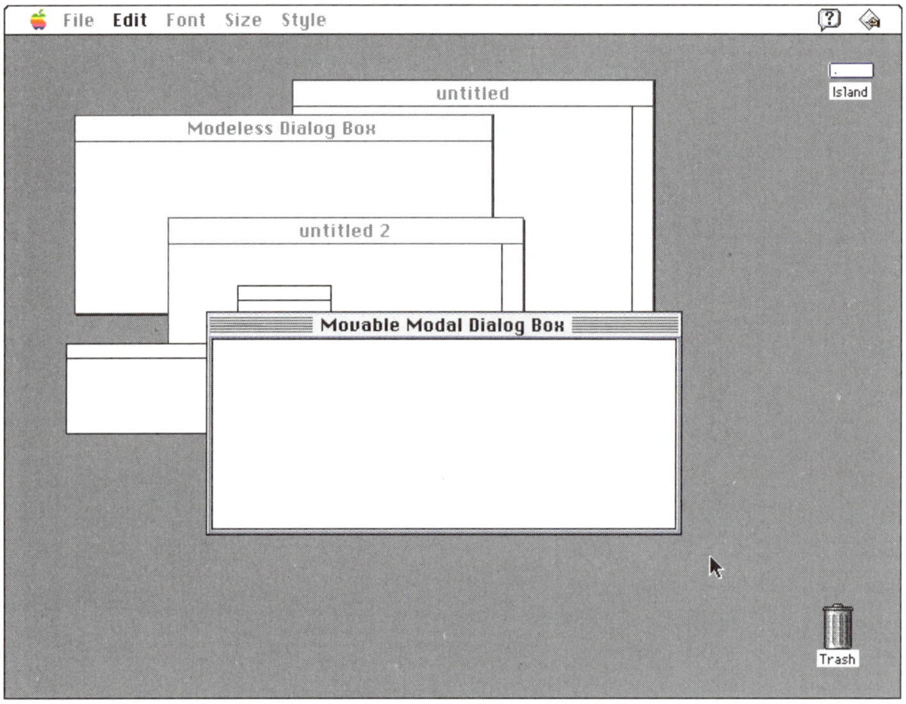

Note that the user *cannot* switch to another application when a fixed-position modal dialog box appears on the screen. Only movable modal dialog boxes allow the user to switch to another application without first dismissing the dialog box. See Chapter 6, "Dialog Boxes," beginning on page 175 for more details on the design and behavior of dialog boxes.

Window Positions

Whenever your application displays a window on the screen, you must decide where to put it and how big it should be. To determine where to place a window, consider what kind of window your application is opening, what other windows are open and where, and the relationship between the content of the window and other windows or dialog boxes. Whenever a change has been made to the initial size or location of a window, maintain the user's preferred size and position for the window.

The sections that follow present examples for the most common situations. You should consider how your application compares to these common situations to determine the best ways to position your application's windows, including dialog boxes and alert boxes.

The Default Position on a Single Screen

When your application opens a new document window, position it in the upper-left corner of the screen. Open each additional new document window below and to the right of its predecessor. Figure 5-15 shows windows positioned on a single screen.

Figure 5-15 Window positions on a single screen

Before closing a window, check to see whether the user has changed its size or position. Save window positions, and reopen windows in the size and position in which the user left them. If a user opens, moves, and closes a document window without making any other changes, save the new window position but don't modify the date stamp of the document. If the user does not change the size or position of the window, don't save the position when the user closes the window.

Before reopening a window, check to make sure that the size and state are reasonable for the user's current monitor or monitors, which may not be the same as the monitor on which the document was last open. For example, a user might start working on a word-processing document on a full-page display at work and then take the document home and work on it on a computer with a 13-inch monitor. In a situation like this, your application should open the document in a window sized appropriately for the smaller monitor and not necessarily in the saved size. See the section "The Zoom Box and Window Behavior," beginning on page 168, for more information on appropriate window size.

Figure 5-16 shows the standard position of a window on a 19-inch screen and a 13-inch screen.

Figure 5-16 The standard window position on two sizes of screens

The Default Position on Multiple Screens

On computer systems with more than one monitor attached, display the first new window in the upper-left corner of the screen that contains the menu bar. If the user doesn't move that first window, display each additional window below and to the right of its predecessor. If the user moves the window, display each additional window on the screen that contains the largest portion of the frontmost window. If there is sufficient room on the screen, display the subsequent windows to the lower right of the frontmost window. If there isn't enough room on the screen, display subsequent windows starting in the upper-left corner on the screen (and then continue to display additional windows in relationship to this new position). For example, if the user creates a new window, drags it to a second screen, and then creates a second window, display this window and any subsequent windows on the second screen.

Figure 5-17 shows the position in which to open a new window when the user has dragged its predecessor from the screen with the menu bar to a second screen.

Figure 5-17 The standard window position on multiple screens

When you open several windows on multiple screens, continue to place the windows on the screen where the user is working, each new one below and to the right of its predecessor. The *initial position* of a window, however, must always be contained on a single screen. It would be awkward to have a window appear initially on screens of different display depths and resolutions. Of course, the user can choose to place a window in such a position.

Figure 5-18 shows a window incorrectly displayed across two screens.

Figure 5-18 A window displayed across two screens

Don't open a window across two screens.

Dialog Box and Alert Box Positions

Open dialog boxes and alert boxes on the screen where the user is working. On a computer system with one monitor, display the dialog box or alert box horizontally centered on the screen. The dialog or alert window should appear with one-fifth of the vertical desktop area (not including the menu bar) above it and the rest below the window. Figure 5-19 shows where to place an alert or dialog box on a single screen if no windows that the alert or dialog box is related to are open.

Figure 5-19 Standard position of an alert box

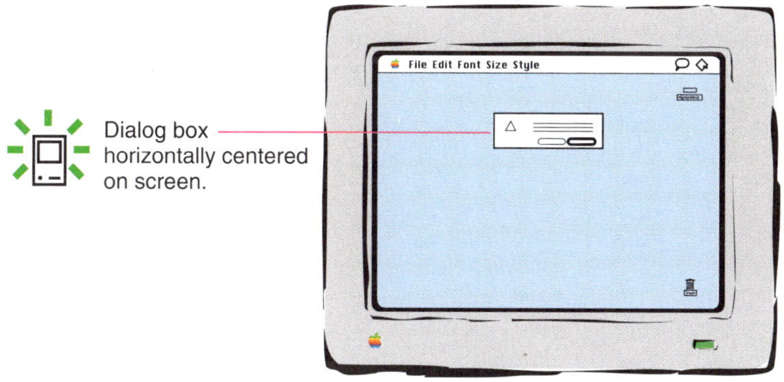

If you are displaying a dialog box or alert box that relates to a specific document, position it relative to the document window. This position reinforces the relationship of the two windows and also puts the box near the user's focus. Leave one-fifth of the document visible above the dialog box or alert box. Figure 5-20 shows where to position an alert or dialog box in relation to the active document window.

Figure 5-20 Alert box position in relation to the active document window

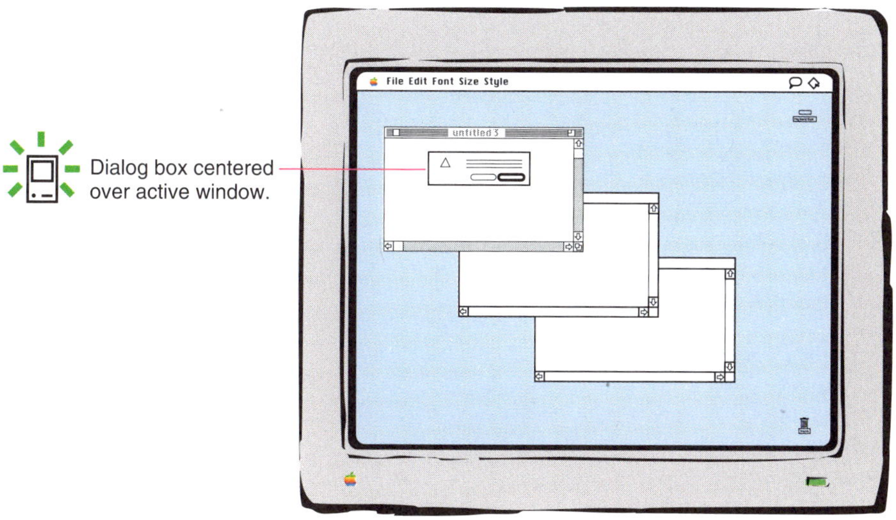

When the user has more than one monitor connected to the computer, display the dialog box or alert box on the screen where the user's attention is. For example, if a text document is active, open a find-and-replace dialog box on the screen where the text document appears, not necessarily on the screen where the menu bar is. Leave one-fifth of the document visible above the dialog box or alert box. Figure 5-21 shows where to place an alert or dialog box when the user has more than one monitor connected to the computer.

Figure 5-21 Standard alert box position with more than one screen

Display dialog boxes where the user is working.

Closing a Window

People can close windows in a variety of ways. They can use the Close command in the File menu, use the keyboard equivalent Command-W, or click the close box. Figure 5-22 shows an enlarged view of the close box.

Figure 5-22 The close box

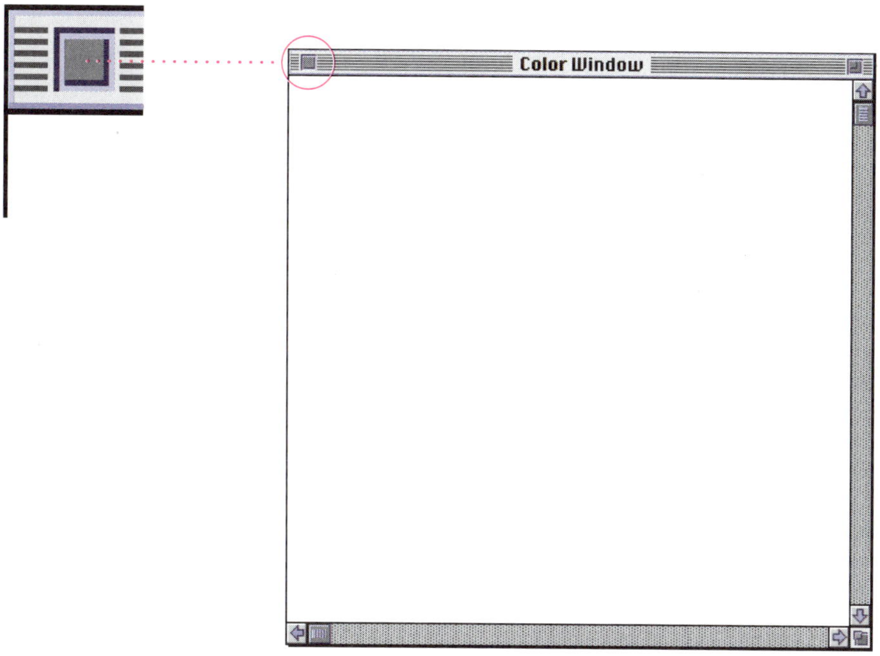

Your application determines what happens with its windows visually and logically when the user closes them. The visible effects may make the window seem to retreat into an icon or to simply disappear.

When a user closes a document window, your application must do something with any user data that may be in the window. The most common case is to save the information by writing it to disk and display it when the user opens the document again. In this case, store the position where the user placed the window on the screen and the last size in which the user had the window as described in "Window Positions," beginning on page 146. When you reopen it, use the size and position information to display the window.

When a user closes a document window, your application must decide whether or not to write the information to disk. If the user has made changes to the contents of the document (the most common situation), display the save changes alert box described in Chapter 4, "Menus," in the section "Close" on page 102. This alert box is shown in Figure 5-23. In addition to saving the contents of the document, you should also store the user state (size and position) of the window and record whether the window was in the system or user state, as described in "The Zoom Box and Window Behavior" on page 168.

Figure 5-23 The save changes alert box

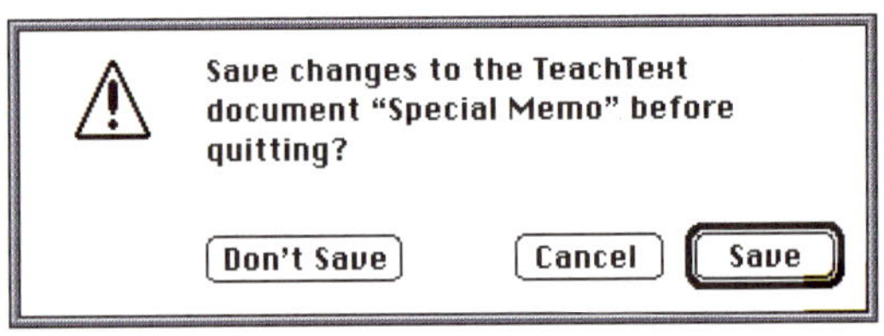

If the user has not changed the contents of the document but has moved, resized, or zoomed the window, it's a good idea to save the new window state (size and position) information, but do *not* change the date stamp. In this situation, the information is saved without prompting the user with the save changes alert box. In either case, the window should have the same content, size, and position the next time the user opens the document (unless they decide *not* to save changes to the content of the document).

Moving a Window

The user moves a window by dragging its title bar. As the user drags, a dotted outline of the window moves with the pointer until the user releases the mouse button. At the release of the button, the full window and its contents appear at the new location. Moving a window doesn't affect the appearance of the document within the window. Figure 5-24 shows how a moving window looks to users.

Figure 5-24 Moving a window

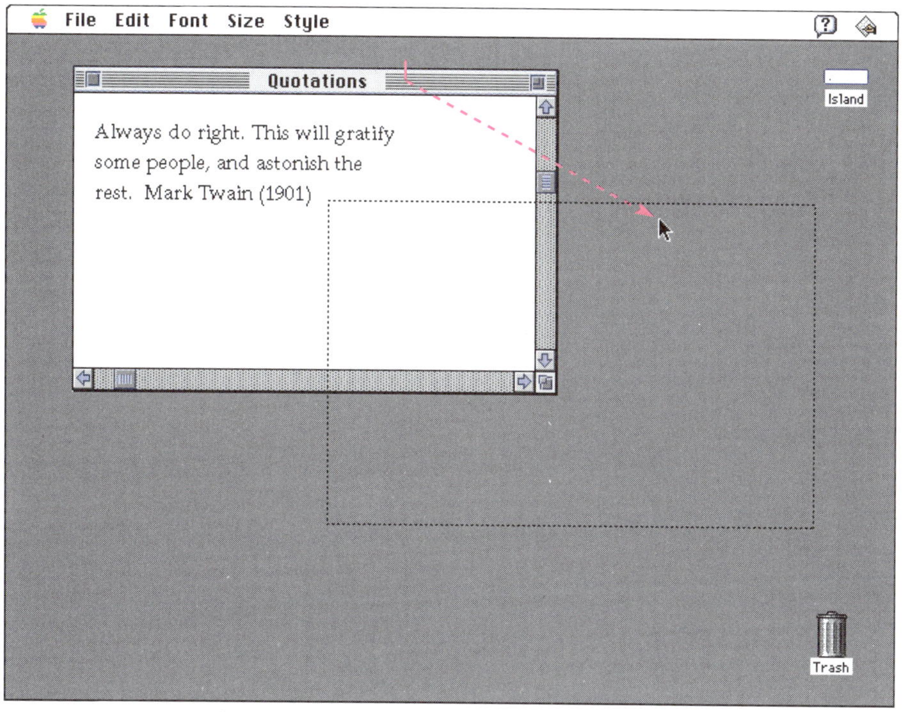

The act of moving an inactive window makes it active. If a user presses the Command key while dragging a window, the window does not become active. The window moves in the same plane (doesn't change stacking order if there are multiple windows within the same application) and remains inactive.

Your application should never allow users to move a window to a position from which they cannot reposition it. For example, don't allow users to move windows completely off the screen.

Changing the Size of a Window

Your application determines the minimum and maximum window size. Base these sizes on the physical size of the display. When a user has more than one monitor attached to the computer system, calculate the display size of all the attached screens. With the Monitors control panel, the user determines the relationship of the screen space on one monitor to that on another. Figure 5-25 shows a conceptual view of the space a user has to work in when more than one monitor is connected to the computer.

Figure 5-25 Multiple monitors and conceptual work space

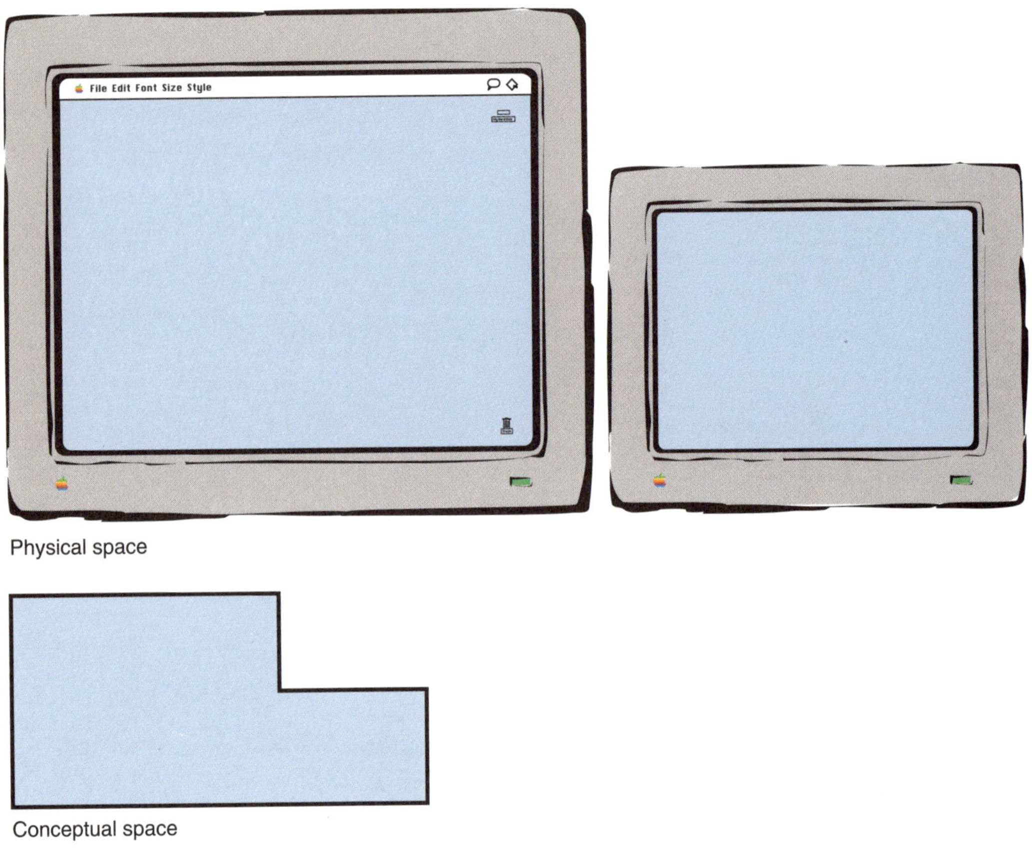

The user changes the size of the window by using the size box in the lower right corner of the window (if a window has one). When the user presses the size box and drags the pointer, a dotted outline of the window moves with the pointer. The upper-left corner of the window remains in the same place. It acts like an anchor on the screen; the window shrinks or grows from that point. The outline of the lower-right corner of the window follows the pointer.

When the user releases the mouse button, redraw the window in the shape of the dotted outline. Figure 5-26 shows how a window changing size appears to the user.

Figure 5-26 A window growing larger

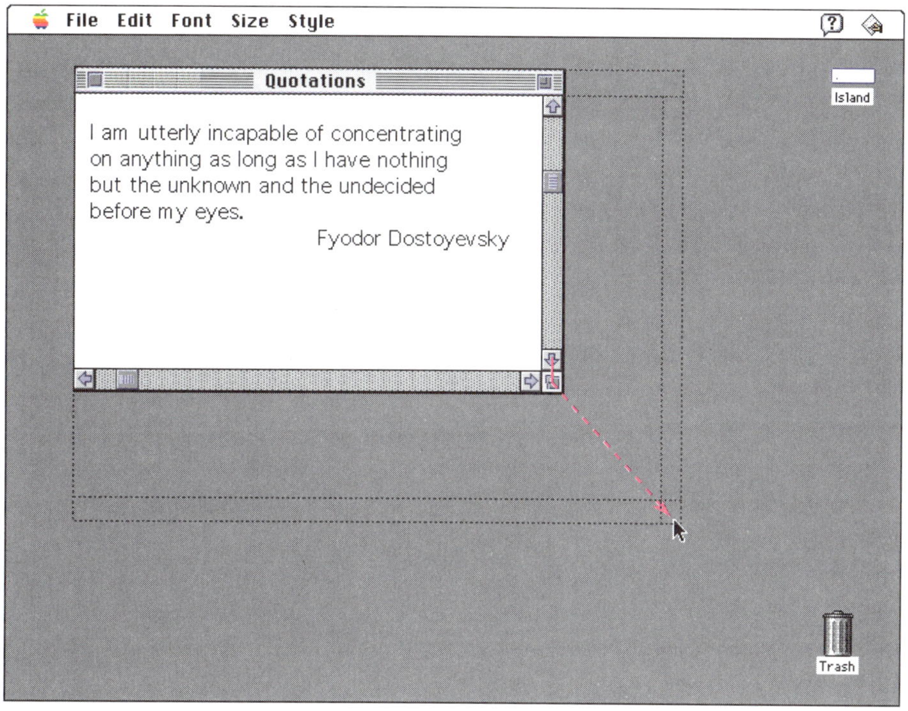

When a user changes the size of a window, it affects only how much of the document is visible in the window. It doesn't affect the position of the upper-left corner of the window or the appearance of the part of the view that's still showing.

Exceptions to this rule are commands that by definition change the view of the window's contents. An example is a Reduce to Fit command, which changes the scale of the view to fit the size of the window. If the user chooses this command, and then resizes the window, your application should change the scale of the view appropriately. See the chapter "Window Manager" of *Inside Macintosh: Macintosh Toolbox Essentials* for details on changing the size of a window.

Scrolling a Window

People use scroll bars to change which part of a document is shown in a window. Only the active window can be scrolled. This section describes the appearance and behavior of scroll bars and their controls. Figure 5-27 shows a conceptual view of a document and the portion of it that appears in a window.

Figure 5-27 Relationship between a window and a document

Scroll Bars

A **scroll bar** is a light gray rectangle that has an arrow in a box at each end of the rectangle. Windows can have a horizontal scroll bar, a vertical scroll bar, or both. A vertical scroll bar appears on the right side of the associated window. A horizontal scroll bar runs along the bottom of the window. Inside the scroll bar is a rectangle called the **scroll box.** At either end of the scroll bar is an arrow that points towards the portion of a document still hidden from view; clicking the arrow displays more of the document by scrolling it into view. The rest of the scroll bar is called the *gray area.* Figure 5-28 shows the elements of a scroll bar.

Figure 5-28 The elements of a scroll bar

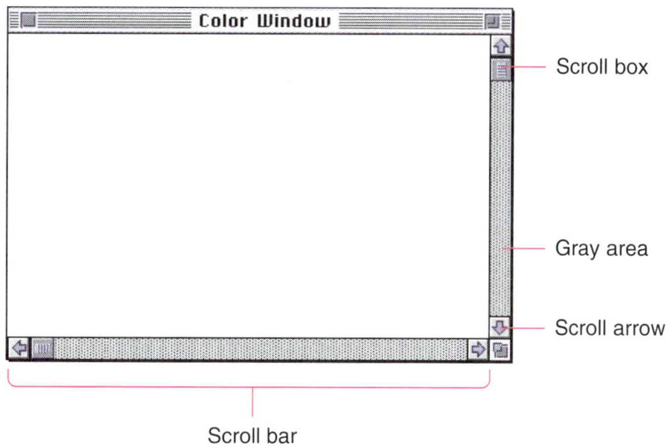

A scroll bar represents one dimension, top to bottom or right to left, of the entire document. The scroll box represents the relative location, in the whole document, of the portion that can be seen in the window.

If the user clicks a scroll arrow or clicks in the gray area, the document "moves" and the scroll box moves along with it. If the user drags the scroll box and releases the mouse button, the document "moves" along with it. Figure 5-29 illustrates these behaviors.

Figure 5-29 Using scroll arrows and the scroll box

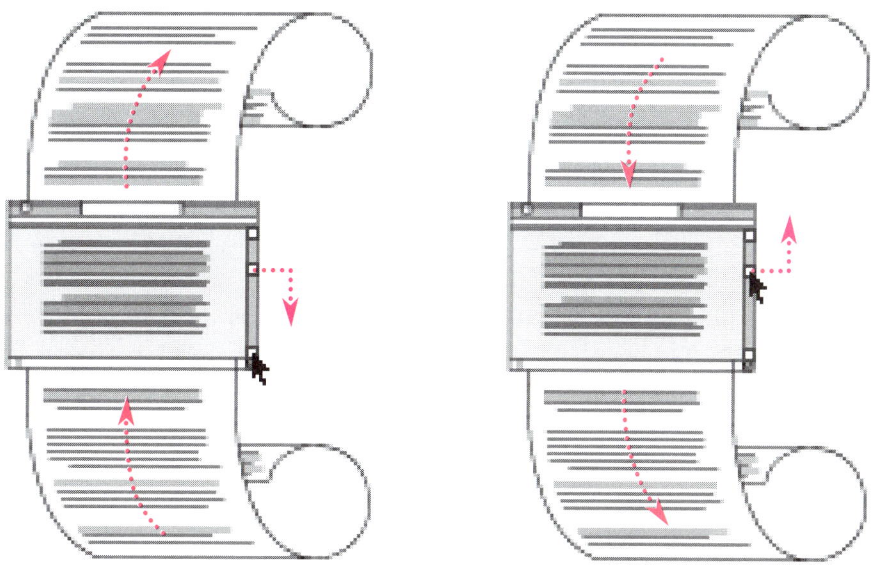

If the document is no larger than the window, the scroll bars are inactive. This means that the rectangles are outlined, but there is no gray area, no scroll box, and the arrows are hollow (their outlines appear). If the document window is inactive, don't show the elements of the scroll bar at all; only the outline of the scroll bar as a whole should appear. Figure 5-30 shows an *active* document window with inactive scroll bars and an *inactive* document window with inactive scroll bars.

Figure 5-30 Inactive scroll bars in active and inactive document windows

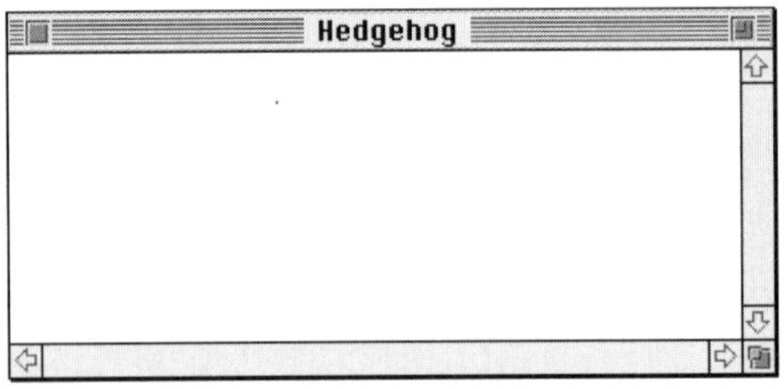

Active window with inactive scroll bars

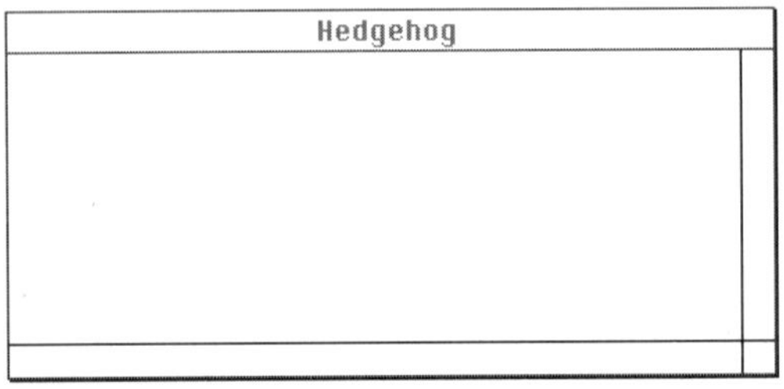

Inactive window with inactive scroll bars

If a document has a fixed size that is smaller than the maximum size of the window, and the user scrolls to the right or bottom edge of the document, your application can display a gray background between the edge of the document and the window frame. This background indicates to the user that the content area has a fixed size that is smaller than the maximum size of the window. Figure 5-31 shows an example of a document with this gray background.

Figure 5-31 Background between the content and the window frame

Many applications add features like controls to windows in the scroll bar region. Since the scroll bars are used frequently, it's best not to add lots of additional controls to this area of the window. Generally it's best to minimize the complexity of your application's interface and use the established graphical language. It's OK to add one control, like a split bar, which allows users to split a window into panels, to the top of the vertical scroll bar. But if you add more than one control to this area, it's hard for people to distinguish controls, and to click exactly the desired control. Also from an implementation standpoint, it's difficult to design small symbols and pictures that effectively convey the action of the control.

Another addition to the window that's not too intrusive is a status bar at the left side of the horizontal scroll bar. This bar doesn't take up much space, while providing useful information to the user. It also doesn't reduce the working size of the scroll bar by too much.

Figure 5-32 shows scroll bars with acceptable additions; the horizontal scroll bar has a page indicator and the vertical scroll bar has a split bar.

Figure 5-32 Acceptable additions to the scroll bar region

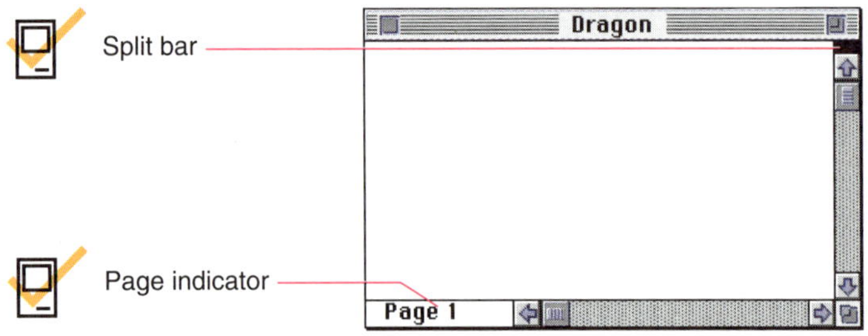

Some applications include a page number inside the scroll box to indicate the position of the document. This allows the user to see the page number change as the document scrolls. It also provides information without adding complexity to the window.

To ensure that the controls that you include in the window are easy to use and understand, it's best to place the majority of your features in the menus as commands. Figure 5-33 shows a window with too many controls in the scroll bars. If you really want to provide additional access to features, consider creating a utility window such as a palette with buttons. For more information on palettes, see "Tear-Off Menus and Palettes" on page 92 in Chapter 4, "Menus."

Figure 5-33 Too many controls in the scroll bar

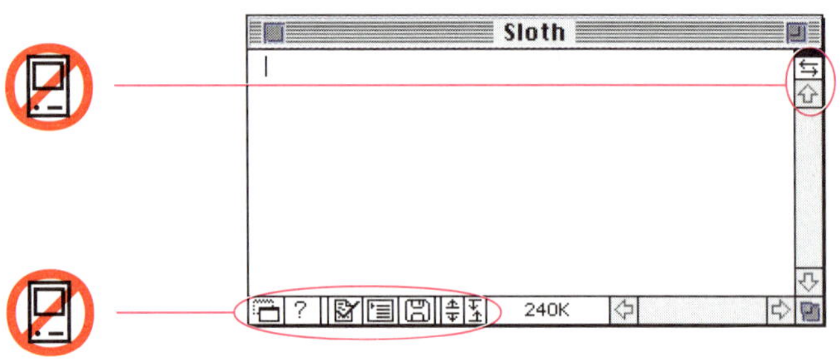

Scrolling With the Scroll Arrows

When the user clicks or presses one of the scroll arrows, more of the document in the direction of the scroll arrow appears, so the document seems to move in the opposite direction. Clicking the arrow means, "Show me more of the document that's hidden in this direction." When the user clicks the bottom scroll arrow, for example, the document moves up, bringing what was just below the window into view. Pressing the scroll arrow causes continuous movement in the appropriate direction. Figure 5-34 shows the change in a document when a user scrolls by clicking a scroll arrow.

Figure 5-34 Scrolling by clicking a scroll arrow

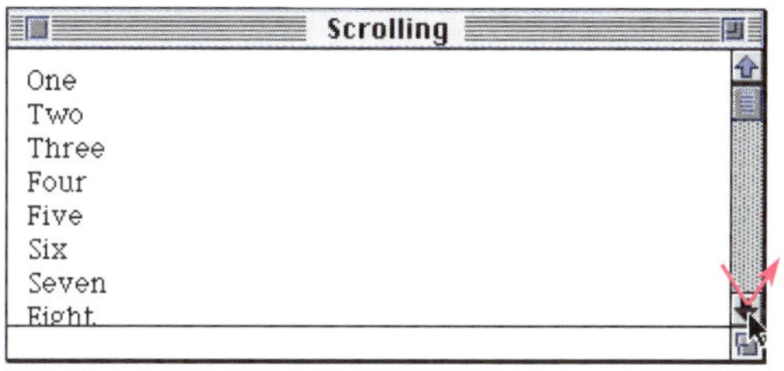

1.

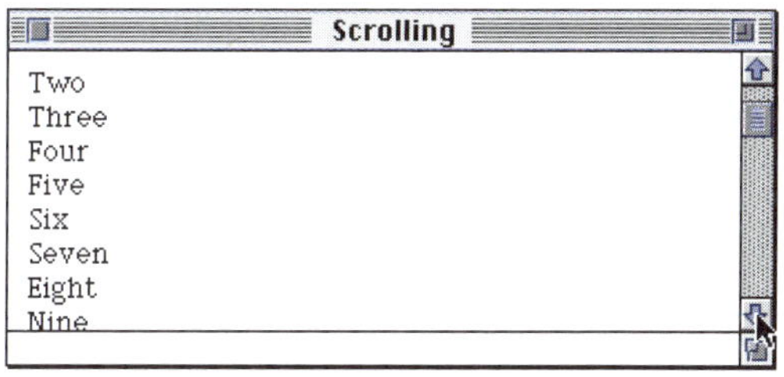

2.

The scroll box moves in the direction of the arrow being clicked. It continues to represent the approximate position of the visible part of the document in comparison to the whole document.

Each click in a scroll arrow causes movement of the content a distance of one unit in the chosen direction. Your application determines what one unit equals. For example, a word processor would move one line of text for each click in the arrow. A spreadsheet would move one row or one column depending on the direction of the arrow. To ensure smooth scrolling effects, it's usually best to specify units of the same size throughout a document.

Scrolling With the Gray Area

Clicking in the gray area of the scroll bar advances the document by a windowful. The scroll box and the document view move toward the location where the user clicked. For example, when the user clicks in the area below the scroll box, the document view moves to the next windowful toward the bottom of the document. Figure 5-35 shows how a user scrolls by clicking in the gray area.

Figure 5-35 Scrolling by clicking in the gray area

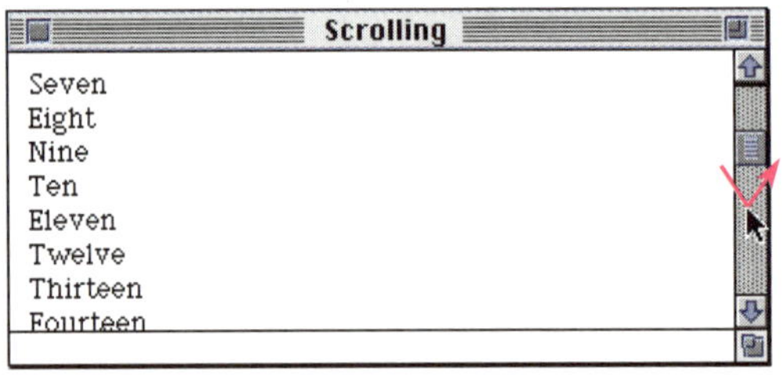

1.

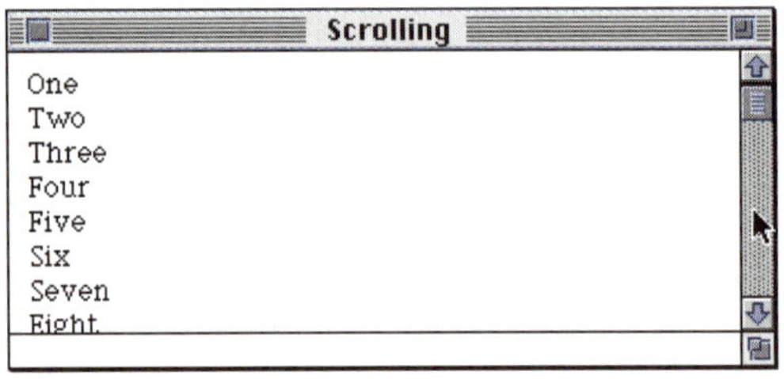

2.

Pressing in the gray area causes the display of consecutive windowfuls of the document, until the user releases the mouse button, or until the location of the scroll box catches up to the location of the pointer. A windowful equals the height or width of the window, minus at least one unit of overlap to maintain the user's context. This unit of overlap is the same measurement determined for scroll arrow movement. By retaining this unit of information, you provide a reference point for the user.

On keyboards with function keys, the Page Up and Page Down keys also move the document view by a windowful.

Scrolling by Dragging the Scroll Box

The scroll box shows the position of the visible portion of the document in relationship to the whole document. If the scroll box is halfway between the top and bottom of the scroll bar, then what the user sees is about halfway through the document. To scroll the document, the user drags the scroll box.

To see the beginning of the document, the user drags the scroll box to the top of the scroll bar; to see the end, the user drags the scroll box to the bottom. This behavior allows the user to quickly move around in the document. The user can get from one end of a long document to the other faster by dragging the scroll box than by clicking in the gray area or pressing the scroll arrows. Figure 5-36 shows how a user scrolls by using the scroll box.

Figure 5-36 Scrolling by dragging the scroll box

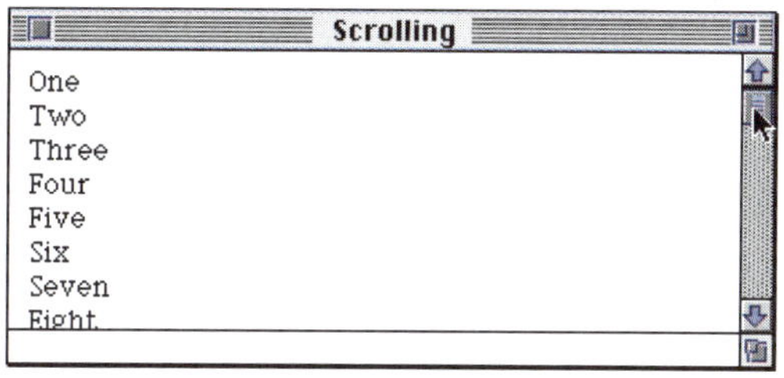

1.

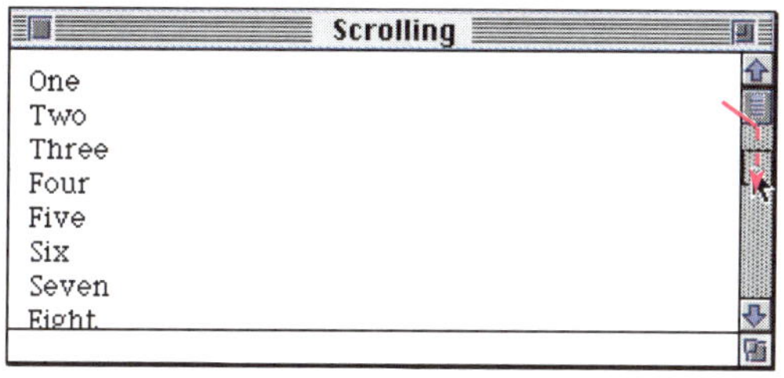

2.

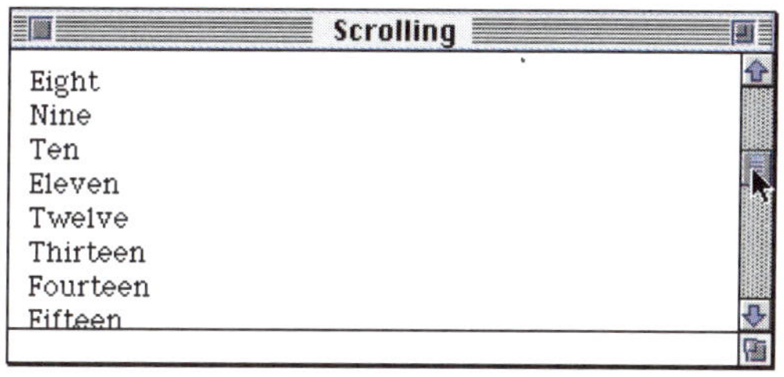

3.

If the user starts dragging the scroll box, then moves the pointer out of the scroll bar, the scroll box stops following the pointer and snaps back to its original position. The user can move the pointer out of the scroll bar region by a little more than the width of the scroll box before the scroll box snaps back. If the user then releases the mouse button, no scrolling occurs. But if the user, still holding down the mouse button, moves the pointer back into the scroll bar, the scroll box resumes its movement in the direction of the pointer. This type of tracking is standard behavior for controls in general, such as buttons, checkboxes, and radio buttons.

Automatic Scrolling

In all the discussions of scrolling behavior and appearance in the previous sections, the user controls scrolling behavior by deciding which control to use and how long to use it. Most of the time, the user should be in control. However, there are four cases where your application must scroll the document.

- When your application performs an operation whose side effect is to make a new selection or move the insertion point, scroll the document to show the new selection.

  For example, when the user searches for some text, your application locates the desired text. If this text appears in a part of the document that isn't currently visible, scroll the document to the location to show the selection. Another example might occur after the user pastes something. If the insertion point appears after the end of whatever was pasted, scroll the document until the selection and the new insertion point are visible. Figure 5-37 shows the effect of automatic scrolling.

Figure 5-37 Automatic scrolling

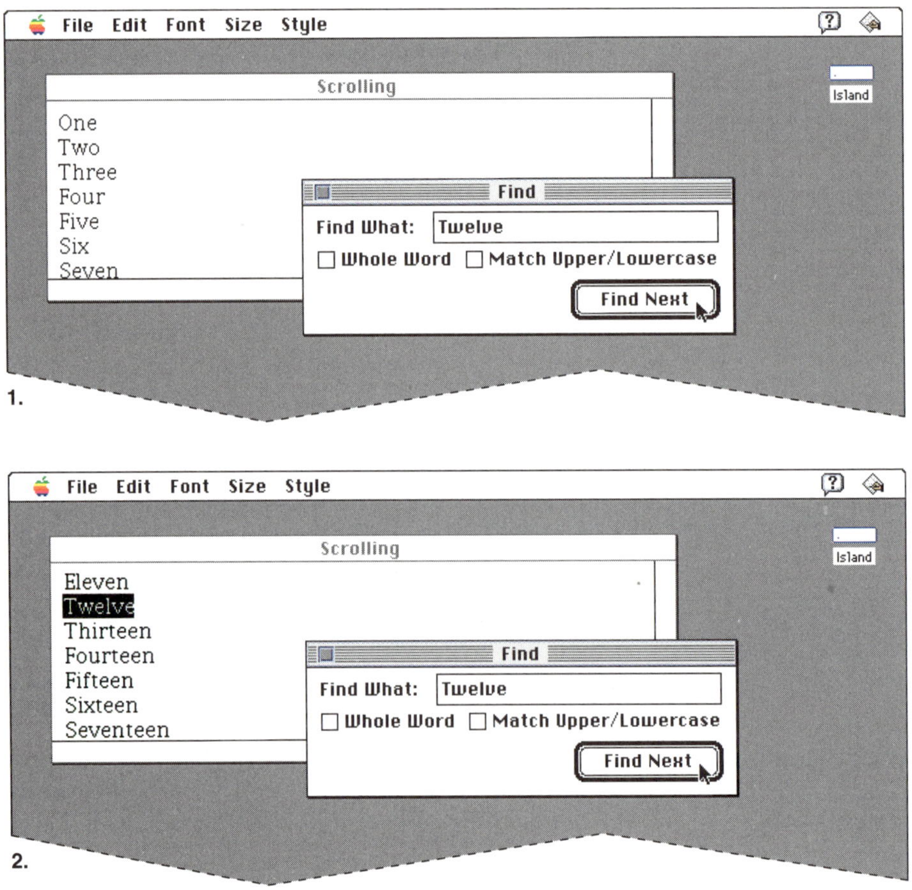

- When the user enters information from the keyboard at the edge of a window, scroll the document automatically to incorporate and display the new information.

  The user's focus will be on the new information, so don't try to maintain the document's position and record the new information out of the user's view. Your application determines the distance to scroll. In general, a word processor scrolls one line of text, a database or spreadsheet scrolls one field. Graphics applications should scroll to display an entire object when possible. Otherwise, determine how quickly your application can redraw the window contents during scrolling and adjust the amount of scrolling to reduce the amount of flashing or redrawing that is necessary. Try to ensure that the scrolling is sufficiently fast that it allows users to see the information at a rate that's useful, but don't scroll so fast that people get lost.

- When the user moves the pointer past the edge of the window while holding down the mouse button to make an extended selection, scroll the document automatically in the direction the pointer moves. The rate of scrolling can be the same as if the user were pressing on the corresponding scroll arrow. In some cases, it makes sense to vary the scrolling speed so that it is faster as the user moves the pointer farther away from the window edge.

- Sometimes the user selects something, scrolls the document to a new location, and then tries to perform an operation on the selection. In this case, scroll the window so that the selection is showing before your application performs the operation. Showing the selection makes it clear to the user what is being changed.

Whenever your application scrolls a document automatically, avoid unnecessary scrolling. Users want to control the position of documents, so your application should move a document only as much as necessary. This means that if part of a selection is showing in the window after the user performs some operation, don't scroll at all. One exception to this rule is when the part of the selection that is hidden is more important than the part that is showing; then scroll to show the important part. For example, if a user has a large text selection, only the bottom of which is currently visible and the user types a character, your application must scroll to the location of the newly typed characters so they are visible.

If your application can scroll in one orientation to reveal the selection, don't scroll in both orientations. That is, if you can scroll vertically to show the selection, don't also scroll horizontally.

When you can show context on either side of a selection, it's useful to do so. It's also better to position a selection somewhere near the middle of a window than right up against a corner. When the selection is too large to show the entire selection in the window, it might be a good idea to show some context next to it rather than having the selection fill the window. For more information about document scrolling, see *Inside Macintosh: Macintosh Toolbox Essentials*.

The Zoom Box and Window Behavior

Your application sets values for the initial size and position of a window. This is called the **standard state** of the window. The user can change the size and location of the window to a state that is more useful or convenient, the **user state.** The user can then toggle between the standard state and the user state by using the zoom box. Figure 5-38 shows an enlarged view of the zoom box.

Figure 5-38 The zoom box

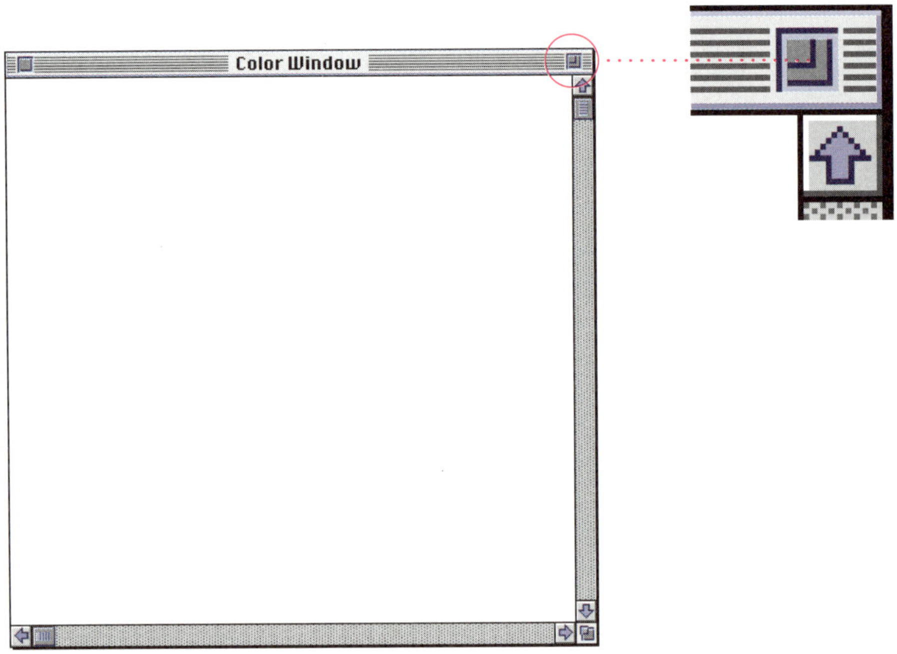

Using the zoom box, the user can quickly manipulate windows to have access to other icons or windows or to look at a document in a larger size or different location. The user must drag or resize a window at least seven pixels to cause a change in the user state.

A window's standard state depends on the size and location that are best suited to working on the document. Macintosh monitors come in many sizes, and multiple monitors can be configured in many different ways, so applications should never simply assume that the standard state should be as large as the screen. Frequently the monitor is larger, sometimes much larger, than the most useful size for a window. Screen real estate is valuable, so use screen-sized windows only when they make sense. Figure 5-39 shows the standard state and the user state of a window on the same size screen.

Figure 5-39 The standard state and the user state of a document

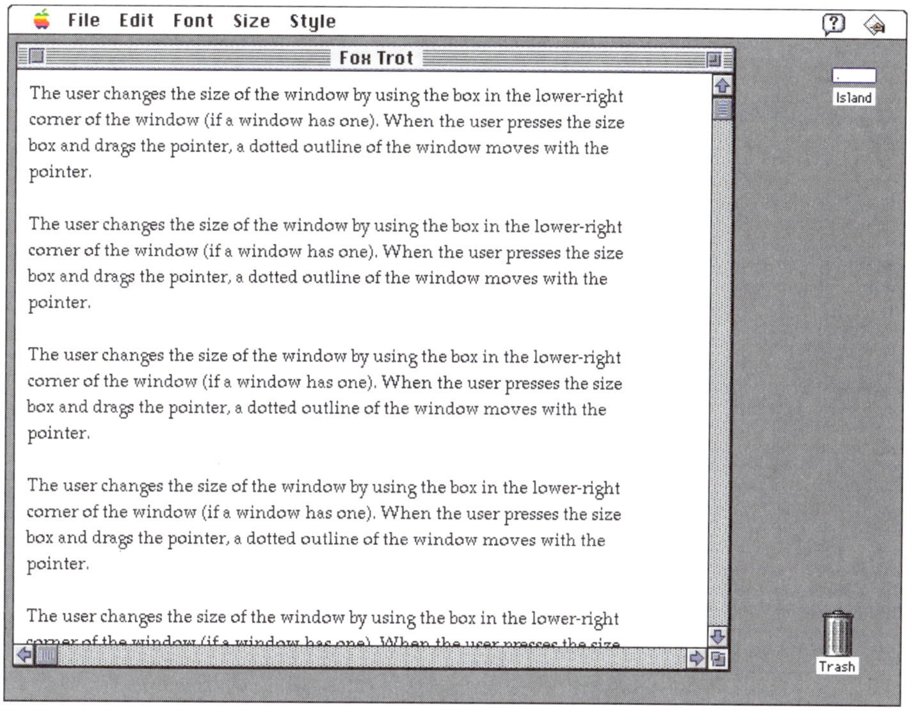

Standard state

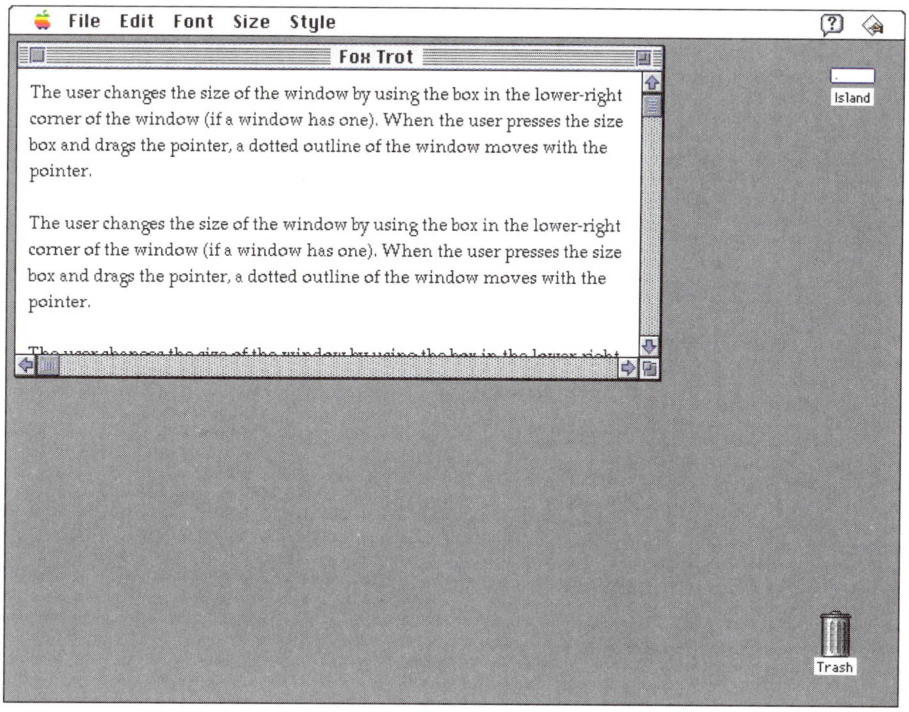

User state

A document for a word-processing program has a well-defined most useful width (the width of a page) and most useful height (the height of the screen). Therefore the width of the standard state should be the width of a page or the width of the screen, whichever is smaller. (When determining the width of the standard state, it's a good idea to leave room on the right side of larger monitors so that desktop icons are not obscured when the user switches to the Finder.) The height of the standard state should be the height of the screen or the length of a page, whichever is smaller.

When a user clicks the zoom box to change a window from the user state to the standard state, first determine the appropriate size of the standard state. Move the window as little as possible to make it the standard size, and keep the window on the screen.

Zooming behavior in multiscreen environments should not violate any of the guidelines described in this chapter, but it does introduce one additional guideline. The standard state should be on the monitor containing the largest portion of the window, not necessarily on the monitor with the menu bar. This means the standard state for a single window may be on different monitors at different times if the user moves the window around. In any case, the standard state for any window must always be fully contained on a single screen.

The user can't change the standard size and location of a window, but your application can change the standard state when appropriate. For example, a word processor might define the standard size and location as wide enough to display a document whose width is specified in the Page Setup dialog box. If the user specifies a wider or narrower document, the application might change the values for the standard state to reflect that change.

As described in the section "Window Positions," earlier in this chapter, open a window in the last state it was in when possible. Your application must make sure that the user state fits on the current screen. That is, if the window was previously open on a different screen, you need to determine the correct size and location for the current screen. Don't open a window off of a user's screen.

Splitting a Window

You can provide the ability for people to look at different parts of a document simultaneously by implementing a split bar. The **split bar** is a control, five pixels high by the width of the scroll bar, contained in the scroll bar. Users drag the split bar to separate a document into separate scrolling sections, called **window panes.** A **split line** appears to visually separate the panes. (Note that there should a one-pixel space between the two lines that make up the split line.) For example, the user might want to look at the opening paragraphs and review the conclusion of a document in a word-processing program at the same time. In a programming environment, you might want to see the include statements at the beginning of a document while looking at routines in another part of the document. Split windows are useful for copying data from one part of a document and pasting it into another part. The user drags the split bar to a location in the scroll bar where the new pane is to begin. To remove a window pane, the user drags the split bar to within three pixels of the top or right of the scroll bar. Figure 5-40 shows a window split into two panes.

Figure 5-40 A split window

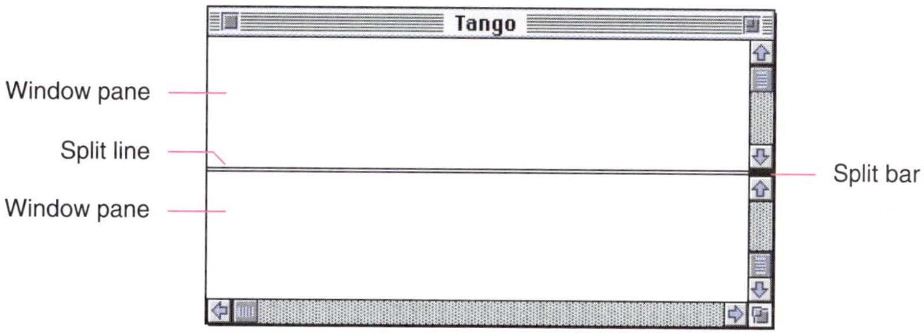

The split bar should be large enough for the user to accurately place the pointer on it, but not so large that it attracts attention. Figure 5-41 shows an example of the correct size for a split bar and some comparison sizes.

Figure 5-41 Split bar size

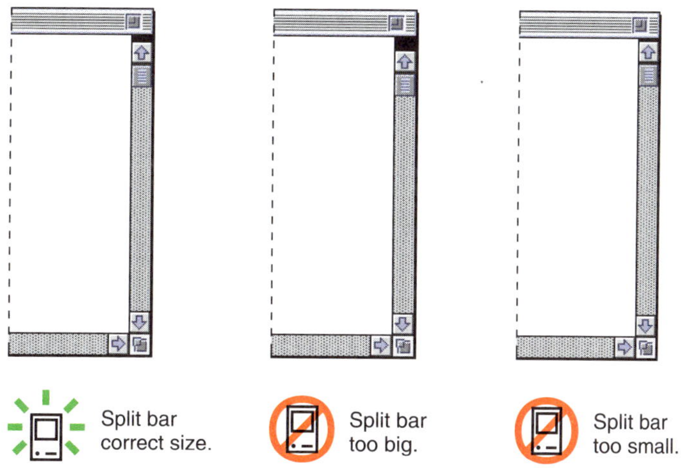

Window Pane Behavior

When you implement window splitting capabilities, place the split bar at the top of the vertical scroll bar or to the left of the horizontal scroll bar, or in both positions if you support both types of splits. The user can drag the split bar anywhere along the scroll bar. Implement an outline of the split line to follow the pointer so that the user can tell where the new pane will appear. (This is similar to the outline of a scroll box being moved.) Releasing the mouse button splits the window into panes there, and divides the appropriate scroll bar into separate scroll bars for each pane.

After a single split, there are separate scroll bars for each pane. Usually the panes scroll independently in the orientation opposite of the split. That is, if the split is horizontal, the vertical scrolling is controlled separately for each pane using the two scroll bars along the right of the window. The horizontal scrolling is still synchronous, or locked, using the scroll bar along the bottom of the window. Figure 5-42 shows how window panes scroll, independently or together.

Figure 5-42 Independent and locked scrolling of window panes

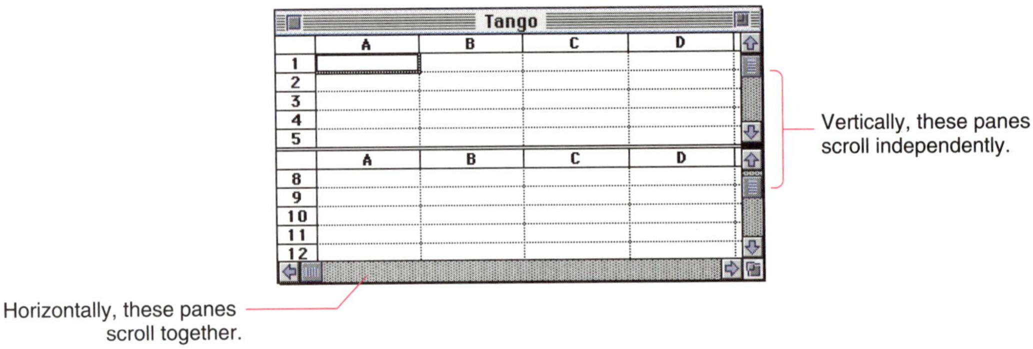

When the user splits a window, any part of the window's contents obscured by the split line or scroll bar should move down so that it is visible. For example, if the user drags a split bar to create a horizontal split, the window's contents that would have disappeared underneath the split line should scroll down by the height of the split line, plus some additional space.

The user can make a selection in one pane, and where the same data appears in another pane, the user can Shift-click to extend the selection. See the section "Editing Text" beginning on page 300 in Chapter 10, "Behaviors," for more information on selecting text. The user should also be able to drag to extend a selection and have the pane scroll automatically as an entire window would.

Your application should save and restore the location of split lines and the content of window panes whenever the user closes a document that is divided into panes.

One Split per Orientation

You can choose to allow only one split in a window. Usually the panes are locked in the direction of the split and the panes move independently in the opposite direction. For example, in a text document if you allow one horizontal split, then the panes move together when the user scrolls horizontally, but the user can scroll to different locations in the vertical direction to see different parts of the content.

Dialog Boxes

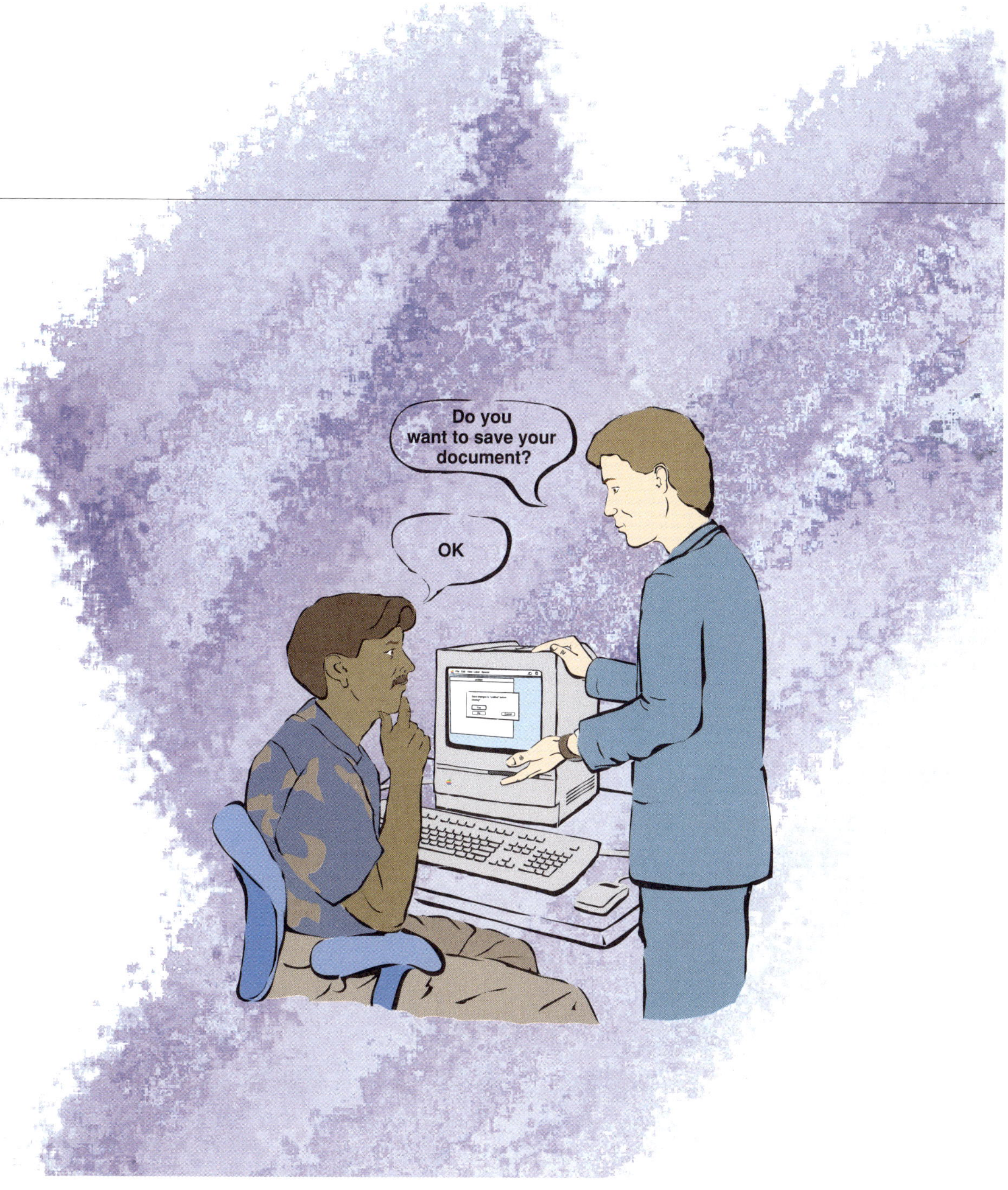

Dialog Boxes

This chapter describes the dialog boxes that you use in your products. It gives recommendations for when to use each kind of dialog box and what behaviors you need to implement for dialog boxes. This chapter also provides information on the standard layout of dialog boxes, the language to use in dialog boxes, and the standard appearance and behavior of the standard file dialog boxes and the save changes alert box.

Dialog boxes are windows that provide a standard framework in which the computer can present alternatives from which the user can choose. The purpose of dialog boxes is to elicit responses from the user, typically several responses at one time. For example, the Print dialog box allows the user to specify the number of copies to be printed, the pages to be printed, whether there should be a title page, and other print-related options. When the user chooses a menu item that is followed by the ellipsis character (…), a dialog box appears. (Note that the appearance of a dialog box does not necessarily mean there should be an ellipsis character after a menu item.) All requests for information in dialog boxes should be phrased in plain language and in a nonthreatening manner.

Alert boxes appear when the system software or an application needs to communicate information to the user. Alert boxes provide messages about error conditions and warn users about potentially hazardous situations or actions. An alert box is a type of dialog box and thus follows many of the same guidelines.

From a programming perspective, dialog boxes and alert boxes are windows. In the language of the human interface, dialog boxes and alert boxes are considered unique elements, each with a specific appearance and behavior, as described in this chapter. A dialog box is a rectangle that may contain text, controls, and icons. Each dialog box contains some text to indicate which command or condition caused it to be displayed and what its function is. In some cases this text is a title for the dialog box. The text in a dialog box should be in the system font size, which is normally 12-point type. Text that is smaller than the system font size sometimes cannot be localized.

Controls, such as buttons, radio buttons, and checkboxes, are described in Chapter 7, "Controls," which begins on page 203. Text entry fields in a dialog box follow the guidelines given in Chapter 10, "Behaviors," which begins on page 267.

In general you use four types of dialog boxes in your application:

- Modeless dialog boxes, which are useful for getting user input and for making changes to a document. Once open, they are available until the user closes them.

- Movable modal dialog boxes, which are useful for requesting user input and for making changes to a document *while* allowing the user to switch to another application. Also useful for allowing the user to see parts of a document that might be obscured by a modal dialog box.
- Modal dialog boxes, which are useful for forcing the user to provide necessary information before carrying out the current operation.
- Alert boxes (a type of modal dialog box), which are useful for communicating error conditions or preventing any other activity until the user responds to the error condition.

Figure 6-1 shows examples of these types of dialog boxes. The sections that follow describe the appearance and behavior of each type of dialog box. See the chapter "Dialog Manager" in *Inside Macintosh: Macintosh Toolbox Essentials* for information on implementing these types of dialog boxes.

Be aware that users can change the colors of standard dialog boxes by using the Color control panel; this is particularly important if you decide to create custom alert boxes, modeless dialog boxes, movable modal dialog boxes, or modal dialog boxes. If you use the default window color table with your custom window definitions, you can be sure that the colors you use are consistent with any color that the user has access to with the Color control panel. You can use the Palette Manager to associate a color palette with a window definition. For more information, see the discussion of the Palette Manager in *Inside Macintosh.*

Figure 6-1 Examples of dialog box types

Modeless dialog box

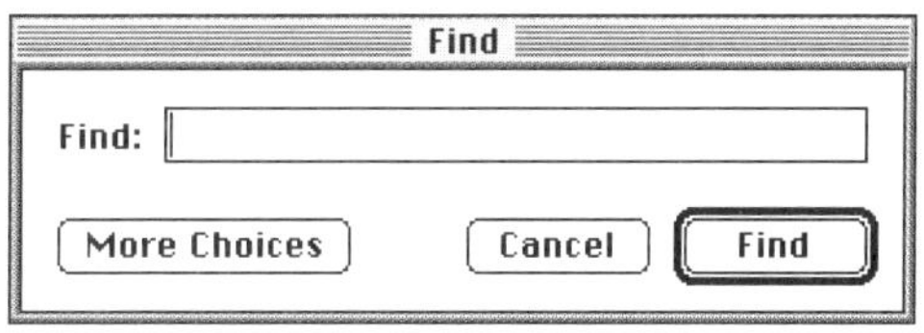

Movable modal dialog box

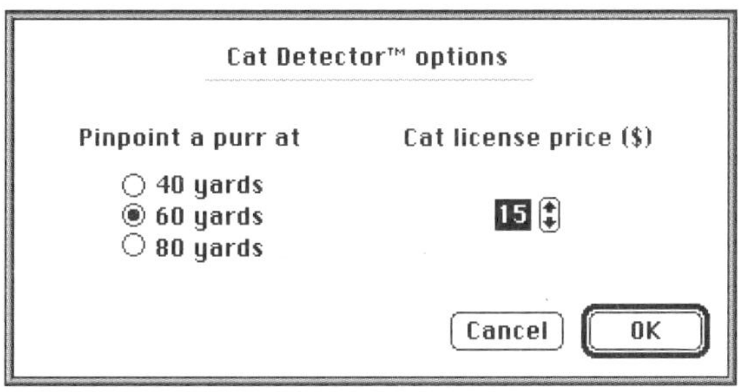

Modal dialog box

Alert box

Modeless Dialog Boxes

A **modeless dialog box** looks like a window without a size box, zoom box, or scroll bars. The user can move a modeless dialog box, make it inactive and active again, and close it like any document window. Modeless dialog boxes provide the most flexibility for your users. They preserve user control so that the user can do any task at any time or in any order. They don't interrupt people's workflow by locking out all other actions. With modeless dialog boxes, people can change things in their documents, perform actions with the data in their documents, or get information about their documents or applications.

Modeless dialog boxes allow people to repeat an action as many times as necessary while the dialog box remains open—that is, the dialog box doesn't close and need to be reopened each time they want to repeat an action. This feature is useful for tasks such as finding and replacing text in a word processor or numbers in a spreadsheet.

Use a modeless dialog box instead of a movable modal dialog box whenever possible so that you can preserve the user's ability to perform tasks in any order. Figure 6-2 shows a typical modeless dialog box.

Figure 6-2 A typical modeless dialog box

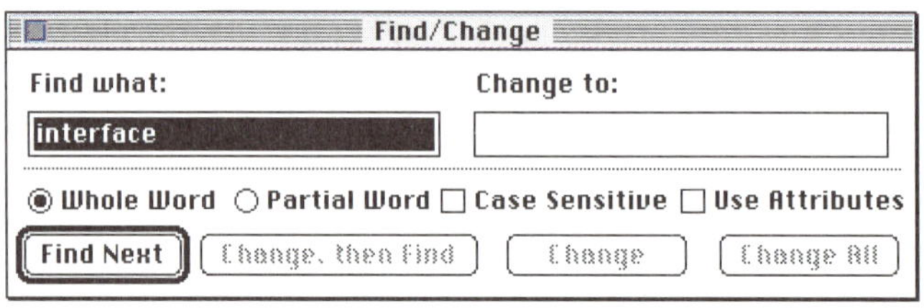

Because modeless dialog boxes are movable, people can place them out of the way of the current point of interest in their documents. People can also keep modeless dialog boxes open and available. This option might be useful if a person wants to compare information about several documents, which is possible with Info windows in the Finder. Figure 6-3 shows two such windows on a desktop.

Figure 6-3 Two open modeless dialog boxes

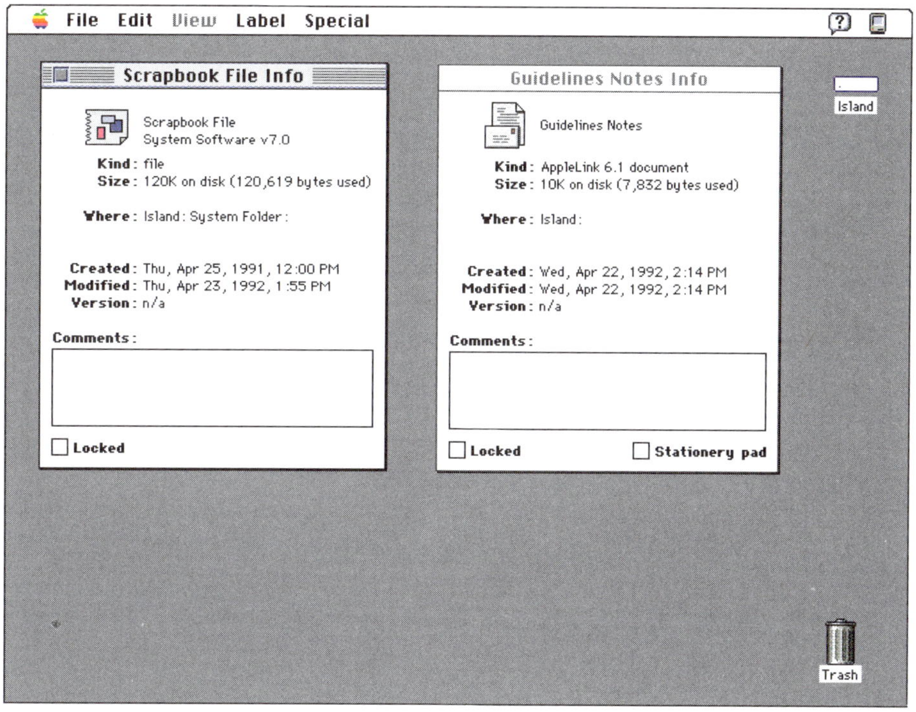

When your application displays a modeless dialog box, it should preset any controls to some logical values. Also, whenever possible, your application should supply appropriate text in any text entry fields; users can verify the information rather than generate it from scratch. In any case, display a selection or an insertion point in *one* of the text entry fields (usually the "first" field) when you display the dialog box.

Modeless Dialog Box Appearance

Modeless dialog boxes look like basic document windows. A modeless dialog box has a title bar that displays its title, which should be the same as the name of the menu item that displays it. If that item includes an ellipsis character, *don't* include it in the title of the dialog box.

Figure 6-4 shows the appearance of a modeless dialog box.

Figure 6-4 The essential elements of a modeless dialog box

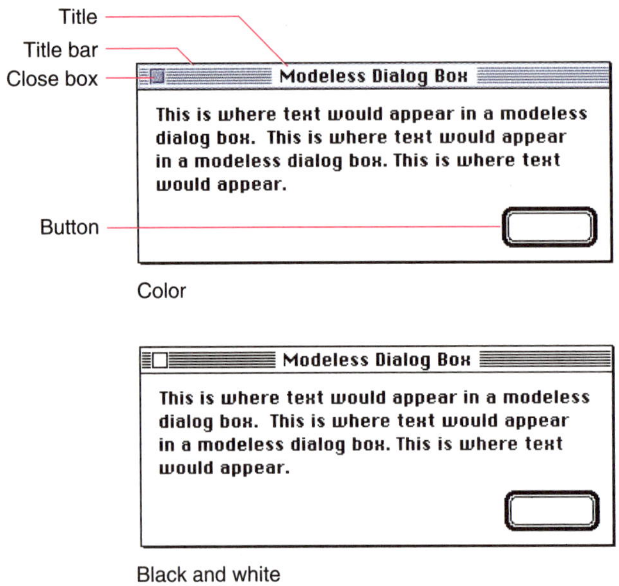

Modeless dialog boxes have the same behaviors as document windows—that is, the user manipulates them in the same way. For example, the user closes a modeless dialog box by using the close box or the Close command in the File menu. If you support keyboard equivalents for menus, support Command-W to close modeless dialog boxes as well as windows.

A modeless dialog box always has a close box; don't implement buttons to make the window disappear. The user expects that modeless dialog boxes stay on the screen until he or she explicitly dismisses them with the close box, *not* when he or she clicks a button in the dialog box.

Using a button to close a modeless dialog box also confuses the distinction between modeless dialog boxes and modal dialog boxes. Further, a modeless dialog box without a close box looks similar to a movable modal dialog box, thereby creating more confusion. Figure 6-5 shows a modeless dialog box that is missing its close box.

Figure 6-5 Incorrect absence of a close box in a modeless dialog box

No close box.

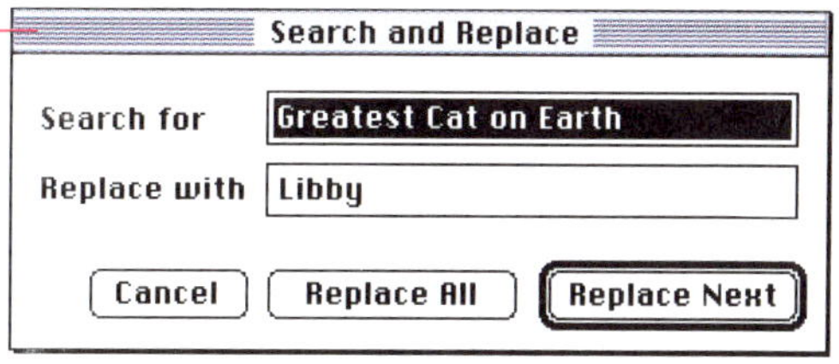

If the user activates another window while a modeless dialog box is open, the window appears in front of the dialog box.

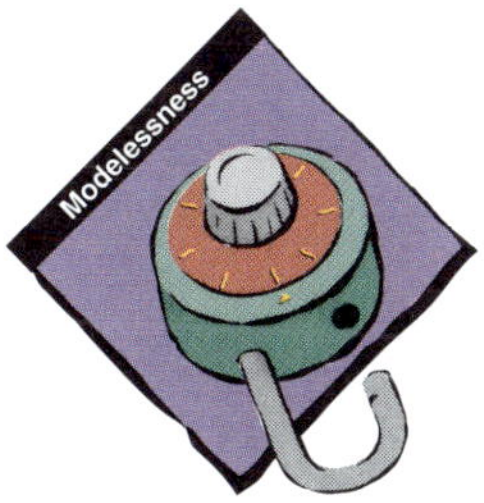

Modeless Dialog Box Behaviors

This section describes the standard behaviors and the issues that you need to resolve when you implement modeless dialog boxes in your application. It includes discussions of how to use modeless dialog boxes to change attributes in a document or an application and how to use modeless dialog boxes to perform actions on a document.

Menu Bar Access

Although system software leaves the Help, Keyboard, and Application menus and their commands enabled, it does nothing else to manage the menu bar when you display a modeless dialog box. Your application is responsible for providing access to the rest of the menus in your menu bar as appropriate. Disable only those menus that contain commands that are invalid in the current context; if the modeless dialog box includes editable text items, enable the Cut, Copy, Paste, and Clear commands (and any other appropriate commands) in the Edit menu. For example, when a modeless dialog box used with a search-and-replace command appears, the application should allow access to the Edit menu to assist the user with the editable text items; it should also allow access to the File menu so that the user can open another file for searching and replacing text. However, your application should disable other menus if the commands in those menus cannot be used inside the active modeless dialog box. After your application removes a modeless dialog box, always restore the menus to their previous states.

Accepting Changes in a Modeless Dialog Box

One purpose for using a modeless dialog box is to give the user an opportunity to change something in the active document or application. For example, you could implement a modeless dialog box for finding text and replacing it with other text. With modeless dialog boxes, people enter information by setting controls or typing text in a text entry box.

In general, all changes that a user enters in a dialog box should appear to take effect immediately whenever possible. There are generally three stages of action in using a modeless dialog box—when keyboard input is entered, when the data is accepted or checked by your application, and when the data takes effect. It is your responsibility to make the three states of using a modeless dialog box as clear as possible to the user. Usually you update controls like checkboxes and radio buttons immediately and display the results as the user clicks the controls. This feedback lets the user see that the information is accurate. If your application doesn't respond immediately to the new settings, it's less clear to the user when the input goes into effect.

Deciding when user input takes effect is a significant issue to resolve with any modeless dialog box. Try to reinforce the consistency of the interface. People usually expect to perform some action, such as clicking a button or closing a window, to cause their input to take effect. For example, the way a user chooses to dismiss a modeless dialog box conveys an obvious meaning to the user. The close box usually means, "I'm done with this task." The Revert button usually means, "Go back to the previous state." Similarly, the way a user chooses to implement changes made in a dialog box conveys an obvious message to the user. For example, an action button such as Apply usually means, "Do this task now." Note that people expect that when they switch to another application, any pending changes that they may have entered in the dialog box and implemented with an action button will take effect.

When the user is finished with the current task and is ready to move to another one, the actions the user performs to dismiss a modeless dialog box should signify that fact. As much as possible, implement modeless dialog boxes to respond to user expectations about the results of their actions.

You need to decide when your application will do error checking on user input. There are several approaches you can take depending on the circumstances and the user's expectations.

One approach is to implement the input as the user tabs from one field to the next. The drawback to this approach is that it isn't clear to the user that the changes are taking effect. The user doesn't click a button, and so isn't aware of completing an action. The user may decide to go back to a field and change the current value. In this case, your application needs to cycle through the event loop again to process the input.

Another approach is to save user input in a queue and activate it when the user clicks a button, closes the dialog box, or switches to another application. This method also presents certain complications for your application. If your application waits to check any user input for errors until the user tries to dismiss the dialog box and move on, you may end up having to present a modal dialog box to inform the user of some input error and thereby force the user to start the process again. If you do your error checking as the user enters input, it takes more time up front, but you can warn the user immediately.

In addition to error checking, you need to decide when to activate user input. This input can take effect immediately in some cases. If it's appropriate to wait until the user performs an action like clicking a button or switching applications, an intermediate state where user settings are pending can cause security problems. For instance, if a user changes permissions on a file server by using checkboxes in a modeless dialog box and your application does error checking immediately, there's a delay during which the user can't finish setting all the new access permissions and the system may be temporarily less secure and open to trespass. You should consider the tradeoffs between the danger of leaving a system less secure for some period of time versus any inconvenience to the user of waiting to have the error checking done after all values are set.

Applications differ in the order in which they check user input. Some applications check numerals in text entry boxes as the user enters them, some applications check the data when the user clicks in another field or presses Tab to move out of the current field, and others check when the user clicks an action button. Each of these techniques can work if you provide appropriate feedback to users so that they know what to expect and how to handle any error conditions.

After you have decided when to check user input for errors and when to activate it, you need to determine whether your application should automatically launch an operation based on the input or whether the user should try to launch the operation by clicking a button or the Close box of a dialog box. To help you make your decision, try to estimate how long an operation will last. It's probably OK to run an operation that happens quickly and returns control to the user within a couple of seconds. The user should initiate any operation that will take a long time to execute. You can then provide information that warns the user that the operation will last for a while, estimating the length of time when possible.

The Info window for applications provides an example of behaviors for acting on user input immediately and waiting until the user explicitly initiates an action. The Locked checkbox in the Info window immediately takes effect when the user clicks it. The file remains locked until the user clicks the box again to unlock the file. This system works to the advantage of the user because the checkbox reflects the user's action and the action is immediately in effect. A different process occurs with the application-size text entry box in the Info window. The text entry box immediately displays the user's input.

The application memory size is verified and accepted when the user closes the window. In this case, it's not dangerous to wait to accept the input until the user closes the Info window, and the user feels like the input is in effect immediately because the text entry field provides feedback that the input is acceptable by updating its contents. (This feedback is accurate unless the user enters 0, in which case the previous value is used.)

Carefully evaluate each situation in each of your modeless dialog boxes and choose the approach that meets the users' needs and expectations as closely as possible. It's a good idea to do some usability testing to verify your choices. See the section "Involving Users in the Design Process" beginning on page 41 in Chapter 3, "Human Interface Design and the Development Process," for information about performing user observations to test your product.

Completing Commands

Another purpose for using a modeless dialog box is to complete an action begun with a command in a menu. In this case the user gives additional information to the application in a modeless dialog box. The information might consist of additional parameters to the command, such as, "Do the task . . . in this way." The user might give specific information that an operation needs. For example, with the command that allows a user to search for words in a document, the user needs a place to type the word or characters being searched for, as shown in Figure 6-6.

Figure 6-6 Provide a place for the user to enter information in a modeless dialog box

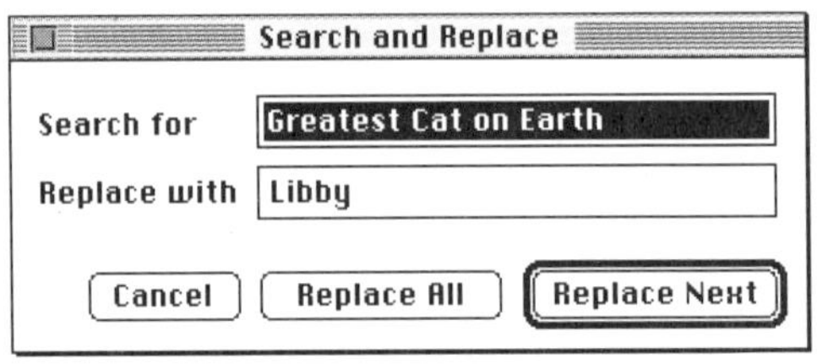

Modeless dialog boxes should be dynamic in nature, updating the document continuously while open. If the dialog box for a particular feature is not designed to interact dynamically with the user, you might think about implementing that feature in a modal dialog box.

Movable Modal Dialog Boxes

A **movable modal dialog box** is a modal dialog box that has a title bar that allows the user to move the dialog box. Movable modal dialog boxes are an adaptation of the modal dialog box that borrows the ability to move around the screen from the modeless dialog box. Movable modal dialog boxes suspend other actions within your application, but allow the user some flexibility. The user can switch to another application while you display a movable modal dialog box. If the user clicks another window of the current application, your application should play the system alert sound. If the user clicks a window from another application or the desktop, the windows of that application or the Finder come to the front. Figure 6-7 shows a typical movable modal dialog box.

Figure 6-7 A typical movable modal dialog box

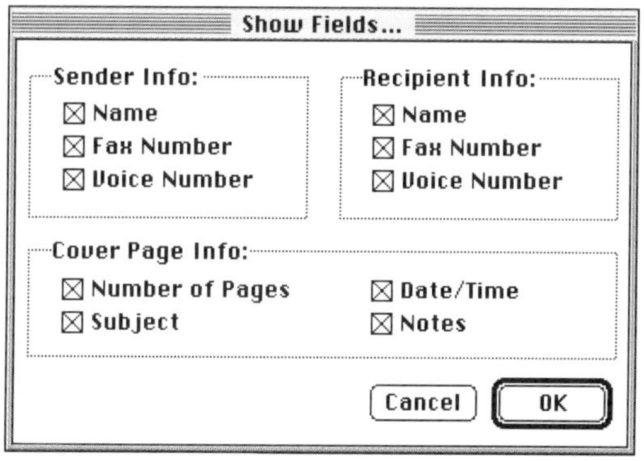

Movable modal dialog boxes typically do not include a close box, meaning that a user closes such a box by clicking a button. See the section "Button Names" on page 206 in Chapter 7, "Controls," for detailed descriptions of how to name buttons and what actions users expect from appropriately named buttons.

Use a movable modal dialog box when the user may need to see the document contents that a modal dialog box obscures. For example, if the dialog box makes style changes to a selection in a document, the user may want to see the selection. If you display a modal dialog box over the selection, the user won't be able to see it.

You can also use a movable modal dialog box when your application needs more information from the user, but it's not imperative to get the information before the user performs another action in another application. (Movable modal dialog boxes are still modal to the application.) Another good use of the movable modal dialog box is to display the status of an operation that takes a long time but can run in the background. This case is described in detail in the section "Movable Modal Dialog Box Behaviors," on page 187.

Movable Modal Dialog Box Appearance

The design of the movable modal dialog box adds a title bar with racing stripes to the standard modal dialog box window. A movable modal dialog box does not have a close box or zoom box. This design gives the user visual feedback that the dialog box is modal, and must be responded to before completing any other action in the active application, but the user can move it. Figure 6-8 shows the appearance of a movable modal dialog box.

Figure 6-8 The essential elements of a movable modal dialog box

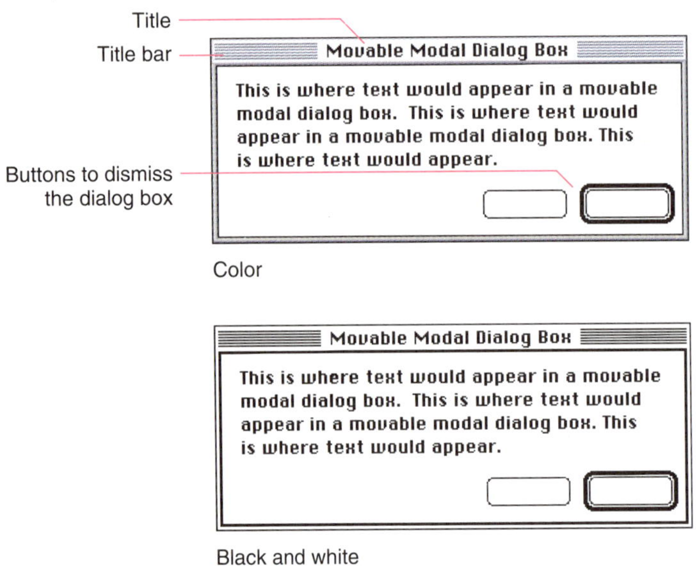

Don't use a close box in a movable modal dialog box. As described in the next section, "Movable Modal Dialog Box Behaviors," the only way to close a movable modal dialog box is by clicking a button. If you add a close box, it confuses the appearance of the dialog box with the modeless dialog box. A close box could also create a situation for users where they wouldn't know what to expect. For example, would the close box mean "accept the changes I've made" or "close the dialog box without using the input"? Figure 6-9 shows a movable modal dialog box with a close box, which is incorrect.

Figure 6-9 Close box used incorrectly in a movable modal dialog box

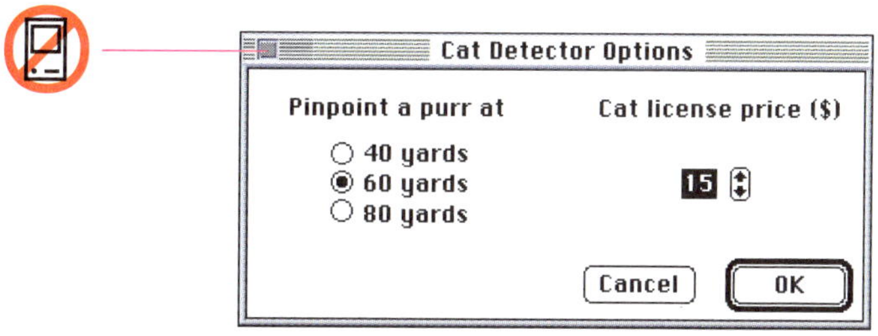

Movable Modal Dialog Box Behaviors

Movable modal dialog boxes should respond like modal dialog boxes in most ways. (See the section "Modal Dialog Boxes" on page 188 for a discussion of modal dialog boxes.) You must make certain that the dialog box is modal within your application. That is, the user should not be able to switch to another of your application's windows while the dialog box is active.

For movable modal dialog boxes, there are certain behaviors you need to support. Allow your application to run in the background when you display a movable modal dialog box. For example, System 7 uses movable modal dialog boxes to show that an application is busy with a time-consuming operation, yet a user can still switch the application to the background. Figure 6-10 shows a movable modal dialog box displayed by the Finder when it is copying files.

Figure 6-10 A Finder movable modal dialog box

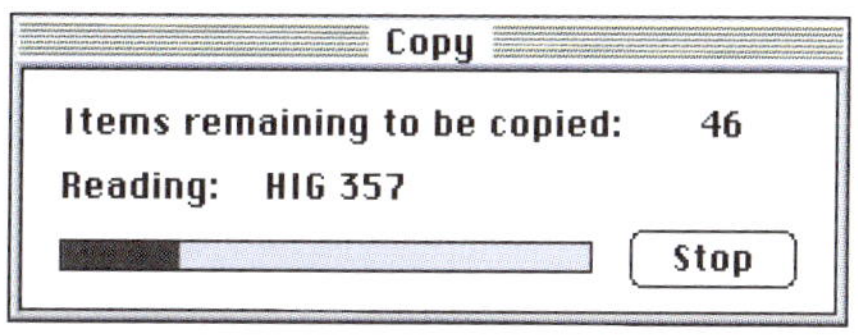

Menu Bar Access

When your application displays a movable modal dialog box, the system software enables the Application menu, the Help menu, and the Keyboard menu; the system software does nothing else to manage the menu bar. Your application should allow or disallow access to the rest of your menu bar as appropriate. Your application should leave the Apple menu enabled so that the user can use it to open other applications while the movable modal dialog box is on the screen. Also, if the movable modal dialog box contains editable text items, your application should enable the Cut, Copy, and Paste commands in the Edit menu as well as other context-appropriate commands in the Edit menu and other menus. Note that it is the responsibility of your application to always restore the menus to their previous states after removing movable modal dialog boxes. Figure 6-11 shows the Application menu open while a movable modal dialog box is on the screen.

Figure 6-11 Menu bar access while a movable modal dialog box is open

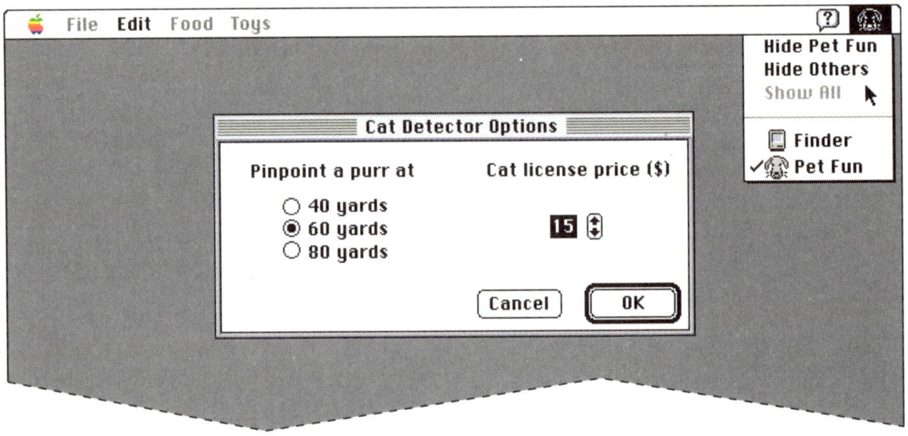

Modal Dialog Boxes

A **modal dialog box** puts the user in the state, or mode, of being able to work only inside the dialog box. It temporarily suspends all other actions in an application and the computer. It forces the user to make decisions before doing any other actions, such as working on a document or switching to another application. Users can cancel a modal dialog box, they can respond to a message, or they can use a modal dialog box to set parameters or assign values to content in the active document. Modal dialog boxes are restrictive in that they require the user to stop any other activity and pay attention only to the current modal dialog box. The user cannot move a modal dialog box, and the user can dismiss it only by clicking its buttons. If the user clicks any other window or on the desktop, the system beeps, but nothing else happens. See the section "Button Names" on page 206 in Chapter 7, "Controls," for detailed descriptions of how to name buttons and what actions users expect from appropriately named buttons.

An alert box is a special case of a modal dialog box. Use alert boxes when you need to get the user's attention to respond to an immediate need, to warn the user of an impending situation, or to force a necessary decision. For example, the dialog box that asks the user what to do with a document with unsaved changes is an alert box; in effect, it warns the user that if the user doesn't save changes to the document, those changes will be lost. Alert boxes are described in the section "Alert Boxes" on page 193.

Modal dialog boxes allow the user to make unambiguous state changes. The action buttons in the dialog box confirm the action and indicate when the changes take effect. With modal dialog boxes you can avoid intermediate states that can occur with a modeless dialog box, where the user's changes take effect without the user being aware that this is happening. Figure 6-12 shows one example of a modal dialog box.

Figure 6-12 An example of a modal dialog box

Use modal dialog boxes when it's appropriate to restrict user input to a certain order, that is, when your application needs information before it can continue. A modal dialog box is fairly simple to implement, but that doesn't mean that you should use modal dialog boxes too freely. You should rarely restrict the user's actions by forcing the user into a mode.

When your application needs to preserve a user selection in order to act on it, use a modal dialog box. This should be a task-specific, limited interaction that affects only the current task.

Modal dialog boxes are good for implementing tasks that are short and simple because they typically allow the user to complete an action and dismiss the dialog box with the click of a single button. That is, the user doesn't have to explicitly close the dialog box as a separate step to initiate the action, as is sometimes the case with modeless dialog boxes.

Use a modal dialog box for an action that the user needs to perform infrequently. For example, the Page Setup command displays a modal dialog box that contains settings that the user will probably set once for each document. This is a case where it makes sense to implement a modal dialog box because the user can set how the document will be displayed and doesn't need to have constant access to the dialog box. You could use a modeless dialog box in this case, but you wouldn't get any extra flexibility or use from its being modeless. Also, modal dialog boxes are typically easier to implement than modeless dialog boxes.

Modal dialog boxes are also useful for providing temporal status. The status may reflect a change from one version to another or an attribute of a document that is subject to change over the use of an application. One example would be a modal dialog box that informs a user that a document was created using a different version of the application. Another example of this is the status dialog box shown in Figure 6-13, which shows the progress of converting a document to a new format.

Figure 6-13 A status dialog box

Modal Dialog Box Appearance

Modal dialog boxes are framed by a double-outline border that doesn't include a drag region. The outer line is one pixel thick and the inner line is two pixels thick. A modal dialog box cannot be moved or resized. Figure 6-14 shows the appearance of a modal dialog box in color and black and white.

Figure 6-14 The essential elements of a modal dialog box

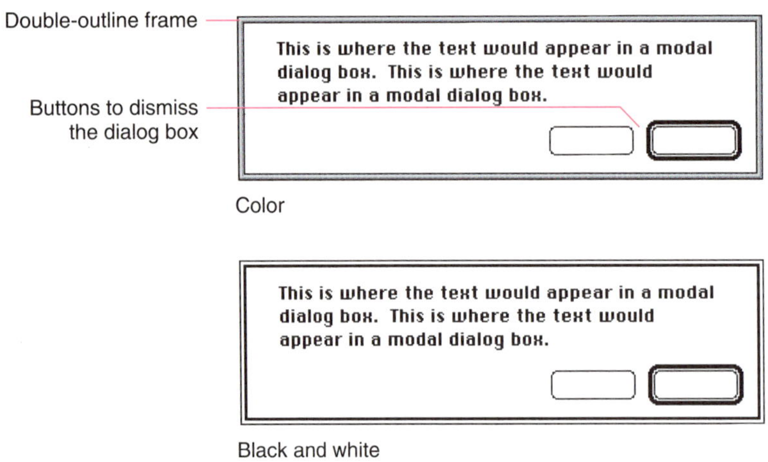

Modal Dialog Box Behaviors

This section describes the standard behaviors and issues that you need to consider when you implement modal dialog boxes in your application. It includes discussions of providing access to the menu bar when your application displays a modal dialog box and why to avoid displaying more than one modal dialog box at a time.

Menu Bar Access

When a modal dialog box is displayed, most menus are inaccessible, but sometimes it's useful for the user to have access to certain menus. The Help menu and the Edit menu are usually active. You can choose to enable some commands in some of your application's menus while your application displays a modal dialog box.

The Dialog Manager and the Menu Manager interact to provide various degrees of access to the menus in your menu bar. For modal dialog boxes without editable text items, you can simply allow system software to automatically provide the appropriate access to your menu bar. However, your application should handle its own menu bar access for modal dialog boxes with editable text items by disabling the Apple menu (or the first item in the Apple menu) in order to take control of its menu bar access, and by disabling all of the application's menus except the Edit menu, as well as any inappropriate commands in the Edit menu. Figure 6-15 illustrates how an application disables all of its own menus except its Edit menu when displaying a modal dialog box containing editable text items. Access to the Edit menu can be very helpful for the user who prefers to use the commands in the Edit menu to copy and paste text from one text field to another rather than retyping the text.

Figure 6-15 Access to the Edit menu when displaying a modal dialog box

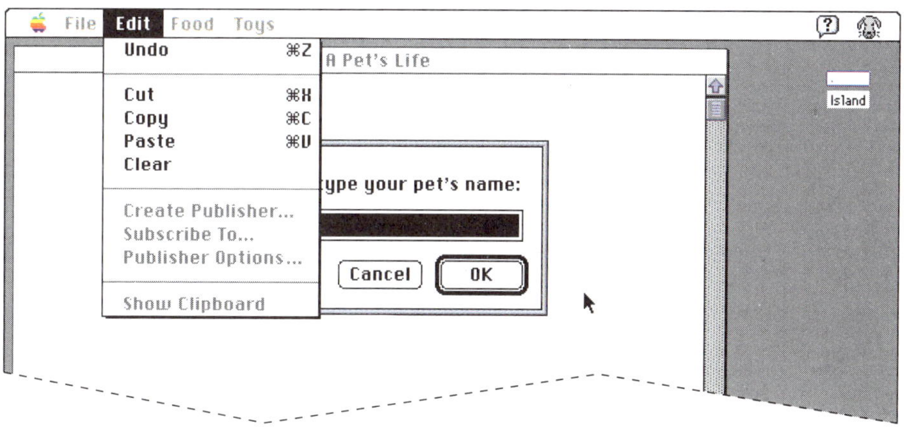

When the user dismisses the modal dialog box, the Menu Manager restores all menus to the state they were in prior to the appearance of the modal dialog box—unless your application handles its own menu bar access, in which case you must restore the menus to their previous states.

See *Inside Macintosh: Macintosh Toolbox Essentials* for more information about providing access to the menu bar while a modal dialog box is onscreen.

Stacking Modal Dialog Boxes

Ideally a user should see only one modal dialog box at a time. The user should never see more than two modal dialog boxes on the screen at any time. One example where a second modal dialog box appears is when the user saves a file with the same name as another file. Then the Standard File Package displays an alert box on top of the standard file dialog box. The alert box questions the user about whether to replace the existing file. If the user answers the question by clicking the Replace button, the alert box and the standard file dialog box both disappear and the action is completed. If the user clicks the Cancel button, the alert box disappears and the standard file dialog box remains on the screen; this allows the user to perform another action, such as saving the file with a different name.

If you find that you can't avoid displaying a second modal dialog box, make sure to obscure as little as possible of the first modal dialog box. Also make sure that the first dialog box (the one in the background) is dimmed when the second dialog box appears. (You dim the dialog box by dimming the border and buttons, and by unhighlighting any text selection; make sure your application stores the text selection so that it can restore it when the second dialog box is dismissed.) By dimming the dialog box in the background, you focus the attention of the user on the active dialog box—the one in which the user must click. Figure 6-16 shows two modal dialog boxes correctly displayed. Notice that the alert box appears on top of the dialog box for saving files, but doesn't totally obscure it. In this way, users still get some context for the current action.

Figure 6-16 Second modal dialog box on top of first one

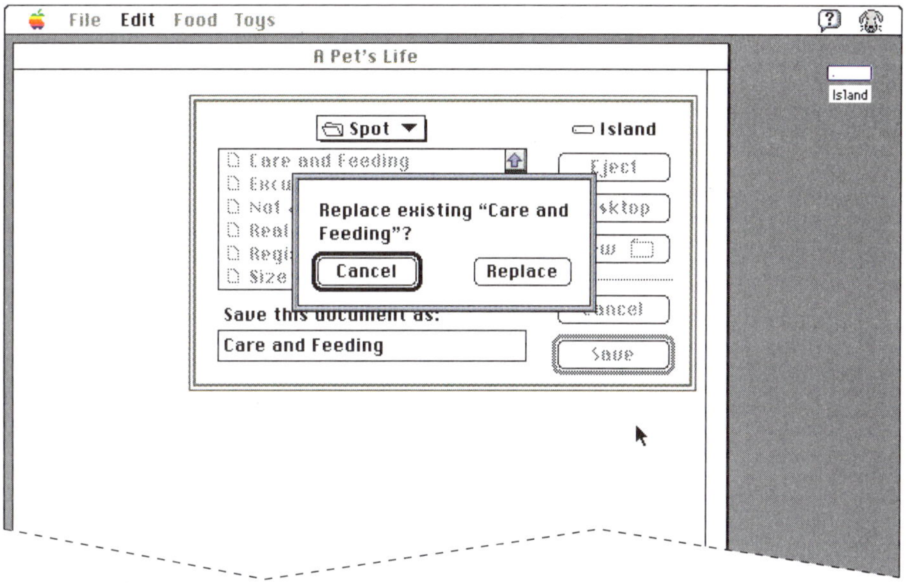

Avoid closing a modal dialog box and displaying another modal dialog box in response to a user action. This situation creates a "tunneling modal dialog box" syndrome from which it is difficult to recover. Since the previous modal dialog box is not there for context, the user can't predict what will happen next, and can't get back to the last place. In other words, don't create a situation where the user is caught in a maze of dialog boxes.

Alert Boxes

Alert boxes are a special case of modal dialog boxes. **Alert boxes** display messages to users to inform them of situations that run from interesting to dangerous. Each type of alert has a corresponding icon that appears in the alert box as described in the sections that follow. An alert box contains only an icon, text, and buttons. There are no other controls in alert boxes.

Alert boxes are modal to the application and don't allow a user to switch to another application. The only way to close an alert box is to click a button. In deciding when to use an alert box, follow the same guidelines as for modal dialog boxes in general.

Alert Box Appearance

In addition to the standard modal dialog box frame, alert boxes contain an icon that signifies the degree of severity of the alert message. Figure 6-17 shows the essential elements of an alert box. The types of alert boxes you can use are described in the sections that follow.

Figure 6-17 The essential elements of an alert box

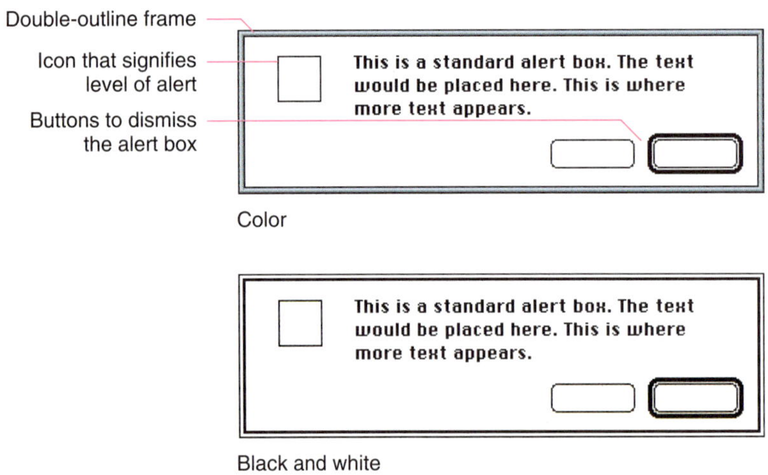

See the section "Dialog Box Messages" on page 310 in Chapter 11, "Language," for more information on writing appropriate alert box messages.

Note Alert Boxes

The note alert box is the first level of alert box. It contains the talking face icon. The note alert box provides nonthreatening information to the user. Usually note alert boxes have only one button, the OK button. In this case, the user can respond to the information only by acknowledging it. Figure 6-18 shows an example of a note alert box.

Figure 6-18 An example of a note alert box

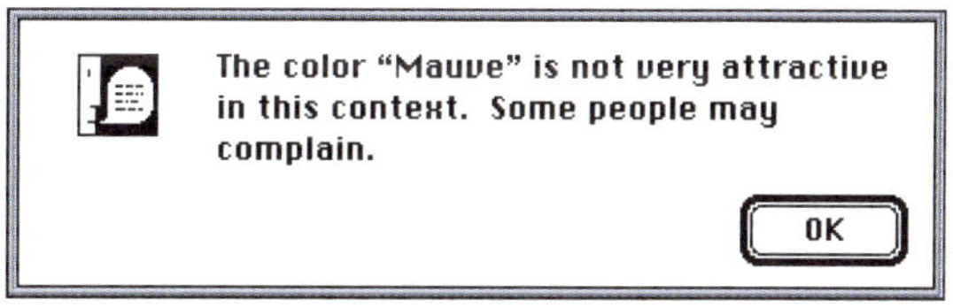

Use the note alert box to convey information that is useful to the user but doesn't present any threat such as a loss of data.

Caution Alert Boxes

The caution alert box is the second level of alert box. It is a more severe alert than the note alert box. The caution alert box icon is the triangle with an exclamation point. Caution alert boxes warn the user in advance of a potentially dangerous action. This kind of feedback provides a safety net for users. Caution alert boxes always contain two buttons, an OK or Continue button and a Cancel button. The caution alert box allows the user to continue the potentially dangerous action or to cancel the action and do something else. The OK or Continue button should be the default button, unless the user has to perform some other task in order to prevent the loss of data. Figure 6-19 shows an example of a caution alert box.

Figure 6-19 An example of a caution alert box

Use a caution alert box to warn users whenever they are about to complete an action that causes irretrievable data loss or any other potentially dangerous situation.

Stop Alert Boxes

The stop alert box is the third, and most severe, level of alert box. The stop alert box icon is the hexagon with an open hand, which resembles a stop sign in some locales. (If this icon is offensive in a region or country where you want to market your application, make sure you replace it with a more appropriate stop icon when you localize your application.) Stop alert boxes notify the user that an action cannot be completed. Stop alert boxes typically have only one button, the OK button. As with the note alert box, the user can only acknowledge the warning and dismiss the alert box. Figure 6-20 shows an example of a stop alert box.

Figure 6-20 An example of a stop alert box

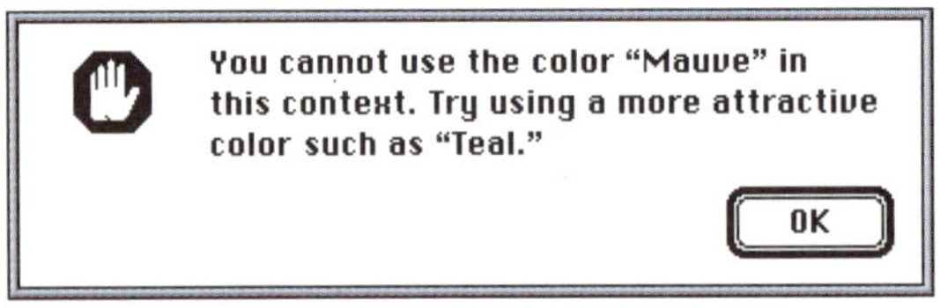

Use stop alert boxes when the user tries to complete an action that is impossible in the current context.

Basic Dialog Box Layout

In dialog boxes, you should place buttons in locations that are functional and consistent—consistent both within your particular application and across other applications that you develop. Note that alert boxes are a *type* of dialog box and thus adhere to the same basic guidelines for proper layout. Place the action button in the lower-right corner with the Cancel button to its left. The default button is not necessarily the button in the lower-right corner; it should be the one for the action that the user is most likely to want to perform. This rule keeps the action button and the Cancel button consistently placed. If the default button were always in the lower-right corner, the buttons would change location depending on which one was the default choice. See the section "Button Behavior," Chapter 7, "Controls," on page 205 for more information on assigning the default button.

Use a consistent amount of white space between the border of the dialog box and its elements. This creates a balanced appearance in the dialog box.

Figure 6-21 shows the recommended location for buttons and text in dialog boxes; it also shows the proper placement of the alert icon in an alert box. Note that the measurements shown in Figure 6-21 reflect the visual appearance of a dialog box on the screen, not the actual settings that you would use when creating dialog boxes with a resource-editing tool such as ResEdit. See the chapter "Dialog Manager" in *Inside Macintosh: Macintosh Toolbox Essentials* for a detailed description of how to place buttons and text correctly in dialog boxes as well as alert boxes.

Figure 6-21 Recommended spacing of buttons and text in dialog and alert boxes

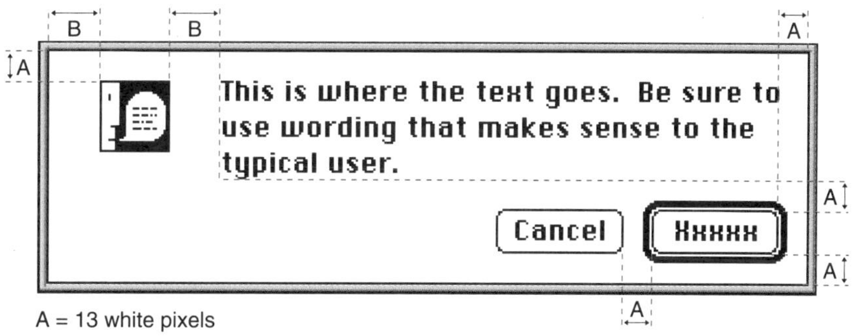

A = 13 white pixels
B = 23 white pixels

The Western reader's eye tends to move from the upper-left corner of the dialog box to the lower right. Put the initial impression that you want to convey in the upper-left area (like the alert icon), and place the buttons that a user clicks in the lower right. Following this guideline makes it easier for users to identify what's important in a dialog box.

When a dialog box is localized for worldwide versions of system software, the text in the dialog box may become longer or shorter. The alignment of the items in the dialog box may vary with localization. For example, Arabic and Hebrew are written right to left, so the items in an Arabic or Hebrew dialog (alert) box should be aligned on the right. The Control Manager, Menu Manager, and TextEdit routines handle the alignment of dialog box components. For more information, see the chapters that describe those managers in *Inside Macintosh: Macintosh Toolbox Essentials* and *Inside Macintosh: Text*. Be sure to create dialog items of the same size, so that they align properly when a user has a script that reads from right to left. This guideline is discussed in the section "Worldwide Compatibility" on page 16 in Chapter 2, "General Design Considerations."

Keyboard Navigation in Dialog Boxes

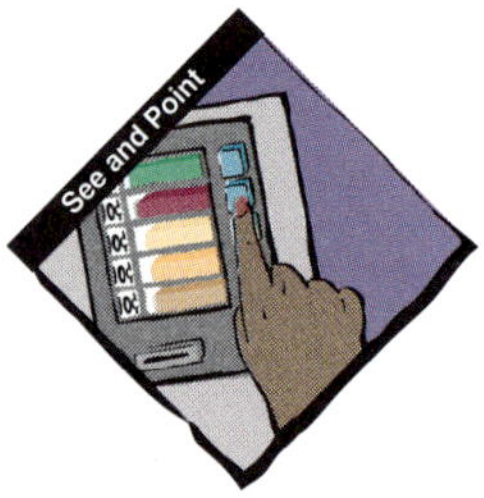

In a dialog box, the user can navigate through the interface elements that accept keyboard input, such as text boxes and scrolling lists, in several ways. The user can click the desired element or press the Tab key to cycle through the available elements. The user can move backward through the available elements by pressing the combination Shift-Tab.

Some scrolling lists in dialog boxes can also accept keyboard input for navigating within the list. The user can use the arrow keys to move through the list one item at a time in the direction of the arrow. Users can also select an item from the list by typing the beginning character or characters of its name; this technique is called **type selection.** In versions of system software earlier than System 7, type selection worked only in the standard file dialog box for opening files. In System 7, type selection has been extended to work in other lists, such as the list of files in a Finder window and the list of available devices in the Chooser.

When a dialog box contains more than one element that can accept input from the keyboard, it's necessary to indicate to users which element is currently accepting input from the keyboard. For text entry boxes, a blinking insertion point or selected text range is a standard way of showing that the text entry box is the active element receiving keyboard input.

When a scrolling list is the active element in a dialog box, its visual indicator is a rectangular border of two black pixels, which is separated from the list by one pixel of white space. Figure 6-22 shows the AppleTalk Zones list in the Chooser as an active scrolling list area.

Figure 6-22 An active scrolling list

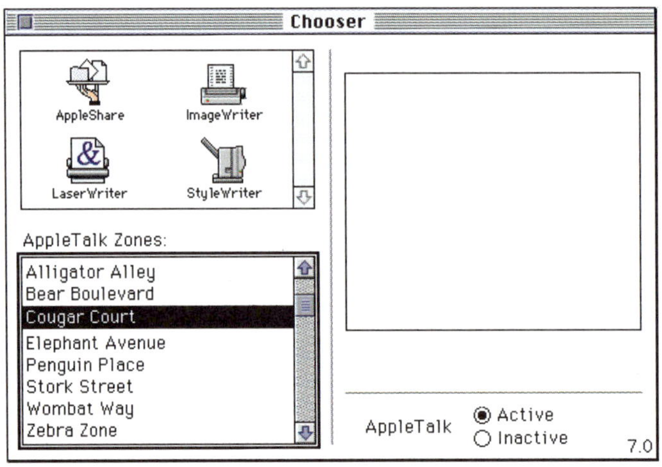

Since all typing goes to the active window, there should be only one active area and only one indicator at any time. If a dialog box has only one scrolling list and no other elements that can accept keyboard input, it's not necessary to outline the scrolling list. In the standard file dialog box for opening documents, the user can use type selection to identify the desired file in the list of files, but, since there's no other list or text box, the selected list doesn't have a border. See *Inside Macintosh: More Macintosh Toolbox* for information about implementing scrolling lists.

Dialog Box Messages

Write messages in dialog boxes and alert boxes that make sense to the user. Use simple, nontechnical language; don't provide system-oriented information that the user can't respond to. When possible, give the user information that helps explain how to correct the problem. Figure 6-23 shows an example of a well-written dialog box message that replaces the message users used to see: "The application is busy or missing."

Figure 6-23 A well-written dialog box message

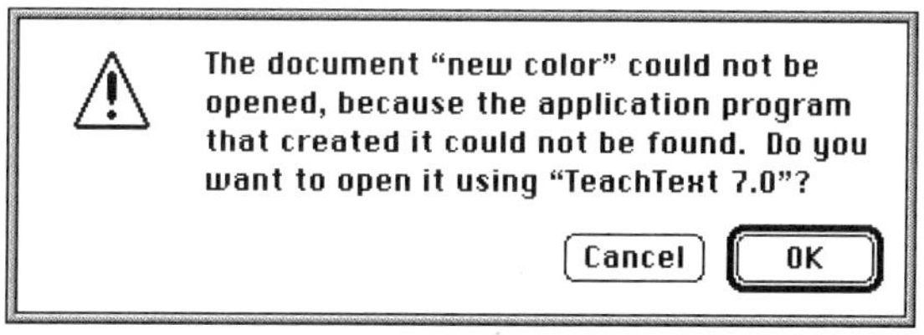

Use the name of the document or application in a dialog box to help users understand the message. For example, a dialog box that appears when a user chooses Shut Down after working on the company's annual report using the TeachText application should say "Save changes to the TeachText document "Annual Report" before quitting?" rather than simply "Save changes before quitting?" This kind of labeling helps users who are working with several documents or applications at once to make decisions about each one individually.

See the section "Dialog Box Messages" on page 310 in Chapter 11, "Language," for more information about writing dialog box messages. See the section "Button Names" on page 206 in Chapter 7, "Controls," for more information on naming buttons.

Standard File Dialog Boxes

The **standard file dialog boxes** allow users to operate on files located on some type of storage media, such as a hard disk, floppy disk, or file server; users can perform such tasks as viewing the files on a hard disk, opening and saving a document, and viewing elements on the desktop. Standard dialog boxes are commonly called *directory dialog boxes* in user documentation because they offer a directory listing of files available on storage media. Users can navigate through the levels of folders they have created and they can navigate to other storage media. The standard file dialog boxes show a file's position in relation to the disk it's stored on. The desktop appears as the top level of the hierarchical file system. The user clicks the Desktop button to get to the top level of the hierarchy to see what storage media are currently mounted and available. A user can view and select storage media from the standard file dialog box, but can see other desktop entities such as the Trash folder. The dialog box that appears when the user chooses Save As includes a New Folder button that allows the user to create a folder in which to store the document.

If you don't use the default dialog boxes that the system software provides for opening files and saving files, you should at least replicate the organization and appearance of the standard file dialog boxes. Figure 6-24 shows an example of the standard file dialog box for opening files. For more information, see *Inside Macintosh: Files*.

Figure 6-24 The standard file dialog box for opening files

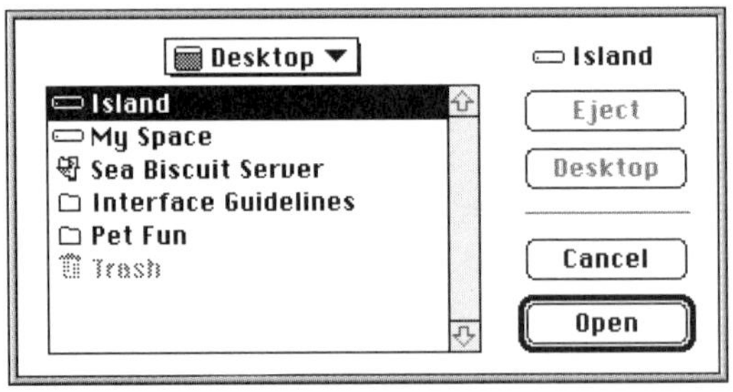

Save Changes Alert Box

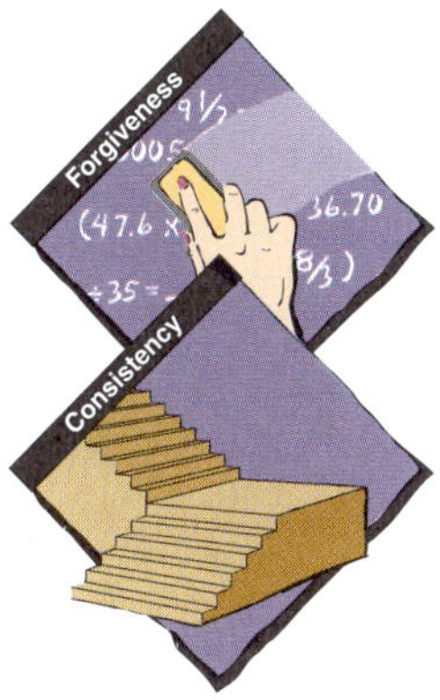

This section describes the standard alert box for saving all changes to a document before a user closes a document with unsaved changes without saving those changes or quits an application when there's an open document with unsaved changes. The design of the save changes alert box standardizes the appearance of the alert box and placement of its buttons so that users can quickly identify a potentially dangerous situation. Follow the guidelines in this section to create your save changes alert box.

Use the caution alert box, which includes the caution icon in the upper-left corner. This icon indicates to users that they need to carefully consider the alert box message before clicking the default button or pressing the Return key. The caution icon should always be in the same, predictable location so that users easily recognize it as a warning and understand its meaning.

The button names in the save changes alert box correlate to the action users perform by pressing the button. The buttons read Save, Don't Save, and Cancel. Using these verbs reinforces the identity of each possible action to the user. In other words, the Don't Save label provides much more context for the user than the word No does.

In order to prevent accidental clicks of the wrong button, you should always keep safe buttons apart from buttons that could cause data loss. Standardizing the location of buttons in a safe configuration provides an additional safeguard for the user. Place the Save button in the lower-right corner with the Cancel button to its left. Place the Don't Save button left-aligned with the message text. Make the Save button the default button, which means that it should be linked to the Return or Enter key. This way, the user is less likely to accidentally click the Don't Save button or activate it with a keystroke and cause irretrievable loss of data. Figure 6-25 shows an example of a standard save changes alert box.

Figure 6-25 The save changes alert box

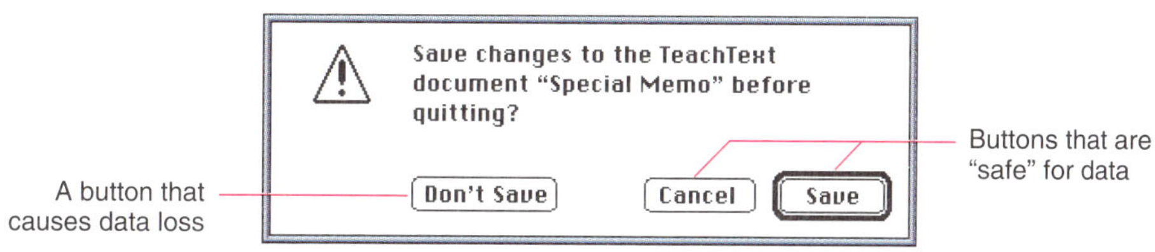

Include the name of your application and the name of the document in the alert box message, as shown in Figure 6-25. When a user shuts down the computer, several save changes alert boxes may appear if there are several open documents on the desktop. This addition of contextual information to the standard message helps the user by identifying to which application and document the message refers.

CHAPTER 7

Controls

This chapter describes the controls that users manipulate in windows, dialog boxes, and alert boxes. These controls are described in terms of their appearance and behavior, which are standardized. This chapter describes controls provided by the Macintosh Toolbox. This group includes buttons, radio buttons, checkboxes, and pop-up menus. (Pop-up menus are described in Chapter 4, "Menus," which begins on page 49.) This chapter also describes controls that are not supported by the Macintosh Toolbox, including sliders, little arrows, and the outline triangle. In addition, this chapter describes text entry fields and scrolling lists. If you need to, you can design your own controls, following the guidelines in this chapter.

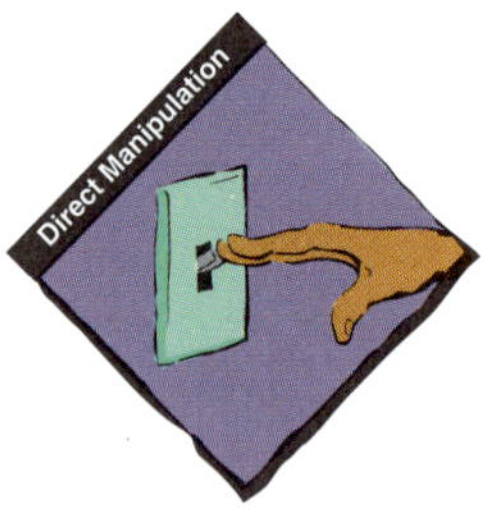

Controls are graphic objects that cause instant actions or audible results when the user manipulates them with the mouse. Users set controls that change settings to modify future actions. Controls also allow users to make choices or assign parameters in a range. Controls display existing choices so that they are visible to users. Because of their appearance and behavior, controls enhance the user's sense of direct manipulation.

When an operation requires more than one object or when it needs additional information before it executes, the Macintosh interface uses dialog boxes or alert boxes to convey and gather information. These dialog boxes and alert boxes use controls that users manipulate to provide the additional input. Controls are also found in windows. Controls provide users with familiar tools and formats for responding to the computer's need for information.

Standard Toolbox Controls

This section describes the controls that are available through the Macintosh Toolbox. It includes descriptions of the appearance and behavior of buttons, radio buttons, and checkboxes.

Buttons

A **button** is a rounded rectangle that is named with text. Clicking a button performs the action described by the button's name. Buttons usually perform instantaneous actions, such as completing operations defined by a dialog box or acknowledging an error message. A button's width is sized to fit the name it surrounds; the standard width for OK and Cancel buttons is 59 pixels.

Standard button height is 20 pixels. Figure 7-1 shows some typical buttons in a dialog box.

Figure 7-1 Buttons in a dialog box

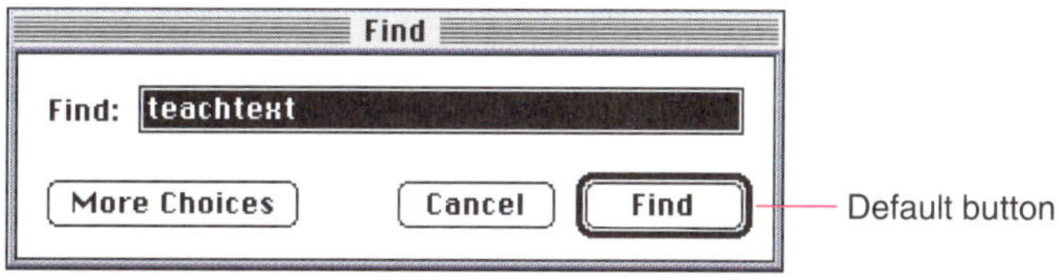

Button Behavior

When the user clicks a button, the button highlights (inverts) to give visual feedback to the user that indicates which item has been clicked. All alert boxes and modal dialog boxes that use the ModalDialog procedure exhibit this behavior. If you implement your own controlling mechanism for dialog boxes or alert boxes, be sure to include this behavior. For buttons that are activated by using a keyboard sequence, the Dialog Manager inverts the button for eight ticks, which is long enough for the user to see that the keyboard event has taken effect. (You must invert the Cancel button when the user presses Command-period or the Escape key; the Dialog Manager does not handle these events.) If the user presses the mouse button while the pointer is over a button, the button stays inverted until the user releases the mouse button or moves the pointer away from the button. The button tracks the mouse movement as long as the user keeps the mouse button depressed. If the user moves the pointer back over the button, it is highlighted. If the user releases the mouse button while the pointer is not over the button, nothing happens. Figure 7-2 shows a button that is highlighted to provide feedback.

Figure 7-2 A highlighted button

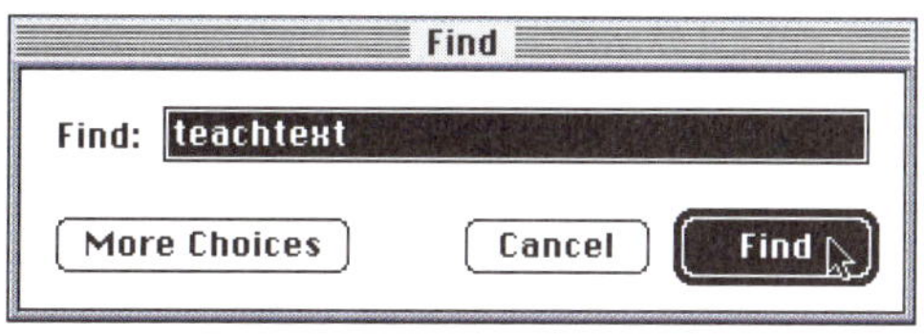

The **default button** should be the button that represents the action that the user is most likely to perform if that action isn't potentially dangerous. To denote a default button, draw an additional border of three black pixels, separated by a border of one white pixel, around it to let the user know that it is the default. (In alert boxes, the Macintosh Toolbox outlines the default button.) When the user presses the Enter key or the Return key, your application should respond as if the user clicked the default button.

Don't use a default button if the most likely action is dangerous—for example, if it causes a loss of user data. When there is no default button, pressing Return or Enter has no effect; the user must explicitly click a button. This guideline protects users from accidentally damaging their work by pressing Return or Enter. You can consider using a safe default button, such as Cancel.

Don't display a default border around any button if you use the Return key in text entry boxes. Having two behaviors for one key can confuse users and make the interface less predictable.

In addition to the action button or buttons, it's a good idea to include a Cancel button. This button returns the computer to the state it was in before the dialog box appeared. It means "forget I mentioned it." Always map the keyboard equivalent Command-period and the Esc (Escape) key to the Cancel button. These keyboard equivalents, along with Return and Enter, are accelerator keys and serve the purpose of letting the user respond quickly to a dialog box or an alert box. In general, it's not a good idea to assign other keyboard equivalents to buttons. If you find it useful to assign keyboard equivalents to some buttons that are used very often in your application, be sure to follow the guidelines in Chapter 4, "Menus," in the section "Keyboard Equivalents," which begins on page 128.

See the chapter "Dialog Manager" in *Inside Macintosh: Macintosh Toolbox Essentials* for information about implementing these behaviors for buttons.

Button Names

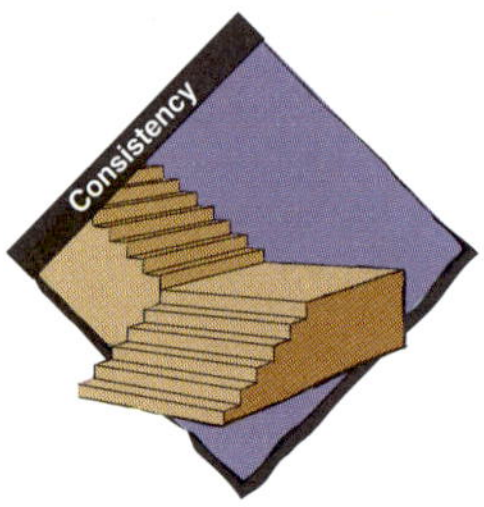

Whenever possible, name a button with a verb that describes the action that it performs. Button names should be limited to one word whenever possible. You should never use more than three words for a button name. Use the caps/lowercase style of capitalization for button names. In general, this means that you capitalize every word except articles *(a, an, the)*, coordinating conjunctions (for example, *and, or*), and prepositions of three or fewer letters. You also capitalize the first and last words of the name; since button names should seldom be more than two words, almost all words in button names should be capitalized. The specific rules for this type of capitalization appear in detail in the *Apple Publications Style Guide.*

Button names usually appear in 12-point Chicago. If a button is not available, it appears dimmed. On a black-and-white monitor, a dimmed button and its name are dithered to 50 percent gray. On color systems, dimmed items appear in true gray. Chicago is designed specifically to display well on the screen in all states, including dithered and gray. Other fonts, such as Geneva, which is sometimes used for button names, are rendered illegible when they are dithered.

Buttons usually cause instant actions, described by the name of the button. Occasionally they require more information before acting. If a button displays another dialog box, use the ellipsis character in the button name to indicate this to the user. (Do not include the ellipsis character if the dialog box appears only to ask users to confirm their actions.) The most appropriate situation for a second dialog box to appear would be when a modeless dialog box needed additional information on a limited basis to complete an action. See the section "Stacking Modal Dialog Boxes," which begins on page 192 in Chapter 6, "Dialog Boxes," for a discussion of the dangers of dialog boxes that generate more dialog boxes.

A user typically reads the text in a dialog box until it becomes familiar and then relies on visual cues, such as button names or positions, to respond. Names such as Save, Quit, and Erase Disk allow users to identify and click the correct button quickly. These words are often more clear and precise than names such as OK, Yes, and No. If the action can't be condensed into a word or two, OK and Cancel or Yes and No may serve the purpose. If you use these generic words, be sure to phrase the wording in the dialog box so that the action the button initiates is clear. Figure 7-3 shows a dialog box with appropriate OK and Cancel buttons.

Figure 7-3 A dialog box with OK and Cancel buttons

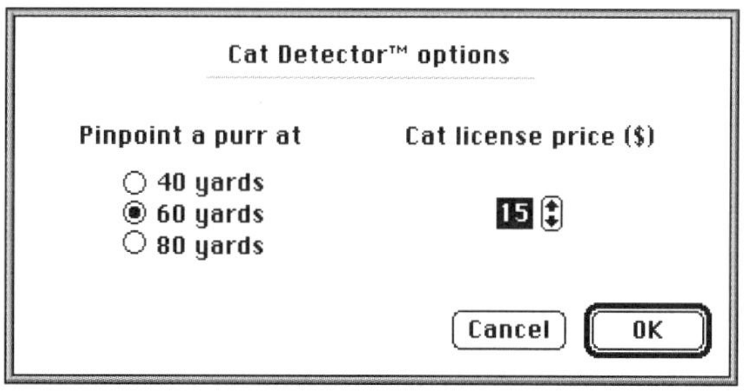

Use Cancel for the button that closes the alert box or dialog box and returns the application to the state it was in before the alert box or dialog box appeared. Cancel means "dismiss the operation I started, with no side effects." It does not mean "I've read this dialog box" or "stop what's going on regardless."

Ideally, you should never put your users in a situation in which they can't return to the state that existed before an operation began (and before the dialog box appeared). But if it can't be avoided, use OK or Stop, depending on the situation, instead of Cancel. Sometimes it is more appropriate to use the word Done instead of OK for the name of a button that closes the alert box or dialog box and that accepts any changes made while the dialog box is displayed. Figure 7-4 shows a dialog box that illustrates this guideline. In this dialog box, the user creates, renames, or deletes fields and then dismisses the dialog box, so the Done button means "I have finished editing fields and want to close the dialog box."

Figure 7-4 A dialog box with a Done button instead of an OK button

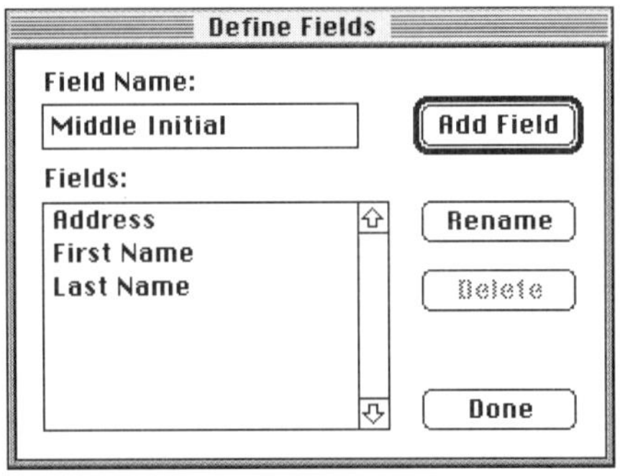

This dialog box uses Done because clicking the Done button maintains any changes that were made subsequent to the display of the dialog box. If the button were named OK, the user might confuse it with the Add Field button, which accepts changes but doesn't close the dialog box and therefore allows the user to make other changes. The Done button is most often used in dialog boxes in which the user can define more than one of an item, for example, field names, without closing the dialog box. In these situations it is often unreasonably difficult to return the user to the state that existed before the operation began, so there is no Cancel button.

Use Stop for a button that halts an operation midstream while accepting the possible side effects. Stop may leave the results of a partially complete task intact, whereas Cancel always returns the computer to its previous state. It's appropriate to change the button name in the middle of the operation from Cancel to Stop if you can determine when it's no longer possible to cancel. The dialog box shown in Figure 7-5 uses a Stop button because clicking the button maintains the text that is already inserted while preventing completion of the insert operation.

Figure 7-5 A progress indicator that uses a Stop button

In an alert box that requires confirmation, use a word that describes the result of accepting the message in the dialog box. For example, if a dialog box says "Revert to the last saved version of this document?" name the button Revert rather than OK. Figure 7-6 shows a dialog box with appropriately named buttons.

Figure 7-6 A confirmation alert box with appropriately named button

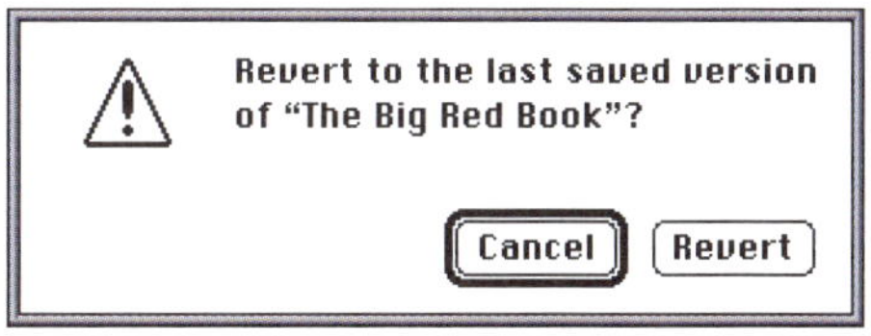

A modal dialog box usually cuts the user off from the task. That is, the user can't see the area of the document that changes when choices are made in the dialog box until dismissing the dialog box. Once the area becomes visible because the user dismisses the dialog box, the user sees whether the changes are the desired ones. If the changes aren't appropriate, then the user has to repeat the entire operation. To provide better feedback to the user, you need to provide a way for the user to see what the changes will be. Therefore, any selection made in a modal dialog box should immediately update the document contents, or you should provide a sample area in the dialog box that reflects the changes that the user's choices will make. In the case of immediate document updating, the OK button means "accept this change" and the Cancel button means "undo all changes done by this dialog box."

Some applications use an Apply button to approximate the behavior of immediately updating the document or using a sample area. This method confuses the meaning of OK and Cancel and is not recommended. If you must implement modal dialog boxes with an Apply button, you need to include a Cancel button. When there is an Apply button, the Cancel button undoes the results of the Apply operation and dismisses the dialog box. The OK button dismisses the dialog box and applies the settings made in the dialog box, even if the Apply button wasn't clicked. The user must always be able to undo any actions caused by the dialog box.

Radio Buttons

A radio button is a Macintosh control that displays a setting, either on or off, and is part of a group in which only one button can be on at a time. They occur in sets and are called radio buttons because they act like the buttons on a car radio. The user can have only one radio button setting in effect at one time, just as you can listen to only one radio station at a time. This means that radio buttons are mutually exclusive. The active setting has a dot in the middle of the button. Clicking one button in a group turns off whichever button was on before. Radio buttons never initiate an action. Figure 7-7 shows a typical set of radio buttons.

Figure 7-7 Sets of radio buttons

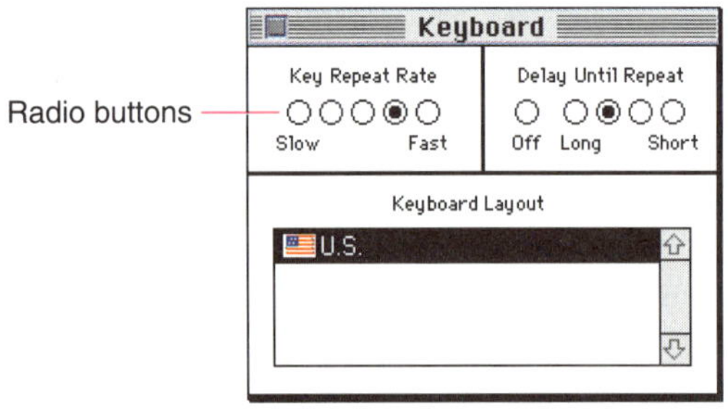

A set of radio buttons should contain from two to approximately seven items. Some sets could be slightly larger, but you must always have at least two radio buttons in each set. Each group of radio buttons usually has a label that identifies the kind of choices the group contains. Usually, each button has a label that identifies what it does. Sometimes a group of buttons represent a range of incremental options, as shown in Figure 7-7, in which case only the buttons at each end of the range are labeled. A label can be a few words or a phrase. A set of radio buttons always has the same set of choices. It is *never* dynamic, changing contents depending on the context. The user can click the button itself or the text that identifies the choice to activate the button.

Radio buttons represent choices that are related, but not necessarily opposite. For example, a set of radio buttons may provide alignment choices in a word processor. The choices would be left aligned, right aligned, and centered on the page. This group of radio buttons is shown in Figure 7-8.

Figure 7-8 Radio buttons for selecting the alignment of text

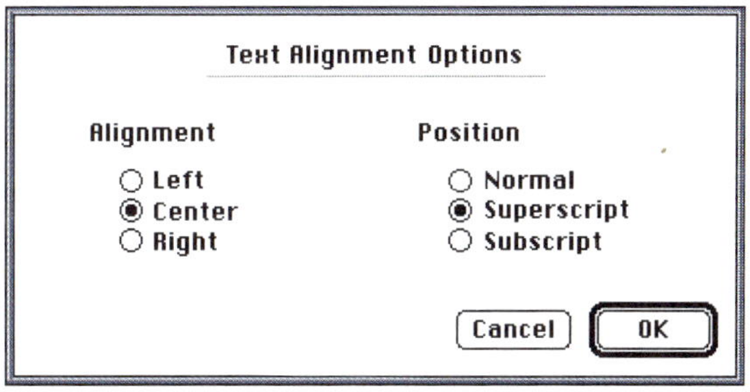

If more than one group of radio buttons is visible at one time, the groups need to be visually separate from each other. The General Controls panel from the Finder, shown in Figure 7-9, shows some examples of radio button sets that are separate and well labeled. Sometimes it's useful to draw a dotted line around a group of radio buttons to separate it from other elements in a dialog box.

Figure 7-9 The General Controls panel

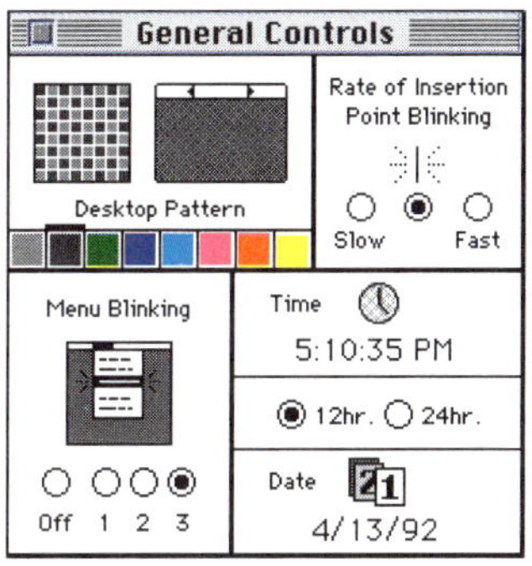

Checkboxes

Checkboxes, like radio buttons, provide alternative choices for users. A **checkbox** is a square with label text next to it. The user clicks the checkbox to select or deselect it. When the option is on, an *x* appears in the box. When the option is off, the box is empty. Checkboxes act like toggle switches, meaning that the setting for each checkbox is either off or on. Use checkboxes to indicate one or more options that must be either off or on. Checkboxes are independent of each other, even when they offer related options.

Any number of checkboxes can be on or off at the same time. Figure 7-10 shows some typical checkboxes.

Figure 7-10 A set of checkboxes

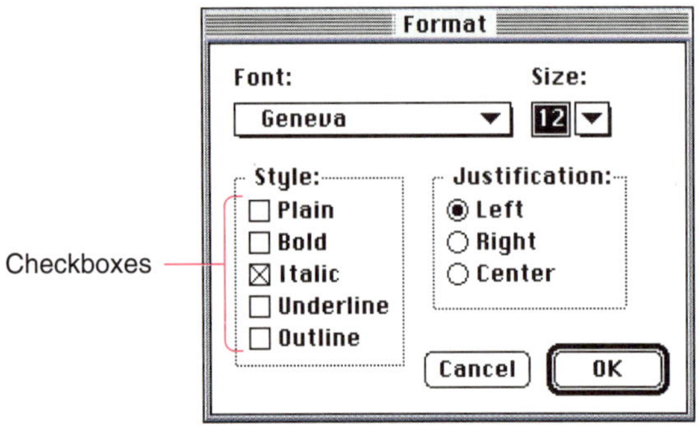

You can have one checkbox or as many as you need. It's a good idea to group sets of checkboxes that are related and to separate the groups from other groups of checkboxes and radio buttons.

Each checkbox has a label. It can be very difficult to label the option in an unambiguous way. The label should imply two clearly opposite states. For example, in a dialog box for opening files, a checkbox provides the option to open a file in a read-only format. The checkbox is labeled Read-Only. The clearly opposite state, when the option is off, is to open files that the user can read *and* write (or make changes to). Figure 7-11 shows this checkbox.

Figure 7-11 A single checkbox in a dialog box

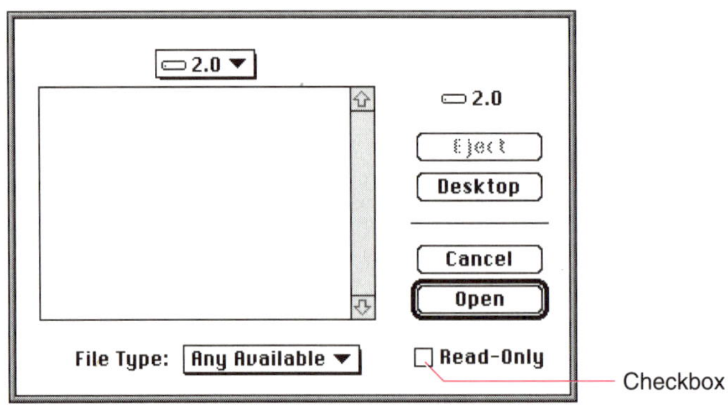

If you can't find a label for the checkbox that clearly implies its opposite state, you might be better off using radio buttons. With radio buttons, you can use two labels, thereby clarifying the states. It's sometimes tempting to use a checkbox because one item takes up less space than two. However, the resulting item may be ambiguous and thus difficult for your users to understand.

When you use one checkbox to provide two options, it makes the user think explicitly about what the significance of the option is. The user must click the checkbox or its label text to enable the option. In this way, you can emphasize the visible choice. For example, when the dialog box that the Find command brings up in System 7 was being designed, two implementations were considered, a set of radio buttons and a checkbox. The radio buttons were to be labeled "all at once" and "one at a time." These choices pertain to how the operating system should search for a text string in filenames. In the first option, all at once, the operating system highlights all the filenames in the open folder that match the text string. This option is similar to how the earlier Find File command operated, displaying all matches in a portion of the window. In the other option, one at a time, the operating system searches until the first item is found and highlights it. To see another match, the user must choose Find Again. One reason to use the checkbox was to reduce the visual clutter of the dialog box. The compelling reason that persuaded the designers to use a checkbox labeled "all at once" was that it emphasized the choice. Not setting the checkbox to on caused the normal state to be searching for one instance at a time. This made users focus on the choice when they wanted the Find operation to act differently than it normally did. Figure 7-12 shows the Find dialog box with the final implementation.

Figure 7-12 The Find dialog box

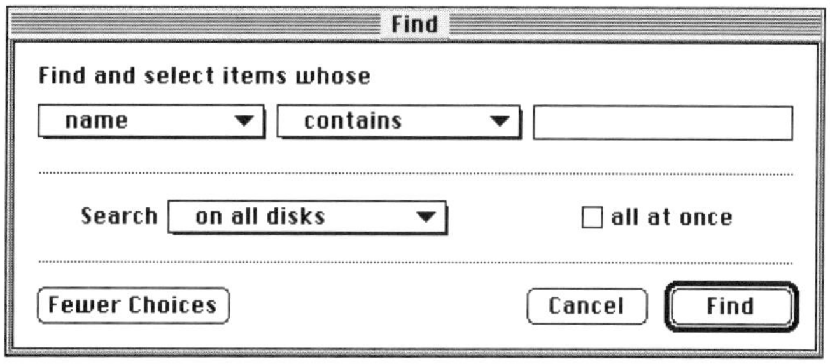

Controls Not Supported by the Macintosh Toolbox

This section describes the appearance and behavior of some common controls that are not supported by the Macintosh Toolbox. These controls include sliders, little arrows, and the outline triangle. You can implement these controls in your application where necessary according to the descriptions presented here.

Sliders

A **slider** (sometimes called a dial) displays the range of values, magnitude, or position of something in the application or system. An indicator notes the current setting. Some sliders allow users to alter the value of the slider by moving the indicator up and down. Sliders can be analog or digital devices that display their values graphically. Figure 7-13 shows an example of a slider.

Figure 7-13 An example of a slider

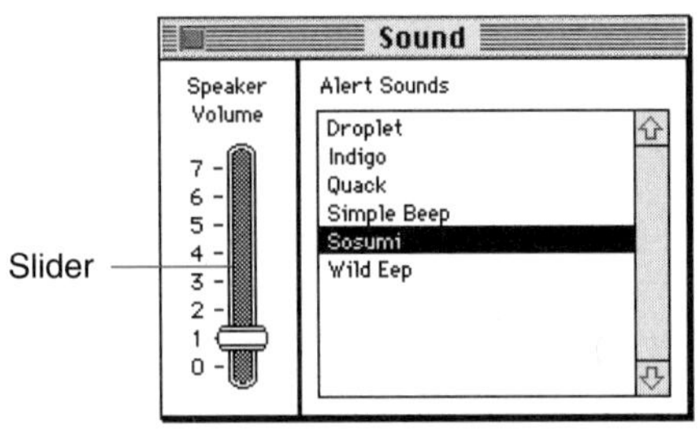

You can design and implement your own sliders as necessary for your application. When you design your sliders, be sure to include meaningful labels that indicate to users the range and direction of the slider. For instance, the Speaker Volume slider in the Sound control panel has numbers from 0 to 7 to indicate the loudness of the sound. It would be much clearer to users if the slider also had labels that stated the loudness in relative terms. The bottom could be labeled Flash Menu Bar. This type of labeling substantially improves the comprehensibility of the graphical interface.

Give users clues about the direction in which the indicator moves and how that relates to the control. For instance, most people assume that moving an indicator up a vertical slider means increasing the value of the setting. However, this assumption could be clarified easily with graphics or words. Figure 7-14 shows an example of a slider with graphical symbols that demonstrate to users which direction to move the indicator to increase or decrease brightness on a monitor.

Figure 7-14 A slider with direction information

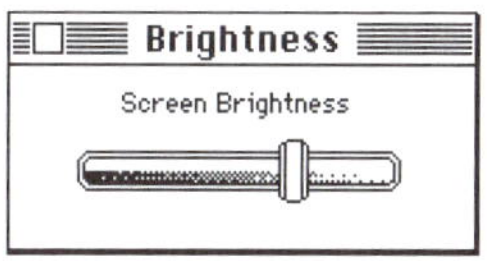

Make sure that you don't use a scroll bar when you really mean to use a slider. Use scroll bars only for representing the relative position of the visible portion of a document and in scrolling lists. Typically a scroll bar represents the amount of data in a document, and the scroll box represents the relative position of the window over the length of the document. Using a scroll box to change a setting confuses the meaning of the element and makes the interface inconsistent. Scroll bars are described in detail in the section "Scroll Bars," which begins on page 158 in Chapter 5, "Windows." Figure 7-15 shows a scroll bar used incorrectly and a slider used correctly in a similar situation.

Figure 7-15 Incorrect use of a scroll bar and correct use of a slider

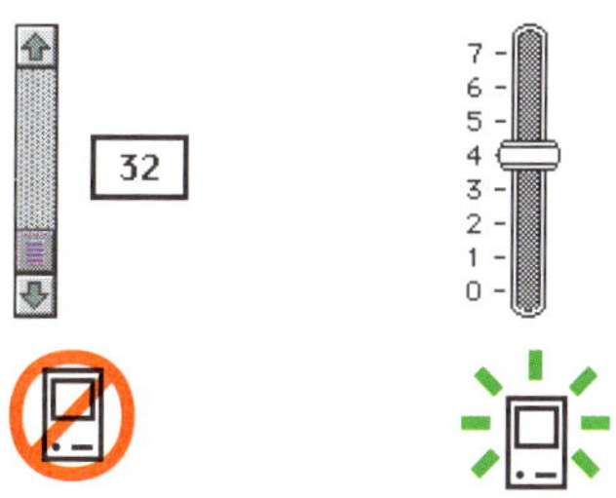

Little Arrows

The control that is two arrows pointing in opposite directions is commonly called **little arrows.** It is used to increase or decrease values in a series. Figure 7-16 shows one example of the little arrows control.

Figure 7-16 Little arrows control

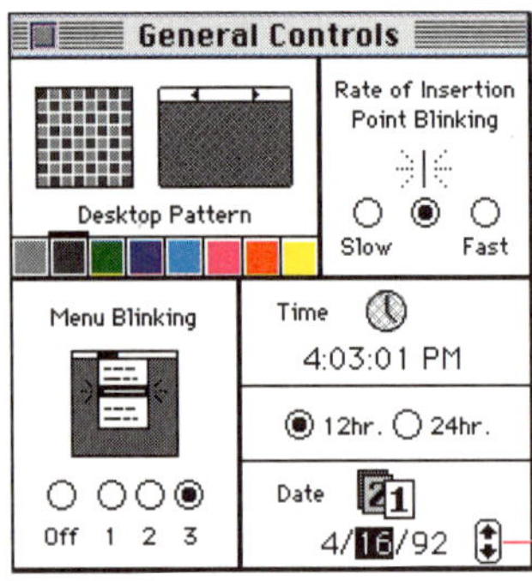

The little arrows control has a label that specifies the content to which it relates. The numerical or textual value appears in a box, which is often a type-in box so the user can type in a value instead of using the little arrows. When the user clicks one arrow, the value changes by a unit of 1. If the user presses the arrow, the value increases or decreases until the user releases the mouse button. While the user clicks or presses the arrow, it is highlighted to provide feedback to the user. The unit of change depends on the content. For example, if the content area displays years, the increment is one year at a time, as shown in Figure 7-17.

Figure 7-17 Content-dependent increment

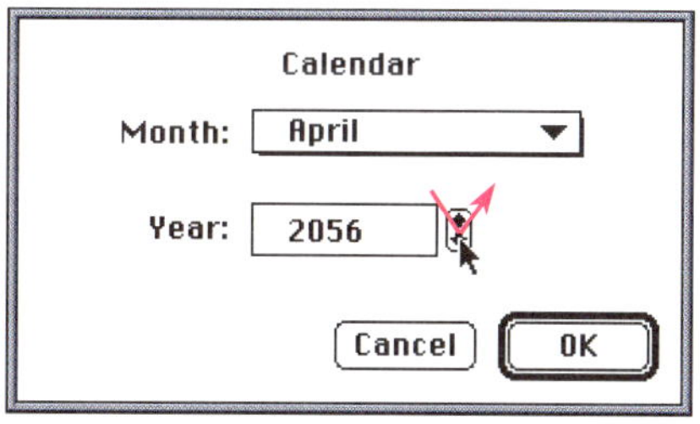

1.

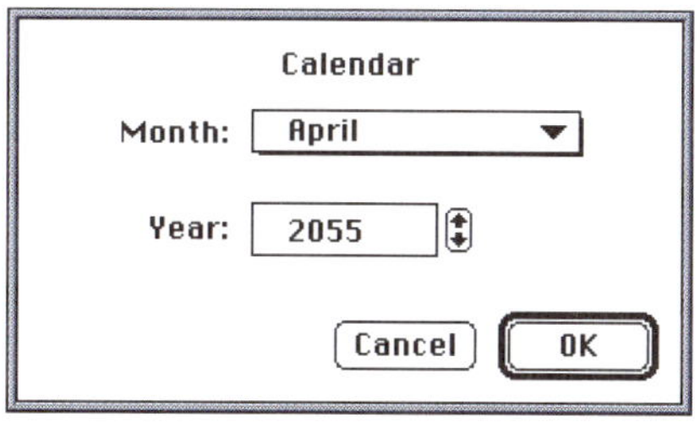

2.

If possible, give some indication what the user can expect by using the up arrow and the down arrow. For example, in Figure 7-17 it may not be obvious which direction the year would increment using either arrow. Clicking the up arrow might change the year from 2055 to 2056 or 2055 to 2054.

The little arrows control works best with numbers in cases in which it's obvious that the up arrow means 1 more than the current value and the down arrow means 1 less than the current value.

Outline Triangles

The **outline triangle** in the Finder is a control that users see when they choose to display the contents of their file system in a list view. The triangle appears next to folders that contain documents. The user clicks the triangle to display a list of the contents of the folder without actually opening it. The triangle then rotates to point downward. This change in position indicates to the user that the folder's contents are listed. Figure 7-18 shows the outline triangle in both positions.

Figure 7-18 Outline triangle control

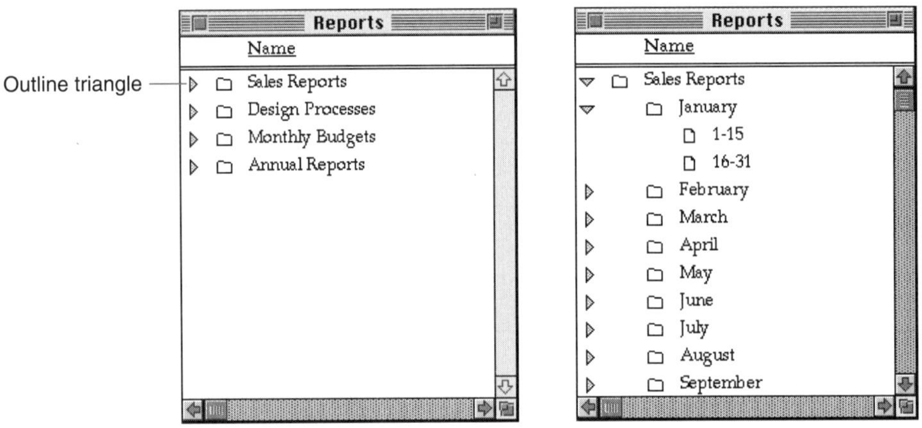

Other Elements for User Interaction

This section describes other elements that users interact with to provide information about what they want to do or what they expect to happen. These elements include text entry fields and scrolling lists. Note that these elements aren't necessarily controls.

Text Entry Fields

The **text entry field** is typically a rectangular box in a dialog box where the user enters some text to identify something. It is also called an *editable text field*. For example, in the Save As dialog box, the user types in the name of a document. Figure 7-19 shows an example of a text entry field.

Figure 7-19 A text entry field

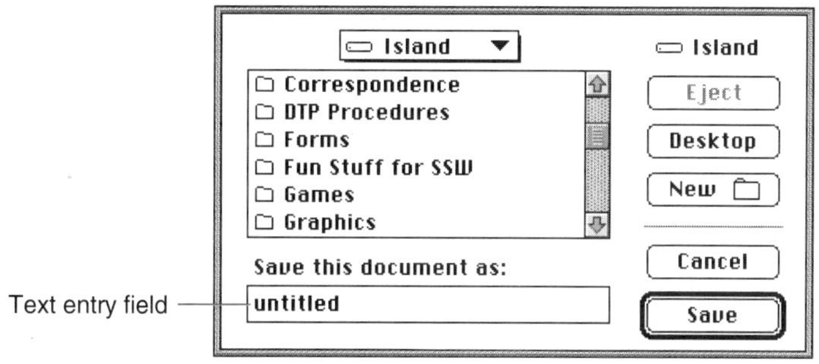

If an application isn't primarily a text application, but does use text in fields, you may not need to provide the full text-editing capabilities. In Macintosh applications, the simplest way to implement text editing is to use TextEdit, or to use the Dialog Manager, which in turn uses TextEdit. You need to make sure that whatever level of text-editing capabilities you implement for text entry fields is upward compatible with the full text-editing capabilities. You should implement these editing capabilities:

- The user can select the whole field and type in a new value, delete text, select a substring of the field and replace it, and select a word by double-clicking.
- The user can choose Undo, Cut, Copy, Paste, and Clear, as described in the section "The Edit Menu" on page 109 in Chapter 4, "Menus."

In addition, you can also implement intelligent cut and paste. (TextEdit does not provide this.) This capability is described in the section "Intelligent Cut and Paste," which begins on page 301 in Chapter 10, "Behaviors."

Even applications with only minimal text editing should perform appropriate edit checks. For example, if the only legitimate value for a field is a string of digits, the application should issue an alert message if the user types any nondigits. For example, the alert message might interrupt the user to remind him or her that the letters *l* and *o* can't be used in place of the numerals *1* and *0*. Alternatively, the application could wait until the user is through typing before checking the validity of a field's contents. In this case, the appropriate time to check the field is when the user clicks anywhere other than within the field or presses the Return, Enter, or Tab key.

Scrolling Lists

A scrolling list is a combination of two other elements. One part of the scrolling list is a list of items, such as a list of document names in the standard file dialog box. The other component is a scroll bar, which allows the user to look at more items in the list that aren't currently visible. The size of the box that displays the list often depends on the amount of space available in the context. The list can contain as many items as necessary. Figure 7-20 shows an example of a scrolling list.

Figure 7-20 A scrolling list

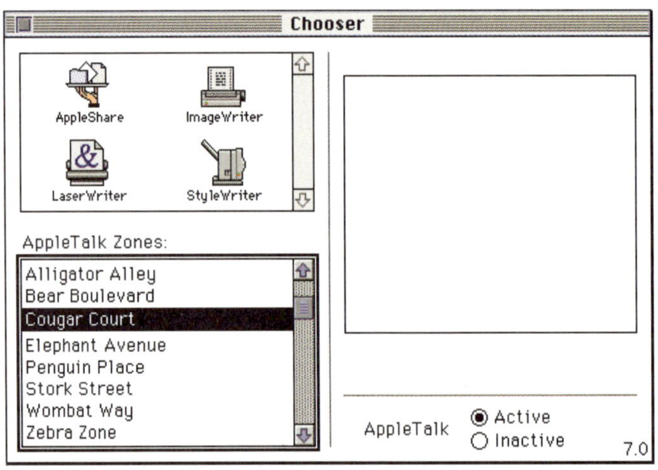

When you create the list of items in a scrolling list, you may find text that is too long to fit in the list. When this is the case, it's best to eliminate text in the middle of the name and insert ellipsis points there, preserving the beginning and ending of the item's name. Users often add version numbers to the end of their document or device names, so if you cut off the end of the text item, they lose that context and must guess which of the several item names that begin the same is the desired one.

The user can click an item in the list to select it, or use multiple selection techniques such as the Shift-click combination to select more than one item. The user can also scroll through the list to peruse its contents without selecting anything. If the list contains folders, the user can use standard techniques to open them and see their contents. Users can also use the keyboard navigation techniques discussed in "Keyboard Navigation in Dialog Boxes" on page 198 in Chapter 6, "Dialog Boxes," to select items in a scrolling list.

Scrolling lists are not appropriate to use for providing choices in a limited range. Since the full range isn't visible all at once in a scrolling list, it's difficult for users to understand the scope of their choices. Sliders work very well for displaying a limited range of values and for letting users choose their preference in the range. Sliders are described in the section "Sliders" on page 214.

CHAPTER 8

Icons

This chapter describes icons, their appearance, and their use in the Macintosh interface. It presents information on how to design icons and general guidelines for designing icons of different sizes and bit depths. This chapter also describes how to customize the standard icons you can provide for your products.

Icons are graphic representations of objects such as documents, storage media, folders, applications, and the Trash. Icons look like their real-world counterparts whenever possible. People can select, open, move, copy, and throw away icons. Figure 8-1 shows some icons displayed in the Finder.

Figure 8-1 Common icons

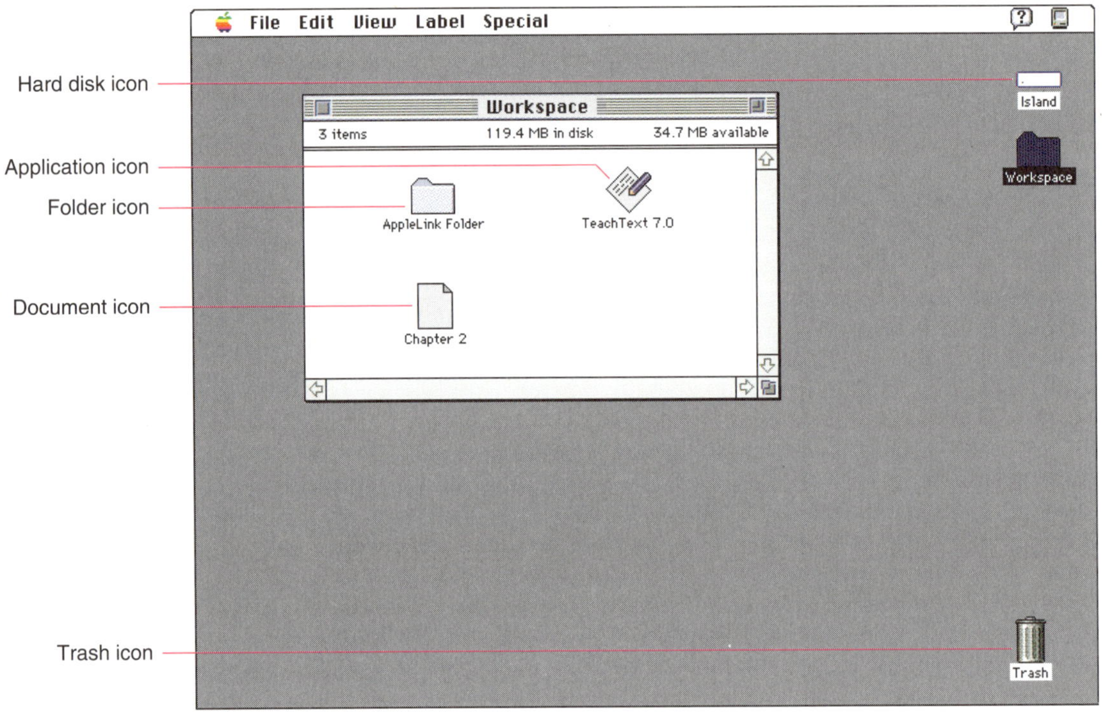

Why Icons Work

Icons work effectively in the Macintosh interface as representations of computer entities for several reasons. People often recognize pictures of things and understand them more quickly than they do verbal representations of the same things. For example, studies have shown that traffic signs that have symbols are more recognizable from a distance than signs that have only words. Figure 8-2 shows several examples of traffic symbols.

Figure 8-2 Examples of common traffic symbols

Symbols cross cultural and language barriers better than words do. Figure 8-3 shows examples of symbols that are used internationally. For example, at the Olympics pictures communicate ideas such as the locations of various events. People from around the globe must recognize the meanings of the signs in order to make their way to events, facilities, and services.

Figure 8-3 Examples of commonly-used international symbols

Symbols also take up less space than words that describe the same concept would. Imagine having to include the words written in many different languages on the signs. You can see that it's much easier in some cases to use graphics to represent concepts.

In the computer realm, it's generally easier to recognize symbols across systems than it is to remember keyboard commands. For example, a mailbox, even if it is of a different kind, is still recognizable as a mailbox. People identify a mailbox with sending and receiving communication. It's much harder for a user to remember that one system uses the command Control-M for mail, another system uses Control-P for post, and a third system uses Control-S for send.

Figure 8-4 shows two examples of mailbox icons and their equivalent keyboard commands.

Figure 8-4 Symbols are easier to understand than keyboard commands

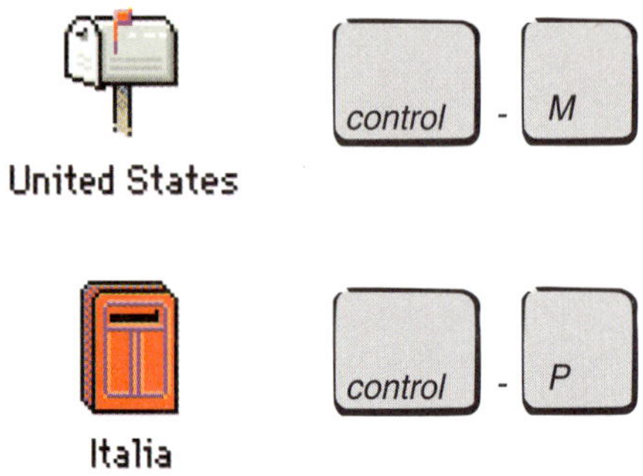

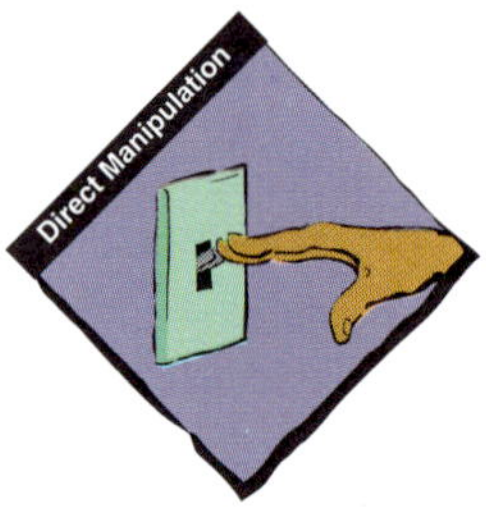

Icons provide direct access to items in the interface. People can see a folder, open it, and see its contents, or they can organize their desktop simply by grouping icons, rather than having to remember a lot of filenames and using lists to keep track of their files. Thus using icons contributes to the clarity and aesthetic integrity of the interface. Figure 8-5 shows a desktop with icon groupings.

Figure 8-5 Grouping icons on the desktop

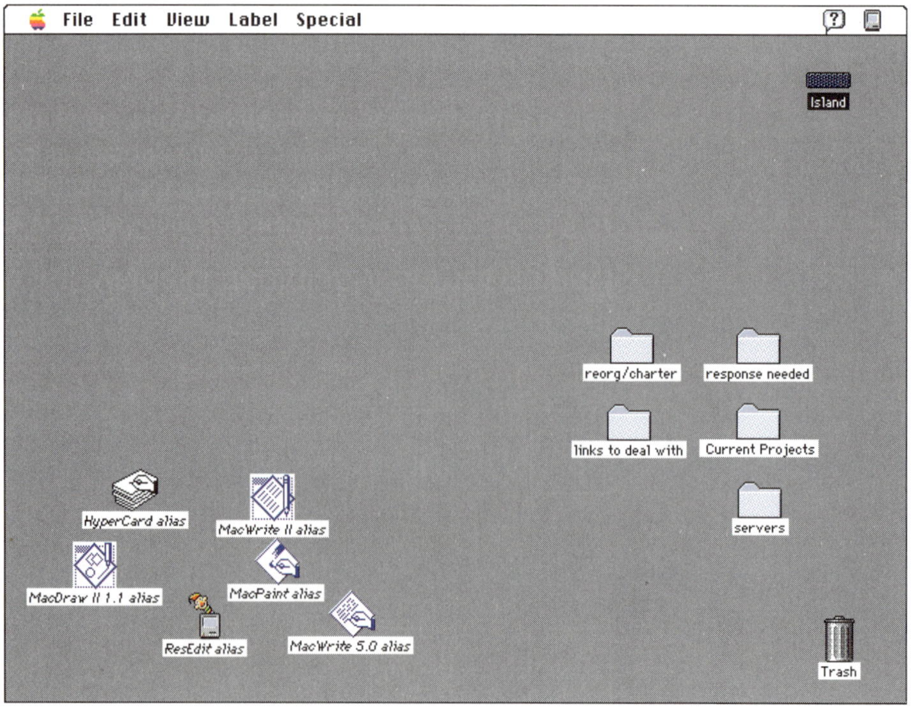

Limitations of Icons

Designing the right icon that conveys your message to most people can be difficult. Sometimes it's difficult because icons need a context to provide successful communication. For example, what does the drawing shown in Figure 8-6 mean? It's a circle that could represent a wide variety of objects in the real world. From this figure, it's not clear what the image represents.

Figure 8-6 A confusing image

This image could represent a circle tool, a degree symbol, a ball, or a planet. It could be as many round things as people could imagine. When it appears in context with another object, the meaning instantly becomes clear, as Figure 8-7 shows.

Figure 8-7 Context clarifies the image

You can clearly see that in this context the circle is a baseball. This picture communicates an idea in a simple, graphic format. By adding the baseball player to the circle image, the context clarifies the meaning of the image.

In general, you can represent most nouns (people, places, and things) quite simply and easily in an icon. For example, you can draw a small picture that looks like a file folder to be a folder icon. Actions are much harder to portray in icons. How would you represent a save operation with an icon? You can overcome this difficulty by representing an action with an icon in combination with text. In fact, icons with label text are always more effective than either text or icons in isolation. Figure 8-8 shows a dialog box that uses icons that change to reflect the choices the user makes. The icons and text together help the icons give the user an idea of what to expect.

Figure 8-8 Icons with label text

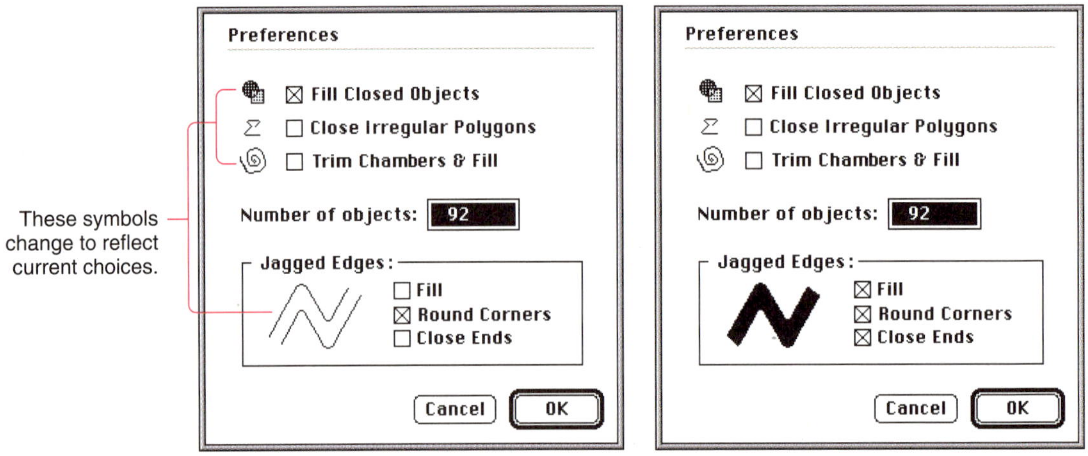

Sometimes another interface element is more appropriate than an icon that isn't clear. For example, you could use text for error messages in dialog boxes more effectively than trying to communicate the same concept with symbols. Sometimes text is the simplest way to convey a concept, depending on the specific interface situation.

Designing Effective Icons

This section presents some basic guidelines for designing effective icons. Remember that all your icon designs must work in the Macintosh context. The desktop interface is based on an office metaphor using a desktop as the primary workspace. You want to build on this basis and diverge from it as little as possible. You must also consider other important facets of the Macintosh interface described here when you're designing icons. For information on designing color icons, see Chapter 9, "Color," beginning on page 257.

Use Appropriate Metaphors

You need to choose the appropriate metaphor to design effective icons. Folders are the appropriate metaphor for a storage container for documents because people use folders to store pieces of paper. In contrast, most people probably wouldn't use a kitchen canister for storing documents. People do use canisters to store things, and the shape of a hard disk platter is round. But it would require a major leap of logic for people to associate a canister as a storage medium for something like paper. Figure 8-9 illustrates this point.

Figure 8-9 A logical and an illogical metaphor

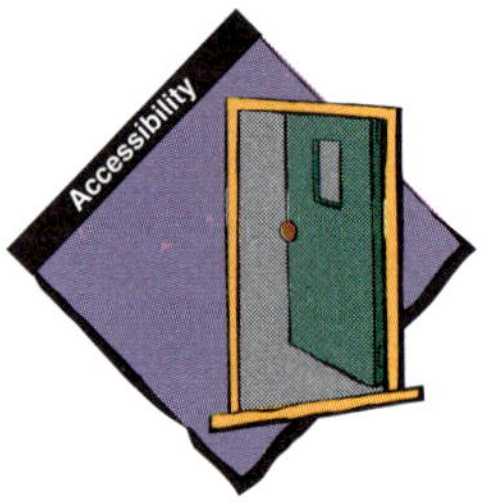

Think About Worldwide Compatibility

Your icon should be localizable for different regions around the world or should be designed with worldwide use in mind. For example, to localize an icon for receiving mail, you would substitute a post box for a mailbox in British system software. A worldwide icon is one that is understood universally. An example of an icon that is understood around the world is the document icon. Even though people in different locations around the world use different sizes of paper and different types of paper stock, they all still recognize the document icon as a representation of a document.

Figure 8-10 shows some examples of mailbox icons that have been localized for use in different countries.

Figure 8-10 Localized mailbox icons

United States Italia France Danmark

In general icons shouldn't be gratuitously cute. Humor typically doesn't translate well to other cultures or languages. Also, don't use inside jokes or pictures that represent code names for your icons. Although it might work to use such icons during your development process for product identification, be sure to remove them and replace them with appropriate icons *before* you ship. Symbols and colloquial language are usually culturally dependent, meaning that what one person relates to may have no meaning or may be an insult in another person's culture.

Avoid Text in Icons

Avoid using text in your icons whenever possible. Text in icons can be confusing, and it's not localizable to other regions, languages, or countries. It's appropriate to label icons to help the user recognize them and so that they can be read to a person with a visual disability. When you ship your product, every icon should have a name, but people can change the name of an icon at any time. Figure 8-11 shows an example of icons with text in them and icons that convey the idea much better without text.

Figure 8-11 Avoid text in icons

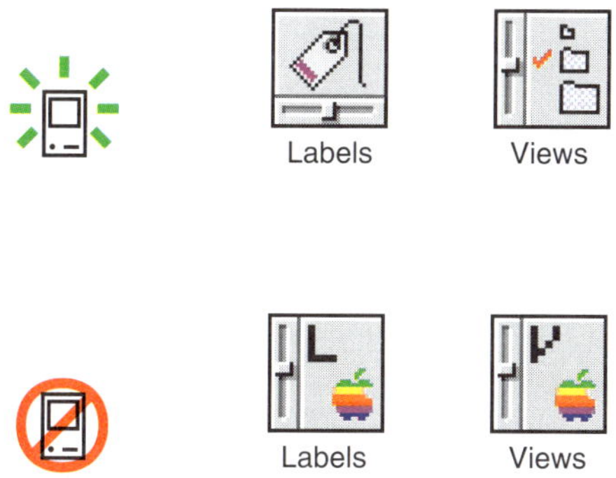

Design for the Macintosh Display

Your icons must look good at the current display resolution. You should use straight lines and 45-degree angles for the best appearance. Curves don't work well because they make the edges appear jagged. Figure 8-12 shows the jagged effects that curves and angles other than 45 degrees produce.

Figure 8-12 Certain shapes don't work well

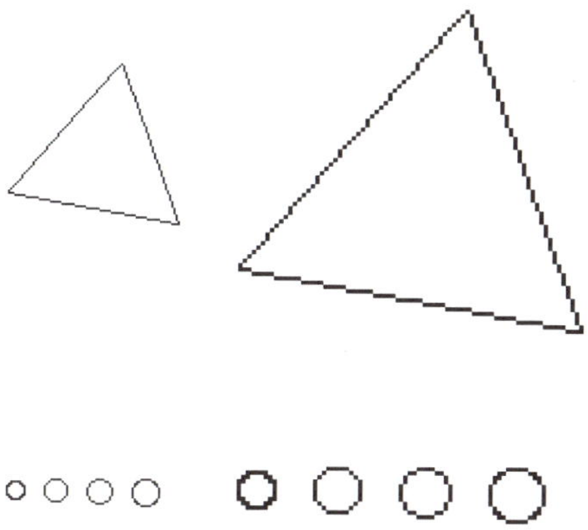

Three-dimensional effects in icons are difficult to achieve in the Macintosh interface because they require shading and more angled lines. A large percentage of users have black-and-white monitors and thus complex shading may not display very well on their screens. If you decide to attempt to incorporate three-dimensional effects in your icons, make sure that a professional visual designer works on the design to ensure aesthetic integrity and compatibility with the Macintosh interface appearance.

Use a Consistent Light Source

On the Macintosh screen the light source always comes from the upper-left corner of the screen. Therefore icons and other elements have drop shadows on the lower-right side. Use the light source consistently, so that shading is consistent throughout the interface. Figure 8-13 shows some desktop entities that have drop shadows consistent with a light source at the upper-left corner of the screen.

Figure 8-13 A consistent light source

Figure 8-14 shows some desktop images that have different light sources and inconsistent drop shadows.

Figure 8-14 Inconsistent light sources

Optimize for Your Target Display

You should optimize your design for the display on which it will most often be seen. For example, some games run on only 4-bit and black-and-white monitors. In this case, you should optimize your design by choosing colors from the 4-bit color palette, rather than starting with the 8-bit version and trying to scale down from there.

Maintain a Consistent Visual Appearance in an Icon Family

Maintain a close visual relationship between all members of an icon family. Color versions of icons should resemble the black-and-white versions. Users should be able to easily recognize standard interface elements and icons across all monitor types. Users can have several monitors connected to a computer and several computers on which they use your applications. Your application icon should look consistent when a user changes the bit depth of a monitor or moves your icon from a color monitor to a black-and-white monitor.

Design the large (32-by-32 pixel) icon first, and then adapt the design to the small icon. You can leave out inessential details in the small version of your icon, but it shouldn't look significantly different from the large version. Figure 8-15 shows how starting with the design of the large icon and adapting it for the small icon works better than starting with the design of the small icon.

Figure 8-15 Design the large icon first and base the small icon design on it

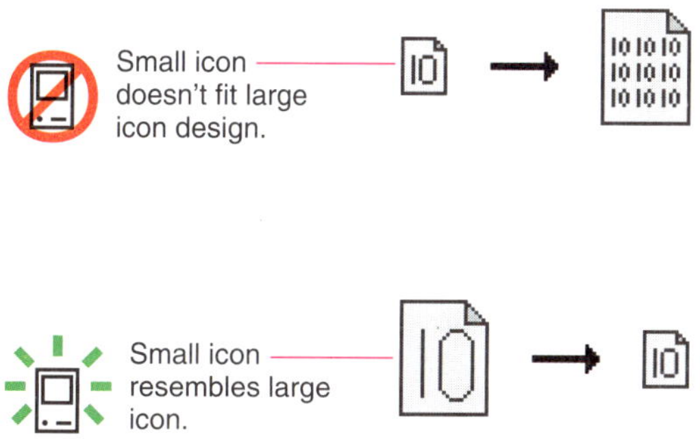

Use Icon Elements Consistently

Use icon elements consistently throughout your designs. If there is an existing shape for an icon element, don't change it. For example, don't invent new designs for entities that have a standard design in system-provided icons, such as folders and documents. For example, in Figure 8-16, the icon of the Macintosh computer is the same when it appears in the Finder, in the Application menu, and within the System Folder icon. Unless you are representing a different model of Macintosh computer, use the Macintosh Classic icon to represent the Macintosh computer. People often assume that different shapes have different meanings and may try to read meaning in where none is intended. Users can learn what icon elements represent when they are used consistently.

Figure 8-16 Consistent use of icon elements

The Finder Icon Family

For display in the Finder, for each icon you should provide an entire icon family, which consists of large (32-by-32 pixel) and small (16-by-16 pixel) icons, each available in three different versions of color: black and white (1-bit color), 4-bit color, and 8-bit color. You also need to provide an icon mask for each size of icon. The Finder uses the icon mask to cut out space on the desktop for the display of the icon. Figure 8-17 shows a family of icons for System 7.

Figure 8-17 An icon family

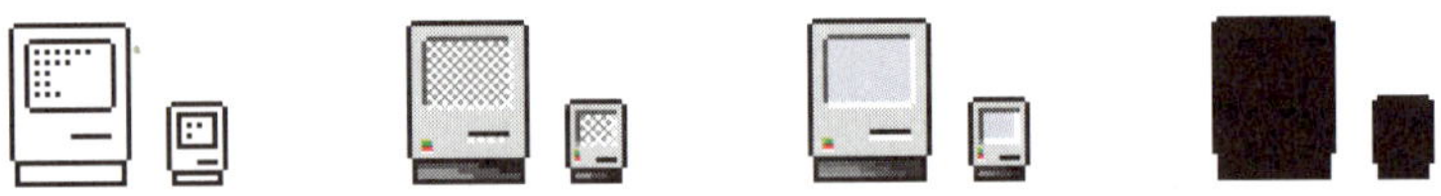

The 32-by-32 pixel icons appear on the desktop, and, if the user chooses "by Icon" from the View menu, these icons also appear in Finder windows. The 16-by-16 pixel icon appears as the Application menu's title when your application is active. It also appears next to your application's name in the Application menu and in Finder windows when the user chooses "by Small Icon" from the View menu. Figure 8-18 shows examples of two sizes of icons and some instances of where they appear in the Macintosh interface.

Figure 8-18 Different sizes of icons

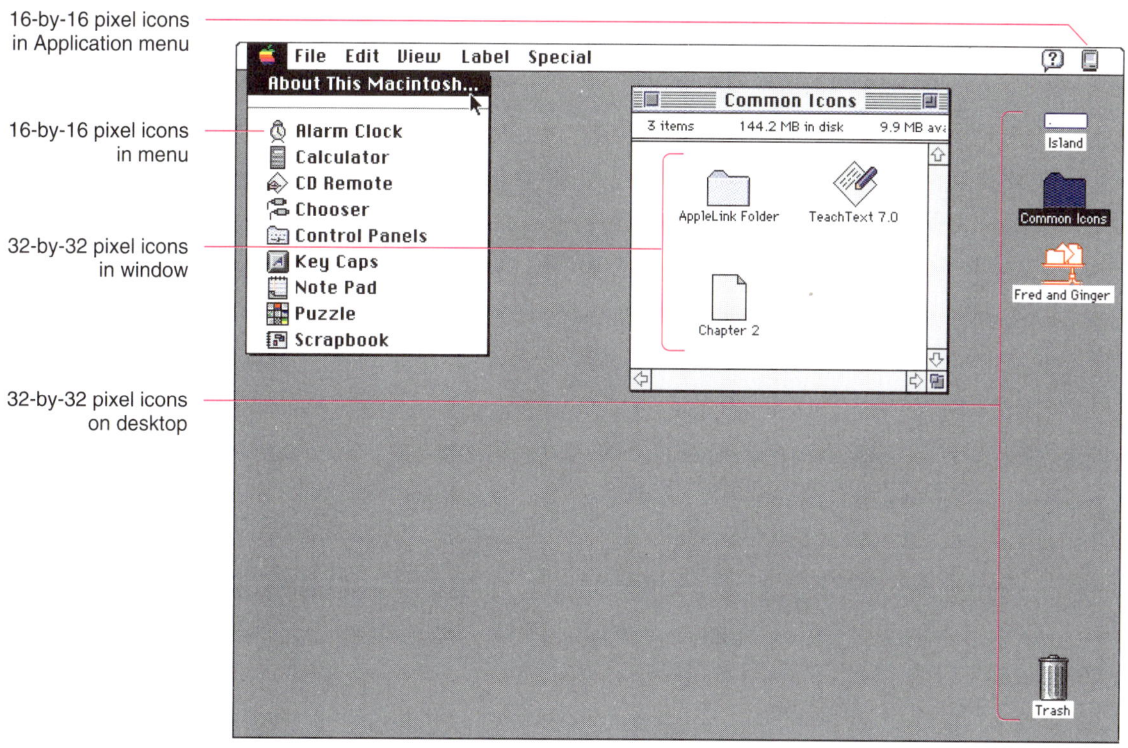

You can also provide icons for other entities that your application creates, such as customized document icons, preferences file icons, and stationery icons. The entire group of icons that you distribute with your product is known as a suite of icons. A suite of icons includes the families of icons for each type of icon that you distribute.

A monitor displays the highest-quality icon that its screen allows. Table 8-1 shows which icons are displayed on monitors with different display capabilities based on the icon families that you provide.

Table 8-1 Icon display on monitors of different bit depths

Icon set provided	What 8-bit color monitor displays	What 4-bit color monitor displays	What black-and-white monitor displays
8-bit, 4-bit, black-and-white icons	8-bit icon	4-bit icon	Black-and-white icon
8-bit, black-and-white icons	8-bit icon	Black-and-white icon	Black-and-white icon
4-bit, black-and-white icons	4-bit icon	4-bit icon	Black-and-white icon
Black-and-white icon	Black-and-white icon	Black-and-white icon	Black-and-white icon

See the chapter "Finder Interface" in *Inside Macintosh: Macintosh Toolbox Essentials* for information about the icons you provide and how to create a bundle resource for your application.

An Icon Design Process

This section presents an icon design process used at Apple. Of course, there are many ways to complete a task, and you may work in a way that doesn't lend itself to using this process. However, you should read this section to find out important principles that contribute to successful and effective icons.

You can't design one icon in your icon family in isolation. All the icons in a family—large, small, and different color depths—are incarnations of the same icon, so the basic design must work for all of them. Be flexible in adapting your design to all bit depths and sizes. Icon design is an iterative process. During the design process, you may need to redesign one version of an icon when you find it doesn't translate well to another version.

If an icon represents hardware that users are familiar with, such as a printer or a disk drive, the icon should resemble the hardware as closely as possible. If the icon represents a desktop entity, such as a document or a folder, it should resemble its physical world counterpart. If you need to design an icon for a more conceptual entity, such as a network or some kind of memory, you can use one of the following approaches. Making the icon representative of the function of the software is a good approach. If the function is complex and hard for novice users to understand, think about how you could explain the idea to someone who doesn't use a computer and try to generate some images that way. Often the terms you use and the analogies you come up with to explain the concept can provide clues for visual images.

You can also make an icon representative of a product name. This may work for your product in one location, but remember that some product names, and thus product icons, are often not localizable. For example, in the United States, an icon for extensions could have something to do with an extension cord. In other languages, the word used for extension cords may have nothing to do with extensions, and therefore an icon based on the word *extension cord* would be meaningless. Another drawback to this approach is that product names are often not finalized until late in the development process, so you might not have much time in which to design an icon based on the final product name.

A final approach to designing conceptual icons is making the icon look like the window that results from opening the icon. For example, if a window that appears when the icon is opened is very distinct in appearance from other windows, you can make an icon look like that window. You need to be very careful that all your icons do not look like miniature windows.

It is often easiest to create icons that represent objects (nouns) rather than actions (verbs). For example, the function of deleting a document is represented by a trash can (an object) rather than by some image of the action of deleting. Thinking of an object that is representative of the function of your icon is the key to good conceptual design. Remember that for every image you generate, you need to consider the advantages and disadvantages of the idea in regard to your audience before deciding on the final design.

Here's an outline of the suggested steps in an icon design process. The sections that follow go into the details of some icon design guidelines.

1. Start by designing the black-and-white version of the large (32-by-32 pixel) icon. Follow the guidelines given in the next section, "Black-and-White Icons."
2. Colorize the black-and-white version of your icon in 8-bit color. Use colors from the Apple icon colors palette (see the section "The Apple Icon Color Set" on page 240). For more information about creating color versions of black-and-white icons, see "Design for Black and White First" on page 263 in Chapter 9, "Color."
3. Translate the 8-bit version of your icon into 4-bit color. If you can't find appropriate colors in the 4-bit palette, try going back to step 2 and swap colors in the 8-bit version. You can use a dithered pattern of two colors to create the illusion of a new color for the 4-bit icon.
4. Create the mask.
5. Create matching small versions (16-by-16 pixel) of the black-and-white, 8-bit, and 4-bit icons.
6. Look at the icon family on different desktop backgrounds and with several effects such as selection and labeling to make sure that the icons look good.
7. Do some usability testing to make sure that your target audience understands your icons, doesn't confuse them with other icons, and identifies them as a family of icons.

ResEdit is a useful tool for accomplishing steps 3, 4, and 6.

Black-and-White Icons

You should begin by designing a black-and-white icon. In general, you should use an outline of one black pixel to create the icon border. Use a minimal number of black pixels in the icon so that the icon's appearance is noticeably different when selected. The Finder automatically inverts the black pixels and the white pixels when the user selects the icon to create the selected appearance. Figure 8-19 shows an example of a well-designed icon that changes significantly when selected.

Figure 8-19 A well-designed icon and its selected version

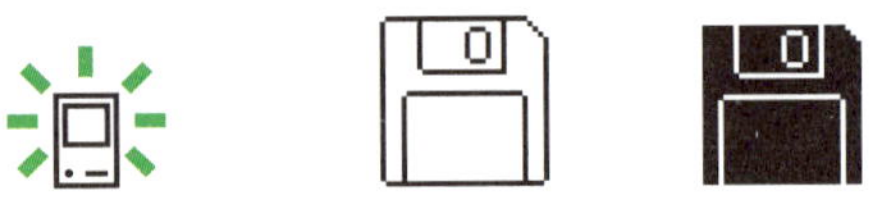

If you use too much black or 50 percent gray in your icon, the icon doesn't appear significantly different when the pixels are reversed for selection. Figure 8-20 shows an example of an icon with too much black and 50 percent gray.

Figure 8-20 A poorly designed icon and its selected version

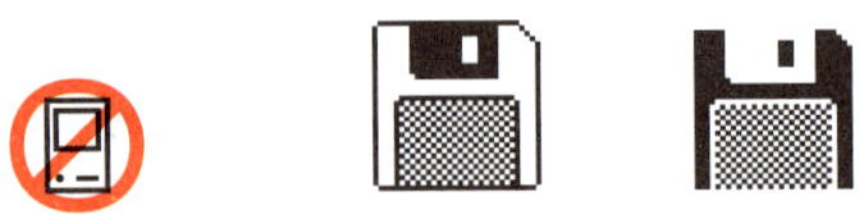

Color Icons

Macintosh system software ships with full-color icons that appear on color monitors. Your application can also provide color icons.

Don't design a color icon that's substantially different from your black-and-white icon. When you add color to an icon, it's best to leave the one-pixel black outline and other black lines that form the icon, and fill the icon in with color. Coloring or graying the icon's outline makes the icon appear less distinct on the desktop. Remember that the user can change the background color of the desktop as well as its pattern, so your icon may not be displayed against the background on which you designed it. If you use ResEdit version 2.1 or later to create your icons, it provides a way to look at your icon against different backgrounds to see whether your design is effective in various environments such as black-and-white displays or color displays of different bit depths. Figure 8-21 shows how icons with a black border look on a gray background.

Figure 8-21 Icons with a black outline

Figure 8-22 demonstrates how an icon appears less distinct from its background without the strong black border.

Figure 8-22 Icons without a black outline

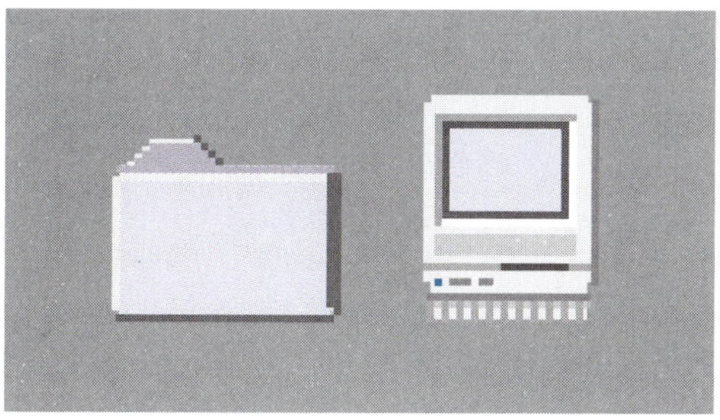

Icon Colors

This section describes the colors and color techniques that you should use when you design your color icons.

The Apple Icon Color Set

Figure 8-23 shows a palette of the standard 256 colors with a mark on each of the 34 colors used for icon design in system software. If you use ResEdit version 2.1 or later to design and create your icons, the Finder icon family editor provides easy access to these colors. Choose Apple Icon Colors from the Color menu. This command sets the palette in the editor (which is similar to the palette in most graphics applications) to contain the 34 colors used for Finder icons. See *ResEdit Reference* for information on using ResEdit.

Figure 8-23 Standard 256-color palette with icon colors marked

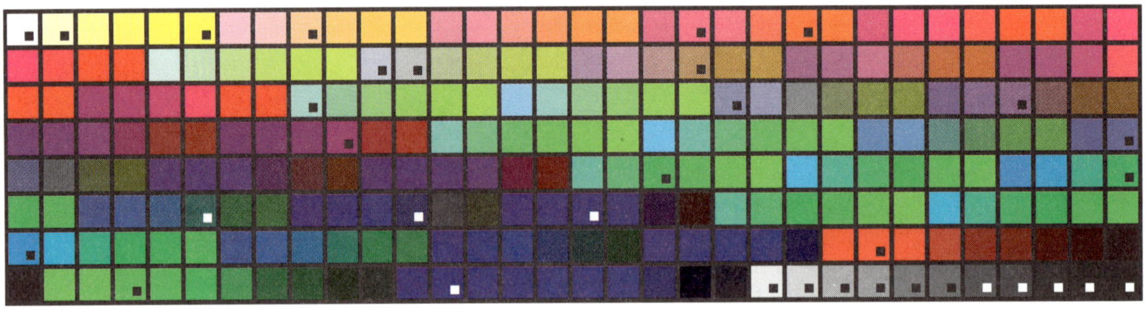

This entire set of 34 colors was chosen to be subtle. Subdued colors avoid a "circus" effect on the screen. If you use too many of the same types of colors, people can't discern what is important as easily. Ramps of color based on the initial colors chosen were created to provide shading and blending capabilities. Some light colors were included in the set to be used for large areas. The colors from the Apple logo were included because those colors have a strong Apple identification. The Apple logo colors are very bright and should be used sparingly. The total set of colors provides maximum flexibility in design. You can combine these colors in a dithered pattern to provide additional color effects. Figure 8-24 shows an example of creating a dithered color to use in your icons.

Figure 8-24 An example of dithered color in an icon

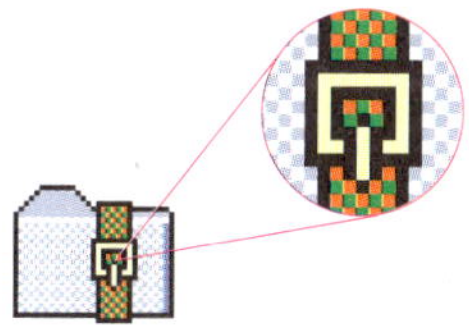

The icon colors were chosen for icon design in system software. It was necessary to limit the number of colors in the set to create consistency across all Apple icons. There are at least 120 system icons. If any number of the 256 system palette colors were used in each icon, the total effect would be a disparate appearance rather than a coherent look to all system icons. Using only 34 colors makes the system icons look like they belong together. In a design scheme that is so large, fewer colors look better.

Degradation of the Color Set Across Monitors

If the default color table colors aren't available, the system software gracefully degrades to black and white. First the operating system tries to match 8-bit colors. If it can't successfully match the colors you specify with those in the system palette, then it displays the 4-bit icon that you supply. If the operating system can't find or match the 4-bit colors, then it displays the icon in black and white. The system software won't substitute colors that aren't visually close to colors that you assigned. If you choose colors other than the 34 marked in Figure 8-23, use them for detail and not for essential parts of your windows or icons.

Selection Mechanism for Color Icons

When a color icon is selected, the color decreases in brightness. This means that the colors appear darker when selected. On a color monitor, a black-and-white icon turns gray when selected. On a black-and-white monitor, a black-and-white icon uses reverse video to show selection. To make selected items appear distinct from unselected ones, use light colors for large areas. Note that only the 34 colors shown in Figure 8-23 get darkened when a color icon is selected. This means that if you use colors other than those 34 colors in large amounts in an icon, that icon will not get darkened and therefore will not look selected.

Figure 8-25 shows a set of control panel icons as they appear on the desktop and the same icons in their selected states.

Figure 8-25 Color icons and their selected states

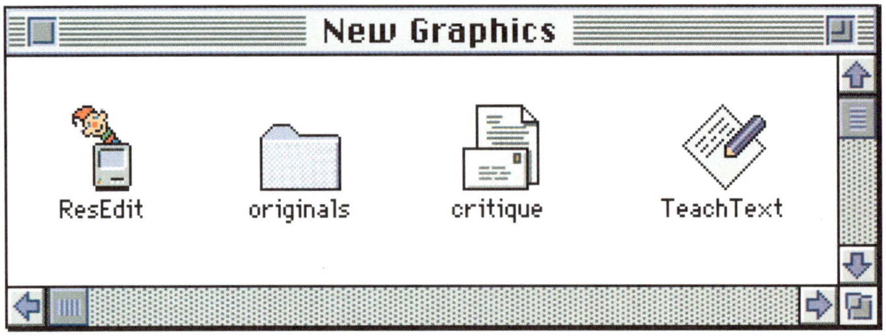

Color icons

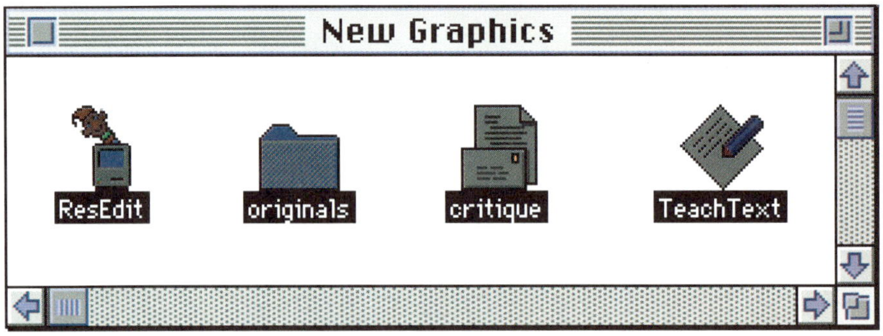

Selected color icons

Color Labeling Mechanism for Color Icons

The labeling mechanism tints color icons toward the label color chosen by the user from the Label menu. Figure 8-26 shows some icons and the same icons in their labeled state. To provide system support for this technique, it was necessary to limit the number of colors used in icons. Using the 34 identified icon colors does not guarantee that labeled icons will look good, only that they will actually look labeled. As with icons that are selected, the tinting applies to only the 34 colors. As a result, if you use colors other than the 34 colors in your icon, the icon will not look labeled when a label color is applied.

Figure 8-26 Color icons and their color-labeled states

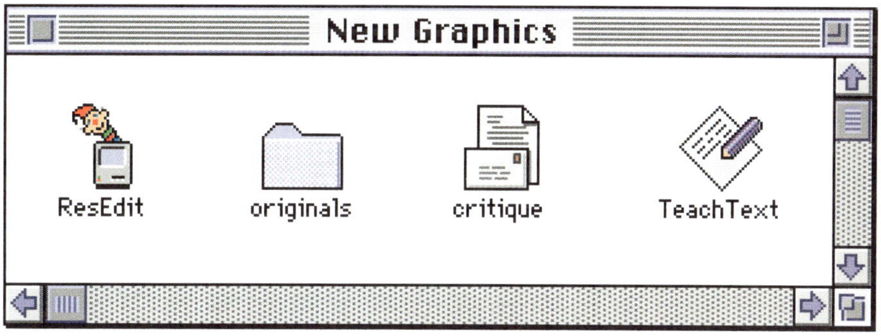

Color icons

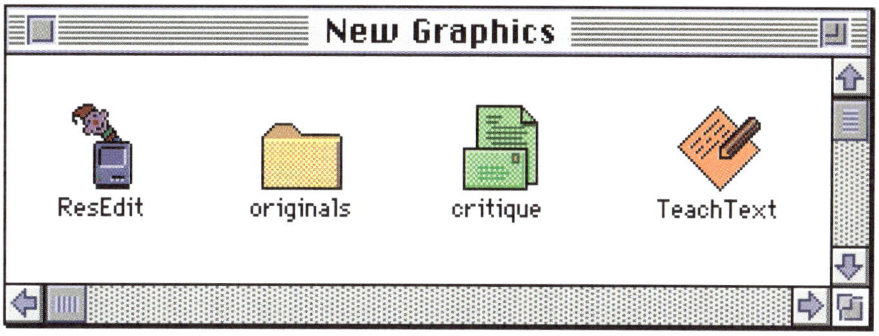

Labeled color icons

Anti-Aliasing

A technique for enhancing the appearance of your icons is to smooth angular or curved lines by coloring pixels on jagged edges. This technique is called *anti-aliasing*. Change the pixel color where you can see a visual break in the outline of a black-and-white icon. Figure 8-27 shows an icon before anti-aliasing, after anti-aliasing, and then in the context of a control panel icon.

Figure 8-27 Correct anti-aliasing

Globe without anti-aliasing   Anti-aliased globe alone   Globe inside control panel

In anti-aliasing, you typically add pixels to an outline shape. Since the Finder uses only one mask for each size in the icon family, make sure that all your icons have the same outline shape. That is, when you anti-alias icons, don't add pixels or shadows to the outline shape of color icons. Figure 8-27 shows how anti-aliasing works well within an icon. The Finder uses the icon mask for alignment and transformation effects, so make sure that the mask and all your icons are appropriate for each other.

If you add too much anti-aliasing to the icons, they appear smooth, but also more fuzzy. While some people prefer this appearance, the Macintosh desktop appearance relies on crisp-looking icons. Gray outlines create a fuzzy image on the desktop. If people perceive something fuzzy on their screen, they may assume that something is wrong with their eyes or their display. Avoid creating this appearance if at all possible.

Small Icons

If you do not provide a 16-by-16 pixel icon, the Finder reduces the 32-by-32 pixel icon based on an algorithmic formula. The algorithm simply shrinks the icon and typically creates black areas, creating less pleasing visual results. If you provide a 16-by-16 pixel icon, however, you can optimize its design by removing pixels when necessary.

When you design a small version of your 32-by-32 pixel icon, preserve as many graphical elements of the icon as possible. In essence you want to provide the same icon in a smaller size. Typically you have to remove some pixels to reduce the visual clutter. However, don't eliminate significant elements, or the smaller version of the icon may look different from the larger version. Figure 8-28 shows icons that a designer carefully scaled and tuned to preserve key elements of the icons' designs.

Figure 8-28 Consistently designed small icons

Small icons preserve elements of large icons.

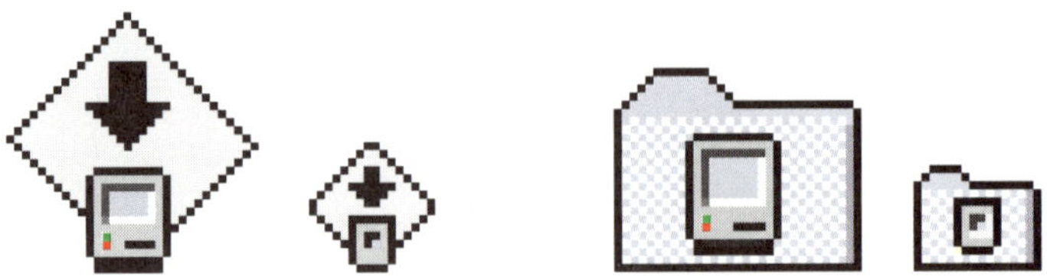

After you've created the small icon, verify the accuracy and clarity of the small icon by trying to design a large icon based on its design. If the large icon you end up with based on your small icon is different from the original large icon, something is not working about your small icon. In this case, you should consider redesigning the small icon, making sure to incorporate the key graphical elements of the original large icon.

In Figure 8-29 the small icons don't match their corresponding 32-by-32 pixel versions. If you have difficulty distinguishing the consistencies or inconsistencies, it's a good idea to consult with someone who specializes in graphic design to design or review your icons.

Figure 8-29 Inconsistently designed small icons

Small icons look different from large icons.

Default and Custom Icons

You can provide custom icons for your application and its associated documents and files. If you don't provide custom icons, the Finder displays default icons in most cases. There are no default icons provided for preferences files or control panels, so you must provide icons for these.

Since there are so many icons that users see and deal with, it's important to create consistent sets of icons. Users should be able to easily identify and locate the icons they're looking for, which is more possible if related icons look related. Each icon family consists of the same icon in two sizes and three bit depths. Each type of icon family needs to look like a class of objects. For example, all document-related icons should look like documents. The entire group of icons that belongs to your product, called a suite of icons, should have a common appearance that identifies all the icons as being related to your product.

Application Icons

Because applications are usually used to create documents, the application icon uses a tilted document page to represent the documents the application creates. In this way, a relationship is established. The hand is also part of the default application icon. Figure 8-30 shows the default icon that appears in the Finder if you don't supply a custom icon for your application.

Figure 8-30 Default application icons

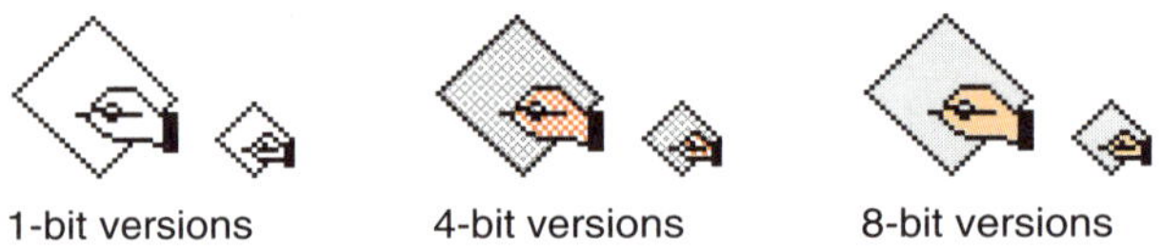

Although it's best to be consistent, if you must design an icon different from the default shape, be sure to use one of the standard application icon elements, either the page or the hand, in your icon. Figure 8-31 shows two custom application icons that use both the tilted document page and the hand elements.

Figure 8-31 Custom application icons

You can customize the application icon by adding graphics to it. Use graphics that convey meaning about what your application does. If you can't think of elements that represent the overall function of your application, it's OK to use your company identification. However, using your logo is limiting because your company will probably make more than one application in its lifetime and you will want a distinct icon for each one.

Don't design an application icon that is completely unrelated to the basic shape of the application icon. People won't get the benefit of visual clues that help them identify your icon as an application. Figure 8-32 shows two examples of application icons that totally violate the guidelines presented here. They don't give the user much information about what they do, although they might be fun to look at.

Figure 8-32 Examples of bad application icons

John's Accounting FlowerWorks

Document Icons

Documents are the files in which users store the content they create in an application. The document icon uses the outline of a page with a turned-down upper-right corner. This shape evokes the concept that a document is like a piece of paper, a typical storage medium for information in an office. Figure 8-33 shows the default document icons that appear in the Finder if you don't supply a custom icon for your documents.

Figure 8-33 Default document icons

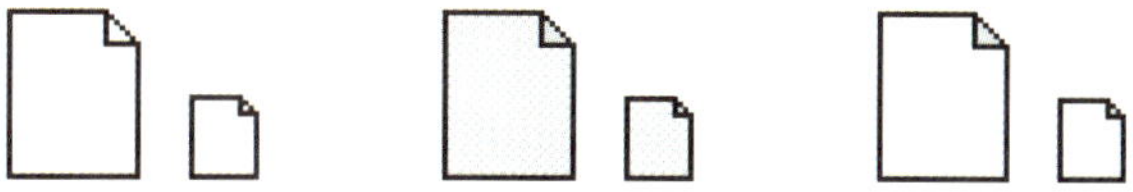

1-bit versions 4-bit versions 8-bit versions

You can customize this document page icon so that it relates to your application icon by adding the same graphics you use in your application icon. Or you can add graphics to the document page that indicate the content that your documents hold. Figure 8-34 shows the relationship between an application icon and its document icon.

Figure 8-34 Application icon and document icon with the same graphic element

As with the application icon, it's OK to use your company identification in a document icon. Be sure not to change the shape of the document icon unless the document that your application creates is fundamentally different from most documents. One example of a document that *is* fundamentally different is a stack. The stack icon is a metaphor that represents a stack of cards, similar to a stack of index cards that you might use to store notes or related information.

Figure 8-35 shows some examples of custom document icons that show the range of acceptable and unacceptable customizations.

Figure 8-35 Acceptable and unacceptable custom document icons

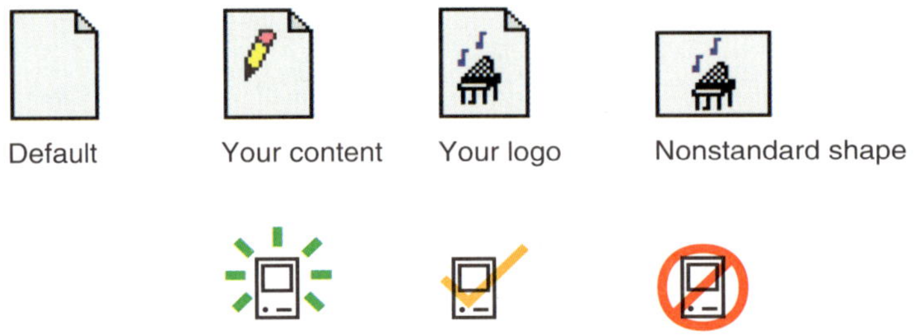

Several conventions exist for conveying document types. You can use these visual clues or others that have meaning for your documents' contents. Documents that are text-only or primarily text use broken lines on the document page. Page layout documents typically include a filled rectangle and broken lines to indicate that the document contains text and pictures. Graphics document icons use geometric shapes or other graphics or graphics tools such as paintbrushes. The standard representation for a file of type 'PICT' is a circle, a square, and a triangle. Use this symbol to indicate files of this type. Figure 8-36 shows document icons with all of these symbols.

Figure 8-36 Document icons with standard symbols

Stationery Pad Icons

A stationery pad is a template with standard contents that the user can create from a document. Each time a user opens a stationery pad, a new document is opened with the same contents as the stationery pad. The stationery pad icon uses the outline of a page, similar to the document icon, but with the lower-right corner turned up and a second page visible in the background.

Figure 8-37 shows the default icons that appear in the Finder if you don't supply a custom icon for stationery pads.

Figure 8-37 Default stationery pad icons

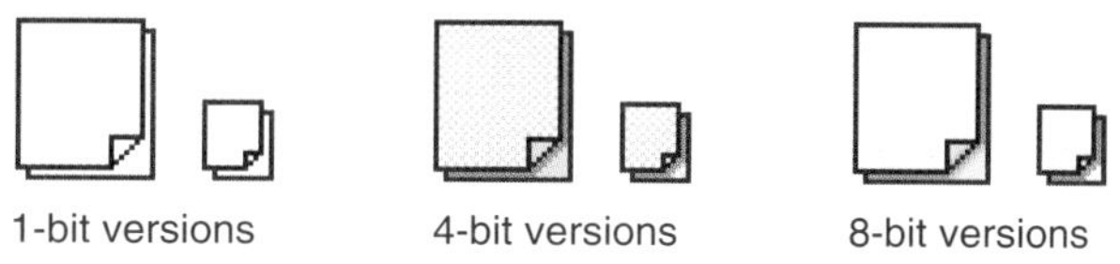

You can customize a stationery pad icon by adding graphic elements to the stationery document page. Your stationery pad icon should look just like your document icon except that it has the second page in the background and the lower-right corner of the first page turned up.

Query Document Icons

Query documents are documents that contain instructions used to get data out of or into a database. The query document icon uses the outline of a document page with a database element attached to its lower right. Figure 8-38 shows the default icons that appear in the Finder if you don't supply a custom icon.

Figure 8-38 Default query document icons

You can customize a query document icon by adding graphics to the document page. Be sure to maintain the outline of the icon and the volume symbol that represents the database. See *Inside Macintosh: Interapplication Communication* for information on using the Data Access Manager.

Edition Icons

An edition is a file that is created when a user chooses Create Publisher from the Edit menu. The edition icon has a rectangular outline in a horizontal orientation. Figure 8-39 shows the default icons that appear in the Finder if you don't supply a custom icon for editions.

Figure 8-39 Default edition icons

You can customize an edition icon by putting a different graphic inside the rectangle. Maintain the horizontal orientation and the double-dotted line of the icon that identify it as an edition icon. See *Inside Macintosh: Interapplication Communication* for information on the Edition Manager human interface and implementing the Edition Manager.

Preferences Icons

Many applications have preferences files that store information about a user's preferences. If you supply this file or create one after the user stores settings for your application or documents, you'll need to create an icon for it. Preferences files icons often contain document icons with radio buttons, as shown in Figure 8-40.

Figure 8-40 Preferences file icons

Extension Icons

Extensions are software that add a feature or capability to the operating system. An extension icon looks like a puzzle piece. Figure 8-41 shows the default icons that appear in the Finder if you don't supply a custom icon for your extension.

Figure 8-41 Default extension icons

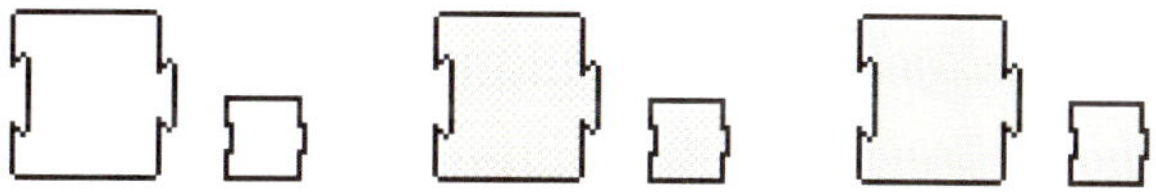

1-bit versions 4-bit versions 8-bit versions

You can customize an extension icon by adding a graphic to the puzzle piece. You can display the puzzle piece in a horizontal or a vertical orientation with the protruding part facing any direction.

One exception to the standard form for extension icons are icons that represent Chooser extensions. Chooser extensions appear in the Chooser and provide people with a visual idea of the service they are choosing. Chooser extension icons should look as much as possible like the devices they represent. Some examples of Chooser icons are shown in Figure 8-42.

Figure 8-42 Examples of Chooser icons

Personal LaserWriter LaserWriter ImageWriter StyleWriter

Control Panel Icons

The control panel icon is a square with a slider on it to identify it. The slider also appears on the Control Panels folder. You can add a graphic to the square to customize the icon. You can display the slider in either a horizontal or a vertical orientation. Figure 8-43 shows the icon family for the Color control panel.

Figure 8-43 Icons for the Color control panel

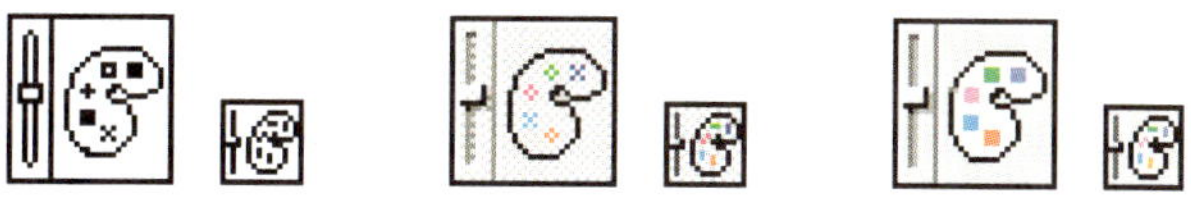

1-bit versions 4-bit versions 8-bit versions

Movable Resource Icons

The Finder displays default icons for fonts, keyboard layouts, and sounds, also known as movable resources. The icon looks like a document icon reversed in orientation. The user installs these resources by dragging the icon to the System Folder icon. The user can remove a movable resource by opening the System file icon (or Font Folder icon) in the System Folder and dragging its icon out of the System file. TrueType fonts have a character in three sizes on the icon, whereas bitmapped fonts only have a single character. When a user opens a font icon, the Finder displays a window with a sample of the font in it. Figure 8-44 shows some font icons.

Figure 8-44 Font icons

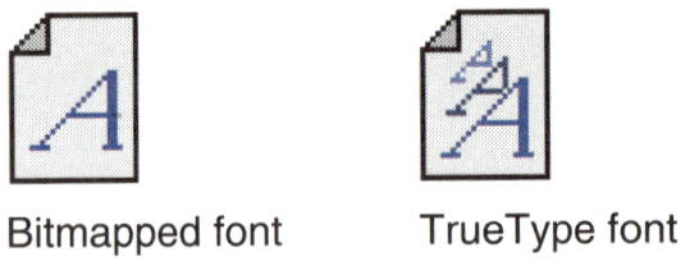

Sound icons have a speaker symbol on them, as shown in Figure 8-45. When a user opens the sound icon, the sound plays.

Figure 8-45 A sound icon

Keyboard Icons

A keyboard icon represents a localized keyboard layout or input method. If you develop keyboards, input methods, script systems, or keyboard resources, you need to provide icons. (Keyboard icons appear in the Keyboard menu and in the Keyboard control panel.) You need to create a 16-by-16 pixel icon in 1-bit and 4-bit color. If you don't create a keyboard icon, then the system provides a default icon. Figure 8-46 shows the default keyboard layout icon and the default input method icon.

Figure 8-46 The default keyboard layout and input method icons

Keyboard icons are a special case of icons. Since they represent a specific type of software they follow design rules different from those for other icons users see on the desktop. The guidelines presented in this section apply only to keyboard icons.

For a keyboard icon, use a solid symbol to represent a keyboard layout for a region that is larger or smaller than an area that can be represented by the flag of a country or province. For example, a diamond represents the Roman Script System, which is used in the United States, Central America, South America, Australia, New Zealand, and most of Europe. Use the flag of a country or province if the keyboard layout is used primarily in that area. For example, the Union Jack represents the keyboard layout localized for use in the United Kingdom. Be sure to use the colors that appear on the nation's flag. Figure 8-47 shows some keyboard icons for script systems and localized keyboard layouts.

Figure 8-47 Examples of keyboard icons

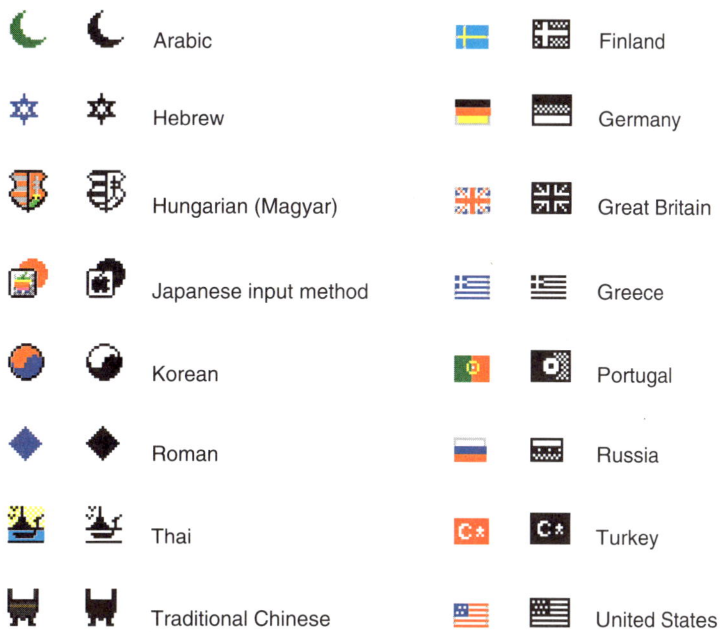

You can also add a visual indicator to the keyboard icon to show some modification. Use a superscript diamond to indicate a QWERTY transliteration, which is a mapping of sounds from a language to the Roman keyboard layout. Figure 8-48 shows some flag symbols with additional indicators.

Figure 8-48 Examples of modification indicators on keyboard icons

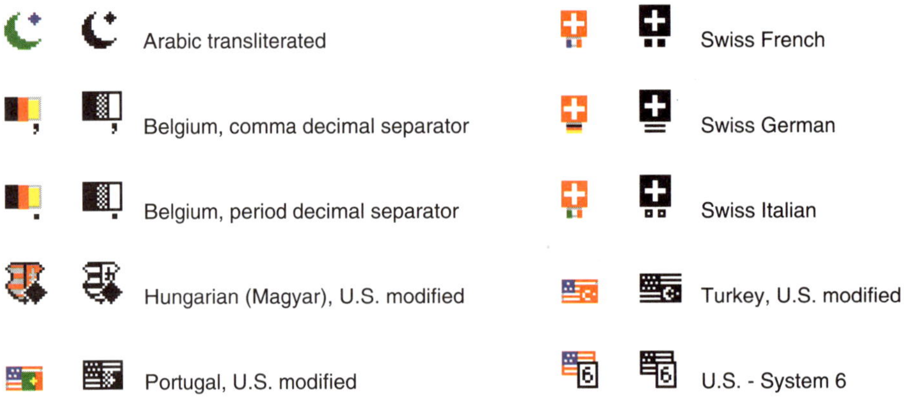

When you design the black-and-white version of a flag icon, use black and a 50 percent gray pattern. These choices provide the best contrast and legibility. To avoid confusion between flags of similar design, use the pattern substitutions for colors shown in Table 8-2.

Table 8-2 Pattern substitutions for colors in keyboard icons

Color	Pattern
Black or blue	Black
Red	50 percent gray
Light blue	25 percent gray
Green	Diagonal stripes
White or yellow	White

Figure 8-49 shows some keyboard icons that use the correct pattern substitutions.

Figure 8-49 Enlarged keyboard icons with correct color substitutions

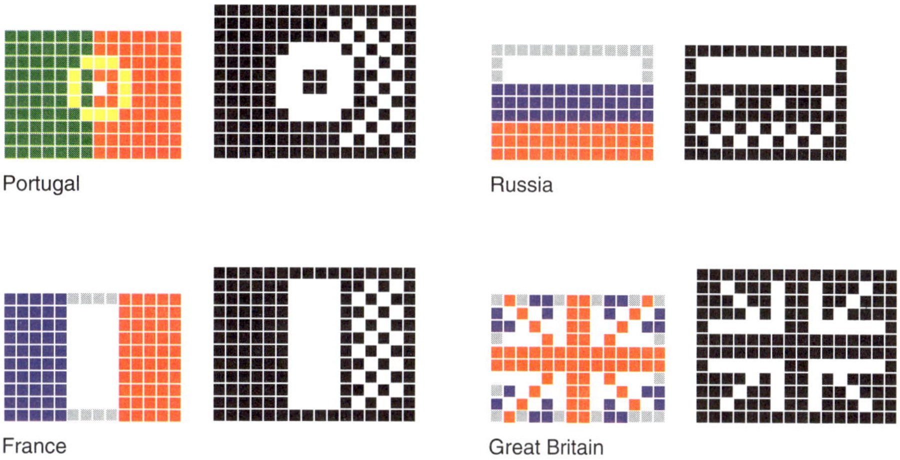

See the section "The Keyboard Menu" beginning on page 125 in Chapter 4, "Menus," and *Inside Macintosh: Text* for information on the Keyboard menu. See the chapter "Finder Interface" in *Inside Macintosh: Macintosh Toolbox Essentials* for more information about displaying custom icons. That chapter also provides information on how to use the bundle resource to associate these icons with your application.

CHAPTER 9

Color

This chapter presents information on how to use color in the Macintosh interface as well as in applications that deal with color. Apple's goal in adding color to the interface is to enhance meaning, not just to color things to improve aesthetics. If used carefully, color can be a valuable additional channel of information to the user.

Ultimately, color is the domain of the user. The user should control color in most cases, modifying or removing any color scheme that your application uses as a default. To implement color successfully in an application, you need to understand some of the complex issues surrounding its use. There are many books available on the use of color. This chapter covers the basic issues of color that relate to its implementation in the Macintosh interface and applications.

Color Design of Standard Interface Elements

This section describes the use of color with standard Macintosh interface elements and provides recommendations about how your application can fit in with the color scheme of system software.

The appearance of the Macintosh interface elements is enhanced by the color capabilities of the Macintosh. Color distinguishes the active window from other windows and enhances user controls on the window frame. Color in the interface should help users focus their attention on their work not draw attention to the interface itself. In general, the use of color makes the interface more visually pleasing.

Windows and Dialog Boxes

The windows and dialog boxes in System 7 are designed for aesthetic consistency across all monitors from black-and-white displays to 8-bit color displays. For display on color monitors, color and shades of gray have been added to the frames of windows and to user controls. The window background remains white on all systems. This updated design takes advantage of the color capabilities of the Macintosh but maintains the consistency of the Macintosh interface. On color screens, the racing stripes in the title bar and the scroll bars are gray. The user controls—close box, size box, zoom box, and scroll box—are colored to make them more apparent. The borders of inactive windows are gray and recede into the background so that the active window's black frame emphasizes its position in front of the other windows. Figure 9-1 shows a colorized window.

Figure 9-1 A colorized window

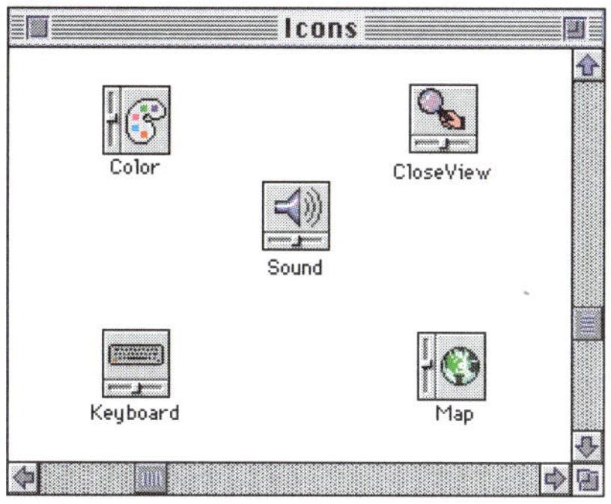

Figure 9-2 shows a dialog box with a colored frame, but black radio buttons and text.

Figure 9-2 A colorized movable modal dialog box

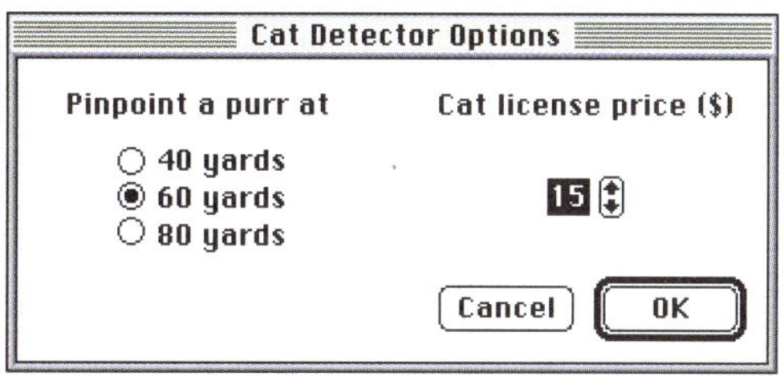

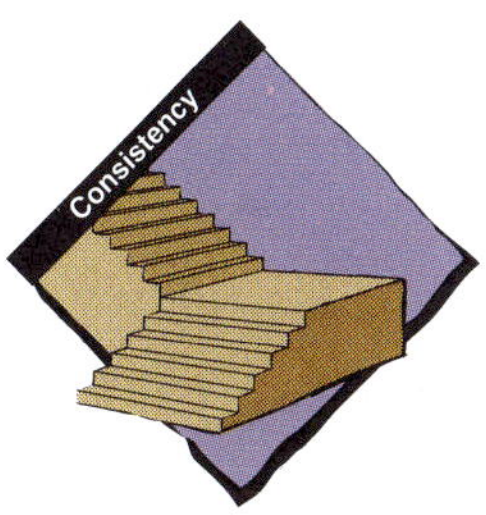

The standard window definition functions display color windows and dialog boxes. Some control definition functions display in color the window's scroll bars, scroll arrows, scroll box, close box, size box, and zoom box. If you use the standard window definition functions and standard control definition functions, your application's windows will match the appearance of standard windows. If you create your own windows, be compatible with the desktop appearance by using the standard window color table and the guidelines described in this section. Be aware that users can change the colors of windows and dialog boxes by using the Color control panel. If you use the default window color table, you can be sure that the colors you use are consistent with any color that the user has access to with the Color control panel. You can use the Palette Manager to associate a color palette with a window definition. For more information, see the discussion of the Palette Manager in *Inside Macintosh*.

Menus

In general, the only use of color in your application's menus should be in menus used to choose colors. However, color could also be useful for directing the user's choices in training and tutorial materials: for example, one color could lead a user through a lesson.

For display on color screens, use true gray wherever you previously used a 50 percent gray pattern. Use true gray in menus for the dotted separator lines between groups of items and for dimmed menu items.

Pointers

The pointer should always be visible. When it's being used for selecting and choosing, it should remain black. A color pointer might not be visible over different colored backgrounds and doesn't give the user any extra information. However, when the user is drawing or typing in color, the drawing or text-insertion pointer can appear in the color that is being used. Except for multicolored paintbrush pointers, the pointer shouldn't contain more than one color at once since it's hard for the eye to distinguish small areas of color. Whether the point is black or colored, make sure the point can be seen when it's placed on a background of a similar color. This can be accomplished by changing the color of the pointer (to contrast it with the background) or by outlining the pointer with a contrasting color (one pixel wide).

Highlighting and Selection

Most things—menu items, icons, buttons, and so forth—should be highlighted when selected by reversing the background with the bits. On black-and-white screens, highlighting means turning white to black and black to white. For example, if the item is black on a white background, it should be highlighted to white on a black background. On color screens, highlighting works differently; colors are darkened when selected, not reversed. For example, if an item appears green on the screen, the green color becomes darker when the item is selected. If the user can set different colors of text, Color TextEdit allows the user to set the highlighting bar color to something other than black to highlight the text better. The user can change the setting; your application should never change it. The default for the highlight color is always black.

Color Application Guidelines

This section describes the use of color in your application. It provides recommendations about how you can use color effectively.

The first task you should complete in creating a color design for your application is to study your users. If you are designing an application that allows users to assign colors to data or that is used to create color graphics, try looking at how people are already using color in their work. You might consider visiting some graphic artists if you are creating a graphic design tool. Look at the types of tools they have and how they organize the tools. See if you can construct your tool palettes and color palettes in a way that matches how people use their color tools such as colored pencils or paint sets.

When designing interfaces to provide color in your application, avoid using the engineer or hardware model of color. Ideally, you want to translate what you know into what your users expect. Although it's essential for you to understand how the computer produces color so that you can deal with the implications of it, your users operate under a very different model. Most users won't understand hue, saturation, and brightness values in terms of numbers. However, they will understand a tool that provides ranges of color expressing hue, saturation, and brightness. Think about how users can understand color, rather than accurately representing the computer's model of color.

Match Complexity to the Level of User

Think about the range of users that your application will be addressing. If you will have novice users and expert users, you need to construct tools that are easy for novice users to understand, but that don't limit your expert users from using their knowledge and skills. For example, you might provide several sets of colors, which can each appear in turn in a palette, that novice users can set and then choose from. In addition, you can build in a way for expert users to create their own sets of colors, including the ability to mix custom colors. This design lets your novice users focus on the simplicity and clarity of your application *and* gives your expert users access to the advanced tools you provide.

Figure 9-3 shows a color palette that novice users can easily use and a color mixing tool that requires more understanding of the interface and the topic.

Figure 9-3 Color palette and custom color mixing tool

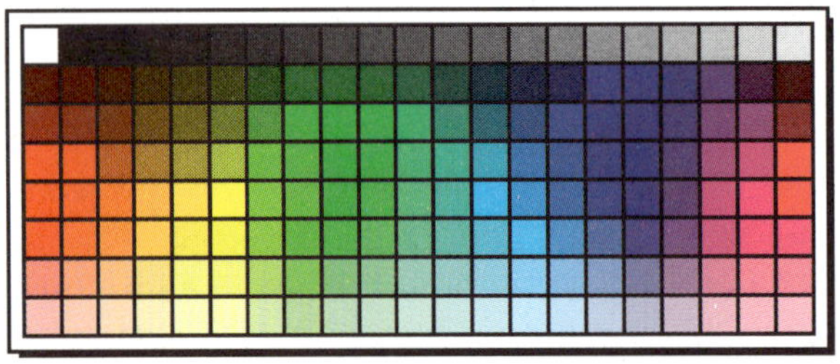

Color palette

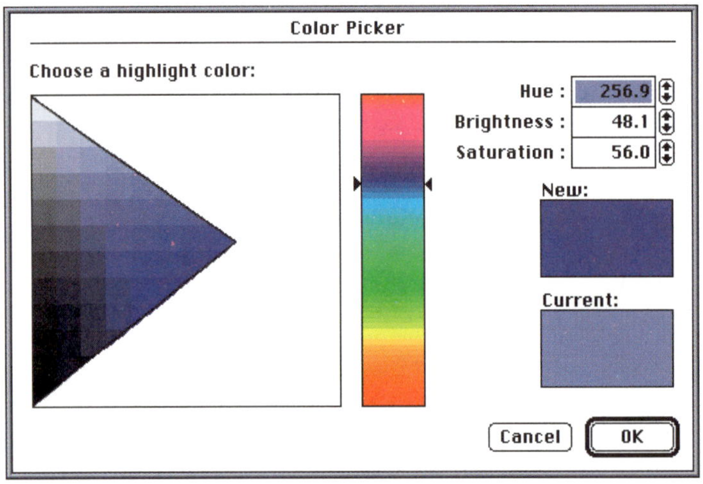

Custom color mixing tool

Design for the Macintosh

When your application uses standard elements or you design custom elements, these elements need to fit into the Macintosh interface framework. This means you should follow the Macintosh design guidelines and not imitate other vendors' designs. The Macintosh has a light source at the upper-left corner of the screen and a two-dimensional appearance. Your designs must be compatible with black-and-white designs, since that is the basis for the Macintosh interface and many users have only black-and-white displays.

Design for Black and White First

Always design for black and white first and then colorize that design. This method ensures that your design looks good on all Macintosh computers. One example of why this is important is the text selection mechanism. On a color monitor you might be tempted to change the color of text to indicate that it has been selected; however, this technique wouldn't translate to a black-and-white monitor. In addition, people with color-deficient vision wouldn't recognize the use of color to indicate selection. Therefore, you shouldn't use color as the only means of communicating important information. Color should be used redundantly. It shouldn't be the only thing that distinguishes two objects; there should be other cues, such as text labels, shape, location, pattern, or sound.

Figure 9-4 shows the correct process of designing for black-and-white monitors and then adding color to those designs. It demonstrates the consistency of the appearance of the icons and how the aesthetic integrity is maintained across the designs.

Figure 9-4 Design for black-and-white monitors first

Keep black-and-white designs two-dimensional. It's important to maintain the visual consistency of the Macintosh interface across applications and computer systems. Don't cause unnecessary visual clutter by trying to mimic color effects, such as shadows, in black-and-white designs. Figure 9-5 shows what can happen to black-and-white icons when you try to mimic color effects.

Figure 9-5 Don't mimic color effects in black-and-white designs

Maintain a close visual relationship between a black-and-white design and its colorized version. Users should be able to easily recognize standard interface elements and icons across all monitor types. Users can have several monitors connected to a computer and several computers on which they use your applications. Your application should look consistent when a user changes the bit depth of a monitor or moves your icon or window from a color monitor to a black-and-white monitor.

Limit the Number of Colors

In order to maintain consistency with the Macintosh interface, use as few colors as possible in your designs. The fewer colors you use, the less flashing occurs when the screen's color table is updated during screen redrawing. The color table contains the colors currently available for display on the screen. Using fewer colors also results in less visual clutter on the screen. Figure 9-6 shows an example of a palette with a limited number of colors used for art design. If you use a graphics application to do design work, make sure that the colors you use are available in the default color tables in system software. For more information, see the discussion of the Palette Manager in *Inside Macintosh*.

Figure 9-6 A limited palette of colors

Colors on Gray

Colors look best against a background of neutral gray. Colors within your application will stand out more if the background and surrounding areas are gray or black and white.

Beware of Blue

The color that is most difficult to distinguish is light blue, which should be avoided for text, thin lines, and small shapes. Adjacent colors that differ only in the amount of blue should also be avoided. However, for things that you want to make unobtrusive, such as grid lines, blue is the perfect color.

Small Objects

People cannot easily distinguish colors in small areas. In order for people to be able to tell what color an object is, that object must be large enough for them to see without effort. If more than one color is used in a small object, the differences must be obvious, not subtle, especially if the different colors are conveying significant information.

Color for Categorizing Information

If you use color to code categories of information in your application, try to limit the use of color elsewhere in the application. Using color to code categories—for example, to label or distinguish groups of items—can make information clear. Providing the user with a small initial selection of distinct colors—for example, from four to seven—and with the capability to change those colors or add more is the best solution.

CHAPTER 10

Behaviors

This chapter describes the aspects of the Macintosh interface that are essential to its "feel." It covers the interaction between the user and the computer, detailing how the computer should respond. This chapter contains information about the mouse and the pointer, the keyboard, and the behavior of different types of objects such as text, graphics, and arrays. It discusses the behaviors associated with the primary user input devices—the mouse and keyboard. It also describes responses generated by your application, such as selection behavior and keyboard navigation through lists.

The Pointing Device

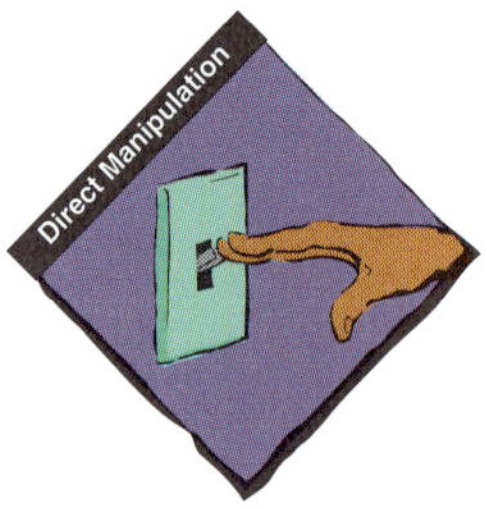

In some computer systems, the keyboard is the primary input device. People type in commands and the computer responds with typed responses or prompts. In the Macintosh interface, the pointing device is central to the user's input. A pointing device makes possible the direct manipulation that is an important aspect of the interface. The user communicates with the computer by manipulating graphic objects on the screen. The user can grab (or seem to grab) an object, then indicate what is to be done with it. The user accomplishes this interaction with the pointing device.

In the Macintosh interface the standard pointing device is the mouse. There are other pointing devices, such as trackballs and stylus pens, that perform the same functions. Figure 10-1 shows several different pointer devices.

Figure 10-1 Different pointing devices

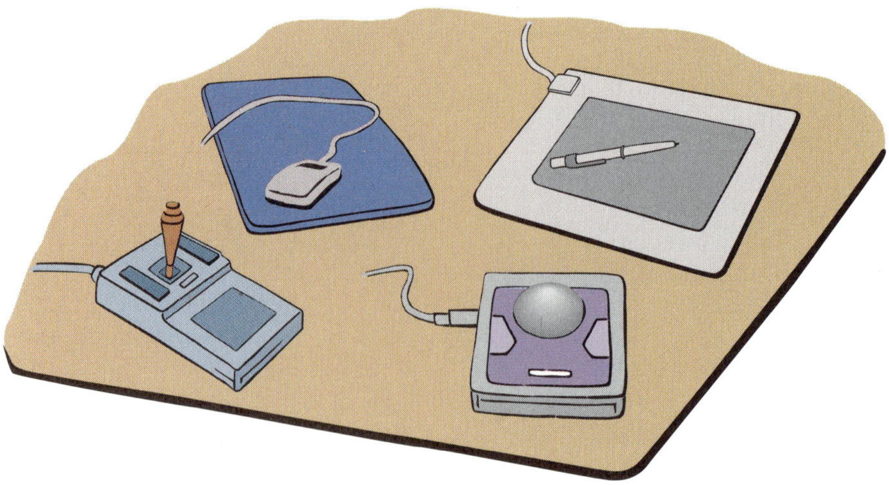

The mouse is a hand-held device, usually (but not necessarily) connected to the computer by a long, flexible cable. There's a single button on the mouse. The user holds the mouse and rolls it on a flat, smooth surface. On the screen, a **pointer,** which can assume different shapes according to the context of the application, follows the motion of the mouse.

Simply moving the mouse (without pressing the mouse button) just moves the pointer. Most actions take place only when the user positions the pointer over an object on the screen, then presses and releases the mouse button.

Traditional character-oriented command-line interfaces rely on a **cursor** to indicate the place on the display where the next character that is typed will appear. The user uses arrow keys (sometimes called *cursor keys*) to move the cursor around the screen. Because there is nothing else to point at, no pointer is needed.

In the Macintosh interface, there may be many graphic objects on the screen, unrelated to the text insertion point. Thus there are lots of objects to point at and a pointer is necessary in the interface. The screen pointer is logically attached to the mouse or other pointing device. The user manipulates the pointer to show your application what to do next and where to do it. The place where the next characters to be typed will appear is indicated by an **insertion point.** In text, the pointer shows where the insertion point will be moved to if the user clicks at that location. Figure 10-2 shows the insertion point and the pointer in a text document.

Figure 10-2 The insertion point and the pointer

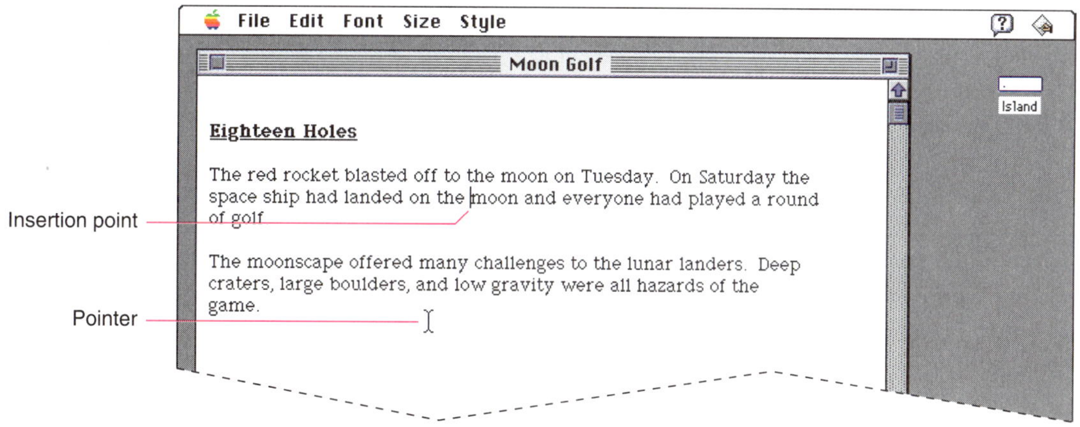

Each pointer has a **hot spot**—the portion of the pointer that must be positioned over a screen object before mouse clicks can have an effect on that object. The hot spot should be intuitive, such as the tip of an arrow pointer or the center point of a crosshair pointer. Similarly, screen objects have a **hot zone**—the area that the pointer's hot spot must be within in order for mouse clicks to have an effect.

As the pointer moves about the screen, it may change shape. For example, in a text-oriented application, the pointer takes the I-beam shape while it's over the text, to show where the insertion point will move to if the mouse button is pressed. When the pointer moves outside of the text, it becomes an arrow. In general, the pointer should change shape *only* to provide information to the user. In other words, it shouldn't change shape randomly. For example, the pointer could change shape to give feedback on the range of activities that make sense either in a particular area of the screen or in a current mode. If the result of mouse actions depends on the item under the pointer when the user presses the mouse button, the pointer could change shape depending on the object. Where an application uses modes for different functions, the pointer could be a different shape in each mode. Table 10-1 shows some examples of pointers and their effects. You can create additional pointers as needed for other contexts.

Table 10-1 Pointers

Pointer	Name	Used for
	Arrow	Scroll bar, other controls, size box, title bar, close box, zoom box, menu bar, desktop
+	Crosshairs	Drawing, shrinking, or stretching graphic objects
	I-beam	Selecting and inserting text
	Plus sign	Selecting fields in an array
	Wristwatch	Showing that a lengthy operation is in progress

During a particularly lengthy operation, when the user can do nothing else but wait until the operation is completed or switch to another application, the pointer may change its shape and become a status or progress indicator. This indicator lets the user know that the system hasn't died—it's just busy. The standard pointer for this case is the wristwatch; however, if the operation will take longer than a few seconds, your application should display an indicator to show the user the estimated total time and the elapsing time of the operation. These measurements can be shown in absolute terms, as proportions of the total, or both. Figure 10-3 shows a status indicator from the Finder that is implemented as a movable modal dialog box to indicate to the user that he or she can switch to another application while waiting for the operation to finish.

Figure 10-3 A status indicator

Mouse Actions

The basic mouse actions in the Macintosh interface are pointing, clicking, double-clicking, pressing, and dragging.

In general, just moving the mouse changes nothing except the location, and possibly the shape, of the pointer. Pressing the mouse button indicates the intention to do something, and releasing the mouse button completes the action. Pressing by itself should have no more effect than clicking has—except in well-defined areas, such as scroll arrows, where it has the same effect as repeated clicking. For example, if you click an icon in the Finder, you select the icon and no more.

Clicking

Clicking has two components: pushing down on the mouse button and then quickly releasing it while the mouse remains stationary. (If the mouse moves between button down and button up, dragging—not clicking—is what happens.) Some uses of clicking are to select an object, to move an insertion point, to activate a button, and to turn on a control such as a checkbox. The effect of clicking should be immediate and evident. If the function of the click is to cause an action (such as clicking a button), the *selection is made* when the button is pressed, and the *action takes place* when the button is released.

Figure 10-4 shows the action of clicking a button.

Figure 10-4 Clicking a button

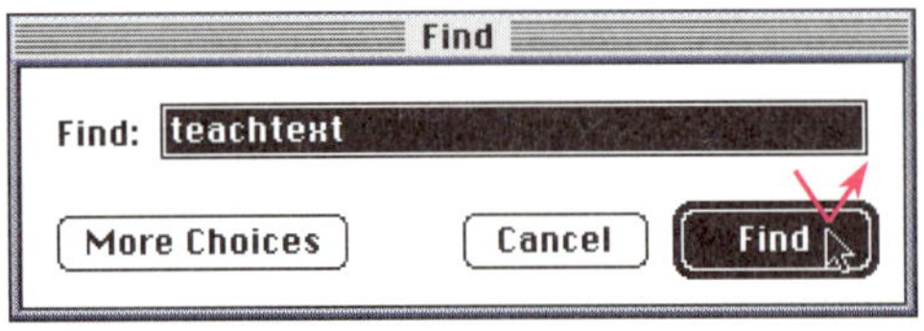

Double-Clicking

Double-clicking involves a second click that follows immediately after the first click. If the two clicks are close enough to one another in terms of time (as set by the user in the Mouse control panel) and of screen location (usually within one or two pixels), they constitute a double click.

The most common use of double-clicking is to provide a shortcut to other actions. For example, clicking an icon twice is a faster way to open it than clicking once to select it, then choosing Open from the File menu. Clicking a word twice to select it is faster than dragging through it. Figure 10-5 shows the effect of double-clicking a word in a text document.

Figure 10-5 Double-clicking to select a word

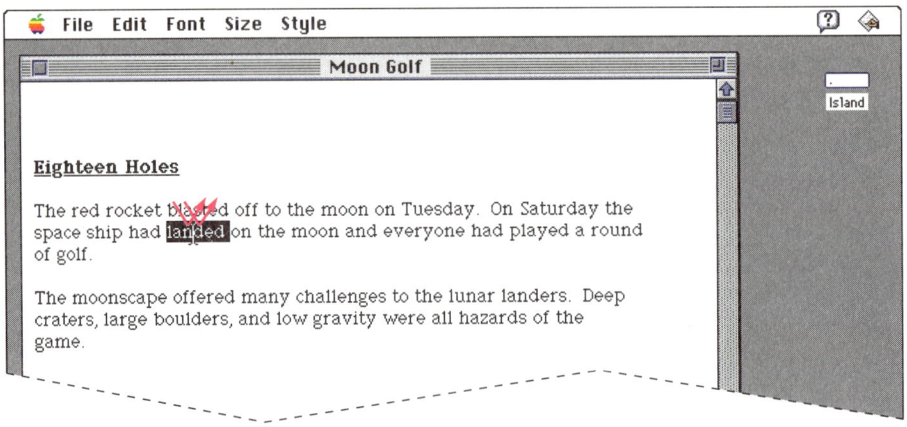

Double-clicking is a shortcut for those users who are physically able to use it. Double-clicking must *never* be the only way to perform a given action. Many novice users, children, and people with certain physical disabilities may have a hard time double-clicking.

Some applications support selection by double-clicking and triple-clicking. The second click extends the effect of the first click, and the third click extends the effect of the second click. For example, in a text-oriented application, the first click sets an insertion point, the second click selects the whole word containing the insertion point, and the third click might select the whole sentence or paragraph. In a graphics application, the first click might select a single object, and double and triple clicks might select successively larger sets of objects.

Three clicks is probably the practical limit, and even that is difficult for many people. If an application defines the effect of only single- and double-clicking, a third click should have no effect. If triple-clicking is defined, then the fourth click should have no effect.

Pressing

Pressing means holding down the mouse button for a time while the mouse remains stationary. For example, pressing a menu title displays the menu contents. For certain kinds of objects, pressing on the object has the same effect as clicking it repeatedly. For example, clicking a scroll arrow causes a document to scroll one line; pressing a scroll arrow causes the document to scroll continuously until the user releases the mouse button or reaches the end of the document. Figure 10-6 shows the effect of pressing the mouse button while the pointer is on a scroll arrow.

Figure 10-6 Pressing a scroll arrow

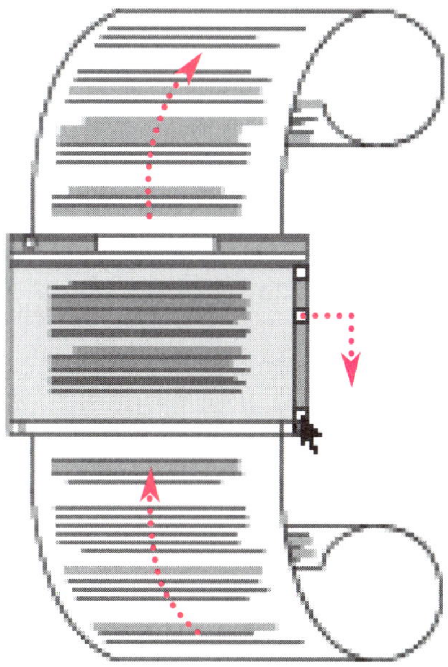

Dragging

Dragging means pressing the mouse button, moving the mouse to a new position, and then releasing the mouse button. Dragging can have different effects depending on what's under the pointer when the mouse button is pressed. The uses of dragging include selecting blocks of text, choosing a menu item, selecting a range of objects, moving an icon or other object from one place to another, and shrinking or expanding an object.

Graphic objects can be moved by dragging. The application either moves the entire object or attaches a dotted outline of the object to the pointer and moves the outline as the user moves the pointer. When the user releases the mouse button, the application redraws the complete object at the new location. Figure 10-7 shows the process of moving an object by dragging.

Figure 10-7 Dragging to move an object

1. Position pointer over icon to be dragged.
2. Press to select.
3. Drag outline to right.
4. Release button.

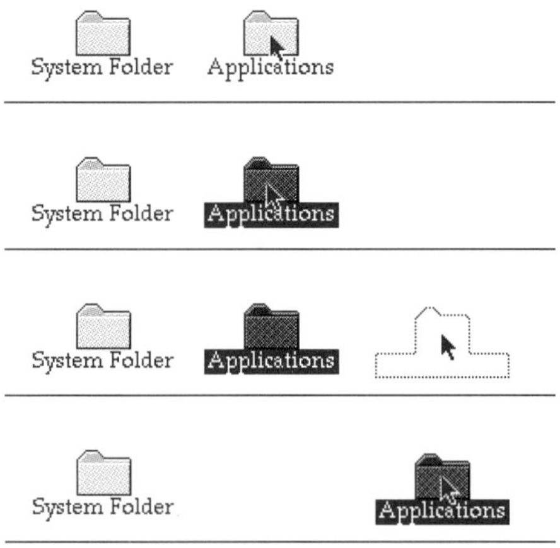

Your application can restrict an object from being moved past certain boundaries, such as the edges of a window. If the user moves the pointer outside the boundaries, the application stops drawing the dotted outline of the object. If the user releases the mouse button while the pointer is outside the boundaries, the object doesn't move. However, if the user moves the pointer back within the boundaries before releasing the mouse button, the object appears in the new location. If the user moves the object beyond the boundary of a window, your application can also scroll the document (using automatic scrolling) or even move the object from one window to another.

The Keyboard

In the Macintosh interface the user points to and manipulates objects on the screen with the pointing device. The user doesn't have to enter commands from the keyboard, which leaves entering text as the primary use for the keyboard. The keyboard may also be used for navigation. (Keyboard navigation methods are always shortcuts to navigating with the mouse; they should never be the only method of navigation.)

There are two kinds of keys: character keys and modifier keys. A **character key** sends characters to the computer. When held down, a **modifier key** can alter the meaning of the character key being pressed, or alter or amplify the meaning of a mouse action.

Character Keys

Character keys include keys for letters, numbers, and punctuation, as well as the Space bar. If the user presses one of these keys while entering text, the corresponding character is added to the text. Nonprinting characters such as the Enter, Tab, Return, Delete (or Backspace), Clear, and Escape (Esc) keys are also treated like character keys. Although the result of pressing one of these keys depends on the application and the context, it is essential that your application use them consistently, as described in the following paragraphs.

Enter

The Enter key tells the application that the user is through entering information in a particular area of the document, such as a field in an array or table. Most applications add information to a document as soon as the user types or draws it. However, the application may need to wait until a whole collection of information is available before processing it. In this case, the user presses the Enter key to signal that the information is complete. The user can press Enter (like Return) to dismiss dialog boxes and alert boxes, if there is a default button. While the user is entering text into a *text* document, pressing Enter has no effect.

Tab

In text-oriented applications, the Tab key is used to move the insertion point to the next tab stop. In other contexts, Tab is a signal to proceed: it signals movement to the next item in a sequence, as shown in Figure 10-8. Pressing Tab often causes data to be entered before moving to the next item.

Figure 10-8 Using the Tab key to cycle through fields

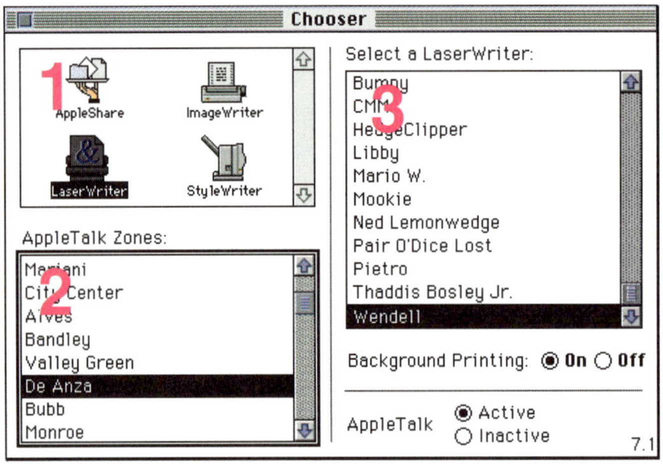

Return

In text, the Return key inserts a carriage return at the current insertion point. It moves the insertion point to the beginning of the next line, as shown in Figure 10-9. In arrays, the Return key signals movement to the leftmost field one step lower on the display (like a carriage return on a typewriter). Return (like Tab) can cause data to be entered before moving down a step. The user can press Return (like Enter) to dismiss dialog boxes and alert boxes, if there is a default button.

Figure 10-9 Using the Return key to move the insertion point

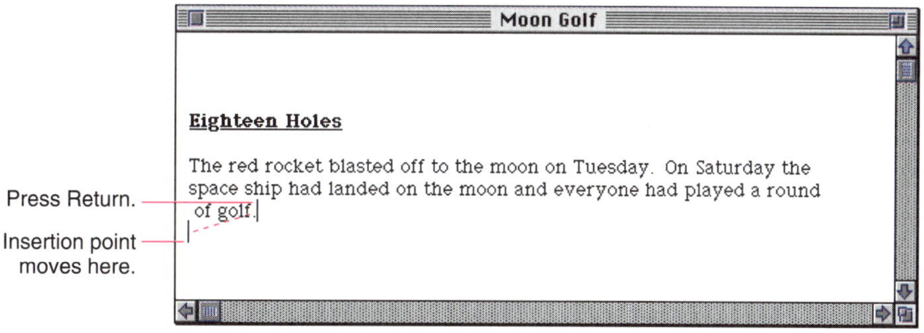

Delete (or Backspace)

The Delete (or Backspace) key deletes text or graphics. Generally, if a selection has been made, pressing Delete removes the selection without putting it in the Clipboard. If there is no selection, pressing Delete removes the character preceding the insertion point without putting it in the Clipboard. The Delete key has an effect like that of the Clear command in the Edit menu.

You can support the keyboard combination Option-Delete to delete the word that contains the insertion point.

Note that the Delete key is different from the Forward Delete key (labeled Del), which removes the character or selection following the insertion point.

Clear

The Clear key has the same effect as the Clear command in the Edit menu; that is, it removes the selection from the document without putting it in the Clipboard. Because not all Macintosh keyboards have Clear keys, no application should ever *require* use of the Clear key.

Escape

The Escape (Esc) key has the general meaning "let me out of here." It's a sort of panic button for the user. In certain contexts its meaning is specific:

- The user can press Escape as an alternate to clicking the Cancel button in a dialog box.
- The user can press Escape to stop an operation in progress, such as printing. Using the Escape key in this way has the same effect as using the keyboard equivalent Command-period.

If an application absolutely requires a series of dialog boxes, the user should be able to use Escape to move backward through the boxes. However, you should avoid getting into this situation for the reasons described in Chapter 6, "Dialog Boxes," in the section "Stacking Modal Dialog Boxes" on page 192.

Pressing Escape should never cause the user to back out of an operation that would require extensive time or work to reenter. Also, pressing Escape should never cause the user to lose valuable information. When the user presses Escape during a lengthy operation, the application should display a confirmation dialog box to be sure that Escape wasn't pressed accidentally. An example of a message you might post is shown in Figure 10-10.

Figure 10-10 A sample confirmation dialog box for the Escape key

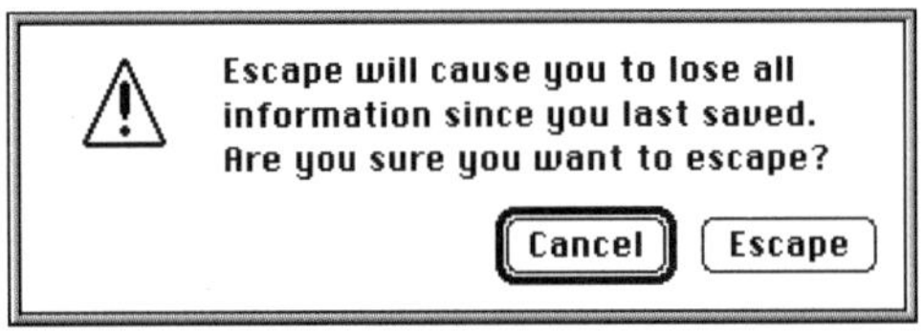

Modifier Keys

Modifier keys are those that alter the way other keystrokes are interpreted. These keys sometimes affect the way the mouse-button actions are interpreted as well. They are the Shift, Caps Lock, Option, Command, and Control keys. Not all Macintosh keyboards contain all of these keys. It is important that you use these keys consistently from application to application, as outlined in these guidelines.

Shift

The Shift key, when held down at the same time a character key is pressed, produces the uppercase letter on alphabetic keys, or the upper character on two-character keys. The Shift key is also used in conjunction with the mouse for extending a selection or for constraining movement in graphics applications. For example, in some graphics applications holding down the Shift key while using a rectangle tool limits the tool to drawing squares.

Caps Lock

The Caps Lock key latches in the down position when pressed and releases when pressed again. (On PowerBook computers this key is a soft switch, so it doesn't latch.) Note that the Caps Lock key operates for Roman languages only; in other words, it works as described in this section for languages that include uppercase and lowercase letters. When down, it gives the uppercase letter on alphabetic keys. Caps Lock has the same effect on alphabetic keys that the Shift key has, but Caps Lock has no effect on any other keys. In other words, even when Caps Lock is down, the user must press the Shift key to produce the upper characters (#, ?, and so on) on the nonalphabetic keys.

Option

The Option key, when used in combination with other keys, produces a set of international characters and special symbols. For example, in many Macintosh fonts, Option-4 produces the ¢ symbol, Option-R produces ®, and Option-G produces ©. Shift and Option can be used together, in combination with a character key, to produce yet other symbols. For example, Option-Shift-? produces the Spanish ¿ character. The Key Caps desk accessory lets the user preview these combinations in all available fonts.

The Option key can also be used in conjunction with the mouse to modify the effect of a click or drag. For example, in some graphics applications, if the user selects an object and holds down the Option key while dragging the object, the application makes a copy of the object and moves it to wherever the user releases the mouse button. This example is illustrated in Figure 10-11.

Figure 10-11 Using Option-drag to make a copy of an object

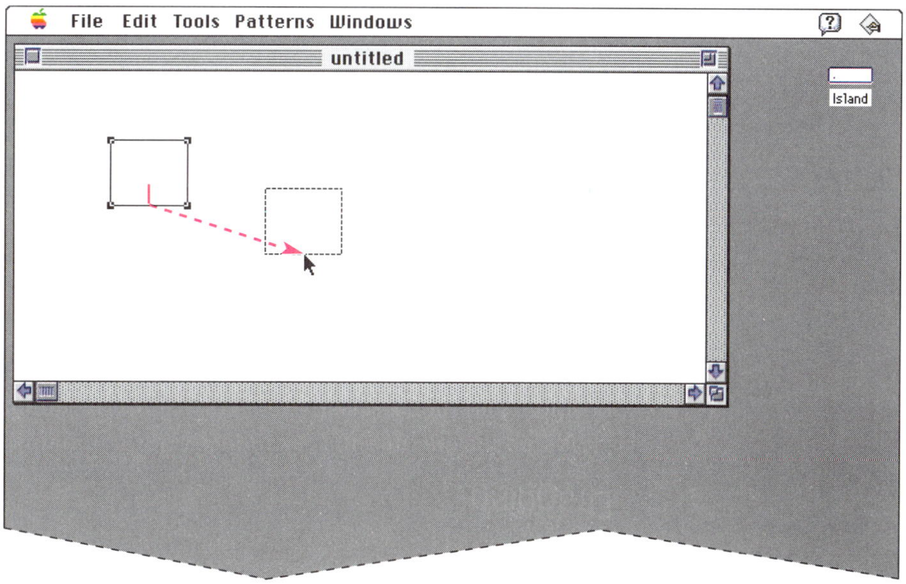

Command

The Command key is labeled with a propeller (⌘) symbol and, on some keyboards, an Apple symbol () as well. Pressing a character key while holding down the Command key usually tells the application to interpret the key as a command, not as a character. These combinations are called *keyboard equivalents*, as described in Chapter 4, "Menus," in the section "Keyboard Equivalents" on page 128.

In some applications, the Command key is used with other keys to provide special functions or shortcuts. For example, pressing Command-Shift-3 on a Macintosh saves a snapshot of the current screen on disk. The Command key can also be used in conjunction with the mouse to modify the effect of a click or drag.

Control

The Control key is used with terminal-emulation programs for Control-key sequences. For all other applications, it is reserved for shortcut key sequences that the user defines using a macro-key facility.

Type-Ahead and Auto-Repeat

If the user types when the computer is unable to process the keystrokes immediately or types more quickly than the computer can handle, the extra keystrokes are queued for later processing. This queuing is called **type-ahead.** There's a limit (varying with the computer) to the number of keystrokes that can be queued, but this limit is usually not reached unless the user types while the application is performing a lengthy operation.

When a character key is held down for a certain amount of time, it starts repeating automatically. This feature is called **auto-repeat.** The user can set the delay and the rate of repetition with the Keyboard control panel. An application can tell whether a series of keystrokes was generated by auto-repeat or by the same key being pressed several times. Your application can choose to disregard keystrokes generated by auto-repeat; this is usually a good idea for menu commands chosen with keyboard equivalents such as Command–character key combinations. Be judicious in ignoring these sequences because users can find them useful in certain situations.

In general, if the user holds down a modifier key, it has the same effect as if the user presses it once. If the user holds down a modifier key *and* a character key at the same time, the effect is the same as if the user holds down the modifier key while pressing the character key repeatedly.

Auto-repeat does not function during type-ahead. It operates only when the application is ready to accept keyboard input.

International Keyboards

Keyboard layouts used in the United States resemble those on standard U.S. office typewriters. The layouts used outside the United States are designed to conform to the International Standards Organization (ISO) standard. In different countries, international keyboards have different labels on the keys, but the overall layout is still based on the ISO standard.

Arrow Keys

Some Macintosh keyboards include four arrow keys: Up Arrow, Down Arrow, Left Arrow, and Right Arrow. These keys are shown in Figure 10-12.

Figure 10-12 Arrow keys

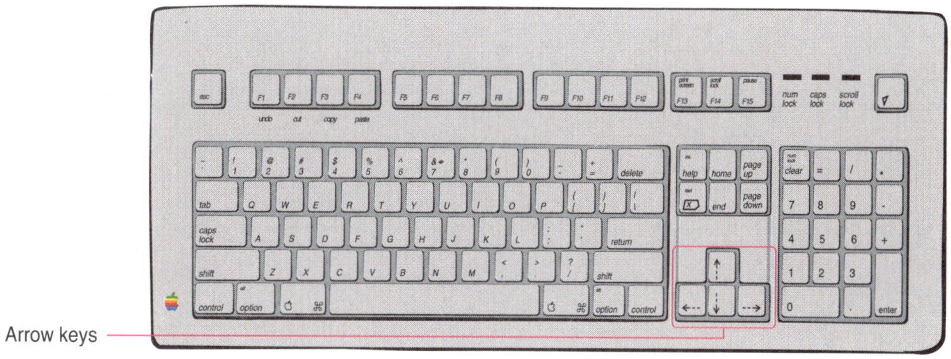

Appropriate Uses for the Arrow Keys

As a general rule, arrow keys are used to move the insertion point and, when used with the Shift key, to extend or shrink selections. The guidelines in this section apply both to moving the insertion point and to making selections. They are the minimum guidelines for arrow keys. You may expand these guidelines if you need to, keeping in mind their spirit.

Arrow keys are never used to duplicate the function of the scroll bars or to move the mouse pointer. They may be used as a shortcut to move the insertion point and, under some circumstances, to make selections.

An application should use the arrow keys only when appropriate to the task. Applications that deal with text or arrays, such as word processors, spreadsheets, and databases, have an insertion point. This insertion point could be moved both by the mouse and by the arrow keys.

If the user makes a selection and then presses the Right Arrow or Left Arrow key, your application should shrink the selection to zero length and place the insertion point at the right or left edge of the selection. This action doesn't move the location of the selection.

In a graphics application, the arrow keys can be used for fine movement of selected objects, particularly since graphics applications typically have no insertion point. If a graphics application uses arrow keys, it should be only to move the selected object by the smallest possible increment (one pixel or one grid unit). For example, the user could select an object and use the arrow keys to move one pixel per keystroke in the direction of the arrow key pressed. Generally, graphics applications shouldn't use arrow keys to change a selection or use modifier keys to multiply the effect of arrow keys. (Note that the Finder uses arrow keys to change the selection.)

Moving the Insertion Point

The Left Arrow and Right Arrow keys move the insertion point one character left and right respectively. Up Arrow and Down Arrow move the insertion point up and down one line respectively.

During vertical movement of the insertion point, horizontal screen position is maintained in terms of screen pixels, not characters. (Character boundaries seldom line up vertically when proportional fonts are used.) When the insertion point moves to a new line, move it slightly left or right, to the nearest character boundary on the new line. During successive movements up or down, the application should keep the insertion point as close as possible to the original horizontal position as it moves from line to line.

Moving the Insertion Point in Empty Documents

Various text-editing programs treat empty documents in different ways. Some assume that an empty document contains no characters, in which case clicking at the bottom of a blank screen causes the insertion point to appear at the top. In this situation, Down Arrow cannot move the insertion point into the blank space because there are no characters there.

Other applications treat an empty document as a page of space characters, in which case clicking at the bottom of a blank screen puts the insertion point where the user has clicked and lets the user type characters there, overwriting the spaces. In this sort of application, Down Arrow moves the insertion point straight down through the spaces. Whichever of these methods you choose for your application, it's essential that you be consistent throughout.

Using Modifier Keys With Arrow Keys

In some cases it's appropriate to use modifier keys such as Option and Command to extend the action of moving the insertion point in a document. This allows users to move the insertion point using keyboard combinations as an alternative to the mouse. Keep in mind that these keyboard combinations are only shortcuts for mouse actions. It is *optional* to extend these behaviors to applications but it is *never* appropriate to implement only a keyboard shortcut and not provide a mouse-based way to perform the same action.

You can support using modifier keys with arrow keys to move the input focus, extend a selection, or move objects. The most common uses of these keyboard combinations are to extend selections and to move the insertion point. The paragraphs that follow suggest typical uses for modifier key–arrow key combinations.

The Option key and the Command key are both used as semantic modifiers with the arrow keys. A semantic modifier changes the semantic unit that the arrow keys affect. The application determines what the semantic units are. For example, in word-processing applications, semantic units are characters, words, lines, paragraphs, and documents. In general, the Option key increases the size of the semantic unit by 1 compared to the arrow keys alone, and the Command key enlarges the semantic unit again. Table 10-2 shows how the Option key and Command key could change the effect of arrow keys in a word-processing application.

Table 10-2 How modifier keys change the movement of the insertion point with the arrow keys

	Arrow key alone	With Option key	With Command key or Shift key
Left Arrow	Left one character	Left one word	To beginning of line
Right Arrow	Right one character	Right one word	To end of line
Up Arrow	Up one line	To start of paragraph	To top of window
Down Arrow	Down one line	To end of paragraph	To bottom of window

If there aren't any paragraphs or an additional paragraph marker after the insertion point in the document, then Option–Down Arrow can't move the insertion point to its end. In this case, you should map Option–Down Arrow to have the same action as Down Arrow. For example, if the insertion point is already at the end of the document and the user presses Option–Down Arrow, play the system beep to call the user's attention to the position of the insertion point.

In an application (such as a spreadsheet) that represents data in an array, the basic semantic unit would be the cell. Option–Left Arrow (or Option–Right Arrow) would designate the cell to the left (or right) of the currently active cell as the new active cell. Using modifier keys with arrow keys doesn't change the data; Option–Left Arrow just causes the data to be entered and moves the selection to the next cell to the left.

Though the use of multiple modifier-key combinations (such as Command–Option–Left Arrow) is discouraged, it's all right to use the Shift key with any one of the other modifier keys for making a selection. (See "Selecting With the Arrow Keys" on page 295 for more information.) If multiple keys must be pressed simultaneously, they should be fairly close together, otherwise, some people won't be able to use that combination.

Note that for non-Roman script systems, Command–Left Arrow and Command–Right Arrow are reserved for changing the direction of keyboard input. Specifically, Command–Right Arrow changes the keyboard layout to Roman and Command–Left Arrow changes the keyboard layout to the system script. This capability is especially useful for bidirectional script systems such as Arabic and Hebrew since it allows users to change the direction of keyboard input. See Table 4-2 in Chapter 4, "Menus," on page 128 for more information. Also, Command–Shift–Left Arrow and Command–Shift–Right Arrow move the insertion point to the beginning and end of the line, respectively.

In all cases, if you can't complete a user action for some reason, provide feedback to indicate this. For example, you can flash the menu bar or play a sound on the first instance of a user action that can't be completed. You can also display an alert box that describes the situation and gives suggestions to the user about what can be done in the current context.

Function Keys

Some Macintosh keyboards include function keys. There are two types of function keys, dedicated and nondedicated. The nondedicated function keys—labeled F1 through F15—are definable by the user, *not* by the application. F1 through F4 represent Undo, Cut, Copy, and Paste in any applications that use these commands.

The six dedicated function keys are labeled Help, Del, Home, End, Page Up, and Page Down. These keys are shown in Figure 10-13.

Figure 10-13 The function keys

Help

Pressing the Help key invokes any application help system that has been installed. This is equivalent to pressing Command-? (or Command-/). The sort of help available varies among applications. If a full contextual help system is not available, some sort of useful help screen should be provided.

Forward Delete (Del)

In most script systems, pressing Forward Delete performs a forward delete: the character following the insertion point is removed, shifting everything following the removed character one character position back. The effect is that the insertion point remains stable while it "vacuums" the character or selection ahead of it.

You can support the keyboard combination Option–Forward Delete to delete the next larger semantic unit as described in the section "Using Modifier Keys With Arrow Keys" on page 282. Deleting more than one word ahead of the insertion point at a time using the keyboard can make users feel uncomfortable. Users prefer to select large amounts of text or content in a document with the mouse so that they have more control over the exact selection.

If Forward Delete is pressed when there is a current selection, it has the same effect as pressing Delete (Backspace) or choosing Clear from the Edit menu.

Home

Pressing the Home key is equivalent to moving the scroll boxes all the way to the top of the vertical scroll bar and to the left end of the horizontal scroll bar. (Note that the Home key may operate differently in a spreadsheet application; it won't necessarily scroll horizontally and it may scroll to the beginning of a row or to the beginning of the spreadsheet itself.) *Pressing the Home key has no effect on the location of the insertion point or any selected material.*

End

Pressing End is the opposite of pressing Home: it's equivalent to moving the scroll boxes all the way to the bottom of the vertical scroll bar and to the right end of the horizontal scroll bar. (Note that the End key may operate differently in a spreadsheet application; it won't necessarily scroll horizontally and it may scroll to the end of a row or to the end of the spreadsheet itself.) *Pressing End has no effect on the location of the insertion point or any selected material.*

Page Up

Pressing Page Up is equivalent to clicking the mouse in the upper gray region of the vertical scroll bar. *Pressing Page Up has no effect on the location of the insertion point or any selected material.*

Page Down

Pressing Page Down is equivalent to clicking the mouse in the lower gray region of the vertical scroll bar. *Pressing Page Down has no effect on the location of the insertion point or any selected material.*

Selecting

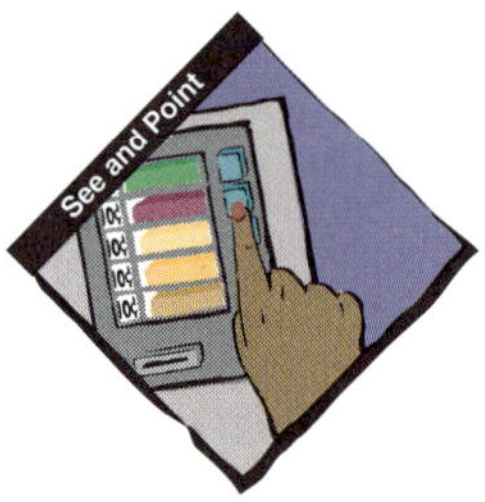

Before performing an operation on an object, the user must select it, usually by clicking it, to distinguish it from other objects. Selecting the object to be operated on before identifying the operation itself is a fundamental characteristic of the Macintosh human interface. The pattern is usually something like this:

1. The user selects an object (a noun, a thing to be operated on).
2. The user chooses an operation (a verb, the thing to be done).

This is often called the "noun-verb paradigm."

There is always a visual clue to show that something has been selected. For example, text and icons in a black-and-white environment usually appear in inverse video when selected. In color environments, icons appear darker and text is highlighted with the color the user set in the Color control panel. In some situations, other forms of highlighting may be more appropriate. The important thing is that there should always be immediate feedback, so the user knows that the click had an effect.

Selecting an object never alters the object itself. Making a selection shouldn't commit the user to anything; there should never be a penalty for making an incorrect selection. The user can undo any selection by making any other selection or clicking outside the selection.

How something is selected depends on what it is. Although there are many ways to select objects, the selection methods fall into easily recognizable groups. Users get used to selecting objects in certain ways, and applications that use these methods are easier to learn. Some of these methods apply to every type of application, and some to only particular types of applications.

It's useful to distinguish among three types of objects—text, lists or arrays, and graphics—because the user deals with each of them in a different way when selecting them. Figure 10-14 shows an example of each.

Figure 10-14 Three ways of selecting information

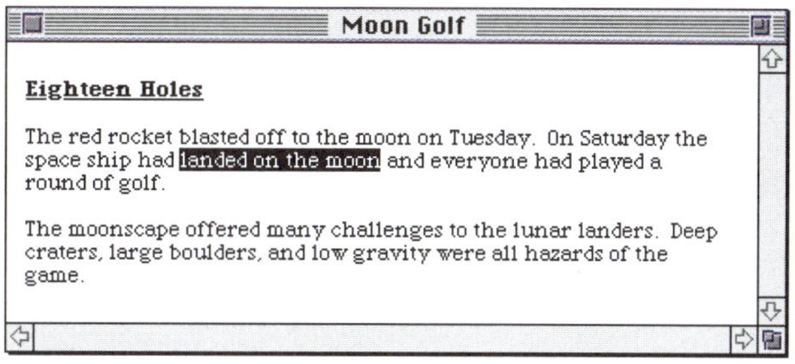

Text

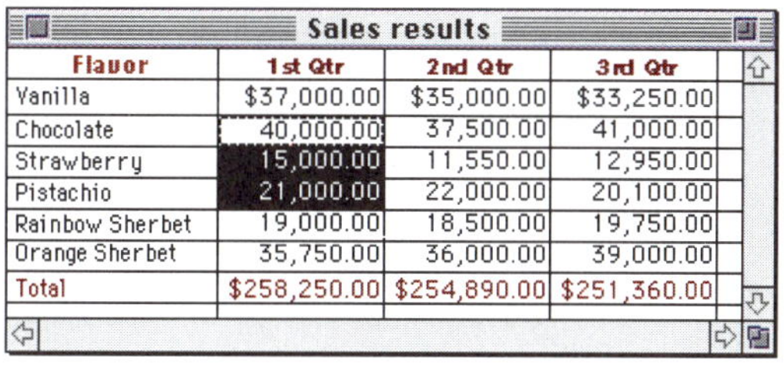

Sales results

Flavor	1st Qtr	2nd Qtr	3rd Qtr
Vanilla	$37,000.00	$35,000.00	$33,250.00
Chocolate	40,000.00	37,500.00	41,000.00
Strawberry	15,000.00	11,550.00	12,950.00
Pistachio	21,000.00	22,000.00	20,100.00
Rainbow Sherbet	19,000.00	18,500.00	19,750.00
Orange Sherbet	35,750.00	36,000.00	39,000.00
Total	$258,250.00	$254,890.00	$251,360.00

Array

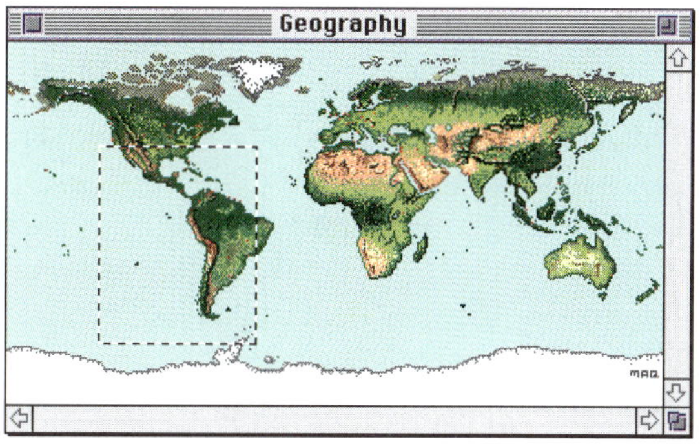

Graphics

Each of these three ways of presenting information retains its integrity regardless of the context in which it appears. For example, a field in an array can contain text. When the user is manipulating the field as a whole, the field is treated as part of the array. When the user wants to change the contents of the field, he or she edits the field in the same way as any other text.

Text can be arranged on the screen in a variety of ways. Some applications, such as word processors, might consist of nothing but text, whereas others, such as graphics-oriented applications, might use text almost incidentally.

It's useful to consider all the text appearing together in a particular context as a block of text. The size of the block can range from a single field, as in a dialog box, to the whole document, as in a word processor. Regardless of its size or arrangement, the application sees each block as a one-dimensional string of characters. Text is edited the same way regardless of where it appears.

Arrays are tabular arrangements of **fields.** One-dimensional arrays are called *lists*, and two-dimensional arrays are called *forms* or *tables*. Each field contains a collection of information, usually text and possibly graphics. A table can be easily identified on the screen as it consists of rows and columns of fields (sometimes called *cells*) separated by horizontal and vertical lines. (Tables are often implemented in spreadsheet applications.) A form is something the user fills out, such as a tax form or credit-card application. Although the fields in a form can be arranged in any appropriate way, your application always considers these fields as being in a well-defined linear order.

Graphics are pictures, drawn either by the user or by the application. Graphics in a document tend to consist of discrete objects, each of which can be selected individually.

The sections that follow discuss the general methods of selecting and the specific methods that apply to text applications, graphics applications, and arrays.

Selection Methods

This section describes various selection techniques: selection by clicking, selection by dragging, extending a selection, and discontinuous selection. Figure 10-15 shows some of the methods.

Figure 10-15 Selection techniques

Clicking B selects B.

Range selection of A through C selects A, B, and C.

Discontinuous selection. (Range selection of A, B, and C is extended to include E.)

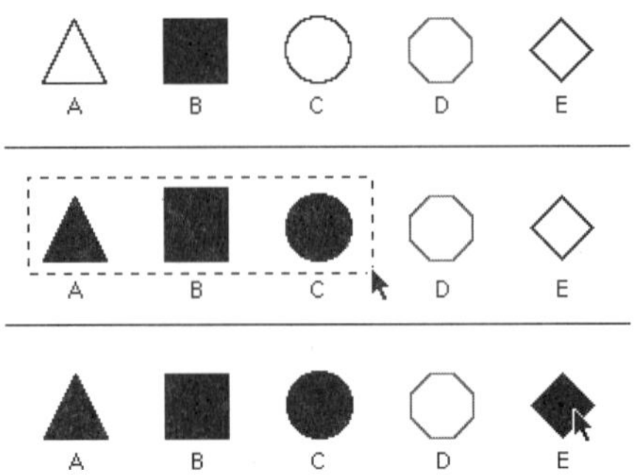

Selection by Clicking

The most straightforward method of selecting an object is by clicking it once. Icons and most other things that can be selected are selected in this way. The user positions the pointer over the desired object, then presses and releases the mouse button.

Selection by Dragging

The user selects a range of objects by dragging through them. Although the exact meaning of the selection depends on the type of application, the procedure is always the same:

1. The user positions the pointer at one corner of the range and presses the mouse button. This position is called the **anchor point** of the range.
2. Without releasing the mouse button, the user moves the pointer in any direction. As the pointer is moved, visual feedback indicates the objects that would be selected if the mouse button were released. For text and arrays, the selected area is continuously highlighted. For graphics, a dotted rectangle expands or contracts to show the range that will be selected. If appropriate, the view should scroll to allow extending the selection beyond one window.
3. When visual feedback shows the desired range, the user releases the mouse button. The point at which the button is released is called the **active end** of the range.

Changing a Selection With Shift-Click

A user can extend a selection by holding down the Shift key and clicking the mouse button. This action is called **Shift-clicking.** Exactly what happens next depends on the context.

In text or an array, the result of the Shift-click is always the selection of a range. The position where the button is clicked becomes the new endpoint of the range. If the user Shift-clicks within the current range, the new range will be smaller than the old range. Usually, if the user then Shift-clicks in another location, the additional data is included in the selection. In arrays, however, a different paradigm can be implemented in which the selection always moves from the current cell to wherever the user Shift-clicks, changing rather than extending the selection. This model works only in applications such as arrays, where the current cell is highlighted and the user can always see the active cell. In this case, the user always knows the fixed point from which the selection will start.

Extended selections can be made, even across the panes of a split window. Figure 10-16 shows the effect of extending and shrinking a range of text using Shift-click.

Figure 10-16 Expanding and shrinking a text selection

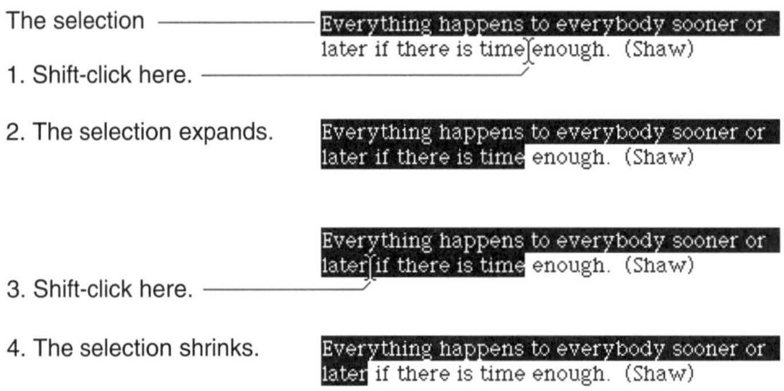

There are two methods for extending a continuous selection using Shift-click: the addition method and the fixed-point method. The **addition method** is based on *adding* new text to a current selection. The **fixed-point method** establishes a fixed location for the insertion point and allows the user to extend the selection on *either* side of the fixed point. Figure 10-16 illustrates the results of three consecutive steps in both the addition method and the fixed-point method.

Figure 10-17 Extending text selections using the addition and fixed-point methods

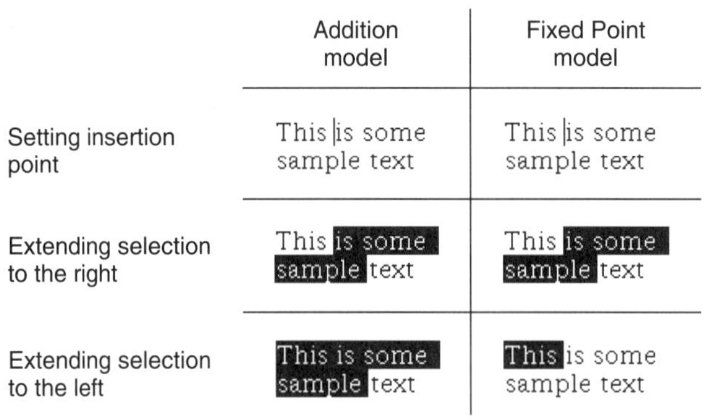

When considering which method to use in your application, keep in mind that the addition method provides more flexibility by allowing users to extend a selection in *both* directions rather than in only one direction, as in the fixed-point method. The addition method also provides greater consistency in terms of *extending* a selection; the fixed-point method can actually end up *shrinking* a selection rather than extending it, as shown in Figure 10-16. In both methods, if the user positions the insertion point within a selection and Shift-clicks, the selection is shortened from the right side of the selection to the location of the insertion point.

In graphics applications, objects aren't usually considered to be in any particular sequence. A selection is extended by adding objects to it, and the added objects do not have to be adjacent to the objects already selected. The user can add either an individual object or a range of objects to the selection by holding down the Shift key before making the additional selection (Shift-click). When the user does this, the objects between the current selection and the new object are not automatically included in the selection. This kind of selection is called **discontinuous selection.** If the user holds down the Shift key and selects one or more objects that are already highlighted, the objects are removed from the selection or are deselected. For more information about discontinuous selections, see *Inside Macintosh: Text.*

Changing a Selection With Command-Click

In the case of graphics, all selections are discontinuous selections because graphic objects are discrete. This is not the case with arrays and text, in which an extended selection made by a Shift-click always includes everything between the old anchor point and the new active end. In arrays and text, discontinuous selections are made by clicking while holding down the Command key.

To make a discontinuous selection in a text or array application, the user selects the first piece in the usual way and holds down the Command key while selecting the remaining pieces. Each piece is selected in the same way as if it were the whole selection, but because the Command key is held down, the new pieces are *added* to the existing selection instead of replacing it. If one of the pieces selected with Command-click is already within an existing part of the selection, then instead of being added to the selection, it's removed from the selection.

Figure 10-18 shows the process of adding cells to and removing cells from a discontinuous selection.

Figure 10-18 Discontinuous selection within an array

1. Cells B2, B3, C2, and C3 are selected.

2. The user holds down the Command key and clicks in D5.

3. The user holds down the Command key and clicks in C3.

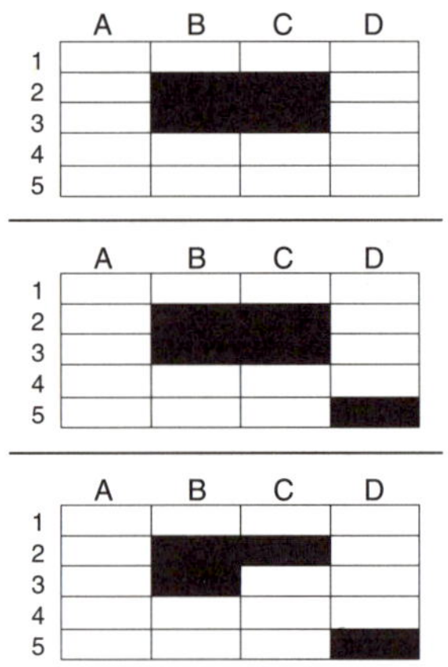

Not all applications support discontinuous selections, and those that do might restrict the operations a user can perform on them. For example, a word processor might allow the user to choose a font after making a discontinuous selection, but not allow the user to type replacement characters. In this situation, it wouldn't be apparent to users which part of the selection the characters would replace. Decide what makes sense in the context of your application and test it with users to make sure that their needs are met.

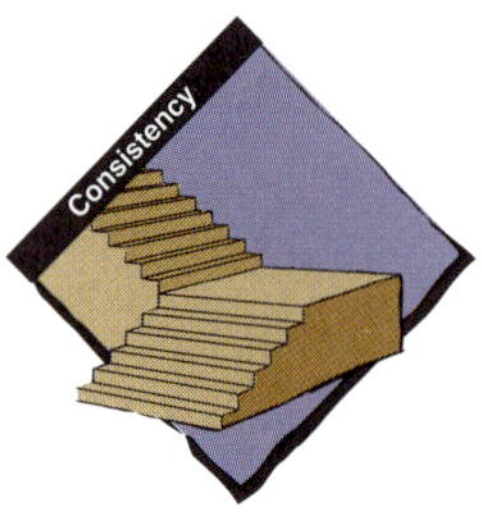

Selections in Text

In most applications, the user is required at some point to edit text. The principle of consistency (both within and among applications) requires that text be selected and edited in a consistent way, regardless of where it appears.

A block of text is a string of characters. A text selection is a substring of this string, which can have any length from zero characters to the whole block. Each of the text selection methods selects a different kind of substring. Figure 10-19 shows different kinds of text selections.

Figure 10-19 Text selections

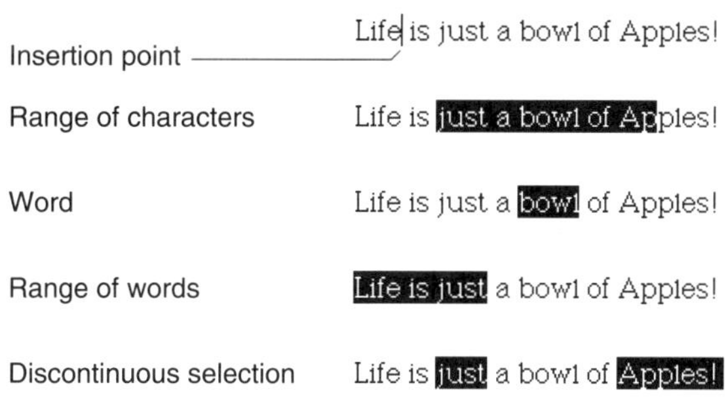

The insertion point is a zero-length text selection. The user establishes the location of the insertion point by clicking somewhere in the text. The insertion point then appears at the nearest character boundary. If the user clicks anywhere to the right of the last character on a line, the insertion point appears immediately after the last character. If the user clicks to the left of the first character on a line, the insertion point appears immediately before the first character.

The insertion point shows where text will be inserted when the user begins typing, or where the contents of the Clipboard will be pasted. As each character is typed, the insertion point is moved to the right of that character.

Selecting With the Mouse

The range selection method can be applied to text. The user selects a range of text by dragging through the range. A range can be a range of characters, words, lines, or paragraphs, as defined by the application. If the user extends the range, the way the range is extended depends on what kind of range it is. If it's a range of individual characters, it can be extended one character at a time. If it's a range of words (including a single word), it's extended only by whole words.

The user selects a whole word by double-clicking somewhere within that word. If the user begins a double-click sequence, but then drags the mouse between the mouse-down and the mouse-up of the second click, the selection becomes a range of words. As the pointer moves, the application highlights or unhighlights whole words at a time.

Selecting Ranges

A word or range of words can also be selected in the same way as any other range; whether this type of selection is treated as a range of characters or as a range of words depends on the operation. For example, in a word processor, a range of individual characters that coincides with a range of words is treated like characters for purposes of extending a selection, but is treated like words for purposes of "intelligent cut and paste" (described in the section "Intelligent Cut and Paste" on page 301).

The following definition of a word applies in the United States and Canada and in some other countries. In many countries, the definition differs to reflect local formats for numbers, dates, and currency. A word is defined as any continuous string that contains any of the following characters:

- a letter
- a digit
- a nonbreaking space (Option-space or Command-space)
- a currency symbol ($, ¢, £, or ¥)
- a percent sign
- a comma between digits
- a period before a digit
- an apostrophe between letters or digits
- a hyphen, but not Option-hyphen (–) or Option-Shift-hyphen (—)

If the user double-clicks any character *not* on this list, only that character is selected.

These are examples of words:

- $123,456.78
- shouldn't
- 3 1/2 (with a nonbreaking space)
- .5%

These are examples of strings treated as more than one word:

- 7/10/6
- blue cheese (with a breaking space)
- "Wow!" (The quotation marks and exclamation point aren't part of the word.)

In some contexts—in a programming language, for example—it may be appropriate to allow users to select both the left and right parentheses in a pair, as well as all the characters between them, by double-clicking either one of them. The same feature could be implemented for braces and brackets. This would mean that the user could select the entire expression

[*x*+*y*–(4*3)^(*n*–1)]

simply by double-clicking [or].

Selecting With the Arrow Keys

To use arrow keys to make a text selection, the user holds down Shift while pressing an arrow key. If it's important that your Macintosh application makes use of the numeric keypad, you shouldn't use these Shift–arrow key combinations. This is because the keypad's codes for the four Shift–arrow key combinations are the same as those for the keypad's +, *, /, and = keys. If the use of a Shift–arrow key combination for making selections is more important to your application than is the numeric keypad, the following paragraphs describe how it should work.

When a Shift–arrow key combination is pressed, the active end of the selection moves and the range over which it moves becomes selected. If both the Shift key and another modifier key are held down, the end of the selection moves as defined for the particular modifier key, and the range over which it moves becomes selected. For example, Option–Shift–Left Arrow selects the whole word that contains the character to the left of the insertion point (just like double-clicking a word).

A selection made by using the mouse is no different from one made by using arrow keys. A selection started with the mouse can be extended by using Shift and Left Arrow or Right Arrow.

In a text application, pressing Shift and either Left Arrow or Right Arrow selects a single character. If the Left Arrow key is used, the anchor point of the selection is on the right side of the selection, the active end on the left. Each subsequent Shift–Left Arrow adds another character to the left side of the selection. In many applications, a Shift–Right Arrow at this point shrinks the selection. In some applications, a Shift–Right Arrow at this point extends the selection, making the right side of the selection the active end (see the description of the addition and fixed-point methods for extending text selections in "Changing a Selection With Shift-Click" beginning on page 289). In this case, each subsequent Shift–Right Arrow adds another character to the right side of the selection.

Figure 10-20 summarizes these two different series of steps.

Figure 10-20 Selecting with Shift and arrow keys

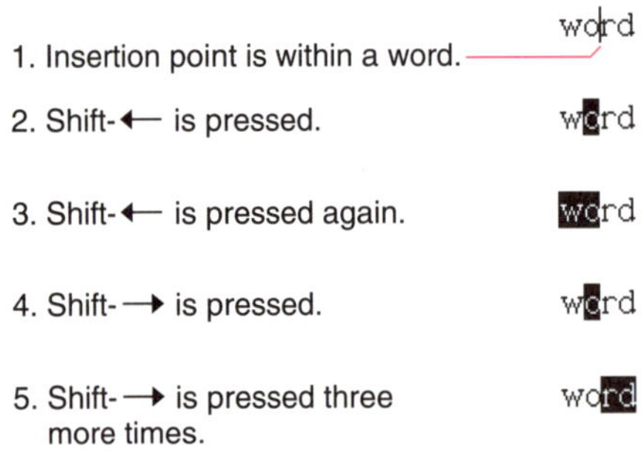

Pressing Option-Shift and either Left Arrow or Right Arrow (in a text application) selects the entire word containing the character to the left or right of the insertion point. Assuming Left Arrow is pressed, the anchor point is at the right end of the word, the active end at the left. Each subsequent Option–Shift–Left Arrow adds another word to the left end of the selection, as shown in Figure 10-21.

Figure 10-21 Selecting with Option-Shift and arrow keys

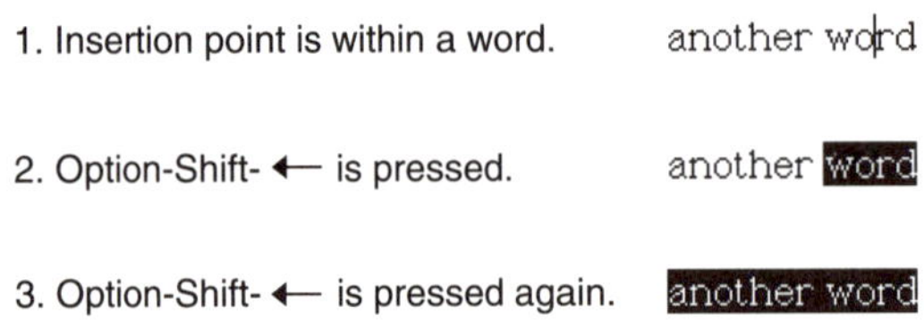

When a block of text is selected, either with a pointing device or with arrow keys, pressing either Left Arrow, Right Arrow, Up Arrow, or Down Arrow deselects the range. If Left Arrow is pressed, the insertion point goes to the beginning of what had been the selection. If Right Arrow is pressed, the insertion point goes to the end of what had been the selection.

Selections in Graphics

Several conventions exist for selecting graphic objects and giving selection feedback. This section describes two ways to show selection feedback. Other situations may require other solutions.

An object-based graphics document is a collection of individual graphic objects. To select one of these objects, the user clicks the object once, which is then bracketed with "handles." (The user can stretch or shrink the object with the handles.) Figure 10-22 shows the selection handles around graphic objects.

Figure 10-22 Selection in an object-based graphics document

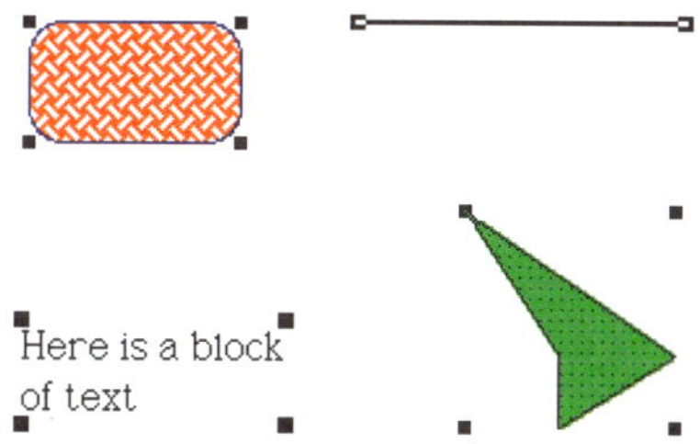

In object-based graphics applications, there are two ways to select more than one object. A range selection includes every object that falls completely within the dotted rectangle outline that encloses the range as the user drags the mouse. A discontinuous selection includes only those objects explicitly selected.

A bitmap-based graphics document, in contrast, is a series of pixels—not discrete objects. Selections are shown surrounded by a moving dashed line, which is sometimes called a *marquee* or *marching ants*. Figure 10-23 shows a selection marquee.

Figure 10-23 Selection in a bitmap-based graphics document

Selections in Arrays and Tables

An array is a one- or two-dimensional arrangement of fields. The user can select one or more fields or part of the contents of a field.

To select a single field, the user clicks in the field. The user can also select a field by moving to it with the Tab or Return key. Selecting a field by clicking is illustrated in Figure 10-24.

Figure 10-24 Field selection in an array

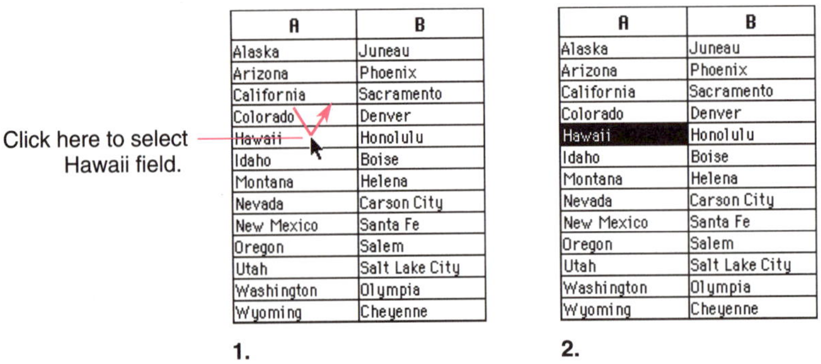

To select part of the contents of a field, the user must first select the field. The user then clicks again to select the desired part of the field. Because the contents of a field are either text or graphics, selections within a field follow the appropriate rules for either text or graphics. A table can support selection of rows and columns. The most convenient way for the user to select a column is to click in the column header. To select more than one column, the user drags through several column headers. The same behavior applies to selecting rows. Figure 10-25 shows column selection in an array.

Figure 10-25 Column selection in an array

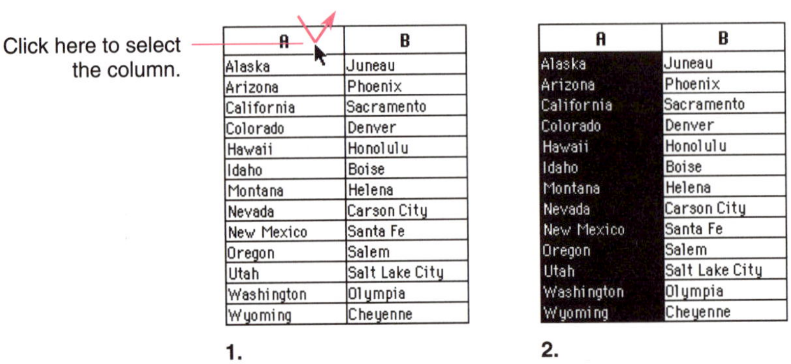

Figure 10-26 shows how a user selects a range in an array.

Figure 10-26 Range selection in an array

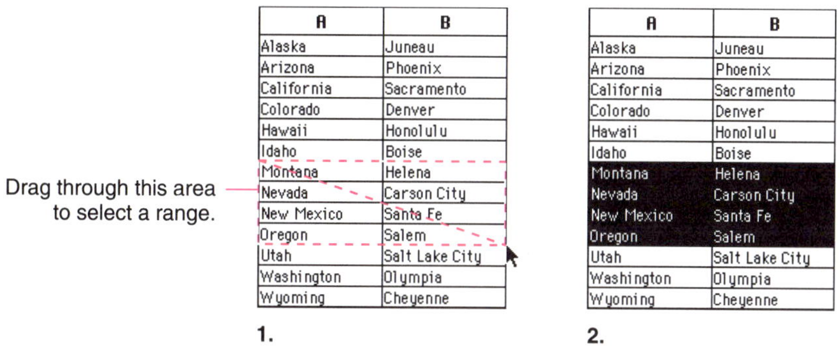

A table can also support discontinuous selection of fields in an array. The user first clicks a field to select it. Then the user holds down the Command key and clicks another field in the array. Figure 10-27 shows this technique.

Figure 10-27 Discontinuous selection in an array

Pressing the Tab key cycles the insertion point through the fields in an order determined by your application. From each field, the Tab key selects the "next" field. Typically, the sequence of fields is first from left to right, and then from top to bottom. When the last field in a form is selected, pressing the Tab key selects the first field in the form. The user can press Shift-Tab to navigate in the opposite direction. That is, Shift-Tab moves the selection back one cell. If there's a good reason, an application may guide the user through the fields in some order other than the order in which the fields appear on the screen.

The Return key selects the first field in the next row. The user can use Shift-Return to navigate up to the previous row in an array. If the idea of rows doesn't make sense in a particular context, then the Return key should have the same effect as the Tab key.

Editing Text

In addition to the different methods for selecting text, there are a number of ways to edit text.

Inserting Text

To insert text, the user positions the insertion point by clicking where the text is to go, then starts typing. The application continually moves the insertion point to the right (or left, depending on the direction of the language) as each new character is added.

Applications with multiple-line text blocks should support **word wrap,** the automatic continuation of text from the end of one line to the beginning of the next without breaking in the middle of a word.

Deleting Text

When the user presses the Delete (or Backspace) key, one of two things happens:

- If the current selection has one or more characters, it's deleted. This behavior is equivalent to choosing Clear from the Edit menu.
- If there is no current selection, but only an insertion point, the character preceding the insertion point is deleted.

In either case, the insertion point replaces the deleted character or characters in the document. The deleted characters don't go into the Clipboard, but the user can undo the deletion by immediately choosing Undo from the Edit menu.

You can also implement the keyboard combination Option-Delete (Backspace) to delete the word that currently contains the insertion point. Be sure to document this behavior if you implement it.

If a keyboard has a Forward Delete (Del) key, the character following the insertion point is deleted each time the user presses the key.

Replacing a Selection

If the user starts typing when the selection has one or more characters, the characters that are typed replace the selection. The deleted characters don't go into the Clipboard, but the user can undo the replacement by immediately choosing Undo from the Edit menu.

Intelligent Cut and Paste

Intelligent cut and paste is a set of editing features that takes into account the need for spaces between words. (Note that the features described in this section don't apply to all languages; for example, the Thai, Chinese, and Japanese languages don't contain spaces.) To understand why this feature is helpful, consider the following sequence of events in a text application *without* intelligent cut and paste:

1. A sentence in the user's document reads

   Returns are only accepted if the merchandise is damaged.

   The user wants to change this to

   Returns are accepted only if the merchandise is damaged.
2. The user selects the word *only* by double-clicking. The letters are highlighted, but neither of the adjacent spaces is highlighted.
3. The user chooses Cut from the Edit menu, clicks just before the word *if*, and chooses Paste.
4. The sentence now reads

   Returns are accepted onlyif the merchandise is damaged.

   Note the extra space between *are* and *accepted* and the lack of a space between *only* and *if*. To correct the sentence, the user has to remove the extra space between *are* and *accepted* and add one between *only* and *if*.

If your application supports intelligent cut and paste, follow these guidelines:

- If the user selects a word or a range of words, the selection itself is highlighted, but spaces adjacent to the selection are not highlighted.
- When the user chooses Cut, if the character preceding the selection is a space, cut that space along with the selection. If the character preceding the selection is not a space, but the character following the selection is a space, cut that space along with the selection.
- When the user chooses Paste, if the character to the left or right of the current selection is part of a word (but not inside a word), insert a space before pasting.

If the left or right end of a text selection is a word, follow these rules at that end, regardless of whether there's a word at the other end. Figure 10-28 shows two examples of intelligent cut and paste.

Figure 10-28 Intelligent cut and paste

1. Select a word.	Drink to me only with thine eyes.
2. Choose Cut.	Drink to me| with thine eyes.
3. Select an insertion point.	Drink to me with |thine eyes.
4. Choose Paste.	Drink to me with only| thine eyes.

1. Select a word.	How, now brown cow
2. Choose Cut.	How,| brown cow
3. Select an insertion point.	How|, brown cow
4. Choose Paste.	How now|, brown cow

Note that the selected text is not necessarily exactly the same range that will be cut and, eventually, pasted. The range may include a space character.

Intelligent cut and paste should be used only if the application supports the definition of a word, described in "Selections in Text" beginning on page 292, rather than the definition of a word as "anything between two spaces." These rules apply to any selection consisting of one or more whole words, no matter how the user made the selection.

Editing Fields

If an application isn't primarily a text application, but does use text in text entry fields (such as in a dialog box), you may not need to provide the full text-editing capabilities described so far. In Macintosh applications, the simplest way to implement text editing is to use TextEdit, or to use the Dialog Manager, which in turn uses TextEdit. It's important, however, that whatever editing capabilities the application provides under these circumstances be upward-compatible with the full text-editing capabilities. The application should support the following editing capabilities:

- The user can select the whole field and type in a new value, delete text, select a substring of the field and replace it, and select a word by double-clicking.
- The user can choose Undo, Cut, Copy, Paste, and Clear, as described in "The Edit Menu" beginning on page 109 in Chapter 4, "Menus."

In addition, you can support intelligent cut and paste. (TextEdit does not provide this.) Even applications with only minimal text editing should perform appropriate edit checks. For example, if the only legitimate value for a field is a string of digits, the application should alert the user if any nondigits are typed. The alert message might remind the user that the letters *l* and *o* can't be used in place of the numerals *1* and *0*. Alternatively, the application could wait until the user is through typing before checking the validity of a field's contents. In this case, the appropriate time to check the field is when the user clicks anywhere other than in the field or presses the Return, Enter, or Tab key.

CHAPTER 11

Language

11

This chapter describes how you should use language in your product. Although the Macintosh interface uses graphics as the primary means of user-computer interaction, much of the user interface still involves text of some kind—names in buttons, labels for checkboxes and radio buttons, messages in dialog boxes, online help systems, and manuals. Consistency in the use of language helps users easily learn to use the Macintosh.

In certain situations, the computer displays textual messages to describe a particular situation or ask the user for a specific decision. This chapter provides guidance on how to construct these messages in language that users understand. This chapter also contains information on how to write balloon help and how to construct a useful online help system for your application.

This chapter presents guidelines for using language clearly, consistently, and concisely throughout every aspect of your product, ranging from the user interface to paper documentation. Any time words are involved in your product, the design team should include a skilled writer who is responsible for not only the documentation but also the use of language on the screen.

Style

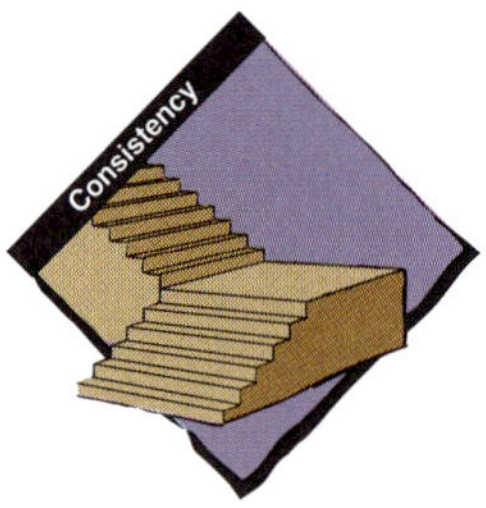

Apple Computer, Inc., publishes the *Apple Publications Style Guide,* which codifies the way in which Apple documentation uses language. This publication contains information about the specific terms that are used to describe interface elements. It also defines style and usage issues such as how certain terms are used and the preferred capitalization, spelling, and hyphenation of those terms. Some parts of the style guide are excerpted in this chapter to provide quick reference for key elements of the user interface. Whenever you are constructing language for your application, you can consult the *Apple Publications Style Guide* to help you to create consistent and usable language. You can obtain this publication through APDA.

For issues that aren't covered in the *Apple Publications Style Guide*, publication departments at Apple Computer rely on three other works: *The American Heritage Dictionary, The Chicago Manual of Style,* and *Words Into Type.* In cases where these reference books give conflicting rules, *The Chicago Manual of Style* takes precedence for questions of usage and *The American Heritage Dictionary* for questions of spelling.

Terminology

This section describes a few terminology issues to be aware of when you are creating your product.

Developer Terms and User Terms

It's very tempting to use the words that you're familiar with when you're developing documentation, training materials, or elements on the screen. However, it's best to use terms that your *users* are familiar with and that are consistent across the Macintosh product line and developer products. Don't use technical jargon or computer science terminology. It's especially important not to use programming terms in menus, dialog boxes, or user books.

Don't use file type names to refer to Finder documents that users see. Call documents by the terms that appear in the Kind column in Finder windows. Table 11-1 lists the terms to use in place of the four-character type names, as well as a few other preferred terms for user documentation.

Table 11-1 Translation chart for user documentation

Previously-used term	Suggested terminology	Examples
adev	Network extension	EtherTalk network extension
cdev	Control panel	Mouse control panel
DA	Desk accessory	Calculator desk accessory
ddev	Database extension	Data Access Language (DAL) database extension
FKEY	Function key	F1 function key
INIT	System extension (*not* startup document)	File Sharing system extension
MultiFinder icon	Active-application icon	
RDEV	Chooser extension	LaserWriter Chooser extension, AppleShare Chooser extension
Standard file dialog box	Directory dialog box	Directory dialog box for opening files

Terms That Are Often Misused

This section contains specific terms that are often misused in user documentation for the Macintosh.

Click

Click is the action of positioning the pointer over an object and briefly pressing the mouse button. The user *clicks* objects, not *clicks on* objects. Thus your documentation should say

- Click the disk icon.
- Click the Open button.
- Click Auto Page Numbering.

It is OK to say *click in* a window, but the user *clicks* all other onscreen elements. Also, it's not appropriate to say *click and drag*. The user clicks or the user drags.

Checkbox

A checkbox is a standard Macintosh control that displays a setting, either checked (on) or unchecked (off); it appears as a square with label text next to it. The user *clicks* a checkbox, not *checks* a checkbox, to select or deselect the corresponding option. When the option is on, an *x* appears in the box. When the option is off, the box is empty.

Document

Document refers to a file the user creates and can open, edit, and print. HyperCard documents are called **stacks.** Use the term *document* in user-level documentation and avoid the use of the term *file*, because it is more technical and less well-defined.

File

File refers to any entity stored on a disk, regardless of whether the user can open, edit, or print it. This use of the term has its origins in computer science and is best avoided when possible. In developer documentation, it's permissible to use this term as long as it's well defined.

Utility Window

Utility window refers to a window appearing in some applications that has some but not all of the features of a regular window. This window is sometimes called a *palette* or *miniwindow. Don't* use the term *windoid* or *floating window* to describe these windows.

Labels for Interface Elements

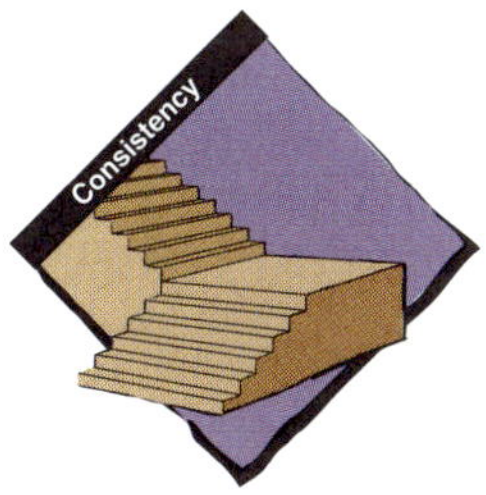

Make labels for interface elements easy to understand in order to help users use your product. When you write labels for screen elements, try to speak in the user's language.

In labels or names for menu items, checkboxes, radio buttons, and push buttons, use book title capitalization style. This style is referred to as caps/lowercase. In general, this means that you capitalize every word except articles (*a*, *an*, *the*), coordinating conjunctions (for example, *and*, *or*), and prepositions of three or fewer letters (except when a preposition is part of a verb phrase). The specific rules of this type of capitalization appears in detail in the *Apple Publications Style Guide*. Figure 11-1 shows some examples of elements that follow these capitalization rules.

Figure 11-1 Proper capitalization of screen elements

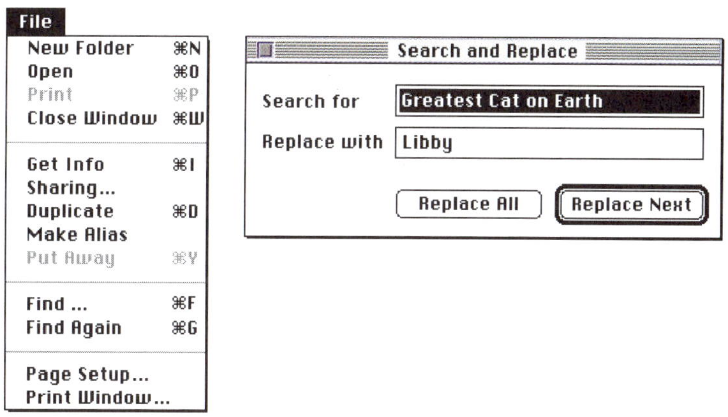

Make sure that the title of the menu fits the items in the menu. For example, the Font menu can contain names of font families such as Helvetica, Geneva, and New York, but it should *not* include editing commands such as Cut and Copy. Use singular for menu titles unless a particular menu title doesn't make sense in the singular (such as Graphics). Apple recommends a number of standard menu titles such as File, Edit, and Font. The most important factor is that you be consistent in your use of menu titles. In other words, try not to create a menu bar that contains both plural and singular menu titles–for example, use Size and Style, *not* Sizes and Style.

Try to be as specific as possible in your labels or names for radio buttons, push buttons, and checkboxes. It can be difficult to name a particular action or option in a word or two, but it's important to be concise and clear. In any case, don't sacrifice clarity for space. Figure 11-2 shows a good example of push button names that are short and accurate.

Figure 11-2 Clear button names

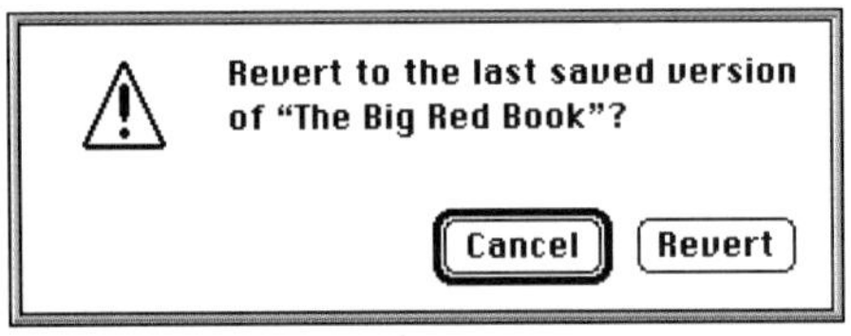

For more information on names for push buttons, see "Button Names" on page 206 in Chapter 7, "Controls."

Dialog Box Messages

This section focuses mostly on messages in caution alert boxes and stop alert boxes, but you can apply the principles to messages in other dialog boxes.

Dialog boxes and alert boxes communicate to the user. It is your responsibility to make sure that the user can understand what is going on when you can't be there to explain. Dialog box and alert box messages should be descriptive rather than evaluative. When you're writing messages, try to put yourself in the place of your users and imagine how they will feel when confronted with your message.

A good alert box message says what went wrong, why it went wrong, and what the user can do about it. Try to express everything in the user's vocabulary. Figure 11-3 shows an example of an alert box message that provides little information and doesn't suggest to the user what is really going on.

Figure 11-3 A poorly written alert box message

You could improve this message by describing the problem in the user's vocabulary, as shown in Figure 11-4.

Figure 11-4 An improved alert box message

To really make this alert box useful to the user, you need to provide some suggestion about what the user can do to get out of the current situation. Figure 11-5 shows the optimal alert box message for this condition.

Figure 11-5 A well-written alert box message

Some dialog boxes include categories of options presented as lists of radio buttons or checkboxes with options. Often a phrase introduces the set of options. Don't include a colon after the phrase that introduces a list if that list is a complement or object of a verb or preposition in the introductory statement. In other words, don't use a colon when the introductory phrase is not a complete sentence and the items in the list complete the sentence. For example, the phrase that follows does not contain a colon:

The objects included are

- □ radio buttons
- □ checkboxes
- □ push buttons
- □ text boxes

Though you may find some situations in which a colon is used to introduce a bulleted list, Apple's publications generally follow the style given in the *The Chicago Manual of Style* and *Words Into Type*, which recommend *not* using a colon in that kind of construction. Another example that illustrates when you would *not* use a colon is shown in Figure 11-6.

Figure 11-6 Correct absence of a colon to introduce a list of options

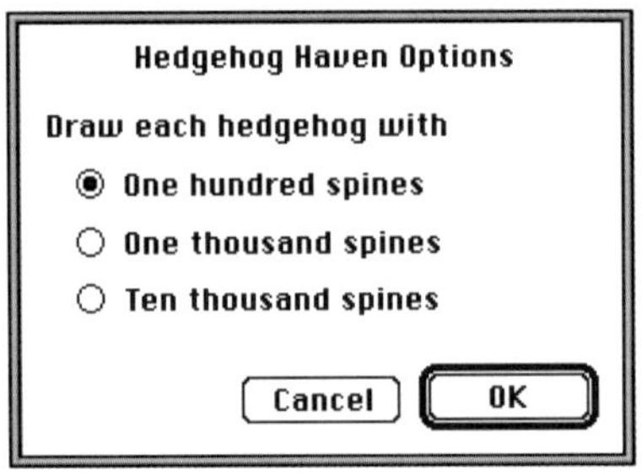

Use a colon after an introductory statement that contains the words *as follows* or *the following*. Figure 11-7 shows an example of when to use a colon.

Figure 11-7 Correct use of a colon

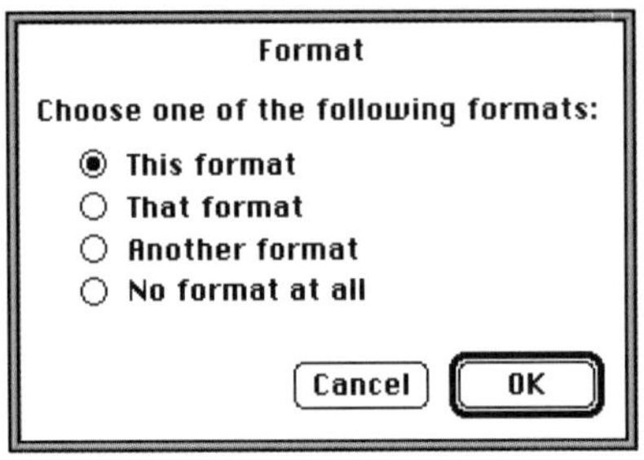

User Documentation

Documentation for users is an essential part of the user interface that you provide. Try to give it the same degree of consideration and attention that you give to your application's user interface. Consider the audience that you address with your product and tailor the documentation to its needs. It's often useful to provide alternate types of documentation for the different types of users who make up your audience. Beginners have different needs from those of expert users.

Plan an overall learning path for your users. This can help target your documentation to specific types of users. A well-designed learning path can help users approach the documentation according to their style of learning. For example, some users may want to be shown exactly how to do something and they may have an easier time learning about a product by practicing using it. A tutorial would be perfect for this type of user. Other users may want to explore and learn by their mistakes; they may read the documentation only to learn about advanced features or to troubleshoot a specific problem. A specific task-oriented set of instructions would be ideal for this type of user. The following list presents a general model for a learning path.

- Setting up or installing the product.

  Provide easy-to-follow, brief instructions that help users to set up the hardware and install the software necessary to begin using the product.

- Learning how to use the product.

  Include a tutorial that introduces core concepts and fundamental skills, and that explains why a user would want to use the product. Ideally this kind of information should be interactive and lead users, via a series of exercises, through several scenarios where they can learn the most common features of the product.

- Using the product.

  Provide detailed instructions about how to accomplish specific tasks, troubleshoot problems, and take advantage of advanced features.

Develop task-oriented documentation that teaches users how to accomplish the tasks that you designed your application to perform. Avoid system-oriented documentation that describes everything that your application can do rather than teaching practical skills.

Use standard terminology and nontechnical language in user documentation. Don't pass on technical jargon to users; they may not understand it. When you must use technical terms, be sure to define them at first occurrence, and include a glossary if your document has many specialized terms. Be consistent in your use of terminology. Make sure that messages and terms that users see on the screen match what appears in the documentation.

When you localize your software product, you'll need to translate all user documentation, including tutorials, online help, and books. Making your documentation available in a user's native language greatly enhances the usability and marketability of your product.

Tutorials, manuals, online help, and other forms of documentation cannot compensate for an interface that is hard to use. Documentation can't "fix" problems that need to be resolved in the interface itself. Thus, try to treat all documentation as part of the end user product and as part of the interface with which users must interact.

Online Help Systems

This section discusses the basic principles and guidelines for building a useful online help system for your application. You can include your help system in the Help menu by adding one or more menu items to it. For more information about the Help menu, see "The Help Menu" on page 125 in Chapter 4, "Menus."

Provide Concurrent Help

A usable help system must present instructions within the users' working context so that they can actually do the actions that they are instructed to perform. If a help system obscures or replaces users' work, they might forget the specifics of their problem. In addition, users would have to read and memorize the help before returning to their work. When users activate help, do not switch them to a separate application or mode for delivering the information. Rather, display the information within the working context so that the user's application remains active or in control. In other words, allow the user to find the necessary help information while working on their particular task. Balloon Help is an example of help that doesn't take users out of their current context, but allows them to see the problem and solution simultaneously. See "Balloon Help," beginning on page 316, for a description of Balloon Help.

Provide Multiple Levels of Help

Users who are just starting to learn how to use an application need a type of help different from that which experienced users need. It's a good idea to provide more than one type of help so that you can meet the needs of users at all levels. Use the Help menu to divide your help into components for different levels of users. For example, an application might add three commands to the Help menu: Tutorial, Help, and Shortcuts.

The Tutorial command would provide an introduction for users who are new to an application or need an overview of its features. The Help command would assist casual and regular users who have reached an impasse using the application. The Shortcuts commands would provide intermediate users with tips to increase the efficiency with which they use the application.

Assist Users by Answering Their Questions

When users need help, they often have at least one question in mind. Users' questions fall into a number of distinct categories, and those categories call for different types of assistance. Provide different types of help for different categories of questions. For example, there is a clear distinction between the question "what is this?" and the question "how do I do this?" The first question asks more about the nature of an object or task while the second question requests instructions about performing a task. The ideal help system tries to support three categories of questions: procedural, descriptive, and troubleshooting. Table 11-2 gives examples of each type of question.

Table 11-2 Categories of questions for help systems

Category	**Type of question**
Procedural	How do I copy a paragraph?
Descriptive	What is an alias?
Troubleshooting	Why do extra characters appear when I print?

Balloon Help provides descriptive information for items that appear on the user's screen. The help system should augment these descriptions as necessary especially for items that do *not* appear on the screen or that require a more in-depth explanation.

Involving users in your product design process can help you identify the types of questions that your users may ask about your products—especially questions about tasks that users will want to perform. See the section "Involving Users in the Design Process" in Chapter 3, "Human Interface Design and the Development Process," for information about how to conduct user observations.

Showing users how to accomplish work should form the core of the help system. Once you have a set of user questions, you can organize the answers—and the ways to get to those answers—in ways that best serve your users.

Keep the Help System Simple

Help systems should present a sensible set of core actions to users without overloading them with too many complex features. Although you can use a few words of instruction to prompt users on how to use the help system (like "click here" or "select a topic"), don't turn the help system into a complicated application that requires lengthy instructions. In general, users don't really want to spend time using a help system. They just want to find the information they need and get back to their work.

Design Online Help as an Interactive Coach

As a method for communication, computers provide opportunities that books can't provide. The full benefits of online help appear when a help system can interact with a user and make use of the context in which the user is working. Where appropriate, a help system can also play sounds, run animations, and play movies. Rather than producing an online document, a help system should bring relevant information to users when they need it and guide them through the interface just as a human teacher would. Your help system needs to assist users with a problem as efficiently as possible without requiring the users to study a topic in depth.

Balloon Help

Balloon Help provides onscreen descriptions of items in balloons shaped like cartoon speech balloons. The user turns on Balloon Help when he or she wants to find out something about an interface element. Once Balloon Help is turned on, the balloon for an item appears when the user moves the pointer to an item. The balloon stays on the screen until the user moves the pointer away from the item. In this way, users get context-sensitive, task-oriented information exactly when they need it. Figure 11-8 shows an example of a help balloon.

Figure 11-8 A help balloon

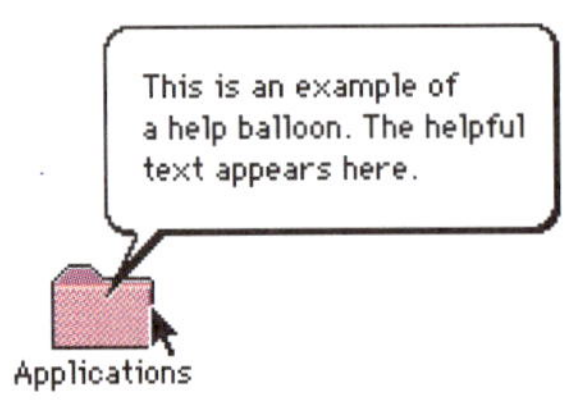

This section briefly describes the kinds of items for which you can add balloons and provides some guidelines for writing the text in balloons. For information on implementing Balloon Help in your application, see *Inside Macintosh: More Macintosh Toolbox.* For complete information on writing the text in balloons, see "How to Write Balloons," a supplement to the *Apple Publications Style Guide.* For additional information on creating balloons, refer to the *Balloon Writer User's Guide,* which is available from APDA.

When to Use a Help Balloon

Balloon Help is designed always to be available to users, even when a modal dialog box is on the screen. This is so that users can get help when they need it, without having to stop what they are doing and look in a separate location for information about what they are doing.

Use help balloons to explain elements of your application's interface that might confuse a new user or elements that could help a user become an expert user. The information provided in help balloons should identify interface elements in your application or explain how to use them. When considering whether or not to use a help balloon, try to think about the types of questions users are most likely to have about elements in your application. For example, are there any elements in your application that don't usually appear in other Macintosh applications? It's helpful to think about the types of users who will be using your application: are they novices or are they experienced computer users? And finally, think about the terminology used in your application that users may not be familiar with.

Help balloons should be short and easy to understand. Don't include lengthy instructions or numbered steps in balloons. Use clear, concise language in balloons. Write help messages that describe what an object in your application does; the user wants to know what will happen if he or she uses that particular object.

It's not necessary to name every object in your application in the balloons, especially if they're already named on screen. It's more important that the user find out how to use an object than it is for the user to know the object's exact name. Some exceptions to this guideline include items whose names help describe how to use the item. These include tools in palettes, controls on a ruler, controls in a paint program, or icons that don't already have names on the screen.

It's a good idea to provide separate help balloons for each state of a menu item or dialog item. For example, write separate balloons for the selected, unselected, and unavailable state of radio buttons and checkboxes. Where appropriate, use parallel wording for the balloons belonging to a single item.

It's especially important to write a separate help balloon for a situation the user might find difficult to figure out. For example, if a selection in a Preferences dialog box causes some menu command to be dimmed, a special balloon for that command should appear when that selection is on.

For groups of controls, it may make sense to use one help balloon to describe the whole group rather than providing a separate help balloon for each control. For example, the help balloon for a group of radio buttons used to set the margins of a document might describe all three options: left, right, and center. Help balloons can also describe a complicated dialog box by telling users what they can accomplish by using each of the features or options in the dialog box.

How to Write a Balloon

Users turn on Balloon Help when they need information about something they don't understand. Sometimes this happens when they are exploring the interface. Other times, users are looking for some helpful information to get them out of a situation that confuses them. Users are most likely to read and understand your balloons in either situation if you use the fewest possible words. If your balloons will be translated from English into another language, the text will most likely get longer. The text in balloons can be up to 255 characters long, or it can use up to 32 KB if you include graphics such as styled text. In order to keep translated balloons within this limit, it's a good idea to limit messages to a maximum of approximately 180 characters in English.

Use active voice in your help balloons. Active voice uses fewer words and is easier to read than passive voice. For example, you could say "To resize the window, drag this box." In passive voice the same explanation would be "This size box is used to resize the window. The box is dragged to resize the window." The second example is a lot longer than the first and requires the user to think about two sentences before acting.

In help balloons, you can use sentence fragments, leaving out the subject of the sentence if the item is named on screen. Put the thing that the user really wants to know first in the balloon. For example, you could write "Saves changes to the active document" to describe what the Save command does. This sentence fragment makes it immediately clear to the user what the command will do if the user chooses it. Use sentences fragments with menu commands, checkboxes and radio buttons that aren't available, and radio buttons that are selected.

Define unfamiliar words by using other words that explain the concept, especially for menu items and buttons. This helps users who aren't sure what the item means. For example, don't describe the Undo command by writing "Undoes your last action." Instead, use different wording that has the same meaning, such as "Cancels your last action."

When you are describing how to use an onscreen element, include only one way of doing something. You can include descriptions of other ways to do actions in your printed or online documentation. In help balloons, describe just the simplest method.

You can use help balloons to draw a user's attention to a few interesting features in your application that the user may not readily discover on his or her own. But be selective about the features for which you provide hints. Don't provide help balloons for obscure features that few users will ever need. And if you do include a hint, place it on a separate line at the end of the balloon. Be careful not to include too many hints because this will make your balloons longer and more difficult to understand.

Wording for Specific Balloon Types

Use similar wording in similar balloons to make it easier for the user to read the balloon messages. Unnecessary variations in wording are distracting. Using phrasing similar to that described here will help your users quickly assimilate the information since the structure of the information will be familiar.

Buttons With Words

For buttons that appear in dialog boxes, use the construction

"To [perform action], click this button."

Figure 11-9 shows an example of a help balloon for a button.

Figure 11-9 Help balloon for a button

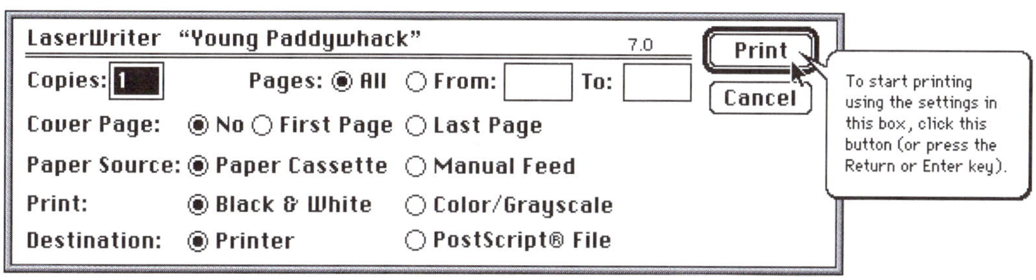

Menu Titles

For pull-down menu titles, give the title of the menu and then describe what kinds of commands are in the menu. You provide the title of the menu because some menus on the menu bar are icons, not words. Figure 11-10 shows an example of this type of help balloon.

Figure 11-10 Help balloon for a menu title

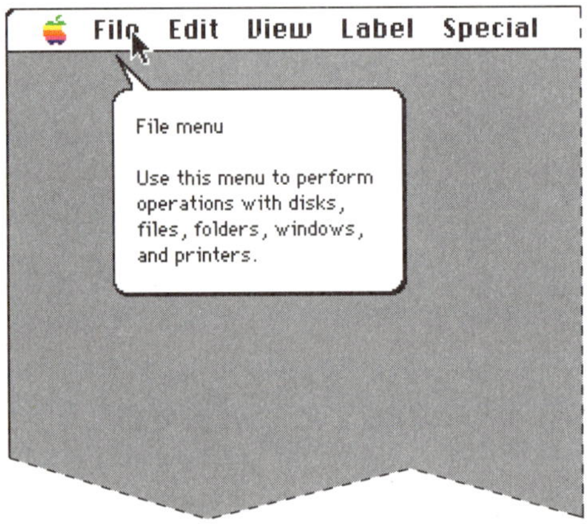

For pop-up menus, describe what to do with the menu. Don't give the menu a name. For example, you could say, "Use this pop-up menu to describe items you want to find."

Menu Items

Don't name the individual items in a menu. Begin with a verb describing what happens when you choose the item. Figure 11-11 shows an example of a help balloon for a common menu item and an example of how to write a help balloon for the same menu item when it's unavailable (dimmed).

Figure 11-11 Help balloon for a menu item

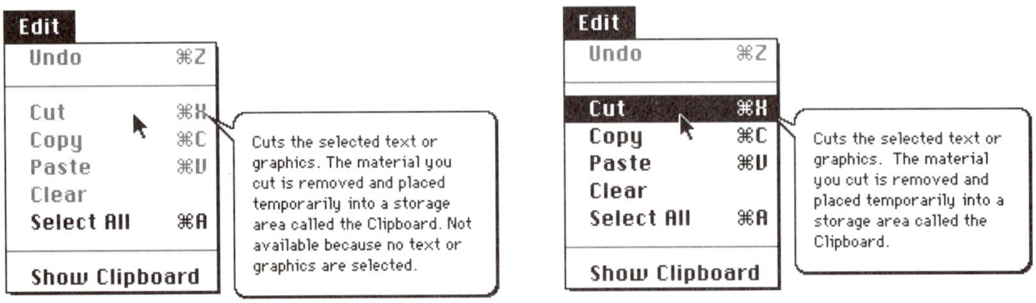

For menu items that require more information and display a dialog box, it's not necessary to say that a dialog box appears. The user wants to know what choosing the menu item ultimately accomplishes.

Radio Buttons

It's best to provide separate balloons for selected, unselected, and unavailable radio buttons. For selected radio buttons, describe what the button does, beginning with a verb. At the end of the balloon, say that the button is selected. Figure 11-12 shows an example of this.

Figure 11-12 Help balloon for a selected radio button

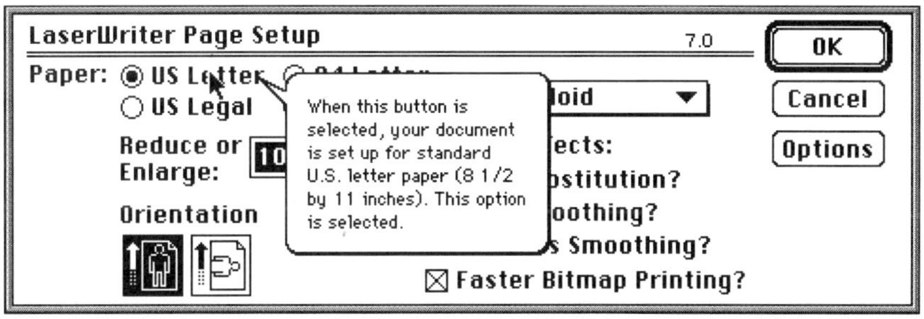

For an unselected radio button, describe what happens when you select the button. For example, you could say, "To align the objects at the left margin of the document, click this button." For a button that's not available, describe what the button does when selected using a sentence fragment beginning with a verb. Then explain why it is not available. For example, a balloon might say, "Aligns objects at the left margin of the document. Not available because no objects are selected."

Checkboxes

For checkboxes, you need to provide several pieces of information. Describe the current state of the system (what the system does currently, given whether the option is selected or not), an explanation of the option provided by the checkbox, and how to turn it on or off. Don't describe the current state of the system if it's obvious or if it would involve saying merely, "This option is *not* on." Also, don't include an explanation of the option if your users don't need one.

Figure 11-13 shows an example of a help balloon for a checkbox.

Figure 11-13 Help balloon for a checkbox

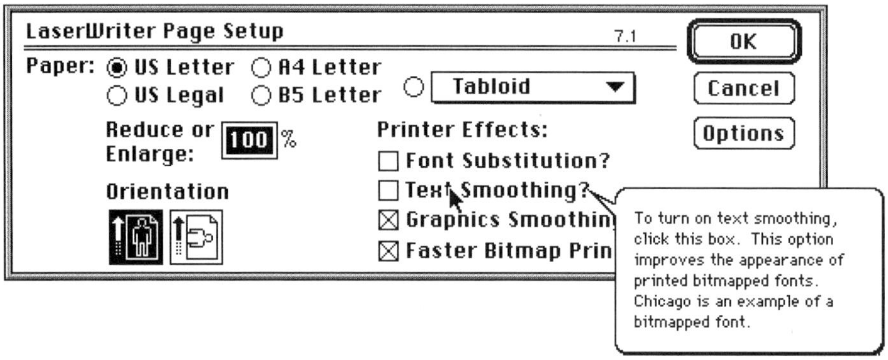

Note that the help balloon shown in Figure 11-13 tells the user about the current state of the system by the way it phrases the sentence: "To turn on text smoothing, click this box." (This means that text smoothing is *not* currently being used.) If the sentence were phrased like this: "To turn *off* text smoothing, click this box," it would tell us the opposite information about the current state of the system (that text smoothing *is* currently being used).

For unavailable checkboxes, describe what the box does when it's selected and then explain why it is not available. This case is similar to that of an unavailable radio button.

Groups of Checkboxes or Radio Buttons

You can provide a single balloon for an entire group of radio buttons, or for a group of closely related checkboxes. When providing one balloon for a group of options, describe what you can do with the options, how to implement the options, and how you can tell whether an option is selected.

Figure 11-14 Help balloon for a group of radio buttons

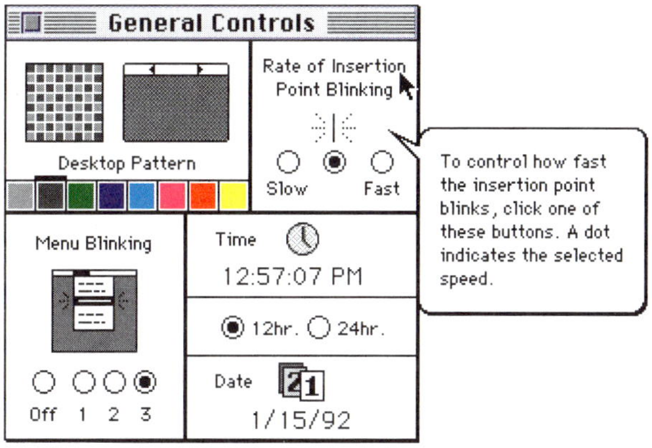

Tools in Palettes

It's a good idea to name tools in palettes, because the name can help the user figure out what the tool is for. After naming the tool, describe one or two likely ways to use it. Don't describe every shortcut or trick you can do with the modifier keys. Figure 11-15 shows one example of a help balloon for a tool in a palette.

Figure 11-15 Help balloon for a tool palette

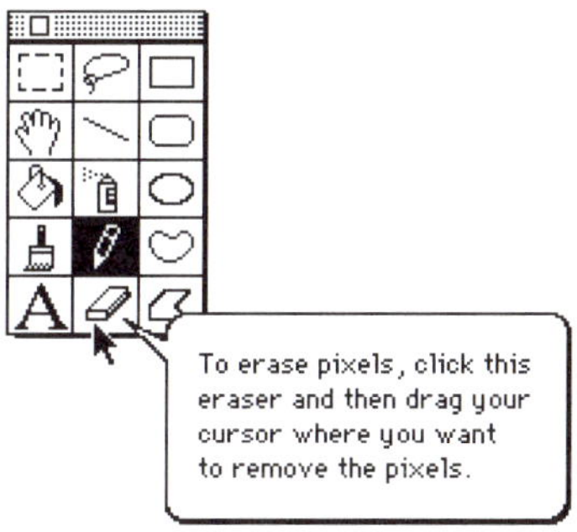

Window Parts

Apple provides standard balloons for standard window parts. If your windows have nonstandard parts, use the general guidelines for writing balloons to describe them. Name only the parts of the window that it's necessary for the user to know.

Modal Dialog Box on the Screen

When there is a dialog box on the screen, you can add the following wording to the end of each balloon that refers to an unavailable item:

> "Not available because a modal dialog box is on the screen."

Icons

Apple provides standard balloons for icons. If you wish, you can provide your own balloons for your application and its associated special files, but don't provide balloons for your application's document icons.

You don't need to describe how to open icons; you can assume that Macintosh users know how. Figure 11-16 shows the standard help balloons for an application icon and a document icon.

Figure 11-16 Help balloons for an application icon and a document icon

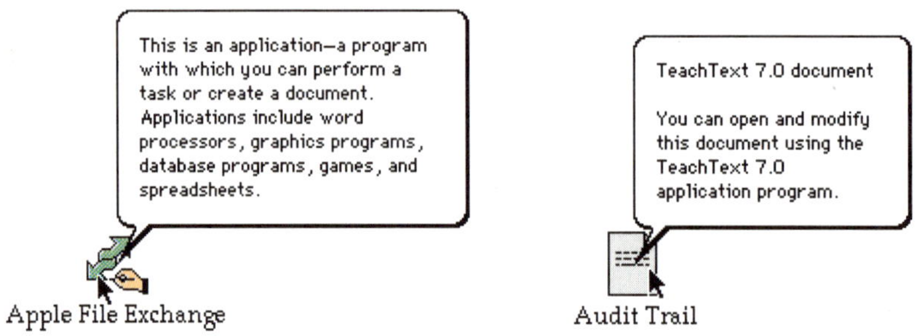

Text Entry Boxes

When you describe text entry boxes in dialog boxes, use *here* to describe the area. You don't have to name the area, or describe standard Macintosh editing procedures. Figure 11-17 shows an example of a help balloon for a text entry box.

Figure 11-17 Help balloon for a text entry box

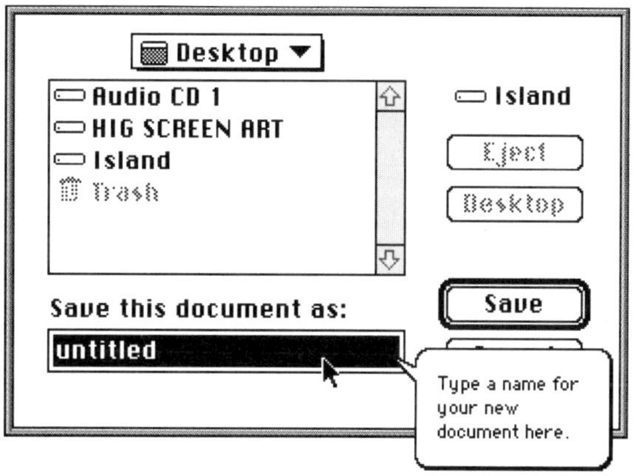

Appendixes

The appendixes provide additional information about the topics discussed in this book. Appendix A describes resources such as professional societies and conferences from which you can get additional information. Appendix B is a bibliography that presents major works on topics discussed in the book. Refer to this appendix when you want to find where to get more extensive information or training on a topic such as color or menus. Appendix C provides a checklist for you to use when evaluating your product to make sure it meets the intent and purpose of the Macintosh human interface guidelines.

Resources

This appendix lists some resources that provide more information about human interface design or human-computer interaction.

Association for Computing Machinery (ACM)

The ACM is a large organization consisting of many special interest groups, or SIGs. It is dedicated to the development of information processing as a discipline and to the responsible use of computers in an increasing diversity of applications. Contact the ACM at

Association for Computing Machinery
11 West 42nd Street
New York, NY 10036
212-869-7440

Communications of the ACM

Communications of the ACM is a journal published monthly by the ACM. It contains topical articles, a calendar of events, and listings for available positions in the fields of computer science, information science, and engineering.

SIGCHI

SIGCHI (Special Interest Group in Computer Human Interaction) is a special interest group of the ACM concerned with computer and human interaction. SIGCHI encompasses all aspects of the human-computer interaction process, including research and development efforts leading to the design and evaluation of user interfaces. This group focuses on how people communicate and interact with computer systems.

There are some local SIGCHI groups that meet monthly and present programs on human-computer interaction. Contact the ACM for more information.

The *SIGCHI Bulletin* is a journal published by SIGCHI. It contains articles, news about the group's activities, and a calendar of events.

The Computer Human Interaction Conference (called CHI) is a yearly conference on human-computer interaction. The conference has papers, panels, posters, lab reviews, and small group meetings on topics of interest.

This conference is held in the spring. The conference proceedings are published as a special edition of the *SIGCHI Bulletin*.

The Symposium on User Interface Software and Technology is a joint conference of SIGCHI and SIGGRAPH, the special interest group devoted to computer graphics and animation. It is usually held in the fall.

SIGGRAPH

SIGGRAPH (Special Interest Group on Graphics) is a special interest group of the ACM concerned with computer graphics and animation. SIGGRAPH addresses all types of professionals involved in the computer graphics community. SIGGRAPH publishes a research journal and sponsors an annual conference.

There are a number of local SIGGRAPH groups that discuss graphics issues and participate in related projects. Contact SIGGRAPH through the ACM for more information about local groups and events.

Computer Graphics is the official journal of SIGGRAPH. Published three times a year, *Computer Graphics* presents book reviews, conference information, research papers, articles on graphics-related topics, and a calendar of upcoming events.

SIGGRAPH is an annual conference that provides a forum for the presentation and publication of scholarly papers on computer graphics. The conference includes technical programs and courses, discussion panels, exhibits, and technical papers; and provides a marketplace for computer graphics hardware, software, and systems. It is usually held in the summer.

CSCW

CSCW (Computer Supported Cooperative Work Conference) is a biannual conference on cooperative work in the computer environment, sponsored jointly by SIGCHI and SIGOIS (Special Interest Group Office Information Systems). The conference looks at all aspects of CSCW, including meeting-coordination software, mail systems, and other collaborative efforts. In particular, the sessions focus on the social considerations of cooperative work from an anthropological standpoint. The conference proceedings are published by the ACM.

Human Factors Society

The Human Factors Society is an interdisciplinary organization of professional people involved in the field of human factors. The human factors field concerns the characteristics of human beings that are applicable to the design of systems of people, machine, and environments.

The Human Factors Society sponsors various technical groups that focus on particular aspects of the human factors field. The technical groups hold meetings, sponsor symposia and conferences, publish newsletters and proceedings, and sponsor technical sessions at the Human Factors Society Annual Meeting.

The Human Factors Society has chapters throughout the United States and in Europe that sponsor local meetings and publications. Contact the Human Factors Society at

Human Factors Society
P.O. Box 1369
Santa Monica, CA 90406
FAX: 310-394-2410
Phones: 310-394-1811; 310-394-9793

Human Factors Society Annual Meeting

The Human Factors Society Annual Meeting is usually held in September or October. It includes a technical program consisting of research reports, panel discussions, and workshops; a business meeting; exhibits; an awards ceremony and banquet; and tours of local facilities of interest.

Human Factors

The bimonthly journal *Human Factors* presents original papers of scientific merit that contribute to the understanding and advance the systematic consideration of human factors. It features articles on methodology and procedures, literature reviews, broad technical research results; articles on research applications; and papers of general professional interest.

Human Factors Society Bulletin

The monthly journal *Human Factors Society Bulletin* features articles of interest to human factors practitioners; timely information about conferences, elections, publications, employment opportunities, and local chapter and technical group activities; and book reviews, editorials, and letters to the editor.

Apple Developer Information

Apple Computer, Inc. offers developers a number of different sources of information. This section lists several developer organizations and describes how to contact the organizations to learn more about them.

APDA

APDA is Apple's worldwide source for over 300 development tools, technical resources, training products, and information for anyone interested in developing applications on Apple platforms. Customers receive the quarterly *APDA Tools Catalog* featuring all current versions of Apple and the most popular third-party development tools. Ordering is easy; there are no membership fees, and application forms are not required for most APDA products. APDA offers convenient payment and shipping options including site licensing.

To order products or to request a complimentary copy of the *APDA Tools Catalog*, contact APDA at

APDA
Apple Computer, Inc.
P.O. Box 319
Buffalo, New York 14207-0319
Phone: 800-282-2732 (U.S.)
800-637-0029 (Canada)
716-871-6555 (International)
FAX: 716-871-6511
AppleLink: APDA
CompuServe: 76666,2405
GEnie: A.DEVELOPER3
Internet: APDA@applelink.apple.com

Developer Support Center

If you are developing a product you plan to sell commercially, please call 408-974-4897 for information on the developer support programs available from Apple. The Developer Support Center provides technical support only to those developers who are members of these programs.

For information on registering unique Creator and File Types, please contact

Developer Support Center
Apple Computer, Inc.
20525 Mariani Avenue, M/S 75-3T
Cupertino, CA 95014-6299
408-974-4897
AppleLink: DEVSUPPORT

In-House Development Support

If you create custom applications for internal use within your organization, call 1-800-950-2442 for information on how to obtain technical documentation and direct access to Apple development support engineers to help you integrate the Macintosh into existing enterprise computing solutions.

develop

Apple's quarterly technical journal, *develop,* helps reduce development time and enhance programming savvy by providing an in-depth look at code and techniques that show the "Apple way" of doing things. The journal contains full-length articles, columns, and question-and-answer sections. In addition, each issue of the journal comes with the latest Developer CD Series disc, which contains the source code for that issue, all back issues of *develop,* *Inside Macintosh,* technical notes, sample code, and more.

Bibliography

This bibliography contains a list of sources of additional information on the topics discussed in this book. The bibliography lists books and journal articles in sections organized by topic. The following symbols help you to identify the nature of some of the works listed.

- This symbol indicates a work of general interest or an overview of the topic. It's a place to start if you know little or nothing about a topic.

- This symbol indicates a work that is seminal in its field. Consult a reference marked with this symbol to find out about the basic research and original ideas on the topic.

- This symbol indicates a work that requires that you have a great deal of knowledge in the field in order to find the work useful.

This bibliography presents materials on the following topics:

- Animation
- Cognitive Psychology and Human Factors
- Color
- Environmental Design
- Graphic and Information Design
- History of Human Interface
- Human-Computer Design
- Human-Computer Interaction
- Language
- Programming
- Special Applications
- Universal Access
- Visual Thinking
- Worldwide Software

Animation

Blair, Preston. *Cartoon Animation.* In How to Draw and Paint Series. Tustin, CA: Walter Foster, 1989.

Blair, Preston. *How to Animate Film Cartoons.* In How to Draw and Paint Series. Tustin, CA: Walter Foster, 1989.

Muybridge, Eadweard. *Animals in Motion.* New York: Dover, 1957.

Shows step-by-step photographs of 34 different animals in 123 kinds of motion. Contains a selection of plates from the 1887 original work. These illustrations are useful to anyone creating animations of animals.

Muybridge, Eadweard. *The Human Figure in Motion.* New York: Dover, 1955.

Shows step-by-step photographs of 163 different kinds of human action. Contains a selection of plates from the 1887 original work. These illustrations are useful to anyone creating animations of people.

Noake, Roger. *Animation Techniques.* New York: Chartwell House, 1989.

Thomas, Frank, and Ollie Johnston. *Disney Animation, The Illusion of Life.* New York: Abbeville Press, 1981.

Presents animation techniques as they evolved at the Disney studios. This 575-page book, heavily illustrated with Disney characters, covers animation's evolution since 1923 and discusses aspects such as story, character development, backgrounds, and animation techniques.

Cognitive Psychology and Human Factors

Fitts, P. M. "The Information Capacity of the Human Motor System in Controlling Amplitude of Movement." *Journal of Experimental Psychology* 47 (1954): 381–391.

Lindsay, Peter H., and Donald A. Norman. *Human Information Processing: An Introduction to Psychology.* New York: Academic Press, 1977.

An engaging textbook that covers a wide range of issues in cognitive psychology.

Long, J., and A. Whitefield. *Cognitive Ergonomics and Human-Computer Interaction.* Cambridge, England: Cambridge University Press, 1989.

Miller, G. A. "The Magical Number Seven, Plus or Minus Two: Some Limits on Our Capability for Processing Information." *Psychological Review* 63 (1956): 81–97.

A well-written, classic paper describing the size of short-term memory.

Norman, Donald A. *Learning and Memory.* San Francisco: W. H. Freeman, 1982.

Provides a good introduction to the processes involved in learning and memory. An excellent presentation of many of the basic concepts of cognitive psychology in little more than a hundred pages.

Norman, Donald A. *Memory and Attention: An Introduction to Human Information Processing,* second edition. New York: Wiley, 1976.

Provides a thorough treatment of the processes involved in attending to, acquiring, and remembering information. This 254-page book approaches most issues by setting the stage, presenting excerpts from one or more groundbreaking papers in the area, and then discussing and commenting on them. This book is fairly accessible to most audiences.

Sanders, Mark, and Ernest J. McCormick. *Workbook for Human Factors in Engineering and Design.* Dubuque, IA: Kendall/Hunt, 1990.

Tillman, Barry, and Peggy Tillman. *Human Factors Essentials: An Ergonomics Guide for Designers, Engineers, Scientists, and Managers.* New York: McGraw-Hill, 1991.

Color

Albers, Josef. *Interaction of Color.* New Haven, CT: Yale University Press, 1963.

Favre, Jean-Paul, and Andre November. *Color and Communication.* Zürich: ABC Verlag, 1979.

Itten, Johannes. *The Elements of Color.* New York: Van Nostrand Reinhold, 1970.

Murch, Gerald M. "Physiological Principles for the Effective Use of Color." *IEEE Computer Graphics and Applications* 4, no. 11 (November 1984): 49–55.

Salomon, Gitta. "New Uses for Color." In *The Art of Human Computer Interface Design*, edited by Brenda Laurel, 269. Reading, MA: Addison-Wesley, 1990.

Discusses the use of color in human computer interface design. This article describes a variety of interface-related issues, including interfaces for choosing colors and using color for visualization and mnemonic purposes.

Sloane, Patricia. *The Visual Nature of Color.* Blue Ridge Summit, PA: TAB Books, 1989.

Thorell, L. G., and W. J. Smith. *Using Computer Color Effectively.* Englewood Cliffs, NJ: Prentice-Hall, 1990.

Wyszecki, Gunter, and W. S. Stiles. *Colour Science.* New York: Wiley, 1982.

Environmental Design

Alexander, Christopher, Sara Ishikawa, and Murray Silverstein. *A Pattern Language, Towns/Buildings/Construction*. New York: Oxford University Press, 1977.

Bentley, Ian, and others. *Responsive Environments: A Manual for Designers.* London: Architectural Press, 1985.

Contains design principles and examples directed toward urban designers, architects, and landscape architects. In spite of its practical orientation, the design principles—permeability, variety, legibility, robustness, visual appropriateness, richness, and personalization—can be easily transposed to the human interface domain.

Gehl, Jan. *Life Between Buildings.* Translated by Jo Koch. New York: Van Nostrand Reinhold, 1986.

Discusses attributes of the physical environment that make small urban spaces (for example, squares and streets) more or less supportive of human-human interaction.

Lynch, Kevin. *The Image of the City.* Cambridge, MA: MIT Press, 1960.

A classic work that describes the author's studies of the regularities of mental maps formed by the inhabitants of three cities. His analysis of the five basic elements of city images, and the ways in which they contribute to the legibility and navigability of their environments, can be applied to a variety of representation and navigation problems within the HCI (human-computer interaction) domain.

Places: A Quarterly Journal of Environmental Design. Cambridge, MA: MIT Press.

This journal is aimed at architects, urban and landscape designers, and others concerned with imbuing their designs with a sense of place. It's relevant to the field of human-computer interaction in two ways. First, understanding how the large-scale physical environment shapes human interaction can be important in the design of systems such as public information kiosks. Second, lessons about how the physical environment facilitates human interaction can be transposed to the domain of human-computer interaction. These lessons can be applied directly to the HCI domain as 3-D environments within the computer become more prevalent. The lessons also can be applied indirectly as computer interfaces–whether 2-D or 3-D–take on more of the richness and flexibility that characterize the real world.

Whyte, William H. *City: Rediscovering the Center.* New York: Anchor Books, Doubleday, 1988.

A uniformly fascinating study of the behaviors of people in urban spaces. Focuses particular attention to the physical factors that affect human-human and human-city interaction.

Graphic and Information Design

This section includes resources on several different subjects related to the design of graphic user interfaces.

Graphic Design and Drawing

Bang, Molly. *Picture This: Perception and Composition.* Boston: Little, Brown, 1991.

Introduces the basic principles of graphic composition with elegance and simplicity. Provides an excellent overview of the ideas and concepts involved in graphic design.

Berryman, Greg. *Notes on Graphic Design and Visual Communication.* Los Altos, CA: William Kaufmann, 1984.

Discusses logos, colors, and many other topics related to graphic design.

Bertin, Jacques. *Semiology of Graphics.* Madison: University of Wisconsin Press, 1983.

Galitz, W. O. *Handbook of Screen Format Design.* Wellesley, MA: QED Information Sciences, 1985.

Henri, Robert. *The Art Spirit.* New York: HarperCollins, 1984.

Kerlow, Isaac, and Judson Rosebush. *Computer Graphics for Designers and Artists.* New York: Van Nostrand Reinhold, 1986.

Tufte, Edward. *Envisioning Information.* Cheshire, CT: Graphics Press, 1990.

Tufte, Edward. *The Visual Display of Quantitative Information.* Cheshire, CT: Graphics Press, 1983.

Wurman, Richard S. *Follow the Yellow Brick Road: Learning to Give, Take, and Use Instructions.* New York: Bantam Books, 1992.

Wurman, Richard S. *Information Anxiety: What to Do When Information Doesn't Tell You What You Need to Know.* New York: Bantam Books, 1990.

Icons and Symbols

Diethelm, Walter. *Signet Sign Symbol.* Zürich: ABC Verlag, 1976.

Dreyfuss, Henry. *Symbol Sourcebook: An Authoritative Guide to International Graphic Symbols.* New York: Van Nostrand Reinhold, 1984.

Presents thousands of symbols, presented first by subject, then by shape, and finally in the index by name. This book provides a fertile source for the designer seeking icons or other stylized design images.

Frutiger, Adrian. *Signs and Symbols: Their Design and Meaning.* New York: Van Nostrand Reinhold, 1989.

Holmes, Nigel, with Rose DeNeve. *Designing Pictorial Symbols.* New York: Watson-Guptil, 1985.

Presents 54 case studies of how concepts were transformed into icons. This book is useful because it not only shows the finished icon but also explains the stages and thoughts that the designer went through to create each icon.

Modley, Rudolf. *Handbook of Pictorial Symbols.* New York: Dover Publications, 1976.

Wildbur, Peter. *Information Graphics.* New York: Van Nostrand Reinhold, 1989.

Typography

Bigelow, C., and D. Day. "Digital Typography." *Scientific American* 249, no. 2 (1983): 94–105.

Carter, Rob, Ben Day, and Philip Meggs. *Typographic Design: Form and Communication.* New York: Van Nostrand Reinhold, 1985.

Describes the evolution and function of typography and illustrates several typefaces in different sizes. Devoted almost entirely to print technology, this book provides a thorough understanding of typography's roots.

Frutiger, Adrian. *Type Sign Symbol.* Zürich: ABC Verlag, 1980.

Tinker, M. A. *Legibility of Print.* Ames: Iowa State University Press, 1963.

History of Human Interface

Engelbart, D. C., and W. K. English. "A Research Center for Augmenting Human Intellect."*Proceedings of the FJCC* 33 (1968): 395–410.

Johnson, Jeff, and others. "The Xerox Star: A Retrospective." *Computer* 22, no. 9 (September 1989): 11–26, 28–29.

Describes the Xerox 8010 Star information system, which was designed as an office automation system. The article identifies the distinctive features of Xerox Star and examines changes to its original design. It includes a history of Xerox Star development and relates some of the lessons learned during its design.

Kay, A. "Inventing the Future (Computer Industry)." In *AI Business: The Commercial Uses of Artificial Intelligence,* 103–112. Cambridge, MA: MIT Press, 1984.

Proceedings: ACM Conference on the History of Personal Workstations. New York: ACM, 1986.

Smith, D. C., and others. "Designing the Star User Interface." *BYTE* 7, no. 4 (April 1982): 242–282.

Tesler, Larry. "The Legacy of the Lisa." *MacWorld* (September 1985): 17–22.

A description of how the Lisa computer changed personal computing, written by a member of the Lisa design team.

Human-Computer Design

This section presents information about a number of different subjects related to human-computer design. It includes resources for several of the human interface principles described in Chapter 1, "Human Interface Principles."

Consistency

Grudin, J. "The Case Against User Interface Consistency." *Communications of the ACM* 32 (October 1989): 1164–1173.

Polson, P. G. "The Consequences of Consistent and Inconsistent User Interfaces." In *Cognitive Science and Its Applications for Human-Computer Interaction*, edited by R. Guindon. Hillsdale, NJ: Lawrence Erlbaum Associates, 1988.

Tognazzini, Bruce. "Consistency." In *The Art of Human-Computer Interface Design*, edited by Brenda Laurel, 75–77. Reading, MA: Addison-Wesley, 1990.

Direct Manipulation

Hutchins, E. L., J. D. Hollan, and D. A. Norman. "Direct Manipulation Interfaces." In *User Centered System Design*, edited by D.A. Norman and S. Draper. Hillsdale, NJ: Lawrence Erlbaum Associates, 1986.

Minsky, M. R. "Manipulating Simulated Objects With Real-World Gestures Using a Force and Position Sensitive Screen." *Computers & Graphics* (July 1984): 195–203.

Myers, B. A., and W. Buxton. "Creating Highly-Interactive Graphical User Interfaces by Demonstration." *Computer Graphics* (August 1986): 249–256.

Schneiderman, Ben. "Direct Manipulation: A Step Beyond Programming Languages." *IEEE Computer* 16, no. 8: 57–69.

Schneiderman, Ben. "The Future of Interactive Systems and the Emergence of Direct Manipulation." *Behaviour and Information Technology* 1 (1982): 237–256.

Menus

Miller, D. P. "The Depth-Breadth Trade-off in Hierarchical Computer Menus." In *Proceedings of the Human Factors Society 25th Annual Meeting,* 296–300. Santa Monica, CA: Human Factors Society, 1981.

Norman, K. L. *The Psychology of Menu Selection: Designing Cognitive Control at the Human/Computer Interface.* Norwood, NJ: Ablex, 1990.

Walker, N., and J. B. Silencer. "A Comparison of Selection Times From Walking and Pull-Down Menus." *CHI '90 Conference Proceedings* (April 90): 221–225.

A seminal paper on why pull-down menus are superior to any other kind. Everyone who designs for the screen must read this paper.

Metaphors

Carroll, J. M., and others. "Interface Metaphors and User Interface Design." In *Handbook of Human-Computer Interaction,* edited by M. Helander. North-Holland: Elsevier Science Publishers B.V., 1988.

A comprehensive review of research and theoretical work on metaphors, coupled with a discussion of designing with metaphors.

Erickson, T. D. "Working With Interface Metaphors." In *The Art of Human Computer Interface Design,* edited by Brenda Laurel. Reading, MA: Addison-Wesley, 1990.

A discussion of the role of metaphors in the human interface, and a discussion and example of how to design interface metaphors.

Lakoff, George, and Mark Johnson. *Metaphors We Live By.* Chicago: University of Chicago Press, 1980.

A delightful book that discusses the ubiquity of metaphors in language. It makes the point that metaphors are not so much picturesque uses of words, as systems of concepts that affect how we describe, think about, and experience the world.

Malone, T. W. "How Do People Organize Their Desks: Implications for Designing Office Automation Systems." *ACM Transactions on Office Information Systems* 1 (1983): 99–112.

Wozny, L. A. "The Application of Metaphor, Analogy, and Conceptual Models in Computer Systems." *Interacting With Computers* 1, no. 3 (December 1989): 273–283.

A paper that clearly describes the differences between metaphor, analogy, and conceptual models and discusses their applications in the computer domain.

Product Design

International Design. New York: International Design.

A bimonthly design magazine focusing on product design. It shows innovative designs ranging from toasters and lamps to computer systems.

Norman, Donald. *Design of Everyday Things* (formerly *Psychology of Everyday Things*). New York: Basic Books, 1988.

An engaging and thoughtful book that discusses interface issues that arise in the design of door knobs, VCRs, cameras, and microwave ovens. This book offers an excellent introduction and overview for readers who are new to the field of human-computer interaction (HCI) and provides useful information for experienced HCI professionals.

Usability Testing

Bewley, W., T. L. Roberts, D. Schroit, and W. L. Verplank. "Human Factors Testing in the Design of Xerox's 8010 'Star' Office Workstation." *CHI '83 Conference Proceedings*, 72–77.

Bruning, J. L., and B. L. Kintz. *Computational Handbook of Statistics,* third edition. Glenview, IL: Scott, Foresman, 1987.

Holleran, Patrick A. "A Methodological Note on Pitfalls in Usability Testing." *Behavior and Information Technology* 10 (1991): 345–357.

Ramey, J. "Usability Testing: Conducting the Test Procedure Itself." *Proceedings of the International Professional Communication Conference* (1987): 127–130.

Runyon, R. P., and A. Haber. *Fundamentals of Behavioral Statistics,* third edition. Reading, MA: Addison-Wesley, 1979.

Schriver, K. A, ed. *Designing Computer Documentation: A Review of the Relevant Literature.* Communications Design Center Technical Report No. 31, Pittsburgh, PA: Carnegie Mellon University, 1986.

Suter, W. N., and H. C. Lindgren. *Experimentation in Psychology.* Boston: Allyn & Bacon, 1989.

This book describes how to design tests for studies. It provides information on how to minimize biases and avoid common pitfalls.

User-Centered Design

Carroll, John M., ed. *Designing Interaction: Psychology at the Human-Computer Interface.* Cambridge, England: Cambridge University Press, 1991.

This book consists of articles by a number of leading HCI researchers and practitioners. It focuses on trying to bridge the gap between psychological theory and HCI design practice. Other themes in the book include close examinations of the design process and discussions of what can be learned from looking at real-world artifacts and situations. This collection will be of particular interest to those people with an interest in the theoretical and conceptual foundations of HCI design.

Greenbaum, Joan, and Morten Kyng, eds. *Design at Work: Cooperative Design of Computer Systems.* Hillsdale, NJ: Lawrence Erlbaum Associates, 1991.

An excellent collection that strikes a nice balance between practice and theory. In general, the articles reflect what has been called the Scandinavian approach, emphasizing participatory design and trying to ensure that computer systems enhance human work rather than mechanize it. Although the articles draw on concepts from anthropology, sociology, and linguistics, the book's strength is in its many examples and its practical orientation.

Norman, D. A., and S. Draper, eds. *User Centered System Design.* Hillsdale, NJ: Lawrence Erlbaum Associates, 1986.

Schneiderman, B. "How to Design With the User in Mind." *Datamation* 28, no. 4 (1982): 125–126.

Winograd, Terry, and Fernando Flores. *Understanding Computers and Cognition: A New Foundation for Design.* Reading, MA: Addison-Wesley, 1987.

This book lays a foundation for interface design by grounding it in human behavior, language, and the social and cultural contexts within which they occur. The book provides a perspective on human-computer interface design very different from the more traditional approach described by Card, Moran, and Newell's GOMS (goals, operators, methods, and selectors) model.

Human-Computer Interaction

Baecker, R. M., and W. A. S. Buxton. *Readings in Human-Computer Interaction: A Multidisciplinary Approach.* Los Altos, CA: Morgan Kaufmann, 1987.

A complete reference compendium of papers on human interface. It has a good subject index, so you can look up specific topics without going through the whole book cover to cover. It is a necessity for the serious designer.

Behaviour and Information Technology. England: Taylor & Francis.

This wide-ranging, bimonthly journal contains articles covering topics such as the role of managers in the introduction of new technology and studies on the learnability of HyperCard.

Brown, Lin. *Human-Computer Interaction Guidelines.* Norwood, NJ: Ablex, 1988.

Card, S. K., T. P. Moran, and A. Newell. *Applied Information-Processing Psychology.* Hillsdale, NJ: Lawrence Erlbaum Associates, 1983.

Card, S. K., T. P. Moran, and A. Newell. *The Psychology of Human-Computer Interaction.* Hillsdale, NJ: Lawrence Erlbaum Associates, 1983.

CHI Conference Proceedings. Reading, MA: Addison-Wesley.
Published annually.

Gardiner, Margaret M., and B. Christie, eds. *Applying Cognitive Psychology to User Interface Design.* New York: Wiley, 1987.

Helander, M. *Handbook of Human-Computer Interaction.* Amsterdam: Elsevier, 1990.

Interacting With Computers: The Interdisciplinary Journal of Human-Computer Interaction. England: Butterworth Scientific.

Published three times a year, this journal focuses on human-computer interaction issues. Material covered in journal ranges from empirical studies of the workplace and computer systems to theoretical and review articles.

Laurel, Brenda, ed. *The Art of Human-Computer Interface Design.* Reading, MA: Addison-Wesley, 1990.

This collection of papers covers topics in interface design including various how-to articles, project descriptions, commentary by experts in the field, and more.

Laurel, Brenda. *Computers as Theatre.* Reading, MA: Addison-Wesley, 1991.

Schneiderman, B. *Designing the User Interface, Second Edition.* Reading, MA: Addison-Wesley, 1992.

Suchman, Lucy. *Plans and Situated Actions: The Problem of Human-Machine Communication.* New York: Cambridge University Press, 1987.

Provides a good introduction to the psychology behind interface issues and human-machine interaction. It reviews many of the issues involved in the application of psychology, anthropology, and sociology to people's everyday actions. The author uses examples such as an analysis of Xerox copier machines to argue that people's thought processes occur within a specific framework or context.

Tognazzini, Bruce. *Tog on Interface.* Reading, MA: Addison-Wesley, 1992.

Language

Apple Computer, Inc. *Apple Publications Style Guide.* Cupertino, CA: APDA, 1991.

Duffy, T. M., and R. Waller, eds. *Designing Usable Texts.* New York: Academic Press, 1985.

Elbow, Peter. *Writing With Power: Techniques for Mastering the Writing Process.* New York: Oxford University Press, 1981.

Introduces ways to write and revise that will strengthen, not strangle, your voice. It discusses techniques for separating writing from revising, for addressing an audience, for using feedback, and for writing with power.

Price, Jonathan. *How to Write a Computer Manual. A Handbook of Software Documentation.* Menlo Park, CA: Benjamin/Cummings, 1984.

Simpson, H., and S. M. Casey. *Developing Effective User Documentation: A Human Factors Approach.* New York: McGraw-Hill, 1988.

Strunk, William, Jr., and E. B. White. *The Elements of Style,* third edition. New York: Macmillan, 1979.

Gives a few memorable rules for writing well. The book is short and covers the survival elements of usage, composition, and style. The guidelines, such as "Omit needless words" and "Revise and rewrite," are clear.

University of Chicago Press. *The Chicago Manual of Style,* thirteenth edition. Chicago: University of Chicago Press, 1982.

Provides a complete reference for English punctuation, usage, and style.

Zinsser, William. *On Writing Well: An Informal Guide to Writing Nonfiction,* fourth edition, rev. New York: HarperCollins, 1990.

Programming

Apple Computer, Inc. *Inside Macintosh.* Reading, MA: Addison-Wesley.

A set of books that describe how to write an application for the Apple Macintosh family of computers. *Inside Macintosh* is the definitive guide and reference for anyone writing software for the Macintosh computer. Current titles of the books that comprise *Inside Macintosh* include *Macintosh Toolbox Essentials, QuickTime, Memory, Processes,* and *Files.* This list presents books that are already available on the market or that will be published within several months of the publication date of this book.

Grogono, P., and S. H. Nelson. *Problem Solving and Computer Programming.* Reading, MA: Addison-Wesley, 1982.

Simpson, H. K. *Programming the Macintosh User Interface.* New York: McGraw-Hill, 1986.

Special Applications

This section presents resources for several different types of applications, including applications that support collaborative computing, hypertext, and multimedia capabilities.

Collaborative Computing

Erickson, T.D. "Interfaces for Cooperative Work: An Eclectic Review of CSCW '88." *SIGCHI Bulletin* 21, no. 1 (July 1989). New York: ACM.

Although this nine-page paper summarizes results presented at a particular conference, it is a good summary of many of the most important interface issues that arise in trying to provide computer support for cooperative work.

Foster, G., and M. Stefik. "Cognoter, Theory and Practice of a Collaborative Tool." *CSCW Proceedings* (1986): 7–15.

Greif, Irene, ed. *Computer-Supported Cooperative Work: A Book of Readings.* San Mateo, CA: Morgan Kaufmann, 1988.

A collection of 28 papers on cooperative work. The papers include many of the classic papers from the history of the field as well as more recent work including theoretical discussions, project descriptions, empirical studies of how people use CSCW (computer-supported cognitive work) systems, and more.

Grudin, J. "Why CSCW Applications Fail: Problems in the Design and Evaluation of Organizational Interfaces." *CSCW Proceedings* (1988): 85–93.

Discusses three reasons why commercial CSCW applications often fail.

Hypertext

Barrett, Edward, ed. *The Society of Text, Hypertext, Hypermedia, and the Social Construction of Information.* Cambridge, MA: MIT Press, 1989.

Discusses hypertext, hypermedia, and online information systems design.

Barrett, Edward, ed. *Text, ConText and HyperText, Writing With and for the Computer.* Cambridge, MA: MIT Press, 1988.

Jonassen, D. H., ed. *The Technology of Text.* Vol. 2. Englewood Cliffs, NJ: Educational Technology, 1985.

Nelson, Theodor H. *Computer Lib.* Schooleys Mountain, NJ: Nelson, 1974.

Nelson, Theodor H. *Literary Machines.* Schooleys Mountain, NJ: Nelson, 1981.

Multimedia

Buxton, W. "A Directory of Sources for Interactive Technologies." *SIGCHI Bulletin* (July 1986): 58–63.

Tognazzini, B. "Principles of Multimedia Visible Interface Design." *Multimedia Review* 1, no. 4 (Winter 1990): 18–22.

Online Documentation and Online Help

Aaronson, A., and J. M. Carroll. "Intelligent Help in a One-Shot Dialog: A Protocol Study." In *CHI + GI'87 Conference Proceedings: Human Factors in Computing Systems and Graphics Interface*, edited by J. M. Carroll and P. P. Tanner, 163–168. New York: ACM, 1987.

Brockmann, R. John. "The Documentation Problem." Part I of *Writing Better Computer User Documentation: From Paper to Hypertext, Version 2.0.* New York: Wiley, 1990.

Cohill, A., and R. Williges. "Retrieval of HELP Information for Novice Users of Interactive Computer Systems." *Human Factors* 27, no. 3 (1985): 335–343.

Conklin, J. "Hypertext: An Introduction and Survey." *IEEE Computer* (September 1987): 17–41.

Duffy, T., B. Mehlenbacher, and J. Palmer. "The Evaluation of Online Help Systems: A Conceptual Model." In *The Society of Text: Hypertext, Hypermedia, and the Social Construction of Reality*, edited by E. Barrett, 362–387. Cambridge, MA: MIT Press, 1989.

Horton, William K. *Designing and Writing Online Documentation: Help Files to Hypertext.* New York: Wiley, 1990.

Kearsley, G. *Online Help Systems: Design and Implementation.* Norwood, NJ: Ablex, 1988.

Queipo, L. "User Expectations of Online Information." *IEEE Transactions on Professional Communications* 29, no. 4 (1986): 11–15.

Rubens, P., and R. Krull. "Application of Research on Document Design to Online Displays." *Technical Communication* 32, no. 4 (1985): 29–34.

Schriver, K. A., J. R. Hayes, and M. D. Langston. "The Design of Information for Computer Users: A Review of the Literature on Hardcopy and Online Documentation." In *Designing Computer Documentation: A Review of the Relevant Literature*, edited by K. A. Schriver. Communications Design Center Technical Report No. 31, Pittsburgh, PA: Carnegie Mellon University, 1986.

Walker, J. "Issues and Strategies for Online Documentation." *IEEE Transactions on Professional Communication* 30 (1987): 235–248.

Universal Access

Apple Computer, Inc. *Macintosh Disability Resources Stack.* Cupertino, CA: Worldwide Disability Solutions Group, 1991.

Available as an online HyperCard stack.

Berliss, Jane, ed. *Trace Resource Book: The 1991–92 Edition: Assistive Technologies for Communication, Control and Computer Access.* Madison, WI: Trace Research and Development Center, 1991.

Enders, Alexandra, and Marian Hall. *Assistive Technology Sourcebook.* Washington, DC: RESNA Press, 1990.

This sourcebook provides an exhaustive listing of resources for individuals with a disability and the professionals working with them. It also contains helpful, brief articles explaining major concepts, philosophies, and technical information on all the major areas of assistive technology.

Green, Peter, and Alan J. Brightman. *Independence Day—Designing Computer Solutions for Individuals With Disability.* Allen, TX: DLM/Teaching Resource, 1990.

Vanderheiden, Gregg C., and Katherine R. Vanderheiden. *Accessible Design of Consumer Products: Guidelines for the Design of Consumer Products to Increase Their Accessibility to People With Disabilities or Who Are Aging.* Madison, WI: Trace Research and Development Center, 1991.

Visual Thinking

Adams, J. L. *Conceptual Blockbusting,* second edition. New York: Norton, 1979.

Hanks, Kurt, and Jerry Belliston. *Rapid Viz: A New Method for the Rapid Visualization of Ideas.* Los Altos, CA: William Kaufmann, 1980.

Presents drawing as a way of capturing ideas quickly and casually, not as a means of producing a finished illustration. The book shows how simple techniques such as contour drawing can make drawing a more useful tool for anyone.

McKim, Robert H. *Experiences in Visual Thinking,* second edition. Boston: PWS, 1980.

Discusses thinking and introduces drawing as a means of strengthening the thinking process. The book weaves together research findings, citations for further reading, quotations, mental exercises, and drawing techniques.

Worldwide Software

Apple Computer, Inc. *Guide to Macintosh Software Localization.* Reading, MA: Addison-Wesley, July 1992.

Describes how application software written for the Macintosh computer is localized for Japan, France, Germany, and more than 50 other markets around the globe. It tells you how to give an application the most successful look, feel, and behavior for each market. It is an essential manual for software designers, programmers, publishers, marketers, translators, and localization specialists.

Apple Computer, Inc. *Localization for Japan.* Cupertino, CA: APDA, 1992.

This book is written for software developers and publishers who wish to market their products in Japan. If you are interested in designing, programming, translating, marketing, or republishing software for the Japanese market, you will find valuable information in this book, which is available through APDA.

Hibi, Sadao. *Japanese Detail • Architecture.* San Francisco: Chronicle Books, 1989.

Koike, Kazuko, and Ikko Tanaka, eds. *Japan Color.* San Francisco: Chronicle Books, 1982.

Nielsen, Jakob, ed. *Designing User Interfaces for International Use.* Vol. 13 of *Advances in Human Factors/Ergonomics.* Amsterdam: Elsevier, 1990.

Checklist

This checklist contains questions about the Macintosh interface that you can ask yourself while reviewing software. These questions will help bring to mind the particulars of the guidelines.

The questions here cover all the guidelines except those for selection. The selection standards of the guidelines are detailed, so refer to "Selecting" on page 286 in Chapter 10, "Behaviors," for information about them.

You must be able to answer every question "yes" to ensure conformity with the guidelines. However, sometimes it is necessary to make tradeoffs in your application in order to provide the most usable interface. Remember to maintain the spirit of the guidelines and the principles when reviewing your product.

General Considerations

- Does the application have the "look" of the Macintosh desktop interface (including, but not limited to, desktop, windows, and menus)?
- Does the application have the "feel" of the Macintosh desktop interface (including, but not limited to, pointing, selecting, and keyboard input)?
- If a metaphor is being used, is it suitable for the application? Does the metaphor match a "real" visual and behavioral representation, as with the desktop, so that the users do not have to carry a "map" in their head?
- Does the application always provide some indication that an activity is being carried out in response to a command?
- Is suitable feedback provided during task processing? Is the completion of a processing task indicated somehow? Is the duration of the task indicated?
- Does the user always have the option of finding an object or action on the screen? In other words, does your interface follow the see-and-point principle of design?
- Are the operations consistent with the standard elements of the interface; that is, if a user is familiar with such applications as MacPaint, MacDraw, and MacWrite, will the application seem like familiar territory?
- Is a printout a replica of what the user sees on the screen? In other words, is it WYSIWYG (what you see is what you get)?
- Is an explanation offered if a particular action cannot be carried out? Are alternatives offered?

Checklist

- Are there warnings about risky actions? Are there different warnings for different levels of risky actions? Are there enough warnings without being too many? Are users allowed to back away gracefully from risky territory?
- Is there a feeling of stability?
- If an operation can be interrupted, do you provide a Cancel or Stop button? Can Escape or Command-period be used to cancel or stop these operations?
- Is your application forgiving and explorable by supporting Undo?
- Do you avoid assigning new behaviors to existing objects?
- Do you make all changes clearly visible?
- Do you interpret user's responses consistently?
- Do you use progressive disclosure, as appropriate?
- When your application runs in the background, do you gently call the user's attention to a task completion or request for input by using the Notification Manager? If an immediate response is crucial and the user doesn't respond to a notification request, does your application handle the situation gracefully? A background application should not take control from the user by placing an alert box on the screen when the user hasn't activated the application.
- Is your application MultiFinder friendly? Better workflow is possible when the user can easily switch back and forth between applications.
- If there are modes, is there a clear visual indication of the current mode? Does the visual indication of the mode appear near the object most affected by the mode? Are there enough landmarks to remind the user what area of the application he or she is in? For example, the MacPaint pointer changes to a pencil in draw mode and to a paint brush in paint mode.
- Is each mode absolutely necessary? Do the modes within the application properly track the user's own modes? Do users consistently avoid the kind of errors caused by the program being in a mode other than what the user wants or expects? Making a mode visually apparent is no guarantee that the user will track it: test the application on users and find out what sorts of mistakes they are making. If the errors are caused by modes, eliminate the modes.
- Can the user save a document or quit an application at any time, unless he or she is in a modal dialog box?
- Are the widest possible range of user activities available at any time? The user should spend most of his or her time in the event loop.
- Will a user unable to distinguish colors be able to use the application? Will someone without a color monitor be able to use it? The information conveyed by color coding should also be presented in another form, such as text, position, highlighting, gray-scale variations, or pattern. (These questions do not apply to programs in which the task to be carried out requires full-color vision on a color monitor.)

- Will a user with a hearing disability be able to use the application? Audible messages should be supplemented with visual cues or should allow the user to choose visible instead of audible messages. (This question may not apply to music programs.)

Graphic Design

- Did you use graphics to illustrate commands, features, and parameters of the applications, as well as all of the user's data, whenever possible?
- Do the graphics resemble items that users are familiar with? Did you leave out insignificant detail (which unnecessarily complicates a graphic)?
- Does the screen look "clean" and free from clutter?
- Does the user have control over the design of the workplace, allowing him or her to individualize it?
- Is the information in windows organized so that the most important information can be read first?
- Does your design look good at different bit depths on all Macintosh computers?
- Do you use a consistent light source, one that always comes from the upper-left corner of the screen?
- Do you use white space and graphics to break up long pieces of text?

Color

- Do you always design for black and white first and then colorize your design?
- Are your black-and-white designs two-dimensional?
- Do you avoid using color as the only means of communicating important information?
- Are the colors carefully chosen? Are bright colors used sparingly and only in small areas? Do you use light or subtle colors for large areas?
- Do you maintain a close visual relationship between a black-and-white design and its colorized version?
- Do you use true gray instead of a 50 percent gray pattern when a color monitor is present?
- Do you use the Color Picker where appropriate?
- Do any custom elements, such as tool palettes or special window controls, follow the color scheme of the operating system? Do the colors get updated when the user changes the color in the Color control panel?

Icons

- Do your icons represent objects that users are familiar with?
- Do your icons fit in with the desktop metaphor?
- Do you provide complete icon families, with `'ICN#'`, `'ics#'`, `'icl4'`, `'ics4'`, `'icl8'`, and `'ics8'` icons?
- Are icon colors chosen from the palette of 34 colors?
- If your application supports stationery pads, the Edition Manager, or the Data Access Manager, do you provide icons that distinguish the stationery pads, editions, or query documents for your application?

Windows

- Do the standard window size and position take into account the dimensions of the screen?
- Is the standard state of a window best suited to working on the document (such as no wider than the page width), and not necessarily as large as the full screen?
- Does your application make sense when it chooses to open a window in either the standard or the user-selected state?
- Can each sizable window be made as large as the smaller of either the maximum document size or the maximum size of the displays, including multiple monitor displays?
- Is the default position of a window contained on a single screen?
- Is each additional window opened below and to the right of its predecessor?
- If a user drags a window from one monitor to another monitor, does your application open subsequent windows on the second monitor?
- Do you use the lowercase letters "untitled" in a new window title? Do you avoid using additional punctuation in window titles? Do you avoid using blank titles? Do you avoid adding a number to the title of the first new window?
- Before closing a window, do you check to see if the user has changed its size or position? Do you save window positions, and then reopen windows in the size and position in which the user left them?
- Before reopening a window, do you make sure that the size and position are reasonable for the user's current monitor or monitors, which may not be the same as the monitor on which the document was last open?

- When zooming from the user state to the standard state, do you check if the size of the standard state would fit completely on the screen without moving the upper-left corner? If so, is the upper-left corner anchored? If not, is the window moved to an appropriate default location?
- When a window becomes inactive, do the close box, zoom box, size box, stripes in the title bar, and scroll bars disappear?
- Do you avoid displaying the selection in an inactive window? (You can use a secondary selection technique such as an outline to indicate where the selection is in an inactive window.)

Dialog Boxes

- Are questions in dialog boxes posed in a straightforward and positive way–for example, "Do you want to erase everything on the disk named "James Bond?" rather than "Do you not want to alter the contents of this disk?"
- Do dialog boxes and alert boxes appear on the screen where the user's focus of attention is, not necessarily where the menu bar is?
- Are dialog boxes horizontally centered either on the screen or over the active window if the window is on a large screen or on a screen other than the one the menu bar appears on?
- If a movable modal dialog box is displayed, can the application run in the background?
- Do you provide access to the menu bar when you display a movable modal dialog box? Are the Help, Edit, Keyboard, and Application menus enabled as appropriate?
- Are movable modal dialog boxes truly modal within the application?
- Do movable modal dialog boxes have a drag region (title bar)? Do movable modal dialog boxes not have a close box? For black-and-white monitors, do movable modal dialog boxes have a two-pixel-wide outline within the content region to signify that it is a modal dialog box?
- Can the Help menu be used when a modal dialog box is displayed?
- If there is an active editable text box in a modal dialog box, can the Cut, Copy, Paste, and Undo menu commands in the Edit menu be used?
- Do keyboard equivalents of the standard Edit menu commands operate correctly in a modal dialog box containing editable text items?
- When a scrolling list is present in a dialog box, can type selection be used? Can the arrow keys be used to move the selection by one item in the direction of the arrow?
- Does the active area of a dialog box have an indicator if there is more than one possible active area? (Active areas are those that accept typing such as scrolling lists with type selection or text boxes.)

- Does clicking a desired element move the active area to that element?
- Does pressing the Tab key cycle through the available elements? Does Shift-Tab cycle in the reverse direction?
- When appropriate, are buttons named with a verb that describes the action that it performs, such as Erase rather than OK?
- Do you provide a Cancel button wherever possible, especially in progress dialog boxes? Does pressing Escape or Command-period indicate Cancel in a dialog box or alert box? (Pressing Escape should never cause the user to lose information.)
- If an operation can be halted midstream, with possible side effects, is the button named Stop instead of Cancel?
- Do the Return and Enter keys map to the default button, which is usually the button with the safest result or the most likely response?
- Are default buttons outlined with an additional border of three black pixels, separated by a border of one white pixel?
- Do you avoid displaying a default border around any button when you use the Return key in editable text boxes?
- When a button is activated by keyboard equivalents, is the button highlighted for eight ticks of the clock to give visual feedback that the item has been chosen?
- Are buttons 20 pixels high? Are they wide enough for their text names (with a minimum of 8 pixels on each side of the text)?
- Are buttons placed in functional and consistent locations, both within your application and across all applications that you develop? Is the action button placed in the lower-right corner with the Cancel button to its left or above (for Western readers)?
- Do you use a consistent amount of white space between the border of the dialog box and its elements, thus creating a balanced appearance in the dialog box?
- When a dialog box or alert box refers to a document or an application, do you use the name of the document or application in the text?
- Do you use curly quotation marks (single and double) instead of straight quotation marks? (This also applies to apostrophes.)
- When you must unavoidably nest dialog boxes, do you dim the background dialog box and buttons, so that the frontmost dialog box stands out?
- Do your modeless dialog boxes have a close box? Such dialog boxes should not have buttons that dismiss the dialog box.
- Has room been left to allow the dialog box to grow during localization? Most languages require more characters than English to convey equivalent messages.

- Are display rectangles of dialog box items (for example, radio buttons and checkboxes) the same size? When the alignment of dialog box items is reversed, the items should align on the opposite side.

Alert Boxes

- Do alert boxes have the proper level of severity and show the proper icon associated with each severity level?
- Are alert boxes vertically positioned so that one-fifth of the remaining desktop area is above the alert box?
- Do the alert icon and message fit the situation?
- Does your application use the system alert sound (SYSBEEP) so that the user's menu bar automatically flashes (inverts rapidly) if the sound is turned off when they receive an alert message?
- Does the alert message not only tell the user what is wrong, but also offer suggestions as to what to do to correct it? The best alert messages answer the following questions: What happened? Why did it happen? What can I do about it?
- Is this alert box necessary? Often, the user can be prevented from making an error. For example, if the application cannot handle an 80-character filename, don't display an 80-character field in which to enter it.

Scrolling

- Does the window use either the standard scroll bar mechanism or the hand for scrolling? If it uses the hand, does the pointer either always become a hand in the window or appear highlighted in a tool palette?
- Does clicking a scroll arrow cause the document to move a distance of one unit in the chosen direction? (The unit should be appropriate and meaningful for the application.)
- Does clicking in the scroll bar below the scroll box advance the document by a windowful? (A windowful is the height or width of a window, minus a one-unit overlap.) Does clicking above the scroll box move the document back by a windowful?
- If the user drags the scroll box and then moves the pointer well outside the scroll bar, does the scroll box snap back to its original position?
- Is the function of the arrow keys different from the function of the scroll bar? (Arrow keys should not substitute for scroll arrows.)
- Are the scroll bars inactive when the document is no larger than the window?

- Are the scrolling keys on the keyboard (Page Up, Page Down, Home, End) supported? Note that these keys do not move the insertion point and do not affect the selection.
- Does the scroll box indicate the approximate position of the visible part of the document in comparison to the whole document?

Menus

- Are the Apple, File, and Edit menus present, with at least the standard items? (These menus are needed for desk accessories, even when the application doesn't use them.)
- Has enough room been left on the right side of the menu bar for the menu that some desk accessories add to the menu bar? Is there also enough extra room to allow for the expansion that almost always occurs during translation into other languages?
- Do the unique menus of the application have names that are appropriate? Are the names sufficiently different from the standard menu names? Can the user understand and remember their meaning?
- Are frequently used menu items available at the top level rather than in a submenu or a dialog box? If not, can the user move them up?
- When an item in a menu is currently disabled, is it dimmed in the menu rather than missing from it?
- If all the items in a menu are currently disabled, is the menu title dimmed? Can the user still pull down the menu and see the dimmed names of the operations?
- Are toggled menu items either unambiguously a verb or unambiguously a state of being?
- Are menu titles and items in caps/lowercase unless there is a compelling reason to have a different style, such as ALL CAPS in a Style menu?
- Do menu items have an ellipsis character (...) if more information is required from the user before completing the command?
- Do menu items blink briefly, and is the menu title highlighted until the command is complete?
- Are the dotted lines in menus (as well as dimmed items) unselectable? These items should not be highlighted when the user moves the mouse pointer over them.
- Are the menu items truly menu items? Menu items should not be used as text, section titles, or status indicators.
- In a hierarchical menu, does the title of the submenu have a right-pointing triangle? Are submenus used only for lists of related items?

- Can the user see all the commands, items, and submenu titles in a menu without scrolling? Scrolling should be necessary only for menus that users have added to or for menus that spill over because the user has selected a large system font.
- Does the application support Undo, Cut, Copy, and Paste?
- If the application is text oriented, can the user change the font and style by using menu commands?

Pop-Up Menus

- Do pop-up menus have a downward-pointing triangle and a one-pixel drop shadow? While the menu is showing, is its title inverted and is the current value checked? If the menu must be scrolled, is this indicated by a triangle pointing up or down?
- Are pop-up menus used to allow the user to choose only *one* of a set of several choices? Pop-up menus should not be used for choosing more than one item from a set of several choices.
- Do you avoid adding menu items that contain verbs (actions) in pop-up menus?
- Is the same font used for the normal state and the open state of a pop-up menu?
- Do you avoid making the pop-up menu narrower in the open state than in the closed state?

Palettes and Tear-Off Menus

- If a tool palette is present, is the selected symbol (icon, pattern, character, or drawing) highlighted?
- Do palettes provide tracking feedback when the mouse button is down?
- Does any change in selection in palettes occur only when the mouse button is released?
- If a menu has been torn off and moved, can the user still get access to it from the menu bar? When it is torn off a second time, does the first instance disappear?
- Do tear-off menus have a drag region with a 25 percent black-and-white pattern and a close box?
- Do tear-off menus always appear on top of open document windows?

Mouse Standards

- If the user initiates an action by pressing the mouse button, does the action take place only when the button is released?
- Are there ways other than double-clicking to perform a given action? Double-clicking should never be the only way to do something; it should only be a shortcut.

Text

- Can arrow keys be used in all text boxes (including dialog boxes)? Can the Shift key be used with the arrow keys to extend the selection (including in dialog boxes)?
- If text is selected, does pressing an arrow key cause the insertion point to go to the corresponding end of the range and deselect it?
- Are discontinuous selections made with the Command key modifier (for text and arrays)? The Shift key is used for graphics selections.
- Do you support intelligent cut-and-paste where appropriate?
- Do you use Command-arrow and Option-arrow for moving the insertion point in larger semantic units? (Note that when multiple script systems are available, Command–Left Arrow and Command–Right Arrow are intercepted by the Script Manager and used for changing the script system.)
- If your application supports TrueType fonts, do you support all font sizes instead of imposing a size limit?
- Do the users have a way to choose whatever font size they desire?
- Does the active font size in a menu have a checkmark next to it?
- Are available font sizes shown in outline in the menu items?
- Do you avoid making assumptions about font sizes? For example, the system font may have a different size in other countries.

Balloon Help

- Do you provide Balloon Help for items in dialog boxes, alert boxes, and menus?
- Do you provide Balloon Help for application window contents?

- Do you provide a custom help balloon for your application icon, if appropriate?
- Do your help balloons answer at least one of these questions:
  - □ What is this?
  - □ What does this do?
  - □ What happens if I click this?
- Is the content of the help balloons short and easy to understand?
- Do you use clear, concise phrases and active constructions?
- Do you use terminology consistently?
- When a balloon appears, is it positioned so that it does not obstruct any interface elements being referred to by the balloon?
- Do you provide different balloon messages for different states of an item (such as enabled, disabled, and checked)?
- Do you add a menu item for help-related information to the Help menu? Does this menu item use the name of your application?

Keyboard Equivalents

- Are Apple-reserved keyboard equivalents used properly? Even if your application doesn't support one of these menu commands, it shouldn't use these keyboard equivalents for another function.
- Do you avoid using Command–Space bar and Command–*modifier key*–Space bar in your application, since they are reserved for use by the Script Manager?
- Do keyboard equivalents appear where appropriate? Are the keyboard equivalents case-independent? (This second rule does not apply if the product uses both cases in the keyboard equivalents and enables the user to predict which case to use.)

Edition Manager

- If your application implements the capabilities of the Edition Manager, do you provide the following commands in the Edit menu, separated from the standard commands by a gray line?
  - □ Create Publisher…
  - □ Subscribe To…
  - □ Publisher/Subscriber Options… (context-sensitive toggle command)
  - □ Show/Hide Borders (optional context-sensitive toggle command)
  - □ Stop All Editions (optional command)

- Do publishers have borders that are three pixels wide with 50 percent gray lines, when appropriate?
- Do subscribers have borders that are three pixels wide with 75 percent gray lines?
- Are the contents of the section separated from the border itself by one pixel of white space?

Documentation

- Does the manual include a glossary of potentially confusing terms that relate to the application or to the application's topic?
- If the manual refers the user to another document, is the reference more appropriate than having the information in the manual itself?
- For those who cannot handle book-form manuals, is any part of the manual available in electronic form?
- Is the manual written for its audience?

Glossary

accumulating attribute group A group of attributes of which any number of attributes can be in effect at the same time. For example, the Style menu allows users to apply a number of different style attributes, such as italics, bold, and underline, to a single piece of text. (In dialog boxes, accumulating attributes are represented by checkboxes.) Compare **mutually exclusive attribute group.**

activate To make an inactive window active by clicking anywhere inside it.

active application The application with which the user is currently interacting. Its icon appears on the right end of the menu bar.

active end The point at which the user releases the mouse button when selecting a range of objects (text, arrays, and graphics) by dragging through them. Compare **anchor point.**

active window The frontmost window on the desktop; the window where the next action will take place. The active window is the window on the screen that has horizontal lines in its title bar.

addition method A method for extending a continuous selection of text, using Shift-click, which *adds* new text to a current selection. Compare **fixed-point method.**

additive color A model of color based on adding the basic hues together to make additional colors.

alert A warning or report of an error in the form of an alert box, a sound from the computer's speaker called an alert sound, or both.

alert box A window that appears on the screen to warn the user or to report an error. An alert box may or may not be accompanied by an alert sound.

alert sound An audible warning from the computer speaker that warns the user of an unusual or potentially undesirable situation. An alert sound may or may not be accompanied by an alert box.

anchor point The point at which the user presses the mouse button to begin selecting a range of objects by dragging through them. The anchor point is at one corner of the range of objects. Compare **active end.**

Apple menu The menu farthest to the left in the menu bar, indicated by an Apple symbol, which contains items the user puts in the Apple Menu Items folder.

application A program that performs a specific task, such as word processing, database management, or graphics. An application's file type is 'APPL'.

Application menu The menu farthest to the right in the menu bar, which displays a list of the applications that are currently running on a user's computer. Allows users to change applications by choosing an item, typically the name of an application, in this menu.

array An arrangement of fields containing information (text or graphics) through which a user navigates using the Tab key.

arrow keys The four directional keys in the lower-right corner of the keyboard. The user can use the arrow keys to move around in an application.

auto-key event An event generated repeatedly when the user presses and holds down a character key on the keyboard or keypad.

auto-repeat See **auto-key event.**

Balloon Help An onscreen help system consisting of balloons that describe items on the screen. A help balloon appears when the user moves the pointer to an item and disappears when the user moves the pointer away from the item.

bitmap A set of bits that represents the positions and states of a corresponding set of items, such as pixels.

bitmap-based graphics application A graphics application that creates images by turning on individual pixels on the screen. Each graphic is a collection of pixels.

brightness A measurement of the amount of black in a color—the less black, the brighter the color. Brightness is equivalent to lightness in the HLS color system, and it is equivalent to value in the HSV color system.

button An image, often resembling a push button, in dialog boxes that the user clicks to designate, confirm, or cancel an action. Compare **mouse button, radio button.**

Cancel button A button that appears in many dialog boxes. Clicking it closes the dialog box and returns the computer to the state it was in before the dialog box appeared.

caret A generic term for a symbol that indicates where the next text will be inserted. The caret used in Macintosh text is a vertical bar (|).

cell The intersection of a row and a column in a spreadsheet. A cell can hold a number, label, function, or formula.

character Any symbol that has a widely understood meaning and thus can convey information. Some characters—such as letters, numbers, and punctuation—can be displayed on the monitor screen and printed on a printer.

character code An integer representing the character that a key or key combination stands for.

character key A key on a keyboard that sends characters to the computer. Compare **modifier key.**

checkbox A standard Macintosh control that displays a setting, either checked (on) or unchecked (off). Clicking a checkbox or its text label reverses its setting. One or more checkboxes can be checked. Compare **radio button.**

Clear A command in the Edit menu that removes selected material without placing it on the Clipboard. The user can restore the material with the Undo command.

Clear key A key on the numeric keypad that has the same effect as choosing the Clear command from the Edit menu.

click (v.) To position the pointer on something, and then press and quickly release the mouse button. (n.) The act of clicking.

Clipboard The holding place for what the user last cut or copied; a buffer area in memory. Information on the Clipboard can be pasted into documents.

close To turn a window back into the icon that represents it by choosing the Close command or by clicking the close box on the left end of the window's title bar.

close box The square box on the left end of the title bar of an active window. Clicking it closes the window.

Close View A control panel, included with system software, for people with a visual disability. It enlarges everything on the screen up to sixteen times the standard size and allows users who have difficulty seeing black on white to invert screen images to white on a black background.

collaborative computing A shared computing environment or an application that facilitates communications and teamwork among a group of people.

command An instruction that causes a device such as a computer or printer to perform some action. A command can be selected from a menu with a hand-held device (such as a mouse), typed from a keyboard, or embedded in a program.

Command key A key that, when held down while another key is pressed, causes a command to take effect. The Command key is marked with a propeller-shaped symbol. On some keyboards, the Command key has both the propeller symbol and the Apple symbol on it.

context sensitive Able to perceive the situation in which an event occurs. For example, if an application program presents help information specific to the particular task the user is performing, rather than a general list of commands, that help is said to be context sensitive.

control An object in a window on the Macintosh screen with which the user, by using the mouse, can cause instant action with visible results or change settings to modify a future action. The control is internally represented in a control record.

control panel A utility that lets the user change global features such as the speaker volume, the keyboard repeat speed and delay, mouse tracking, and number of colors displayed.

cursor See **pointer.**

database (1) A collection of information organized in a form that can be readily manipulated and sorted by a computer user. (2) Short for *database management system.*

default A value, action, or setting that a computer system assumes unless the user gives an explicit instruction to the contrary.

default button In an alert box or a modal dialog box, the button whose effect occurs if the user presses Return or Enter. In an alert box, it's boldly outlined; in a modal dialog box, it's boldly outlined or it's the OK button.

delete To remove something, such as a character or word from a file, or a file from a disk. Keys such as the Delete key and the Backspace key can remove one character at a time by moving to the left (in languages that read from left to right). The Cut command removes selected text and places it on the Clipboard; the Clear command removes selected text without placing it on the Clipboard. (The Undo command can reverse the action of Clear and of the Delete or Backspace key if it is used immediately.)

Delete key A key that moves the insertion point backward, removing the previously typed character, or that removes the current selection. Its function is identical to that of the Backspace key on the original Macintosh keyboards. Compare **Forward Delete key.**

desk accessory A small application that provides a specific, limited capability for a particular task, for example, the Calculator, the Note Pad, and Key Caps. In versions of system software earlier than System 7, desk accessories were always in the Apple menu. In System 7, a desk accessory can be in the Apple menu or anywhere in the file system. From the user's point of view, there is little distinction between desk accessories and applications.

desktop The working environment on the computer—the background on which icons and windows are displayed (minus the menu bar).

dial See **slider.**

dialog box A box that appears on the screen to solicit information from the user or to report that the computer is waiting for a process to complete. For example, a typical printing dialog box requests the user to specify such options as number of copies of a document to print. A dialog box is internally represented in a dialog record. See also **modal dialog box, modeless dialog box,** and **movable modal dialog box.**

dimmed Used to describe words or icons that appear in gray. For example, menu commands appear dimmed when they are unavailable; folder icons are dimmed when they are open.

dimmed icon An icon that represents an opened disk or folder or a disk that has been ejected.

disabled Describes a menu item or an item in a dialog box or alert box that cannot be chosen; the item appears dimmed.

discontinuous selection A selection that consists of objects that are *not* adjacent to one another.

document A file the user creates and can open, edit, and print. See also **file.**

document window The window that displays the content of a document.

double click (n.) Two clicks in quick succession, interpreted as a single command. The action of a double click is different from that of a single click. For example, clicking an icon selects the icon; double-clicking an icon opens it.

double click (v.) To press and release the mouse button twice in quick succession without moving the mouse.

drag To position the pointer on something, for example, a window icon, press and hold the mouse button, move the mouse, and release the mouse button.

drag region A region in a window frame; usually the title bar. Dragging inside this region moves the window to a new location and makes it the active window. (The window doesn't become active if the Command key is down while the window is dragged.)

Easy Access A feature of system software that assists people who have difficulty typing on the keyboard or manipulating the mouse. See also **Mouse Keys, Slow Keys, Sticky Keys.**

edit To change or modify. For example, to insert, remove, replace, or move text in a document.

edition The data written to an edition container by a publisher. A publisher writes data to an edition whenever a user saves a document that contains a publisher, and subscribers in other documents may read the data from the edition whenever it is updated. See also **publisher, subscriber.**

Edit menu A menu that contains editing commands such as Copy, Cut, and Paste.

Enter key A key that notifies the application that the user is through entering information in a particular area of the document, such as a field in a database record. The user can also press the Enter key (like the Return key) to dismiss dialog boxes and alert boxes.

ergonomics The science of designing work environments that allow people and products to interact efficiently and safely. Examples include screen ergonomics and workplace ergonomics. Sometimes called *human engineering.*

Escape key A key that allows the user to quickly get out of a situation while working on a computer. In many applications, pressing the Escape key allows the user to stop an operation in progress. The user can also press the Escape key as an alternate to clicking the Cancel button in a dialog box.

event-driven Describes a kind of program that responds to user input in real time by repeatedly testing for events posted by interrupt routines. An event-driven program does nothing until it detects an event such as a click of the mouse button.

extension A software program that adds some feature to the operating system.

field A data item separated from other data by blanks, tabs, or other specific delimiters. A particular type or category of information in a database.

file Any named, ordered collection of information stored on a disk. Application programs and operating systems on disks are files as well as documents that users create. A Macintosh file consists of a data fork and a resource fork. See also document.

File menu A menu that contains commands that affect whole documents such as Open, Save, Print, and Quit.

file server A combination of controller software and a mass-storage device that allows computer users to share common files and applications through a network. A file server on an AppleTalk network system typically consists of a Macintosh computer with AppleShare software and one or more hard disks.

Finder The application that maintains the Macintosh desktop and starts up other programs at the request of the user. The user uses the Finder to manage documents and applications, and to get information to and from disks.

fixed-point method A method for extending a continuous selection of text, using Shift-click, which extends the selection on *either* side (but not both) of a fixed point. Compare **additive method.**

folder A holder of documents, applications, or other folders on the desktop. Folders act as subdirectories, allowing users to organize information in any way they want.

font A complete set of characters in one design, size, and style. In traditional typography usage, fonts may be restricted to a particular size and style or may comprise multiple sizes, or multiple sizes and styles, of a typeface design.

Font menu A menu that contains text fonts, such as Geneva and Chicago, available on a system (residing in a user's System Folder). See also **font.**

font size The size of a font of characters in points; equivalent to the distance between the ascent line and the descent line of one line of text. Examples of font size are 12 point and 18 point.

font style A set of stylistic variations other than size, such as italic, bold, and underline.

Forward Delete key A key on the Apple Extended Keyboard that causes the character to the right of the insertion point to be deleted in left-to-right systems. The insertion point does not move: the characters to its right are "vacuumed" in toward it as each is deleted. Compare **Delete key.**

graphics Information presented in the form of pictures or images. Compare **text.**

grow region A window region, usually within the content region, where dragging changes the size of an active window.

Help menu The menu directly to the left of the Application menu in the menu bar, indicated by a help balloon symbol, which contains on-screen help information. (Users can turn on Balloon Help from the Help menu.)

hierarchical menu A menu in which one or more individual menu items can themselves contain a submenu.

highlight To make something visually distinct, typically when it's selected. Usually done by reversing black and white areas or by darkening colors.

hot spot The portion of the pointer that must be positioned over a screen object before mouse clicks can have an effect on that object.

hot zone The area that the pointer's hot spot much be within in order for mouse clicks to have an effect.

icon A symbol that graphically represents an object or a concept. Screen icons represent such objects as disks, documents, tools, and application programs. Icons on the outside of the computer can be used to show where to plug cables, such as the disk drive icon on the back panel that marks the disk drive connector.

Info window The window that appears when you select an icon and choose Get Info from the File menu. It supplies information such as size, type, and date, and it includes a comment box for adding information.

input Information transferred into a computer from some external source, such as the keyboard, a disk drive, or a modem. Compare **output.**

input device A device that sends information to the microprocessor. The mouse and keyboard are the Macintosh computer's primary input devices. Compare **output device.**

insertion point The position where text will be inserted, usually marked by a blinking vertical bar.

Installer A utility program that users can use to update system software or add resources.

invert To highlight by changing white pixels to black and vice versa.

keyboard equivalent Keystrokes that invoke a menu item from the keyboard. A keyboard equivalent is usually the combination of a modifier key and a character key.

keyboard layout Software that specifies the mapping of keys on a physical keyboard to character codes.

Keyboard menu A menu, located between the Help menu and the Application menu icons in the menu bar, that contains script system, keyboard layout, and input method items. It appears when more than one script system is installed and enabled or when a localizable flag is set.

keyboard shortcut A keystroke that you can use instead of a mouse action to perform a task. For example, pressing the Command and the X keys at the same time is the same as choosing the Cut command from the Edit menu.

little arrows A control, consisting of two arrows pointing in opposite directions, that allows users to increase or decrease values in a series by clicking or pressing the arrows.

localization The process of adapting software to a particular region, language, and culture. Script and language adaptations are necessary but not sufficient for this process. Localization also includes date and time formats, number formats, text behavior formats, keyboard resources, and fonts.

locked file A file whose data cannot be changed.

Macintosh Operating System The combination of ROM-based and disk-based routines that together perform basic tasks such as starting the computer, moving data to and from disks and peripheral devices, and managing memory space in RAM.

Macintosh user interface The standard conventions for interacting with Macintosh computers. The interface ensures users a consistent means of interacting with all Macintosh computers and the applications designed to run on them.

main event loop In a standard Macintosh application program, a loop that repeatedly calls the Event Manager to get events and then responds to them as appropriate.

mainstreaming programs Educational programs in which children with special needs (including those with physical disabilities) are included in "mainstream" classes with children who don't necessarily have special needs.

menu A list of choices presented by a program. In the desktop interface, menus appear when users point to and press menu titles in the menu bar. Dragging through the menu and releasing the mouse button while a command is highlighted chooses that command.

menu bar The horizontal strip at the top of the screen that contains menu titles.

menu item A choice in a menu, usually a command to the current application.

menu title A word, a phrase, or an icon in the menu bar that designates a menu. Pressing on the menu title causes the title to be highlighted and its menu to appear below it.

modal dialog box A dialog box that puts the user in the state or "mode" of being able to work only inside the dialog box. (A modal dialog box resembles an **alert box.**) The user cannot move a modal dialog box, and the user can dismiss it only by clicking its buttons. Compare **modeless dialog box** and **movable modal dialog box.**

modeless dialog box A **dialog box** that looks like a document window without a size box or scroll bars. The user can move a modeless dialog box, make it inactive and active again, and close it like any document window. Compare **modal dialog box** and **movable modal dialog box.**

modifier key A key on a keyboard that changes the behavior or action of a character key when pressed at the same time as the character key. A modifier key can also change or accentuate the meaning of a mouse action. Compare **character key.**

movable modal dialog box A modal dialog box that has a title bar (with no close box) that allows the user to move the dialog box. Compare **modeless dialog box.**

monitor See **video monitor.**

monochrome monitor A monitor capable of displaying in only one color.

mouse button The button on the top of the mouse. In general, pressing the mouse button initiates some action on whatever is under the pointer, and releasing the button confirms the action.

Mouse Keys An Easy Access feature that lets users use keys on the numeric keypad to control the pointer.

mutually exclusive attribute group A group of attributes of which only one attribute can be in effect at any time. For example, the Left, Center, and Right commands in a graphics menu are a set of three commands, only one of which can be in effect at any time. (In dialog boxes, mutually exclusive attributes are represented by radio buttons.) Compare **accumulating attribute group.**

network A collection of interconnected, individually controlled computers, together with the hardware and software used to connect them. A network allows users to share data and peripheral devices such as printers and storage media, to exchange electronic mail, and so on.

operating system Low-level software that controls a computer by performing basic tasks such as input/output, memory management, and interrupt handling.

Option key A modifier key that gives a different meaning or action to another key or to a mouse action.

outline font A collection of outline glyphs in a particular typeface and style with no size restriction. The Font Manager can generate thousands of point sizes from the same TrueType font. See also **TrueType font.**

outline triangle A control that allows users to view the contents of a folder without opening it. (The triangles appear when the user chooses to view the contents of their file system in a list view.)

output Information transferred from a computer to some external destination, such as the display screen, a disk drive, a printer, or a modem. Compare **input.**

output device A device that receives information from the microprocessor. The monitor is the Macintosh computer's primary output device. Compare **input device.**

palette The name for a **tear-off menu** when it's been torn off. A palette remains visible on the screen so you can use it without having to pull down the menu. A palette can also be part of a window that provides tools or choices such as colors or patterns.

password A unique word or set of characters used to ensure security. For example, a user enters a password to log on to a volume on a file server.

paste To place the contents of the Clipboard—whatever was last cut or copied—at the insertion point.

peripheral card A removable printed-circuit board that plugs into one of the computer's expansion slots, allowing the computer to use a peripheral device or to perform some subsidiary or peripheral function.

peripheral device A piece of hardware—such as a video monitor, disk drive, printer, or modem—used in conjunction with a computer and under the computer's control. Peripheral devices are often (but not necessarily) physically separate from the computer and connected to it by wires, cables, or some other form of interface. Such devices sometimes require peripheral cards.

pixel Short for *picture element;* the smallest dot you can draw on the screen. Also a location in video memory that corresponds to a point on the graphics screen when the viewing window includes that location. In the Macintosh monochrome display, each pixel can be either black or white, so it can be represented by a bit; thus, the display is said to be a bitmap. For color or gray-scale video, several bits in RAM may represent the image. Thus, the display is not a bitmap but rather a pixel map.

pixel map A set of values that represents the positions and states of the set of pixels making up an image.

point (1) A unit of measurement for type. Twelve points equal 1 pica, and 6 picas equal 1 inch; thus, 1 point equals approximately 1/72 inch. (2) The intersection of a horizontal grid line and a vertical grid line on the coordinate plane, defined by a horizontal and a vertical coordinate.

pointer A small shape on the screen that follows the movement of the mouse or shows where the user's next action will take place. The pointer can be an arrow, an I-beam, a crossbar, a wristwatch, or other appropriate image. Called the *cursor* in Macintosh technical manuals. See also insertion point.

pop-up menu A menu not located in the menu bar, which appears when the user presses the mouse button in a particular place.

progressive disclosure A technique by which the most common options are presented in a simple interface and additional choices or information are disclosed by activating some control.

publisher A portion of a document that makes its data available to other documents or applications. A publisher stores its data in an edition whenever a user creates or edits the data in the publisher and then saves it. See also **edition** and **subscriber.**

pull-down menu A menu that is hidden until you move the pointer to its title and press the mouse button.

radio button A standard Macintosh control that displays a setting, either on or off, and is part of a group in which only one button can be on at a time.

Read Me document A plain text document that is included on application and system software disks and provides late-breaking information about the product.

resource Data or code stored in a resource file and managed by the Resource Manager.

Return key A key that causes the cursor or insertion point to move to the beginning of the next line. It's also used in some cases to confirm a command and to dismiss dialog boxes and alert boxes.

RGB Abbreviation for *red-green-blue*; a method of displaying color video by transmitting the three primary colors as three separate signals. There are two ways of using RGB with computers: TTL RGB, which allows the color signals to take on only a few discrete values; and analog RGB, which allows the color signals to take on any values between their upper and lower limits, for a wide range of colors.

RGB monitor A type of color monitor that receives separate signals for each color (red, green, and blue).

saturation A measurement of how much white a color contains—the less white, the more saturated the color.

save To store information by transferring it from main memory to a disk. Work not saved disappears when you switch off the computer or when the power is interrupted.

screen The part of the monitor where information is displayed. Also called *display screen*.

script A writing system, such as Cyrillic or Arabic. The English language uses Roman script.

script system A collection of software facilities that provides for basic differences between writing systems, such as character sets, fonts, keyboards, text collation, and word breaks. Examples of script systems are Roman, Japanese, Arabic, Traditional Chinese, Simplified Chinese, Hebrew, Greek, Thai, and Korean.

scroll To move a document or directory in its window so that a different part of it is visible.

scroll arrow An arrow at either end of a scroll bar. Clicking a scroll arrow moves a document or directory one line. Pressing a scroll arrow moves a document continuously.

scroll bar A rectangular bar that may be along the right or bottom of a window. Clicking or dragging in the scroll bar causes the view of the document to change.

scroll box The solid box in a scroll bar. The position of the scroll box in the scroll bar indicates the position of what's in the window relative to the entire document.

See Files The AppleShare file server access privilege that gives the right to open and copy documents and applications in a folder.

See Folders The AppleShare file server access privilege that gives the right to see folders within a folder.

select To designate where the next action will take place. To select using a mouse, you click an icon or drag across information.

selection A series of characters, or a character position, at which the next editing operation will occur. Selected characters in the active window are inversely highlighted. Also called *selection range.*

shared resource A resource, such as a document, an application, or a storage medium, that is being used, often simultaneously, by a group of users on a computer network.

Shift-click To click while the Shift key is down. Shift-clicking extends or shortens a selection.

Shift-drag To drag while the Shift key is down. Shift-dragging allows users to select multiple objects.

Shift key A key that, when held down, causes the subsequent letter typed to appear in uppercase or the top symbol on a two-character key to be produced. The Shift key can also modify mouse actions. See also **Shift-click, Shift-drag.**

size box A box in the lower-right corner of some active windows. Dragging the size box resizes the window.

Size menu A menu that contains sizes, measured in points, for fonts.

slider A control that graphically represents the ranges of values that a user can set or that simply displays the value, magnitude, or position of something. Also called a *dial.*

Slow Keys An Easy Access feature that lets the user set a delay before each keystroke is accepted by the computer.

Space bar The long, unlabeled bar along the bottom of the keyboard that generates a space character.

space character A text character whose printed representation is a blank space. Generated by pressing the Space bar.

split bar A control appearing in a scroll bar that allows users to split a window into separate window panes. See also **split line, window pane.**

split line The line, which appears when a user splits a window, that visually separates the resulting window panes. See also **split bar, window pane.**

stack A HyperCard document.

standard file dialog box A dialog box that allows users to perform actions (such as viewing, opening, and saving) on files residing on any type of storage media. Also allows users to view elements on their desktops.

Standard File Package A Macintosh package for presenting the standard user interface when a file is to be saved or opened.

standard state The initial size and location of a window. This state is determined by the application.

Sticky Keys An Easy Access feature that lets the user type combination keystrokes without actually pressing the keys simultaneously.

Style menu The menu that contains style attributes, such as bold, italic, and condense, for fonts.

subscriber A portion of a document that automatically obtains current data from other documents and applications. A subscriber reads data from an edition. See also **edition** and **publisher.**

system font The font that the system uses (in menus, for example). In Roman-based writing systems, the system font is 12-point Chicago.

TeachText An application that lets you open text and graphics documents, particularly if the original application that created the document is not available.

tear-off menu Any menu that you can detach from the menu bar by pressing the menu title and dragging beyond the menu's edge. The torn-off menu appears in a window or a utility window on the desktop. Once torn off, these menus are called *palettes*.

text Information presented in the form of readable characters. Compare graphics.

text box The place or places in a dialog box where information can be typed. Also called *text entry field*.

TextEdit The part of the Toolbox that supports basic text entry and editing capabilities of a standard Macintosh application.

text entry field An area, usually a rectangular box, located in a dialog box and into which the user enters text to identify something, such as the name of a document.

toggled menu item A menu item that has two states. The menu item changes from one state to the other each time a user chooses it.

tokens (1) An abbreviation of a string of characters. (2) A sequence of characters delimited so as to be indentified by a compiler.

TrueType font A type of outline font supplied with Macintosh system software. See also **outline font.**

type-ahead The process by which the computer stores keystrokes (typed faster than the computer can process) in a queue for later processing.

type selection The ability to select an item from a list of items by typing the beginning character or characters of its name.

user interface The rules and conventions by which a computer system communicates with the person operating it.

user state The size and location a user sets for a window.

utility A type of software that helps people manage the computer environment.

utility window A type of box that has some but not all features of a regular window. A utility window has a bar at the top by which it can be dragged and a close box, but does not necessarily have a title, and is nonscrolling. Also called a *miniwindow*. Compare **palette.**

value An item of information that can be stored in a variable, such as a number or a string.

video monitor A display device that can receive video signals by direct connection and cannot receive broadcast signals such as commercial television; it can be connected directly to the computer.

window An object on the desktop that presents information such as a document or message. Each window is internally represented in a window record.

window pane A part of a window after it has been split into two or more parts

word processor An application program that provides tools for creating, editing, and formatting text.

word wrap The automatic continuation of text from the end of one line to the beginning of the next without breaking in the middle of a word.

zoom box A small box with a smaller box enclosed in it found on the right side of the title bar of some windows. Clicking the zoom box toggles the window between the standard state and the user state.

Index

Numerals

A

B

C

D

E

F

G

H

I, J

K

L

M

N

O

P

Q

R

S

Z

This Apple manual was written, edited, and composed on a desktop publishing system using Apple Macintosh computers and FrameMaker software. Proof pages were created on an Apple LaserWriter IINTX printer. Final page negatives were output directly from text files on an AGFA ProSet 9800 imagesetter. Line art was created using Adobe™ Illustrator. PostScript™, the page-description language for the LaserWriter, was developed by Adobe Systems Incorporated.

Text type is Palatino® and display type is Helvetica®. Bullets are ITC Zapf Dingbats®. Some elements, such as program listings, are set in Apple Courier.